Great Escapes
Around the World
Europe • Africa • Asia • South America • North America

Vol. II

Great Escapes
Around the World

Europe • Africa • Asia • South America • North America

Vol. II

Edited & compiled by Angelika Taschen

TASCHEN

HONG KONG KÖLN LONDON LOS ANGELES MADRID PARIS TOKYO

Amhuinnsuidhe Castle, UK 016
Lute Suites, NL 030
The Old Railway Station, UK 024
Domein Scholteshof, BE 036

Wheatleigh, US 560
The Point, US 554
Langdon Hall, CA 548

Le Chaufourg en Périgord, FR 060
Les Maisons Marines d'Huchet, FR 070

Paço de São Cipriano, PT 130
Quinta da Capela, PT 120
Monasterio Rocamador, ES 108
L'Atelier sul Mare, IT 102

Calistoga Ranch, US 662
The Carneros Inn, US 654
Deetjen's Big Sur Inn, US 636
Madonna Inn, US 644
Korakia Pensione, US 630

The Wauwinet, US 568

Kasbah Agafay, MA 148
Riad Enija, MA 156
Riad El Mezouar, MA 162

170

Hotel Congress, US 622

576 Little Palm Island, US

588 Molokai Ranch, US

Ankobra Beach, GH 284

El Monte Sagrado, US 604
The Mabel Dodge Luhan House, US 610

Cibolo Creek Ranch, US 596

Pousada Maravilha, BR 420

Pousada do Quadrado, BR 430
Estrela d'Água, BR 440

Sandibe Sa
Mor

Makalali Privat

explora en Atacama, CL 534
Bodega El Esteco de Cafayate, AR 464
Hotel Casa Real, CL 522

456 Posada La Bonita, AR

448 La Posada Aguaverde, UY

Kensington

Dos Lunas, AR 472
Estancia Ancón, AR 480

484 La Pascuala Delta Lodge, AR
492 Estancia La Candelaria, AR

Ten Rivers & Ten Lakes Lodge, AR 500
Estancia Arroyo Verde, AR 504

514 Los Notros, AR

— 052 Landhaus Börmoos, DE

— 044 Seehotel am Neuklostersee, DE

— 082 La Bastide de Marie, FR
— 092 La Maison Domaine de Bournissac, FR

● 402 Red Capital Club & Residence, CN

— 136 Les Maisons de Cappadoce, TR

● 410 Asaba, JP

Ben Moro, MA

l Marsam, EG 176 ●

l Moudira, EG 182 ●

● 292 Royal Desert Camp, IN
300 Narain Niwas Palace, IN
306 Sardar Samand Palace, IN

Nilaya Hermitage, IN 314 ●

Green Magic Nature Resort, IN 322 ●

● 344 Pansea Angkor, KH
● 398 Whale Island Resort, VN

Shalimar Spice Garden Resort, IN 330 ●

● 392 The Barceló Pearl Farm Island Resort, PH

Sun House, LK 336 ●

● 352 The Datai, MY

190 Hippo Point House, KE

● 362 Banyan Tree Bintan, MY

● 198 Ngong House, KE

ngire Treetops, TZ 202 ●

● 206 Mnemba Island Lodge, TZ
216 Zanzibar Serena Inn, TZ

● 368 Amankila, ID
380 Begawan Giri Estate, ID

● 222 Frégate Island Private, SC

lge, BW 242 ●

● 234 Matetsi Water Lodge, ZW

mp, BW 250 ●

● 228 Le Prince Maurice, MU

e Reserve, ZA 270 ●

262 Sabi Sabi Earth Lodge, ZA

ZA 278 ●

Contents Sommaire Inhalt

Europe

Africa

Contents   Sommaire   Inhalt

Asia

South America

Contents   Inhalt   Sommaire

North America

Europe

Scotland • England • The Netherlands
Belgium • Germany • France • Italy
Spain • Portugal • Turkey

Text by Shelley-Maree Cassidy   *Edited by* Angelika Taschen

"Tourists don't know where they've been,
travelers don't know where they're going."
Paul Theroux

Amhuinnsuidhe Castle 16 ●

SCOTLAND

IRELAND

ENGLAND

The Old Railway Station 24 ●

FRAN

● 60 Le Chaufo

Les Maisons Marines d'Huchet 70 ●

Paço de São Cipriano 130 ●

PORTUGAL

La Maison Domaine de Bournissac 92

Quinta da Capela 120 ●

SPAIN

Monasterio Rocamador 108 ●

MOROCCO

ALGERIA

ndhaus Börmoos 52 ●

● 44 Seehotel am Neuklostersee

● 30 Lute Suites

● 36 Domein Scholteshof

rigord

La Bastide de Marie

Les Maisons de Cappadoce 136 ●

L'Atelier sul Mare 102 ●

A castle of one's own...
Amhuinnsuidhe Castle, Isle of Harris

Amhuinnsuidhe Castle,
Isle of Harris

A castle of one's own

A man's home is his castle, so goes the old saying. Would that this could be one's very own fortress, quite distant from the rest of the world.

Amhuinnsuidhe Castle, on the Isle of Harris, is the most westerly castle in all of Great Britain. Built more than one hundred years ago, it stands at the edge of the sea in dramatic and beautiful surroundings. The castle's domain covers many thousands of acres, and is one of Europe's last unspoilt wildernesses. Although it is privately owned, it can be yours for a week. Set in a rugged landscape of mountains and glens, lochs and rivers, and white sand beaches, it is world famous for its salmon and sea trout fishing. And it was here that the weaving of the classic Harris Tweed fabric first began.

This castle on the beach, sheltered at the head of its own bay, is also a citadel of cuisine. Fortunately, for a place so remote, this is a fortress that is full of great food. Amhuinnsuidhe is well known for its cookery school. Rosemary, the television and real life chef, makes full use of the rich local resources – lobsters and scallops fresh from the sea as well as venison and lamb.

**Books to pack: "Mary Stuart" by Friedrich Schiller
"Ivanhoe" by Sir Walter Scott**

Amhuinnsuidhe Castle

Isle of Harris

Hebrides PA85 3AS

Scotland

United Kingdom

Tel: + 44 (0) 1876 500 329

Fax: + 44 (0) 1876 560 428

E-mail: northuistestate@btinternet.com

Website: www.castlecook.com

Booking: www.great-escapes-hotels.com

DIRECTIONS	There is anchorage in front of the castle and a helicopter landing site. Stornaway airport on Isle of Harris, 1 hour by road, is 40 minutes flying time from Inverness, and 1 hour from Glasgow.
RATES	On application, for a week's fishing, painting classes, or cookery tuition.
ROOMS	8 rooms.
FOOD	Judged as the finest in Scotland.
HISTORY	Built for the Earl of Dunmore in 1867, now home of the Bulmer family.
X-FACTOR	Romantic isolation and picturesque landscape.

Ein Schloss für sich allein

»My home is my castle« lautet ein altes englisches Sprichwort. Dieser Traum von dem eigenen Schloss kann Wirklich-
keit werden an einem Ort weit entfernt vom Rest der Welt.
Das auf der malerischen Isle of Harris gelegene Amhuinnsuidhe Castle ist die am westlichsten gelegene Burg Groß-
britanniens. Sie wurde vor mehr als hundert Jahren direkt
an der Küste inmitten einer aufregenden Landschaft erbaut.
Über mehrere Tausend Hektar erstrecken sich die angren-
zenden Ländereien, welche zu den letzten Flecken unberühr-
ter Natur in Europa gehören. Obwohl sich die Burg in
Privatbesitz befindet, ist es möglich, sie für eine Woche sein
Eigen zu nennen. Eingebettet in zerklüftete Berge und Täler,
Seen und Flüsse sowie weiße Sandstrände, ist sie weltbe-
rühmt für den Fang von Lachs und Meeresforellen. Und
hier war es auch, wo man anfing, den klassischen Harris
Tweed zu weben.
Diese am Strand, im Schutz ihrer eigenen Bucht gelegene
Burg ist zugleich ein Tempel der Kochkunst, der kulinarische Köstlichkeiten bereithält. Amhuinnsuidhe ist bekannt
für seine Kochschule. Rosemary, im Fernsehen wie auch
im wahren Leben die Küchenchefin, macht großzügigen
Gebrauch von dem, was die Natur hier in reichlichem Maße
bietet: Hummer und Kammmuscheln frisch aus dem Meer
sowie Wild und Lamm.

Buchtipps: »Maria Stuart« von Friedrich Schiller
»Ivanhoe« von Sir Walter Scott

Un château pour soi

« Mon chez-moi est mon château » dit un proverbe britannique. Qui n'a pas rêvé parfois de posséder sa propre forteresse
et de vivre dans un château, loin du reste du monde …
Amhuinnsuidhe Castle, sur l'île de Harris, est le château
situé le plus à l'ouest de la Grande-Bretagne. Construit il y a
plus d'un siècle, il se dresse au bord de la mer, à l'abri d'une
baie privative, dans un environnement de toute beauté. Le
domaine, qui couvre quelques milliers d'hectares, est l'un
des derniers sanctuaires sauvages d'Europe. Bien que privée,
cette demeure seigneuriale peut être la vôtre pendant une
semaine. Nichée dans un rude paysage de montagnes, de
glens, de lochs, de rivières et de plages de sable blanc, elle
jouit d'une renommée internationale pour la pêche au
saumon et à la truite de mer. C'est également ici que
naquirent les célèbres filatures Harris Tweed.
Le château est en outre réputé pour sa gastronomie. Malgré
son grand isolement, il offre une table délicieuse et est
aussi très connu pour ses cours de cuisine. Rosemary, chef
cuisinier à la télévision comme dans la vie, tire pleinement
profit des nombreuses ressources locales – les homards, les
coquilles Saint-Jacques, l'agneau et le gibier.

Livres à emporter : « Marie Stuart » de Friedrich Schiller
« Ivanhoé » de Sir Walter Scott

ANREISE	Die Burg verfügt über eigene Ankerplätze und einen Hubschrauberlandeplatz. Von Inverness bis Stornaway Airport auf der Isle of Harris 40 Minuten, von Glasgow eine Stunde Flugzeit; vom Stornaway Airport 1 Stunde Fahrt.
PREIS	Auf Anfrage, für eine Woche Angeln, Malunterricht oder Kochkurse.
ZIMMER	8 Zimmer.
KÜCHE	Sie gilt als die beste in ganz Schottland.
GESCHICHTE	Im Jahre 1867 für den Earl of Dunmore erbaut, heute im Besitz der Familie Bulmer.
X-FAKTOR	Romantische Einsamkeit und malerische Landschaft.

ACCÈS	Il existe un mouillage devant le château et un héliport. L'aéroport de Stornaway sur l'île de Harris est à une heure de route ; il relie Inverness en 40 minutes et Glasgow en 1 heure.
PRIX	Varient selon la formule pour une semaine de pêche, de cours de peinture ou de cours de cuisine.
CHAMBRES	8 chambres.
RESTAURATION	Considérée comme la meilleure d'Écosse.
HISTOIRE	Construit en 1867 pour le duc de Dunmore, aujourd'hui en possession de la famille Bulmer.
LES « PLUS »	Isolement romantique et paysage grandiose.

All aboard...
The Old Railway Station, West Sussex

The Old Railway Station,
West Sussex

All aboard

Trains never arrive or depart on time, or indeed at any time, at this station. You can stay at The Old Railway Station without worrying about timetables and schedules, cocooned in a motionless carriage overlooking the pretty garden. Trains once went through here on their way to and from London and Brighton. Now the only ones left are Alicante and Mimosa, two pre-First World War Pullman carriages that have been beautifully restored into four spacious and elegant rooms, all with en-suite bathrooms. Bearing no resemblance to their previous life as dining cars, the carriages, with their luxurious beds, plush furnishings, and soft colours, are a clever conversion of old to new. Appropriately, they are located next to the historic Victorian railway station. Guests can choose to stay in the carriages or in either of two bedrooms in an annex to the station, whose former waiting room is now a splendid lounge for guests. There is no waiting on a draughty platform or missed connections here, just old-fashioned peace and quiet. A treasure trove of antiques is in the local village.

Book to pack: "Stamboul Train" by Graham Greene

The Old Railway Station	DIRECTIONS	84 km/52 m south of London, 30 minutes drive north of Chichester.
Petworth		
West Sussex GU28 0JF	RATES	£ 36 to 80 per person, including full English breakfast, served in the station or on the platform.
United Kingdom		
Tel: + 44 (0) 1798 342 346	ROOMS	4 rooms on board, 2 in the station.
Fax: + 44 (0) 1798 342 346	FOOD	A 5-minute walk to award-winning local pub, the *Badgers Inn*, for lunch and dinner.
E-mail: query@old-station.co.uk		
Website: www.old-station.co.uk	HISTORY	The railway station was built in 1894.
Booking: www.great-escapes-hotels.com	X-FACTOR	Living in a grown-up's train set.

Alle an Bord?

An diesem alten Bahnhof kommen die Züge weder pünktlich an noch fahren sie pünktlich ab, denn hier fährt überhaupt kein Zug mehr. Sorgen Sie sich also nicht um Fahrpläne und Abfahrtszeiten, sondern genießen Sie unbeschwert Ihren Aufenthalt in The Old Railway Station, in einem der stillgelegten Eisenbahn-Waggons mit Blick auf den bezaubernden Garten. Denn von den Zügen, die hier früher auf dem Weg nach London und Brighton hielten, haben zwei Wurzeln geschlagen: Alicante und Mimosa, zwei Pullman-Wagen aus der Zeit vor dem Ersten Weltkrieg, die liebevoll restauriert wurden und jetzt vier geräumige und elegante Zimmer beherbergen, von denen jedes mit einem Bad ausgestattet ist. Ihre Vergangenheit als Speisewagen sieht man diesen stilvoll eingerichteten Waggons mit ihren luxuriösen Betten und geschmackvoll abgestimmten Farben nicht mehr an. Sinnigerweise wurden sie direkt neben dem historischen viktorianischen Bahnhof platziert, wo die Gäste wahlweise auch in einem der zwei Zimmer im Anbau des Bahnhofs Quartier nehmen können, dessen Wartesaal zu einem romantischen Empfangsraum umgebaut wurde. Vergessen Sie lange Wartezeiten auf zugigen Bahnsteigen und verpasste Anschlusszüge. Hier finden Sie Ruhe und Frieden in nostalgischem Ambiente. Das Örtchen Petworth ist eine Fundgrube für Antiquitätenliebhaber.

Buchtipp: »Orient-Express« von Graham Greene

Fermez les portières

Dans cette ancienne gare, les trains n'arrivent ni ne partent jamais à l'heure : en fait, l'heure n'existe plus. À l'hôtel The Old Railway Station, vous séjournerez confortablement dans un wagon désormais immobile, avec vue sur un ravissant jardin, sans avoir à vous soucier d'horaires ou d'agendas. Les trains reliant Londres à Brighton passaient ici autrefois. Aujourd'hui, il n'en reste plus que deux wagons, Alicante et Mimosa. Ces voitures pullmans d'avant la Première Guerre mondiale, magnifiquement restaurées, abritent désormais quatre chambres spacieuses et élégantes, chacune équipée d'une salle de bains. Judicieusement converties, avec leurs lits luxueux, leur ameublement somptueux et leur décor aux couleurs douces, elles ne gardent aucune trace de leur ancienne fonction de wagon-restaurant. Elles sont stationnées, comme il convient, à côté de la gare datant de l'époque victorienne. On peut loger dans les voitures ou dans les chambres aménagées dans une annexe de la gare dont l'ancienne salle d'attente est aujourd'hui un splendide salon. Ici, tout est calme et repos. Personne n'attend de train dans les courants d'air d'un quai ou ne court pour éviter de manquer sa correspondance. Au village, des trésors attendent les amateurs d'antiquités.

Livre à emporter : « Orient-express » de Graham Greene

ANREISE	84 km südlich von London, 30 Autominuten nördlich von Chichester.
PREIS	36 bis 80 £ pro Person, einschließlich English Breakfast, das im Bahnhof oder auf dem Bahnsteig serviert wird.
ZIMMER	4 Zimmer »an Bord«, 2 im Bahnhof.
KÜCHE	In 5 Gehminuten erreichen Sie den preisgekrönten Pub The Badgers Inn (Mittag- und Abendessen).
GESCHICHTE	1894 wurde der Bahnhof erbaut.
X-FAKTOR	Eisenbahn-Spielen für Erwachsene.

ACCÈS	À 84 km au sud de Londres, à 30 minutes de route au nord de Chichester.
PRIX	De 36 à 80 £ par personne, petit déjeuner anglais complet compris, servi dans la gare ou sur le quai.
CHAMBRES	4 chambres dans les voitures, 2 dans la gare.
RESTAURATION	À 5 minutes à pied d'un pub primé, le Badgers Inn (repas de midi et du soir).
HISTOIRE	La gare existe depuis 1894.
LES « PLUS »	Séjour dans un train nostalgique.

Suite Dreams...
Lute Suites, Ouderkerk aan de Amstel

Lute Suites,
Ouderkerk aan de Amstel

Suite Dreams

When I met Peter Lute and Marcel Wanders for the first time about two years ago in Ouderkerk, the sleepy little town 15 minutes from Amsterdam was still quite unknown – today it is one of Holland's top destinations for design fans. Scene-restaurant chef Lute and designer Wanders, famous for his macramé "Knotted Chair" on show at New York's MoMa, opened the Lute Suites here just a few months ago. This is not a hotel in the classical sense: the suites were created by converting seven listed houses built in 1740 into seven individual apartments, each with a bedroom, living area, kitchenette and bathroom, and each full of Wanders' ideas and accessories. From cream-coloured "soap" bath-tubs you can look out directly at the Amstel, and from your bed at walls full of Bisazza marble or Swarovski crystal; you can walk across lime-green floorboards and up winding teak staircases, or sit under huge orange lamps and glamorous chandeliers. Marcel Wanders combines creative and functional design, antique shapes and modern forms – while Peter Lute provides the high-tech (including flat screen and cordless internet access) and ensures absolute privacy. Anyone who stays in the Lute Suites is not even disturbed by the room service – breakfast, for example, turns up in front of the door as if by magic in a pretty wooden box. In the evening one should, however, leave this home away from home for a couple of hours and eat at the local Lute restaurant, for Peter Lute's cuisine is among the most innovative on offer in Amsterdam and its surroundings at the moment.
Book to pack: "The Discovery of Heaven" by Harry Mulisch

Lute Suites
Amsteldijk Zuid 54-58
1184 Ouderkerk aan de Amstel
The Netherlands
Phone + 31 (0)20 4722462
Fax   + 31 (0)20 4722463
E-mail: info@lutesuites.com
Website: www.lutesuites.com (in Dutch only)
Booking: www.great-escapes-hotels.com

DIRECTIONS	Situated 10 km south of Amsterdam (centre), 15 km from Schiphol Airport.
RATES	Suite for 2 persons from € 300 to € 575 per night (incl. breakfast).
ROOMS	7 suites.
HISTORY	7 designer apartments created out of 7 listed houses located directly on the River Amstel.
X-FACTOR	Dutch design par excellence – a place for individualists.

Suite dreams

Als sich Peter Lute und Marcel Wanders vor knapp zwei Jahren zum ersten Mal in Ouderkerk trafen, war das Städtchen 15 Minuten außerhalb von Amsterdam noch ein unbekanntes verschlafenes Nest – heute gehört es zu Hollands Topzielen für Designfans. Der Szenegastronom Lute und der Designer Wanders, der mit dem Makramé-Thron »Knotted Chair« berühmt wurde und sogar im New Yorker MoMA ausstellt, haben hier vor wenigen Monaten die Lute Suites eröffnet. Dabei handelt es sich um kein Hotel im klassischen Sinn: Für die Suiten wurden sieben denkmalgeschützte Häuser aus dem Jahr 1740 in sieben individuelle Apartments verwandelt – jedes mit Schlafzimmer, Wohnbereich, Kitchenette und Bad; und jedes voller Wanders-Ideen und -Accessoires. Da blickt man aus cremeweißen »Soap«-Badewannen direkt auf die Amstel und vom Bett aus auf Wände voller Bisazza-Marmor oder Swarovski-Kristall, da läuft man über limettengrüne Dielen und Wendeltreppen aus Teakholz oder sitzt unter riesigen orangefarbenen Lampen und glamourösen Kristallleuchtern. Marcel Wanders verbindet kreatives und funktionales Design, antike Anklänge und moderne Formen – Peter Lute liefert Hightech (inklusive Flatscreen und kabellosem Internetzugang) und absolute Privatsphäre mit dazu. Wer in den Lute Suites wohnt, wird selbst vom Zimmerservice nicht gestört – das Frühstück zum Beispiel steht wie von Zauberhand und in einer schönen Holzbox verpackt vor der Tür. Abends sollte man sein Heim auf Zeit aber doch für einige Stunden verlassen und im nahen Restaurant Lute essen, denn auch Peter Lutes Küche gehört zum Innovativsten, was Amsterdam und Region derzeit zu bieten haben.
Buchtipp: »Die Entdeckung des Himmels« von Harry Mulisch

Suite dreams

Lorsque Peter Lute et Marcel Wanders se rencontrèrent pour la première fois il y a à peine deux ans à Ouderkerk, cette petite ville située à 15 minutes d'Amsterdam n'était encore qu'une bourgade endormie, inconnue, alors qu'elle est devenue aujourd'hui l'une des destinations privilégiées en Hollande pour les passionnés du design. Lute, le gastronome tendance, et Wanders, le designer qui a exposé au MoMA (New York) et est devenu célèbre avec son Trône en makramé, « Knotted Chair », ont ouvert ici depuis quelques mois les Suites Lute. Il ne s'agit pas d'un hôtel au sens classique : sept immeubles datant de 1740 et classés aux monuments historiques ont été transformés en sept appartements individuels – chacun avec chambre à coucher, espace salon, kitchenette et salle de bain ... et tout plein d'idées et d'accessoires Wanders. Depuis les baignoires « Soap » blanc-crème, la vue donne directement sur l'Amstel, et depuis le lit sur des murs recouverts de marbre Bisazza ou de cristal Swarovski. On marche sur des planchers vert-citron, on monte ou descend des escaliers tournants en bois de teck, ou l'on s'assoit sous d'immenses lampes de couleur orange et de prestigieux lustres de cristal. Marcel Wanders conjugue design créatif et fonctionnel, connotations antiques et formes modernes – Peter Lute livre de la haute technologie (y compris des écrans plats et un accès Internet sans fil) et garantit une sphère totalement privée. L'hôte d'une Suite Lute n'est même pas dérangé par le service à la chambre – le petit déjeuner, par exemple, est déposé comme par magie devant la porte, protégé dans une belle boîte en bois. Le soir, quittez votre cocon pour quelques heures, et allez manger dans le restaurant Lute tout proche, car la cuisine de Peter Lute fait partie des propositions les plus innovantes qu'Amsterdam et la région ont actuellement à offrir.
Livre à emporter : « La découverte du ciel » de Harry Mulisch

ANREISE	10 km südlich von Amsterdam (Zentrum) gelegen, 15 km vom Flughafen Schiphol entfernt.
PREIS	Suite für 2 Personen von 300 bis 575 € pro Nacht (inklusive Frühstück).
ZIMMER	7 Suiten.
GESCHICHTE	Aus 7 denkmalgeschützten Häusern direkt an der Amstel wurden 7 Design-Apartments.
X-FAKTOR	Niederländisches Design par excellence – und eine Adresse für Individualisten.

ACCÈS	A 10 km au sud d'Amsterdam (centre), à 15 km de l'aéroport Schiphol.
PRIX	Suite pour 2 personnes de 300 à 575 € par nuit (petit déjeuner compris).
CHAMBRES	7 Suites.
HISTOIRE	7 maisons classées monuments historiques, construites sur le bord de l'Amstel, ont été transformées en 7 appartements design.
LES « PLUS »	Le design néerlandais par excellence – et une adresse pour individualistes.

Sage advice...
Domein Scholteshof, Vlaanderen

Domein Scholteshof, Vlaanderen

Sage advice

Not far from the urban bustle of Brussels is a gem of a country house, one that would soothe the most stressed of bureaucrats.

All those in need of rest and relaxation, not too far from the city, will find that Domein Scholteshof is just the place to get it. A restored 18th-century farmhouse that has been furnished with art and antiques, it is set in acres of gardens. A few days spent immersed in these quiet surroundings will soon calm the nerves; and the cuisine is sure to appeal to the appetite. The chef is considered to be one of Belgium's best. The elegant rooms round out the great menu here. While the restaurants have been marked on the epicurean map, the hotel is the icing on the cake.

Each of the rooms bears the Latin name of one of the aromatic plants that grow in the herb garden. In keeping with the gastronomic focus that attracts its guests, freshly picked sprigs of herbs are more often than not placed on the pillows at night. The subtle scent lingers in the air. A good night's sleep is quite likely to follow.

Book to pack: "Maigret and the Flemish Shop" by Georges Simenon

Domein Scholteshof		
Kermstraat 130		
3512 Steveoort-Hasselt		
Belgium		
Tel: + 32 (0) 11 250 202		
Fax: + 32 (0) 11 254 328		
E-mail: info@scholteshof.be		
Website: www.scholteshof.be		
Booking: www.great-escapes-hotels.com		

DIRECTIONS	An hour's drive east of Brussels.
RATES	Rooms from € 100 to 225, apartments € 350.
ROOMS	17 rooms and suites, 2 apartments.
FOOD	The great attraction.
HISTORY	Domein Scholteshof has been built at the beginning of the 18th century. It has been renovated and opened to the public in 1983.
X-FACTOR	A gourmet "Garden of Eden" – without the serpent.

Die Kräuterhexe empfiehlt

Nicht weit vom großstädtischen Trubel Brüssels entfernt liegt ein Landhaus, dessen Schönheit die Nerven selbst gestresstester Euro-Bürokraten beruhigen würde.
Wer nach Ruhe und Entspannung sucht, aber dies nicht zu weit von einer Stadt entfernt, für den ist Domein Scholteshof genau der richtige Ort. Das restaurierte Bauernhaus aus dem 18. Jahrhundert ist mit Kunst und Antiquitäten geschmackvoll eingerichtet und liegt in einer weitläufigen Gartenanlage. Schon nach einigen Tagen Aufenthalt stellt sich ein doppelter Effekt ein: Die Nerven sind beruhigt und der Gaumen ist wach gekitzelt. Kein Wunder, gilt der Küchenchef doch als einer der besten Belgiens. So überrascht es nicht, dass Gourmets das Hotel ganz gezielt ansteuern. Aber die eleganten Zimmer stehen dem großartigen Menü in nichts nach. Jedes Hotelzimmer trägt den lateinischen Namen einer der Aromapflanzen, die im Kräutergarten angebaut werden. Passend zum gastronomischen Schwerpunkt findet der Gast abends oft ein Sträußchen aus frisch gepflückten Kräutern auf seinem Kissen. Ihr zarter Duft durchzieht die Luft und bringt tiefen, wohligen Schlaf.

Buchtipp: »Maigret bei den Flamen« von Georges Simenon

Sage conseil

Non loin de l'agitation bruxelloise se cache une délicieuse maison de campagne, propice à une détente bien méritée. Vous avez besoin de repos et de calme pas trop loin de la ville? Le Domein Scholteshof est ce qu'il vous faut. Cette ferme restaurée du XVIIIe siècle, meublée d'objets d'art et d'antiquités, est située au cœur d'un parc immense. Quelques jours passés dans ce paisible environnement suffiront à calmer vos nerfs... et votre appétit. Le chef est l'une des plus grandes toques de Belgique. Les élégantes salles à manger complètent la carte alléchante. Mais si le restaurant figure sur l'atlas gastronomique, l'hôtel est la cerise sur le gâteau.
Chaque chambre porte le nom scientifique d'une des plantes aromatiques cultivées dans le jardin de l'hôtel.
Conformément à l'esprit gastronomique qui règne en ces lieux, des brins de fines herbes fraîches sont placés le soir sur les oreillers. Leur subtile et apaisante odeur vous mènera vite dans les bras de Morphée.

Livre à emporter : « Chez les Flamands » de Georges Simenon

ANREISE	Eine Stunde Autofahrt östlich von Brüssel.
PREIS	Zimmer von 100 bis 225 €, Apartments 350 €.
ZIMMER	17 Zimmer und Suiten, 2 Apartments.
KÜCHE	Eine der Hauptattraktionen.
GESCHICHTE	Erbaut zu Beginn des 18. Jahrhunderts, als Hotel eröffnet im Jahr 1983.
X-FAKTOR	Ein Paradies für Gourmets – ohne Schlange.

ACCÈS	À une heure de route à l'est de Bruxelles.
PRIX	Les chambres de 100 à 225 €, les appartements 350 €.
CHAMBRES	17 chambres et suites, 2 appartements.
RESTAURATION	L'attrait majeur.
HISTOIRE	Construit au début du XVIIIe siècle, hôtel depuis 1983.
LES « PLUS »	Un « jardin d'Eden » gourmand... sans le serpent !

Remembrance of times passe

Seehotel am Neuklostersee, Mecklenburg

Seehotel am Neuklostersee, Mecklenburg

Remembrance of times passed

This seems like a place that is kept in the memory, of a blissful childhood holiday; a summer spent by a lake. A place there used to be when one was very young and carefree. Long warm days in the sun and fresh air; untroubled by the stresses and strains that come with adulthood.

This is evocative of that age, where "grown-ups" may recall some of the gentle times of their lost youth. The Seehotel is on the shores of Lake Neukloster; in surroundings so peaceful it is almost like being in a dream.

The hotel's simple design is in accord with its country setting. While its style appears to be classic, there is a modern overlay that makes it more chic than rustic.

Being in this tranquil atmosphere, of white and cream, of natural colours and textures, gives a welcome soft focus on the world. In a boat on the lake, drifting through the reeds; cocooned in a wicker bathing chair reading, asleep, or just gazing at the sparkling water; there is no hurry here, no need to do anything taxing. Whether picking wildflowers, fishing from the end of the jetty, or merely daydreaming; staying here can all be part of going back, just for a short time, to a simpler way of life.

Books to pack: "Flights of Love" by Bernhard Schlink
"Elective Affinities" by Johann Wolfgang von Goethe

Seehotel am Neuklostersee	
Seestrasse 1	
23992 Nakenstorf bei Neukloster	
Germany	
Tel: + 49 (0) 38422 254 45	
Fax: + 49 (0) 38422 256 30	
E-mail: seehotel@nalbach-architekten.de	
Website: www.Seehotel-Neuklostersee.de	
Booking: www.great-escapes-hotels.com	

DIRECTIONS	15 km/9 m east from Wismar, 2.5 hours' drive from either Berlin or Hamburg.
RATES	Rooms from € 64, bungalows from € 110; including breakfast.
ROOMS	12 rooms, 1 apartment and 3 bungalows.
FOOD	The restaurant offers traditional rural North German cooking.
HISTORY	The house was built at the beginning of the 19th century. During the GDR it served as a holiday resort. The hotel was opened in 1993.
X-FACTOR	Back to the way things were …

Erinnerung an alte Zeiten

Der Ort wirkt wie ein Bild aus Kindertagen, als man unbeschwerte Sommerferien am See genoss. Dies scheint der Ort zu sein, an dem man weilte, als man noch jung und frei von Sorgen war und lange, warme Tage im Sonnenschein und an der frischen Luft verbrachte ohne jeden Zwang und Druck. Dieser zauberhafte Ort vermag es, Sie in die glückliche Zeit Ihrer Jugend zurückzuversetzen.

Am Ufer des Neuklostersees gelegen, ist das Seehotel eingebettet in eine friedliche Landschaft, wie man sie sonst nur aus Träumen kennt. Die schlichte Bauweise des Hotels steht in Einklang mit der ländlichen Umgebung. Obwohl es auf den ersten Blick recht traditionell erscheint, ist es nach seiner Modernisierung eher schick als rustikal zu nennen. Die beruhigende Atmosphäre von cremefarbenen und weißen Tönen, von Naturfarben und -stoffen macht herrlich gelassen und zufrieden. In einem Boot durch das Schilfrohr treiben, in einem Strandkorb gemütlich lesen, schlafen oder einfach nur auf das vor sich hin plätschernde Wasser blicken – es besteht kein Grund zur Eile, es gibt nichts, was nicht auch warten könnte. Egal ob man Wildblumen pflückt, am Ende der Mole angelt oder einfach nur in den Tag hinein träumt – hier an diesem Ort gelingt es einem, wenigstens für eine kurze Zeit einen kleinen Schritt zurückzutun zu einem einfacheren und sorgloseren Leben.

Buchtipps: »Liebesfluchten« von Bernhard Schlink
»Die Wahlverwandtschaften« von Johann Wolfgang von Goethe

Souvenirs des temps passés

C'est un endroit qui évoque des souvenirs d'enfance, ceux de merveilleuses vacances estivales passées au bord d'un lac. Un de ces endroits que l'on associe à sa jeunesse insouciante, à de longues journées chaudes remplies de soleil et de bon air, exemptes des contraintes et des soucis qu'apporte la vie adulte.

Au Seehotel, les « grands » replongeront avec délices dans les réminiscences de leur jeunesse perdue ... Le complexe s'étend sur les rives du lac Neukloster, dans un cadre si paisible que l'on se croirait dans un rêve.

L'architecture simple de l'hôtel est en parfaite symbiose avec son environnement. En apparence de style traditionnel, l'établissement est doté d'un confort moderne qui le rend plus chic que rustique. L'ambiance paisible, faite de blanc et crème, de textures et couleurs naturelles, adoucit les âmes. Un tour en bateau à travers les roseaux du lac, une sieste, une heure de lecture ou de rêverie, installé dans un confortable fauteuil en osier, au bord de l'eau ... Ici, les journées se déroulent sans hâte ni précipitation. Que l'on aille cueillir des fleurs sauvages, pêcher au bout de la jetée ou que l'on se relaxe tout simplement, séjourner dans cet endroit fait retrouver un mode de vie plus simple, près de la nature.

**Livres à emporter : « Amours en fuite » de Bernhard Schlink
« Les Affinités électives » de Johann Wolfgang von Goethe**

ANREISE	15 km von Wismar, 2,5 Autostunden nördlich von Berlin und östlich Hamburg.	ACCÈS	À 15 km de Wismar et à 2 heures 30 de route au nord de Berlin et à l'est de Hambourg.
PREIS	Zimmer ab 64 €, Bungalows ab 110 €, Frühstück inklusive.	PRIX	Chambres de 64 €, bungalows de 110 €, petit déjeuner compris.
ZIMMER	12 Zimmer, 1 Apartment und 3 Bungalows.	CHAMBRES	12 chambres, 1 studio et 3 bungalows.
KÜCHE	Das Restaurant bietet traditionelle norddeutsche Küche an.	RESTAURATION	Une cuisine traditionnelle d'Allemagne du Nord.
GESCHICHTE	Das Haus wurde Ende des 19. Jahrhunderts gebaut und war zu DDR-Zeiten ein Ferienheim. Als Hotel öffnete es 1993.	HISTOIRE	Construit à la fin du XIXe siècle dernier, le bâtiment était un centre de vacances sous la RDA. L'hôtel a ouvert ses portes en 1993.
X-FAKTOR	Eine Reise zurück in die Vergangenheit.	LES « PLUS »	Comme au bon vieux temps ...

Perfect peace and deep quiet
Landhaus Börmoos, Schleswig-Holstein

Landhaus Börmoos,
Schleswig-Holstein

Perfect peace and deep quiet

They say that the air here is more sparkling than champagne; that the landscape is balm for the soul. High praise and claims indeed for the land of Schleswig-Holstein. This countryside between the two seas, the Baltic and the North Sea, is one of pleasing contrasts. Gentle hills, roads lined with trees, sleepy villages, fresh air, the sun reflecting on the waves; this is country life at its best.

A trip to this part of the world will quite likely cause one to contemplate moving here. The owners of this lovely old farmhouse thought that too, when they saw it nestled in the landscape. So they did.

In the midst of fields and moorland, near lakes and very close to the coast, it is in an idyllic spot. Both Landhaus Börmoos and the barn have been restored to mint condition. Under the thatched roof and beamed ceilings are charming rooms with huge alcove beds; once they have got used to the lack of noise these may be some of the best nights of sleep that guests experience. A weekend or longer here, with good food and wine, and pleasant strolls along the beach or by the lakes, would be bliss indeed.

And for those who must hit a ball, there is a splendid golf course nearby.

Book to pack: "Effi Briest" by Theodor Fontane

Landhaus Börmoos	DIRECTIONS	About 180 km north of Hamburg, nearest town is Flensburg, very near the Danish border.
Grüfft 9	RATES	€ 75 to 95 per apartment, € 10 for breakfast.
24972 Steinbergkirche/Habernis	ROOMS	8 apartments, each for 2-5 people, in the house and adjacent barn.
Germany		
Tel: + 49 (0) 4632 7621		
Fax: + 47 (0) 4632 1429	FOOD	Farmhouse-style breakfasts in the lovely old hall.
E-mail: landhaus.boermoos@t-online.de	HISTORY	The house and the barn were built in 1876 and the Landhaus Börmoos has received guests since 1985.
Website: www.landhaus-boermoos.de	X-FACTOR	The quiet that prevails.
Booking: www.great-escapes-hotels.com		

Tiefer Frieden und vollkommene Ruhe

Man sagt, die Luft hier sei besser als Champagner und die Landschaft Balsam für die Seele – ein hohes Lob für das Land Schleswig-Holstein. Die Region zwischen Ostsee und Nordsee ist reich an Kontrasten: Geschwungene Hügellandschaften, lange Alleen, verschlafene Dörfchen, viel frische Luft und die Sonne, die auf den Wellen der Meere glitzert – so lässt es sich auf dem Lande aushalten!

Eine Reise zu diesem Fleckchen Erde wird in jedem den Wunsch hervorrufen, hier zu wohnen. Nicht anders erging es den Besitzern dieses wunderschönen alten Bauernhauses, das sich harmonisch in die Landschaft einfügt, als sie es zum ersten Mal sahen. Und sie setzten ihren Wunsch in die Tat um. Inmitten von Feldern und Moorlandschaften, in der unmittelbaren Nähe von Seen und der Ostseeküste ist hier ein überaus idyllischer Ort entstanden. Das Haus und die ehemalige Scheune sind beide perfekt restauriert. Unter einem Reetdach und von massiven Holzbalken getragenen Decken befinden sich gemütliche Zimmer mit riesigen Alkovenbetten, in denen die Gäste den vielleicht besten Schlaf ihres Lebens genießen – wenn sie sich erst an die Stille gewöhnt haben. Ein Wochenende oder ein längerer Aufenthalt mit gutem Essen und gutem Wein, mit traumhaften Spaziergängen am Strand oder an den Seen ist wahre Glückseligkeit.

Und wem das zu viel der Ruhe ist, der darf sich auf dem nahe gelegenen Golfplatz betätigen.

Buchtipp: »Effi Briest« von Theodor Fontane

Silence et sérénité

On dit qu'ici, l'air est plus pétillant que le champagne et que la nature apaise les âmes. Bref, on ne tarit pas d'éloges sur le Land de Schleswig-Holstein. S'étirant entre deux mers, la Baltique et la mer du Nord, la région offre de plaisants contrastes. Avec ses paysages vallonnés, ses routes bordées d'arbres, ses villages endormis, son air vif et piquant, son soleil se réfléchissant sur les vagues, elle incarne la douceur de la vie champêtre.

Il y a fort à parier qu'un séjour dans cette partie du monde vous donnera envie d'y rester pour toujours. En tous les cas, c'est l'idée qu'ont eue les propriétaires de Börmoos en découvrant cette ravissante ferme nichée dans la campagne. Ils s'y sont installés.

Börmoos est un endroit tout simplement idyllique, situé au cœur de champs et de landes, non loin de jolis lacs et tout près du littoral. La ferme et la grange ont été entièrement remises à neuf. Le toit de chaume et les plafonds aux poutres apparentes abritent de charmantes chambres dotées d'immenses lits en alcôve. Une fois accoutumés à l'absence de tout bruit, les hôtes pourront goûter un sommeil comme ils en ont rarement connu. Un week-end ou quelques jours passés dans cette auberge, agrémentés d'une cuisine et de vins de qualité ainsi que d'agréables promenades au bord de la plage ou des lacs, vous laisseront un souvenir impérissable.

Pour les inconditionnels, un superbe terrain de golf se trouve juste à côté.

Livre à emporter : « Effi Briest » de Theodor Fontane

ANREISE	Etwa 180 km nördlich von Hamburg und nahe der dänischen Grenze beim Städtchen Habernis gelegen.
PREIS	75 bis 95 € pro Apartment, Frühstück 10 €.
ZIMMER	8 Apartments für je 2–5 Gäste im Haupthaus und anliegender Scheune.
KÜCHE	Gemütlich-gehaltvolles Bauernfrühstück in der hübschen alten Frühstücksdiele.
GESCHICHTE	Haupthaus und Scheune stammen aus dem Jahr 1876. Das Landhaus Bömoos empfängt seit 1985 Gäste.
X-FAKTOR	Ruhe überall.

ACCÈS	Environ 180 km au nord de Hambourg, tout près de la frontière danoise ; la ville la plus proche est Habernis.
PRIX	De 75 à 95 €, petit déjeuner 10 €.
CHAMBRES	8 appartements pour 2 à 5 personnes, dans la ferme ou la grange adjacente.
RESTAURATION	Petits déjeuners «fermiers» pris dans le vestibule au beau mobilier rustique.
HISTOIRE	La ferme et la grange datent de 1876. L'hôtel a ouvert ses portes en 1985.
LES « PLUS »	Calme et paix.

Where the truffle nose comes

Le Chaufourg en Périgord, Dordogne

from...

Le Chaufourg en Périgord, Dordogne

Where the truffle nose comes from

In the ninth century, the Vikings sailed up the River Dordogne near here, raiding many towns on the way. If this house had already been there, no doubt they would have moved in and stayed put.

It was another eight hundred years before Le Chaufourg was built; its doors are open now to guests seeking peace.

Though it is in the heart of the Dordogne, once you are inside the gates that lead to the courtyard, you have a sense of seclusion from the real world. The quite fairytale façade of the house adds to that feeling. Its white-shuttered doors and ivy-laced windows suggest that there is a charming interior to be revealed; one that will more than match up with the outside. That wish comes true. All the rooms are simply romantic; indeed so much so that you might feel inspired to live here happily ever after.

As well as Vikings, others with a nose for good things have come here. This region is the home of the black truffles, "black pearls" that trained dogs can smell and dig out of the ground. And Cyrano, the owner of the most famous nose of all, was from the nearby town of Bergerac.

Book to pack: "Cyrano de Bergerac" by Edmond Rostand

Le Chaufourg en Périgord
24400 Sourzac-Mussidan
Dordogne
France
Tel: + 33 (0) 5 53 81 01 56
Fax: + 33 (0) 5 53 82 94 87
E-mail: chaufourg.hotel@lechaufourg.com
Website: www.lechaufourg.com
Booking: www.great-escapes-hotels.com

DIRECTIONS	1.5 hours' drive east from Bordeaux; 26 km/16 m from Bergerac.
RATES	€ 136 to 274, 2-night minimum. Open March to November and on reservation.
ROOMS	5 rooms and 4 suites.
FOOD	A restaurant serving delicious local specialties.
HISTORY	Built in the 17th century, Le Chaufourg opened as a hotel in 1991.
X-FACTOR	A place to make-believe could be your own.

Auf Trüffelsuche

Im 9. Jahrhundert segelten die Wikinger den nahe gelegenen Fluss hinauf und brandschatzten viele Städte auf ihrem Weg. Hätte dieses Haus damals schon gestanden, wären sie sicher stattdessen dort eingezogen und lebten bis heute hier. Doch Le Chaufourg wurde erst acht Jahrhunderte später erbaut, und seine Türen stehen heute friedlicheren Gästen offen. Sobald man die Tore durchschritten hat, die auf den Innenhof des Hotels führen, fühlt man sich vom wirklichen Leben abgeschottet. Fast wie im Märchenland sieht die Fassade des Hauses aus, und die weiß gestrichenen Türen und Läden, die efeuumrankten Fenster lassen ahnen, dass das Innere des Hauses ebenfalls viel Charme besitzt, vielleicht sogar noch mehr. Und die erste Ahnung wird nicht enttäuscht. Alle Zimmer sind sehr romantisch und lassen den Wunsch aufkommen, hier glücklich und zufrieden bis ans Ende der Tage zu leben.

Neben den Wikingern hielten auch andere Lebewesen mit einem »Riecher« für Gutes und Teures hier Einzug. Denn diese Region ist Heimat der schwarzen Trüffel, des »schwarzen Goldes«, das von Trüffelhunden über die Nase aufgenommen und mit den Pfoten aus dem Boden gegraben wird. Auch der Inhaber der berühmtesten Nase der Welt, Cyrano von Bergerac, stammte hier aus der Nähe.

Buchtipp: »Cyrano von Bergerac« von Edmond Rostand

Au pays des truffes

Au IXe siècle, les Vikings remontèrent la rivière toute proche, attaquant de nombreuses localités au passage. Si cette maison avait été là, ils y auraient certainement élu domicile et l'on n'aurait plus entendu parler d'eux.

Mais Le Chaufourg ne fut construit que huit siècles plus tard. Aujourd'hui, il ouvre ses portes à quiconque recherche la tranquillité. Bien que situé en plein cœur de la Dordogne, l'hôtel semble être à des milliers de kilomètres de toute civilisation. Caché au fond d'une cour, il évoque une maison de contes de fées. La façade aux volets blancs et aux fenêtres couronnées de lierre laisse deviner un intérieur plein de cachet et de charme. De fait, toutes les pièces sont si délicieusement romantiques que vous souhaiterez y vivre heureux jusqu'à la fin de vos jours, comme dans les contes. Outre les Vikings, bien d'autres, ayant le nez fin, sont venus en ces lieux. La région est réputée pour ses truffes noires que des chiens dressés détectent et déterrent. Par ailleurs, celui qui était doté du nez le plus célèbre au monde, Cyrano de Bergerac, est originaire de la ville toute proche.

Livre à emporter : « Cyrano de Bergerac » d'Edmond Rostand

ANREISE	1,5 Fahrstunden östlich von Bordeaux, 26 km von Bergerac entfernt.
PREIS	Zwischen 136 und 274 €, zwei Nächte Minimum. Geöffnet von März bis November.
ZIMMER	5 Zimmer und 4 Suiten.
KÜCHE	Ein angeschlossenes Restaurant serviert köstlichste regionale Spezialitäten.
GESCHICHTE	Erbaut im 17. Jahrhundert, seit 1991 Hotel.
X-FAKTOR	Ein Ort, den man sich wünscht zu besitzen.

ACCÈS	À 1,5 heures à l'est de Bordeaux et 26 km de Bergerac.
PRIX	De 136 à 274 €, 2 nuits minimum. Ouvert de mars à novembre.
CHAMBRES	5 chambres, 4 suites.
RESTAURATION	Délicieuses spécialités locales.
HISTOIRE	Construit au XVIIe siècle, hôtel depuis 1991.
LES « PLUS »	Un endroit où l'on se sent chez soi.

Far from the madding crowd...
Les Maisons Marines d'Huchet, Aquitaine

Les Maisons Marines d'Huchet, Aquitaine

Far from the madding crowd

A tall structure often marks the site of somewhere special. In a distant place in France, far from the crowds that flock to see his famous Parisian tower, there is a small marine beacon built by Gustave Eiffel. It also marks a special spot. On the Atlantic coast between Bordeaux and Biarritz there are many miles of deserted beaches, edged by forests of pine trees. Hidden amongst the sand dunes is a tiny retreat where the motto is "keep it simple". Les Maisons Marines consist of just three beach houses, an unusual trio. The distinctive main house was built some one hundred and fifty years ago as a hunting lodge. The other two houses, once boatsheds, are now charming little guest cottages set apart in this quiet hideaway.

Access to Les Maisons Marines is circuitous; there is no direct route to here, because first you must stay at one of Michel and Christine Guérard's hotels at Eugénie-les-Bains, like Les Prés d'Eugénie, to gain admittance to the beach houses. They are more like a private home than a hotel, one the owners invite you to share, and a special place to take time out and savour the solitude. The sound of the surf will lull you to sleep.

Book to pack: "Les Misérables" by Victor Hugo

Les Maisons Marines d'Huchet	
40320 Eugénie-les-Bains	
France	
Tel: + 33 (0) 5 58 05 06 07	
Fax: + 33 (0) 5 58 51 10 10	
E-mail: guerard@relaischateaux.fr	
Website: www.relaischateaux.fr/guerard	
Booking: www.great-escapes-hotels.com	

DIRECTIONS	150 km/93 m south from Bordeaux Airport.
RATES	€ 183 to 366.
ROOMS	2 houses that accommodate two people.
FOOD	Menus by a master chef.
HISTORY	Built in the middle of the 19th century, Les Maisons Marines opened as guesthouses in December 1999.
X-FACTOR	Solitude and scenery with special surroundings and food.

Abseits des Massentourismus

Es kommt häufig vor, dass ein Ort, der etwas Außergewöhnliches zu bieten hat, durch ein hohes Bauwerk gekennzeichnet ist. In einem entlegenen Winkel an der Westküste Frankreichs, weitab von den Touristenmassen, die sich um seinen berühmten Turm in Paris drängen, steht ein kleines, von Gustave Eiffel erbautes Leuchtfeuer, das mit Sicherheit auf einen ganz besonderen Ort verweist.

Zwischen Bordeaux und Biarritz erstrecken sich entlang der Atlantikküste lange, einsame Strände, die von Pinienwäldern geschützt werden. Versteckt in den Sanddünen liegt ein kleines Refugium, in dem das Motto »weniger ist mehr« stilvoll gelebt wird. Les Maisons Marines sind genau drei Strandhäuser: Das markante Haupthaus wurde vor etwa 150 Jahren als Jagdhütte erbaut. Die beiden anderen Gebäude dienten früher als Bootshäuser und sind heute bezaubernde kleine Ferienhäuschen, die ganz im Verborgenen liegen.

Es ist jedoch ein Umweg nötig, um nach Les Maisons Marines zu kommen, denn Sie müssen zuvor in einem der Hotels von Michel und Christine Guérard in Eugénie-les-Bains, wie etwa dem Les Prés d'Eugénie, zu Gast gewesen sein. In den Strandhäusern sind Sie dann eher privilegierter Hausgast der Besitzer als Hotelbesucher. Nutzen Sie die Abgeschiedenheit, um zur Ruhe zu kommen, und lassen Sie sich nachts vom Rauschen des Meeres in den Schlaf wiegen.

Buchtipps: »Die Elenden« von Victor Hugo

Loin des foules

Il est fréquent qu'un lieu extraordinaire se distingue par un bâtiment de haute taille. Dans un coin reculé de France, loin des foules qui affluent pour visiter la célèbre tour Eiffel à Paris, se trouve un petit phare également construit par Gustave Eiffel, soulignant lui aussi un lieu remarquable.

De Bordeaux à Biarritz, la côte Atlantique s'étend sur des kilomètres de plages désertes, bordées de forêts de pins. Dans les dunes se cache une retraite minuscule où le mot d'ordre est « simplicité ». Au nombre de trois, ces Maisons Marines forment un trio original. La plus grande, d'aspect distinctif, est un ancien pavillon de chasse construit il y a environ 150 ans. Les deux autres, d'anciens hangars à bateaux, sont aujourd'hui de charmantes petites maisons d'hôtes, situées à l'écart dans cette retraite paisible.

L'accès aux Maisons Marines se fait par des chemins détournés : pour y être admis, il faut d'abord séjourner dans l'un des hôtels de Michel et Christine Guérard, à Eugénie-les-Bains ou aux Prés d'Eugénie. Elles ressemblent moins à un hôtel qu'à des demeures privées que leur propriétaire vous aurait invité à partager. Dans ce lieu privilégié dont vous savourerez la solitude, vous vous reposerez, bercé par le clapotis des vagues.

Livre à emporter : « Les Misérables » de Victor Hugo

ANREISE	150 km südlich vom internationalen Flughafen Bordeaux.
PREIS	Zwischen 183 und 366 €.
ZIMMER	2 Häuser für je 2 Personen.
KÜCHE	Menüs gekocht von einem Spitzenkoch.
GESCHICHTE	Les Maisons Marines wurden Mitte des 19. Jahrhundert erbaut und werden seit Dezember 1999 als Gästehäuser genutzt.
X-FAKTOR	Abgeschiedenheit, schöne Umgebung und hervorragendes Essen.

ACCÈS	À 150 km au sud de l'aéroport international de Bordeaux.
PRIX	De 183 à 366 €.
CHAMBRES	2 maisons accueillant deux personnes.
RESTAURATION	Cuisine d'un chef cuisinier.
HISTOIRE	Construites au milieu du XIXe siècle, Les Maisons Marines ouvraient leurs portes en décembre 1999.
LES « PLUS »	Solitude, cadre superbe et gastronomie.

A providential place...
La Bastide de Marie, Provence

La Bastide de Marie, Provence

A providential place

To have a centuries-old house with its own vineyard in one of the most beautiful parts of France, in reach of charming villages, has been a dream of many.

High in the Lubéron Mountains of Provence, that fantasy can come partly true by staying at La Bastide de Marie, a small inn more like a home than a hotel. Set in a vineyard that produces promising red, white, and rosé Côtes du Lubéron, the rustic old farmhouse has been given a new lease of life. Contemporary restful colours, and the peace and quiet of the setting make this a haven for travellers who crave tranquillity and nourishment of body and mind. When the air is scented with lavender, sunlight bathes the walled garden, and delectable food and wine is served beside the pool, one could dream of not going home.

On a nearby hillside is the picturesque village of Ménerbes. This may be as far as guests of La Bastide de Marie might want to venture. For those who feel like going further on shopping expeditions, there are lively weekly markets in the surrounding countryside, specialising in collectables from pottery to antiques.

Books to pack: "The Water of the Hills" by Marcel Pagnol "Perfume" by Patrick Süskind

La Bastide de Marie
Route de Bonnieux
Quartier de la Verrerie
84560 Ménerbes
France
Tel: + 33 (0)4 90 72 30 20
Fax: + 33 (0)4 90 72 54 20
E-mail: bastidemarie@c-h-m.com
Website: www.c-h-m.com
Booking: www.great-escapes-hotels.com

DIRECTIONS	An hour's drive north from Marseille Airport, 40 minutes east from the airport of Avignon; 2.5 hours with TGV south from Paris.
RATES	Rooms from € 370 to 450, suites from € 565 to 640 inclusive of all but lunch or dinner.
ROOMS	8 rooms and 4 suites.
FOOD	The best of Provencal cuisine.
HISTORY	Built in the 18th century, La Bastide de Marie was opened as a hotel in 2000.
X-FACTOR	A taste of Provence the way it should be.

Ein schicksalhafter Ort

Wer hat nicht schon einmal davon geträumt, Besitzer eines jahrhundertealten Hauses mit eigenem Weinberg zu sein, welches in einer der schönsten Regionen Frankreichs liegt, umgeben von charmanten Dörfern?

Zumindest für eine Weile können Sie sich diesen Traum hoch in den Lubéron-Bergen der Provence in La Bastide de Marie erfüllen, einem bezaubernden, kleinen Hotel, das fast wie ein Zuhause ist. Inmitten eines Weinbergs gelegen, der viel versprechenden roten, weißen und rosé Côtes du Lubéron hervorbringt, erlebt dieses rustikale alte Bauernhaus einen zweiten Frühling. Angenehme, ruhige Farben und die friedliche Umgebung machen es zu einer Zuflucht für Reisende, die sich nach stressfreier Erholung für Körper und Seele sehnen. Wenn Lavendelduft in der Luft liegt, die Sonne auf dem von Mauern geschützten Garten liegt und köstliche Gerichte und Weine am Pool serviert werden, lässt es sich leicht davon träumen, für immer zu bleiben.

Auf einem nahe gelegenen Hügel liegt das malerische Dörfchen Ménerbes. Und weiter möchten sich viele Gäste von La Bastide de Marie möglicherweise gar nicht entfernen. Wer aber gern auch mal einen Einkaufsbummel unternimmt, sollte die lebhaften Wochenmärkte in den Dörfern der Umgebung besuchen, wo Sammlerstücke von Töpferwaren bis zu Antiquitäten angeboten werden.

Buchtipps: »Die Wasser der Hügel« von Marcel Pagnol »Das Parfüm« von Patrick Süskind

Un lieu providentiel

Nombreux sont ceux qui rêvent de posséder une vieille maison nichée au cœur des vignes, non loin de charmants villages, dans l'une de ces belles régions de France.

Ce rêve se réalise le temps d'un séjour à La Bastide de Marie, une petite auberge perchée dans les Montagnes du Lubéron, qui évoque davantage une maison de famille qu'un hôtel. Située dans un vignoble produisant d'excellents Côtes du Lubéron rouges, blancs et rosés, cette ancienne ferme a trouvé une nouvelle jeunesse. Le décor aux couleurs reposantes et le cadre serein en font un havre de paix pour qui a soif de quiétude et recherche à la fois des nourritures spirituelles et terrestres. Séduit par l'air embaumant la lavande, par le soleil qui baigne le jardin clos et par les mets et vins délicieux servis près de la piscine, on s'imaginerait bien de ne plus jamais rentrer chez soi.

Sur une colline voisine s'élève le pittoresque village de Ménerbes. Parfois, les hôtes de La Bastide de Marie ne souhaitent pas s'aventurer plus loin. Les marchés hebdomadaires des environs offrent toutes sortes d'objets, des faïences aux antiquités.

Livre à emporter: « Manon des sources » de Marcel Pagnol « Le Parfum » de Patrick Süskind

ANREISE	1 Fahrstunde nördlich vom Flughafen Marseille, 40 Minuten nach Osten vom Flughafen Avignon; 2,5 Stunden Fahrt südlich von Paris mit dem TGV.
PREIS	Zimmer zwischen 370 und 450 €, Suiten zwischen 565 und 640 € einschließlich Frühstück und Abendessen.
ZIMMER	8 Zimmer und 4 Suiten.
KÜCHE	Das Beste aus der provenzalischen Küche.
GESCHICHTE	Im 18. Jahrhundert erbaut, 2000 als Hotel eröffnet.
X-FAKTOR	Die Provence von ihrer Glanzseite.

ACCÈS	À une heure de route au nord de l'aéroport de Marseille, à 40 minutes à l'est de l'aéroport d'Avignon. À 2 heures 30 au sud de Paris en TGV.
PRIX	Chambres de 370 à 450 €, suites de 565 à 640 €, petit déjeuner et dîner compris.
CHAMBRES	8 chambres et 4 suites.
RESTAURATION	Le meilleur de la cuisine provençale.
HISTOIRE	Construite au XVIIIe, La Bastide de Marie est un hôtel depuis 2000.
LES « PLUS »	La Provence authentique.

A place in the country...
La Maison Domaine de Bournissac, Provence

La Maison Domaine de Bournissac, Provence

A place in the country

Just minutes from the town of Saint-Rémy, in the heart of Provence, there is an old country inn. It is still quite a secret place, even in this much-explored area.

Hidden at the end of a long gravel road, a simple house comes into view. Yet the Domaine de Bournissac has a deceptive exterior; the inside is not quite as simple as it appears to be. The centuries-old farmhouse has been restored; revived as an oasis of calm. Style and simplicity have been expertly paired. The pale colours of marble, stone, and bleached wood signal the restful atmosphere to be found within its walls. Each room is different; but all are in soft colours and composed by a sure and artistic hand. Outside, the garden and terrace are places to sit in the sun and dream. A massive old oak tree casts a welcome shade. In the summer, fields of sunflowers and lavender are in bloom. This is the landscape and light that so inspired Van Gogh, and lures people to it still.

However, despite its past, traditional farmhouse style food is not on the menu. The kitchen has a reputation that has spread a long way from its rural setting.

Book to pack: "Lust for Life: the Story of Vincent van Gogh" by Irving Stone

La Maison Domaine de Bournissac
Montée d'Eyragues
13550 Paluds de Noves
France
Tel: + 33 (0) 490902525
Fax: + 33 (0) 490902526
E-mail: annie@lamaison-a-bournissac.com
Website: www.lamaison-a-bournissac.com
Booking: www.great-escapes-hotels.com

DIRECTIONS	South of Avignon, it is just 5 minutes from Saint-Rémy-de-Provence.
RATES	From € 89 to 206.
ROOMS	13 rooms.
FOOD	Renowned, and drawing on the rich local resources.
HISTORY	Part of the building dates back to the 14th century, others are from the 18th century. The Domaine de Bournissac has received guests since 1999.
X-FACTOR	A lovely country house in one of the most beautiful parts of France.

Ein Platz auf dem Lande

Nur wenige Minuten von Saint-Rémy im Herzen der
Provence liegt ein alter Landgasthof. Er ist sogar in dieser
touristisch weitgehend erschlossenen Gegend ein Geheim-
tipp geblieben.

Versteckt am Ende eines langen Kieswegs entdeckt man
plötzlich ein einfaches Haus. Doch dieser Eindruck täuscht:
Die Domaine de Bournissac wirkt nur äußerlich einfach.
Das ehemalige, mehrere Jahrhunderte alte Bauernhaus ist
heute als Oase der Stille wieder zum Leben erwacht. Stil und
Schlichtheit sind eine perfekte Symbiose eingegangen. Die
blasse Farbpalette von Marmor, Stein und gebleichtem Holz
signalisiert, welch entspannende Atmosphäre innerhalb der
Steinmauern zu finden ist. Die Gästezimmer wurden jeweils
individuell gestaltet, alle jedoch gekonnt und stilsicher und in
warmen Farben gehalten. Draußen laden Garten und Terrasse
zum Sonnenbaden und Träumen ein, und eine riesige alte
Eiche spendet angenehmen Schatten. Im Sommer blühen
Sonnenblumen und Lavendel in den Feldern ringsherum.
Landschaft und Licht inspirierten einst Van Gogh und ziehen
bis heute die Menschen an.

Doch etwas überrascht: Trotz der langen Geschichte des Hofs
wird hier keine deftige Landhausküche serviert, sondern
Gerichte, die die ländlichen Wurzeln längst hinter sich
gelassen haben.

**Buchtipp: »Vincent van Gogh. Ein Leben in Leidenschaft« von
Irving Stone**

Dans la campagne provençale

À quelques minutes à peine de Saint-Rémy, en plein cœur
de la Provence, se dresse une vieille auberge de campagne.
C'est un endroit encore secret dans cette région qui n'en
compte plus guère.

Tout au bout d'une longue route de gravier surgit une maison
toute simple. Mais que l'on ne s'y trompe pas : l'intérieur
est beaucoup moins modeste qu'il n'y paraît. Cette ancienne
ferme séculaire a été restaurée, transformée en une oasis
de tranquillité, où raffinement et simplicité vont de pair.
Les teintes discrètes du marbre, de la pierre et du bois brut
annoncent l'atmosphère paisible qui règne entre ses murs.
Chaque chambre est différente des autres, mais toutes sont
dotées de couleurs douces et décorées avec beaucoup de
goût. À l'extérieur, le jardin et la terrasse se prêtent au repos
et à la rêverie, à l'ombre d'un imposant chêne centenaire. En
été, les champs de tournesol et de lavande déploient leurs
symphonies de couleurs. C'est le paysage et la lumière qui
ont inspiré Van Gogh, et qui continuent d'attirer les visiteurs.

En dépit de son passé rural, l'auberge ne sert pas de plats
campagnards : l'excellente cuisine a depuis longtemps oublié
ses origines champêtres.

**Livre à emporter : « La Vie passionnée de Vincent van Gogh »
de Irving Stone**

ANREISE	Südlich von Avignon und 5 Minuten von Saint-Rémy-de-Provence entfernt.
PREIS	Zwischen 89 und 206 €.
ZIMMER	13 Zimmer.
KÜCHE	Renommierte Küche, die sich am kulinarischen Reichtum der Region orientiert.
GESCHICHTE	Teile des Gebäudes stammen aus dem 14. Jahrhundert, andere aus dem 18. Jahrhundert. Die Domaine de Bournissac ist seit 1999 Hotel.
X-FAKTOR	Ein wunderschönes Landhaus in einem wunderschönen Teil Frankreichs.

ACCÈS	Au sud d'Avignon, à 5 minutes de Saint-Rémy-de-Provence.
PRIX	De 89 à 206 €.
CHAMBRES	13 chambres.
RESTAURATION	Réputée, tire profit des ressources locales.
HISTOIRE	Quelques parties du bâtiment sont du XIVe siècle, les autres du XVIIIe siècle; le Domaine de Bournissac est un hôtel depuis 1999.
LES « PLUS »	Une ravissante maison de campagne dans une région non moins superbe.

Changing rooms...
L'Atelier sul Mare, Sicilia

L' Atelier sul Mare, Sicilia

Changing rooms

Without doubt, guests here will ask to stay in a room other than the one in which they spent the last night.

At L'Atelier sul Mare, it is usual to change rooms daily so the guest can profit from being at this unique hotel as much as possible. Just a few steps from the sea in one of Sicily's most beautiful bays, on the coast between Palermo and Messina, the hotel has a rare concept: a place where the rooms double up as exhibition pieces. Well-known artists have created many of the rooms. The interiors that have sprung from their fertile imaginations are quite fantastic and dramatic spaces, all with poetic names. Dreams amongst the Drawings is themed around the growth of writing, The Prophet's Room pays homage to film director Pasolini, and in The Tower of Sigismondo, a circular tower descends from the transparent ceiling. At the base, an enormous round bed rotates slowly.

This might seem more like a museum than a hotel, except for the fact that, as its creator explains, "only when a visitor enters and lives in a room will the work of art be fully realized; the use of the room is an integral and fundamental part of the work."

Books to pack: "The Leopard" by Giuseppe Tomasi di Lampedusa "The Lives of the Artists" by Giorgio Vasari

L'Atelier sul Mare

4, Via Cesare Battisti

98079 Castel di Tusa (Messina)

Sicily

Italy

Tel: + 39 (0) 921 334295

Fax: + 39 (0) 921 334283

E-mail: ateliersulmare@nebro.net

Website: www.mediterraneo.it

Booking: www.great-escapes-hotels.com

DIRECTIONS	2 hours' drive west from Palermo, near the town of Cefalù.
RATES	Standard rooms from € 54, for the Art Rooms from € 80 to 90, breakfast included.
ROOMS	40 rooms and suites; 24 standard rooms decorated by young European artists, 14 rooms created by contemporary artists.
FOOD	Traditional Sicilian fare, artfully served.
HISTORY	Built in the 1970s as a hotel, the Atelier Sul Mare was transformed in the 1980s.
X-FACTOR	Being the living part of an artwork.

Tapetenwechsel

Wenn Sie hier Gast sind, werden Sie sicher jede Nacht in einem anderen Zimmer verbringen wollen. Der tägliche Tapetenwechsel gehört im L'Atelier sul Mare zum guten Ton, denn die Gäste sollen so viel wie möglich von ihrem Aufenthalt in diesem einzigartigen Hotel profitieren können. Nur wenige Schritte vom Meer entfernt in einer der schönsten Buchten Siziliens an der Küste zwischen Palermo und Messina gelegen, verwirklicht dieses Hotel ein außergewöhnliches Konzept, bei dem die Gästezimmer gleichzeitig Ausstellungsräume sind. Viele Räume wurden von bekannten Künstlern gestaltet und tragen entsprechend der fantasievollen Interieurs poetische Namen: »Träume inmitten der Zeichnungen« hat die Entwicklung des Schreibens zum Thema, »Der Raum des Propheten« ist eine visuelle Hommage an den Regisseur Pier Paolo Pasolini und im »Turm von Sigismondo« hängt von der durchsichtigen Decke ein runder Turm herab, – darunter dreht sich ein riesiges Bett langsam im Kreise.

Dieses Haus wirkt eher wie ein Museum als wie ein Hotel, doch sein Gründer erklärt, dass »das Kunstwerk erst dann vollendet ist, wenn ein Besucher sich mit dem Raum auseinandersetzt und darin lebt. Die Nutzung der Räume ist integraler, ja unabdingbarer Aspekt der Werke.«

Buchtipps: »Der Leopard« von Giuseppe Tomasi di Lampedusa
»Pier Paolo Pasolini. Eine Biografie« von Nico Naldini

De chambre en chambre

À coup sûr, les clients de l' Atelier sul Mare voudront changer de chambre toutes les nuits ! Ici, les hôtes ont coutume de déménager chaque jour pour profiter au maximum de cet hôtel hors du commun. Situé entre Palerme et Messine, dans l'une des plus belles baies siciliennes et à seulement quelques pas de la mer, l'hôtel concrétise un concept inédit selon lequel chaque chambre est un objet d'art en soi. La plupart d'entre elles ont été créées par des artistes connus et sont dotées de noms poétiques à l'image de ces intérieurs originaux : celle des « Rêves parmi les dessins » s'inspire de l'évolution de l'écriture, « La Chambre du prophète » rend hommage au metteur en scène Pier Paolo Pasolini et dans « La tour de Sigismondo » une tour circulaire descend du plafond transparent. À son pied, un immense lit circulaire tourne lentement sur lui-même.

On pourrait se croire dans un musée plutôt que dans un hôtel, mais comme l'explique son créateur, « l'œuvre d'art n'est complète que lorsqu'un hôte a pénétré dans la chambre et y vit ; l'utilisation de la chambre forme une partie intégrante et fondamentale de l'œuvre. »

Livres à emporter: « Le Guépard » de Giuseppe Tomasi di Lampedusa
« Pier Paolo Pasolini : Biographie » de Nico Naldini

ANREISE	2 Fahrstunden westlich von Palermo, in der Nähe von Cefalù.	ACCÈS	À deux heures de route de Palerme, près de la ville de Cefalù.
Preis	Standardzimmer ab 54 €, Künstlerzimmer zwischen 80 und 90 €, inklusive Frühstück.	PRIX	Les chambres standard à partir de 54 €, les chambres artistiques de 80 à 90 €, petit déjeuner compris.
ZIMMER	40 Zimmer und Suiten; 24 von jungen europäischen Künstlern gestaltete Standardzimmer, 14 von zeitgenössischen Künstlern gestaltete Zimmer.	CHAMBRES	40 chambres et suites ; 24 chambres standard, décorées par de jeunes artistes européens, 14 créées par des artistes contemporains.
KÜCHE	Traditionelle sizilianische Gerichte, kunstvoll präsentiert.	RESTAURATION	Cuisine sicilienne traditionnelle, servie avec art.
GESCHICHTE	1970 errichtet und in den 1980er-Jahren umgebaut.	HISTOIRE	Hôtel construit en 1970 et transformé dans les années 1980.
X-FAKTOR	Hier sind Sie lebender Bestandteil eines Kunstwerks.	LES « PLUS »	Devenir l'élément vivant d'une œuvre d'art.

Monasterio romántico...
Monasterio Rocamador, Extremadura

Monasterio Rocamador, Extremadura

Monasterio romántico

This striking structure has crowned this hilltop in rural Spain since the 16th century. Although it looks like a small village, it was once a monastery and then a centre of philosophy.

Its most recent reincarnation is as a hotel. Rocamador is a respite for fugitives from a hectic life; at a pace far less serene than the monastic one. Although the furnishing of the guestrooms is simple, they are anything but cell-like in their comforts.

The restaurant, converted from what was once the chapel, is not at all austere in its menu. It proffers cuisine of a superior standard to that which the brothers would have been served. With no set schedule to abide by, guests can spend all the time they like beside or in the infinity pool; play pelota or go horseriding, before enjoying nights of blessed repose after a divine dinner.

On the other hand, this quiet region is known as the "land of the conquistadors". Its rich landscape, dotted with grand castles, chestnut forests, and whitewashed towns, is one that lures the explorer. Expeditions in search of the leather and crafts that the area is known for will bring certain rewards.

Books to pack: "The Consolations of Philosophy" by Alain de Botton

"Raquel, the Jewess of Toledo" by Lion Feuchtwanger

Monasterio Rocamador
Apdo. Correos n.7
Barcarrota
06160 Badajoz
Extremadura, Spain
Tel: + 34 924 489 000
Fax: +34 924 489 000
E-mail: mail@rocamador.com
Website: www.rocamador.com
Booking: www.great-escapes-hotels.com

DIRECTIONS	40 km/25 m south-east from Badajoz, near the border of Spain and Portugal.
RATES	From € 102 to 210.
ROOMS	30 rooms.
FOOD	One of Spain's most talked-about restaurants.
HISTORY	Built in the 16th century, the monastery was opened as a hotel in 1997.
X-FACTOR	A truly romantic hermitage.

Klösterliche Romantik

Bereits im 16. Jahrhundert wurde dieser eindrucksvolle Bau inmitten der hügeligen, ländlichen Landschaft der spanischen Extremadura erbaut. Aus dem einstigen Kloster, das fast wie ein eigenes kleines Dorf wirkt, wurde später ein reges geistiges Zentrum.

In jüngster Zeit machte das Rocamador wieder eine Wandlung durch – diesmal in ein Hotel, das Zuflucht vor dem hektischen Alltagsleben bietet, auch wenn ihm längst nicht mehr die klösterliche Stille innewohnt wie damals. Obwohl die Zimmer sehr einfach ausgestattet sind, liegt der Komfort weit über dem einer Mönchszelle. Auch das Essen im Restaurant, das sich dort befindet, wo früher die Kapelle war, ist alles andere als asketisch. Die Speisen, die dort serviert werden, sind von weitaus höherer Qualität als das, was zu Zeiten der Ordensbrüder auf den Tisch kam. Auch müssen die Gäste hier keinem strengen Zeitplan folgen, sondern können nach Lust und Laune am riesigen Swimmingpool liegen, Pelota spielen oder reiten, um sich schließlich nach einem göttlichen Essen der seligen Nachtruhe hinzugeben. Jedoch ist diese ruhige Gegend auch als das »Land der Konquistadoren« bekannt. Die eindrucksvolle, mit Burgen übersäte Landschaft, die Kastanienwälder und die weiß getünchten Städte waren eine große Verlockung für die Eroberer. Die Expeditionen, die Sie unternehmen, um Lederwaren oder Kunsthandwerk zu erlangen, werden gewiss von Erfolg gekrönt sein.

Buchtipps: »Trost der Philosophie. Eine Gebrauchsanweisung« von Alain de Botton
»Die Jüdin von Toledo« von Lion Feuchtwanger

Monasterio romántico

Cet ouvrage impressionnant fut construit au XVIe siècle au cœur de la campagne vallonnée de l'Extramadura. L'ancien monastère aux allures de village devint plus tard un centre spirituel animé.

Récemment reconverti en hôtel, Rocamador est aujourd'hui un refuge pour tout ceux qui désirent fuir les trépidations d'une vie bien moins sereine que l'existence monacale. Bien que meublées avec simplicité, les chambres sont confortables et ne ressemblent plus en rien à des cellules. Installé dans l'ancienne chapelle, le restaurant est de même dénué d'austérité : il propose une cuisine fort supérieure à celle dont devaient se satisfaire les moines. Entièrement libres de leur temps, les hôtes peuvent se prélasser à leur guise au bord de la piscine, jouer à la pelota ou randonner à cheval, avant de savourer un dîner divin, suivi du plus doux des sommeils.

Cette région si paisible est aussi connue pour être le « pays des conquistadors ». Ses superbes paysages émaillés d'imposants châteaux, de forêts de marronniers et de villages blanchis à la chaux, incitent à la découverte. On fera également de bonnes trouvailles si l'on s'intéresse à l'artisanat et aux articles de cuir pour lesquels l'endroit est réputé.

Livres à emporter : « Les Consolations de la philosophie » d'Alain de Botton
« La Juive de Tolède » de Lion Feuchtwanger

ANREISE	40 km südöstlich von Badajoz, nahe der spanisch-portugiesischen Grenze.
PREIS	Zwischen 102 und 210 €.
ZIMMER	30 Zimmer.
KÜCHE	Eines der meist gepriesenen Restaurants Spaniens.
GESCHICHTE	Im 16. Jahrhundert erbaut, seit 1997 als Hotel in Betrieb.
X-FAKTOR	Stilvolle Auszeit.

ACCÈS	À 40 km au sud-est de Badajoz, près de la frontière du Portugal.
PRIX	De 102 à 210 €.
CHAMBRES	30 chambres.
RESTAURATION	L'une des tables les plus réputées d'Espagne.
HISTOIRE	Bâtiment construit au XVIe siècle, converti en hôtel en 1997.
LES « PLUS »	Un cadre hors du temps.

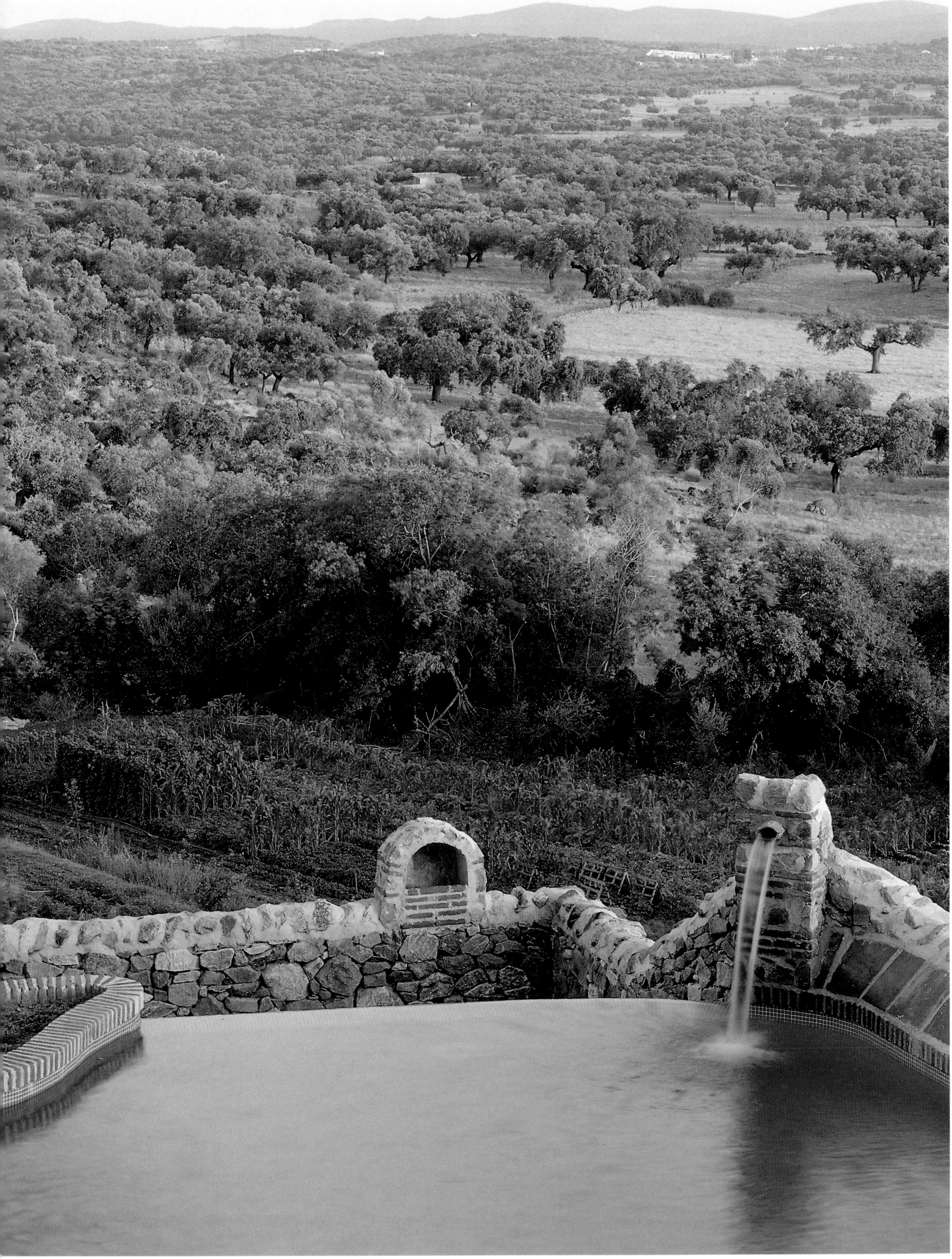

This glorious Eden...
Quinta da Capela, Sintra

Quinta da Capela, Sintra

This glorious Eden

Some of the most famous talkers have had something to say about the town of Sintra. Its virtues have been extolled by poets and writers. For centuries the lovely village was the summer refuge of the royalty of Portugal. Keen to escape the stifling heat of the city, the rest of the nobility came here too. Grand residences were built so that the peers of the realm could holiday in the style to which they were accustomed. Many were set just beyond the town, out in the country, for more peace and quiet. Lush gardens and thick walls thwarted prying eyes.

One of the palatial homes is Quinta da Capela, which is now an aristocratic guesthouse; one with a more modest lineage. It has an exterior that steers clear of decoration. But behind the simple façade there is an elegant interior with high vaulted ceilings, expansive rooms, and wide doors that look out on lush greenery. A discreet and refined sense of luxury is apparent in the very simplicity of the furnishings. Lord Byron would have liked it, especially the classic garden with its peacocks and swans. It was he, hard to please, who called Sintra "perhaps the most delightful place in Europe".

Books to pack: "Fernando Pessoa & Co: Selected Poems" ed. by Richard Zenith

"Byron: Child of Passion, Fool of Fame" by Benita Eisler

Quinta da Capela	
Monserrate Sintra	
Sintra 2710	
Portugal	
Tel: + 351 21 9290170	
Fax: + 351 21 9293425	
No e-mail	
No website	
Booking: www.great-escapes-hotels.com	

DIRECTIONS	30 km/19 m northwest of Lisbon; 4 km/2.4 m from the centre of Sintra.
RATES	Rooms and Suites from € 130 to 185, including breakfast; apartments from € 185 to 320. Closed between November and March.
ROOMS	7 in the main house, and 3 cottages in the grounds.
FOOD	There is a restaurant 5 minutes drive from the Quinta.
HISTORY	The first Quinta was built in the 16th century but was destroyed in the great Lisbon earthquake of 1755. It was rebuilt in 1773 and opened as a hotel in the 1980s.
X-FACTOR	Historical atmosphere with beautiful surroundings.

Hier liegt das Paradies

Nicht wenige berühmte Dichter und Denker haben Sintra
in ihren Werken Denkmäler gesetzt. Über Hunderte von
Jahren war hier die Sommerresidenz des portugiesischen
Königshauses. Ihm auf den Fersen folgte der Adel, der
ebenfalls der drückenden Hitze der Stadt entkommen wollte.
Die Hochwohlgeborenen des Reiches ließen sich prachtvolle
Residenzen errichten, um auch im Urlaub nicht auf den
gewohnten Lebensstil verzichten zu müssen. Oft befanden
sich diese direkt vor der Stadt, doch dabei schon mitten auf
dem Land, und boten Ruhe und Frieden. Vor neugierigen
Blicken schützten üppige Gärten und dicke Mauern.
Auch Quinta da Capela war einst ein solcher Palast. Heute
beherbergt er ein nicht minder aristokratisches Gästehaus,
was sich jedoch in angenehmer Zurückhaltung ausdrückt.
Das Äußere des Palasts verzichtet ganz auf dekorative
Elemente. Hinter der einfachen Fassade verbirgt sich ein
elegantes Inneres: hohe Bogendecken, weite Türen und
großzügige Räume, die auf prächtiges Gartengrün blicken.
Diskret-raffinierter Luxus wird auch bei der Einrichtung
spürbar: Das Mobiliar ist bewusst einfach gehalten. Lord
Byron hätte es hier gefallen. Besonders beeindruckt hätte
ihn sicher der im klassischen Stil angelegte Garten, in dem
sich Pfaue und Schwäne tummeln. Denn er, der bekannter-
weise nicht leicht zufrieden zu stellen war, bezeichnete Sintra
einst als »den wohl schönsten Flecken in ganz Europa«.
**Buchtipps: »Esoterische Gedichte« von Fernando Pessoa
»Byron. Der Held im Kostüm« von Benita Eisler**

Un petit coin de paradis

Sintra a inspiré certains de nos plus grands orateurs, et ses
vertus ont été vantées par maints écrivains et poètes. Des
siècles durant, cette charmante petite ville servit de retraite
estivale à la famille royale du Portugal. Désireuse d'échapper
à l'accablante chaleur de la ville, la noblesse y venait également pendant les mois d'été. De luxueuses résidences furent
édifiées pour que les pairs du royaume villégiaturent dans
le style auquel ils étaient accoutumés. Beaucoup furent construites à l'extérieur de la localité, dans la campagne qui
offrait plus de silence et de tranquillité. De luxuriants jardins
et des murs épais protégeaient des regards curieux.
L'une de ces résidences est la Quinta da Capela, aujourd'hui
convertie en un hôtel aussi sobre qu'élégant. Derrière une
façade dépourvue de tout ornement, se cache un intérieur
d'un grand raffinement. Sous les hauts plafonds voûtés, de
vastes salles et de larges portes donnent sur une nature
verdoyante. De la sobriété du mobilier se dégage un luxe
à la fois chic et discret. Lord Byron aurait fort apprécié cet
endroit, notamment le jardin classique peuplé de paons
et de cygnes. C'est d'ailleurs cet hôte exigeant qui qualifia
Sintra de « peut-être l'endroit le plus délicieux d'Europe ».
**Livres à emporter : « Œuvres poétiques » de Fernando Pessoa
« Lord Byron » de Gilbert Martineau**

ANREISE	30 km nordwestlich von Lissabon; 4 km von Sintra entfernt.	ACCÈS	À 30 km au nord-ouest de Lisbonne et 4 km de Sintra.
PREIS	Zimmer und Suiten zwischen 130 und 185 €, inklusive Frühstück; Apartments zwischen 185 und 320 €. Von November bis März geschlossen.	PRIX	Chambres et suites de 130 à 185 €, petit déjeuner compris, appartements de 185 à 320 €; fermé de novembre à mars.
ZIMMER	7 im Haupthaus, 3 Cottages auf dem Anwesen.	CHAMBRES	7 chambres dans le bâtiment principal, et 3 cottages dans le parc.
KÜCHE	Restaurant in 5 Minuten Fahrt zu erreichen.	RESTAURATION	Il y a un restaurant à 5 minutes de route de la Quinta.
GESCHICHTE	Erstmals erbaut im 16. Jahrhundert; nach der Zerstörung 1755 beim großen Lissaboner Erdbeben 1773 wiederaufge-baut. Als Hotel eröffnet seit den 1980er-Jahren.	HISTOIRE	Construite au XVIe siècle, la Quinta a été détruite pen-dant le grand tremblement de terre à Lisbonne en 1755, rebâtie en 1773 et transformée en hôtel dans les années 1980.
X-FAKTOR	Historisches Flair in wunderschöner Umgebung.	LES « PLUS »	Atmosphère historique dans un beau paysage.

Pilgrim's rest
Paço de São Cipriano, Minho

Paço de São Cipriano, Minho

Pilgrim's rest

This house would have been a welcome sight to pilgrims on their way to the cathedral and shrine of St. James, in Spain. For centuries, thousands of people have trod this road on a journey to see the tomb of the Apostle. Walking the long route to Santiago de Compostela, from France through Portugal and then on to Spain, was a spiritual goal. The sore feet on such a trek would be a sharp daily reminder of one's human frailties.

Resting at Paço de São Cipriano would have been a divine treat to look forward to. It still is for many. The ancient custom of receiving guests carries on; the modern traveller or the pilgrim, by car or on foot, is still welcomed here. This former manor house is set in the midst of lush greenery. As well as gardens, orchards, and vineyards, it has its own chapel, and is also blessed with wine cellars. The house is one of the many old noble seats that have been restored all through the country. While most are still family homes, paying guests can now share their proud history. The past is very much part of the present. Here, the tower room, with its splendid bed, evokes the spirit of the old Portugal.

Book to pack: "The Pilgrimage: A Contemporary Quest for Ancient Wisdom" by Paulo Coelho

Paço de São Cipriano	
Tabuadelo – 4810-892	
Guimarães	
Minho	
Portugal	
Tel: + 351 253 565 337	
Fax: + 351 253 565 337	
E-mail: info@pacocipriano.com	
Website: www.pacosaocipriano.com	
Booking: www.great-escapes-hotels.com	

DIRECTIONS	In the north of Portugal, north-east from Porto. 6 km from Guimarães.
RATES	€ 100.
ROOMS	7 rooms.
FOOD	Only breakfast, restaurants near the hotel.
HISTORY	The house was built in the 15th century and opened as a hotel in 1983.
X-FACTOR	The serene gardens and sense of history.

Nachtlager für Pilger

Dieses Haus wäre ein willkommener Anblick für Pilger auf dem Weg zur Kathedrale des heiligen Jakobus in Spanien gewesen. Im Laufe der Jahrhunderte sind tausende von Menschen hier entlang gepilgert, um das Grabmal des Apostels zu sehen. Der weite Weg nach Santiago de Compostela von Frankreich über Portugal bis nach Spanien war ein großes religiöses Ereignis. Und die vom langen Marsch wunden Füße gemahnten die Menschen täglich an ihre Gebrechlichkeit.

Sich im Paço de São Cipriano zur Ruhe zu legen wäre gewiss ein göttliches Vergnügen gewesen, dem man mit großer Freude entgegengeblickt hätte. Viele können das heute noch genießen, denn der alte Brauch, Gäste zu empfangen, wird fortgeführt. Jeder – vom modernen Reisenden bis zum Pilger, egal, ob mit dem Auto oder zu Fuß – ist hier willkommen. Das ehemalige Herrenhaus ist eingebettet in eine üppige, grüne Landschaft. Neben Gärten, Obstgärten und Weinbergen verfügt es über eine eigene Kapelle und ist noch dazu mit Weinkellern bestückt. Es handelt sich um einen der vielen alten Adelssitze, die im ganzen Land restauriert wurden. Obwohl die meisten von ihnen noch im Familienbesitz sind, können auch zahlende Gäste an ihrer stolzen Geschichte teilhaben. Die Vergangenheit ist in der Gegenwart noch sehr präsent. So lässt das Turmzimmer mit seinem prächtigen Bett den Geist des alten Portugals auferstehen.

Buchtipp: »Auf dem Jakobsweg. Tagebuch einer Pilgerreise nach Santiago de Compostela« von Paulo Coelho

Sur la route des pèlerins

Nul doute que la vue de cette maison n'ait réjoui bien des pèlerins en route vers la cathédrale Saint-Jacques en Espagne. Au cours des siècles, des milliers de personnes ont parcouru le chemin menant à la tombe de l'apôtre. La route de Compostelle, de la France à l'Espagne en passant par le Portugal, avait une finalité spirituelle. Les pieds meurtris rappelaient chaque jour la fragilité de l'homme.

Faire enfin halte au Paço de São Cipriano devait être un moment divin ... et l'est toujours aujourd'hui. L'ancienne coutume d'accueillir les voyageurs perdure : touriste ou pèlerin, en voiture ou à pied, chacun est ici le bienvenu. Cet ancien manoir est situé au cœur d'une nature verdoyante. Outre des jardins, vergers et vignobles, il possède sa propre chapelle et des caves à vin. La demeure fait partie des nombreuses résidences patriciennes à avoir été restaurées dans le pays. Si la plupart sont toujours habitées par les familles d'origine, des hôtes payants peuvent partager leur fier passé. L'histoire semble faire partie du présent : ici, la chambre de la tour, avec son lit splendide, évoque le Portugal au temps jadis.

Livre à emporter : « Le Pèlerin de Compostelle » de Paulo Coelho

ANREISE	Im Norden von Portugal, nordöstlich von Porto, 6 km von Guimarães entfernt.
PREIS	100 €.
ZIMMER	7 Zimmer.
KÜCHE	Nur Frühstück, Restaurants in der Nähe des Hotels.
GESCHICHTE	Das Gebäude stammt aus dem 15. Jahrhundert und wurde 1983 als Hotel eröffnet.
X-FAKTOR	Die herrlichen Gärten und der Sinn für Geschichte.

ACCÈS	Au nord du Portugal, au nord-est de Porto. À 6 km de Guimarães.
PRIX	100 €.
CHAMBRES	7 chambres.
RESTAURATION	Petit déjeuner uniquement, restaurants à proximité de l'hôtel.
HISTOIRE	Construit au XVe siècle, le Paço de São Cipriano a ouvert ses portes en 1983.
LES « PLUS »	Jardins paisibles et cadre historique.

Caving in comfort...
Les Maisons de Cappadoce, Uçhisar

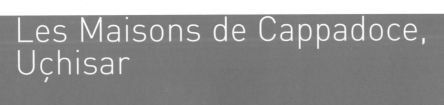

Les Maisons de Cappadoce, Uçhisar

Caving in comfort

There are few places on earth like Cappadocia in Central Turkey. Its otherworldly landscape of volcanic rock has been sculptured by time and the elements into amazing spires and needles, amongst which apple, apricot, and mulberry trees flourish in fertile valleys. The first Christians carved churches, houses, and whole subterranean cities in the soft volcanic tufa rock to escape invaders. Perched at the highest point above this bizarre landscape is the ancient hamlet of Uçhisar. Here, once dilapidated cave dwellings in the oldest part of the village, have been transformed into Les Maisons de Cappadoce, ten stone houses. Sensitively restored, their added contemporary comforts merging easily with the millennial architecture, these unique homes are available to people seeking a holiday in a truly unusual place.

You can pass your time as a temporary troglodyte tasting the delicious Turkish food in the local restaurants, enjoying the hospitality of the village, and perhaps bargaining at the carpet and kilim shops. And you can follow the ancient paths of Cappadocia, walking, riding, driving, or ballooning over it, to wonder at the extraordinary terrain spread out below.

Book to pack: "Memed My Hawk" by Yashar Kemal

Les Maisons de Cappadoce	
Belediye Meydani	
POB 28 Uçhisar Nevshehir	
Turkey	
Tel: + 90 384 219 28 13	
Fax: April 1–October 31: + 90 384 219 27 82;	
November 1–March 31: + 33 (0) 563 46 20 09	
E-mail: info@cappadoce.com	
Website: www.cappadoce.com	
Booking: www.great-escapes-hotels.com	

DIRECTIONS	300 km/180 m south-east from Ankara, 800 km/500 m south-east from Istanbul; Nevshehir is the nearest airport (40 km/25 m), or Kayseri (80 km/50 m).
RATES	From € 113 to 362 per house/studio, per night, minimum 4 nights rental.
ROOMS	11 houses, for 2 to 7 people.
FOOD	Breakfast hampers available, Turkish cuisine in Uçhisar or self-catering.
HISTORY	The guesthouses have been renovated in the 90s, the first opened 1994.
X-FACTOR	Bewitching scenery, enchanting accommodation.

Erhöhlungsurlaub

Nur wenige Regionen auf der Welt sind mit Kappadokien
vergleichbar. Eine bizarre Landschaft aus Vulkangestein ist
im Lauf der Jahrtausende durch die Kraft der Naturgewalten
entstanden. Zwischen den eindrucksvollen Felstürmen und
-nadeln aber blühen Apfel-, Aprikosen- und Maulbeerbäume
in fruchtbaren Tälern. Die ersten Christen meißelten
Kirchen, Häuser und ganze unterirdische Städte aus dem
weichen, vulkanischen Tuffstein und versteckten sich hier
vor ihren Verfolgern.

Auf dem höchsten Plateau dieser Mondlandschaft im Herzen
der Türkei liegt das alte Dörfchen Uçhisar. Hier wurden
einige der verlassenen Höhlenwohnungen, welche sich im
ältesten Teil des Ortes befinden, zu den zehn Steinhäusern
von Les Maisons de Cappadoce umgebaut. Diese einzigartigen,
sehr stilvoll renovierten Häuser, in denen moderner
Komfort und die mehr als tausend Jahre alte Architektur
eine harmonische Verbindung eingehen, sind Traumziele
für alle diejenigen, die einen absolut unkonventionellen
Urlaub verbringen wollen.

Als Einsiedler auf Zeit können Sie sich hier an den hervorra-
genden türkischen Spezialitäten in den örtlichen Restaurants
erfreuen, die Gastfreundschaft der Dorfbewohner genießen
und vielleicht mit den Teppichhändlern um Kelims feilschen.
Die jahrtausendealten Pfade Kappadokiens können Sie zu
Fuß, zu Pferde oder mit dem Auto erkunden, oder gar vom
Heißluftballon aus, um die außergewöhnliche Landschaft
von oben zu bestaunen.

Buchtipp: »Memed, mein Falke« von Yaçar Kemal

Grottes tout confort

Peu d'endroits sur terre égalent la Cappadoce. Des vallées
fertiles où poussent des pommiers, des abricotiers et des
mûriers s'étendent au pied de paysages surréels de roche
volcanique, où la nature a sculpté au fil des siècles des
flèches et aiguilles extraordinaires. Dans le tuf, une roche
volcanique poreuse et légère, les premiers chrétiens ont
creusé des églises, des maisons ainsi que des cités sou-
terraines entières pour se protéger des envahisseurs.

Le hameau ancien d'Uçhisar est perché sur le point le plus
élevé de ce paysage fantastique de Turquie centrale. Dans
la partie la plus ancienne du village, des habitations troglo-
dytiques autrefois délabrées ont été transformées en dix
maisons d'hôtes : Les Maisons de Cappadoce. Restaurées
avec goût, le confort moderne s'intégrant sans heurter
l'architecture millénaire, ces demeures uniques séduiront
ceux qui souhaitent passer des vacances dans un endroit
véritablement original.

Troglodyte le temps d'un séjour, vous savourerez la délicieuse
cuisine turque dans les restaurants locaux, découvrirez le
village et ses habitants accueillants et vous amuserez à mar-
chander dans les boutiques de tapis et de kilims. Vous pourrez
aussi parcourir les chemins anciens de Cappadoce, à pied, à
cheval ou en voiture, ou bien survoler en ballon des paysages
absolument extraordinaires.

**Livre à emporter : « Le dernier combat de Mèmed le Mince » de
Yachar Kemal**

ANREISE	300 km südöstlich von Ankara, 800 km südöstlich von Istanbul. Die nächsten Flughäfen sind Nevsehir (40 km) und Kayseri (80 km).	
PREIS	Zwischen 113 und 362 € pro Haus bzw. Apartment pro Nacht (4 Übernachtungen Mindestaufenthalt).	
ZIMMER	11 Häuser für 2 bis 7 Personen.	
KÜCHE	Selbstversorger sind willkommen, Frühstückskörbe auf Wunsch, türkische Spezialitäten gibt es in Uçhisar.	
GESCHICHTE	Die Häuser wurden in den 1990er Jahren renoviert, das erste 1994 eröffnet.	
X-FAKTOR	Fantastische Landschaft, bezaubernde Unterkünfte.	

ACCÈS	À 300 km au sud-est d'Ankara et à 800 km au sud-est d'Istanbul ; 2 aéroports : Nevsehir (à 40 km) ou Kayseri (à 80 km).
PRIX	De 113 à 362 € par maison/studio la nuitée ; 4 nuits minimum.
CHAMBRES	11 maisons logeant de 2 à 7 sept personnes.
RESTAURATION	Panier de petit déjeuner sur demande ; cuisine turque à Uçhisar ou possibilité de préparer soi-même ses repas.
HISTOIRE	Les maison ont été rénovées dans les années 1990, la première a été ouverte en 1994.
LES « PLUS »	Cadre fantastique, logement original.

Africa

Morocco• Egypt • Kenya
Tanzania • Seychelles • Mauritius • Zimbabwe
Botswana • South Africa • Ghana

Text by Shelley-Maree Cassidy   *Edited by* Angelika Taschen

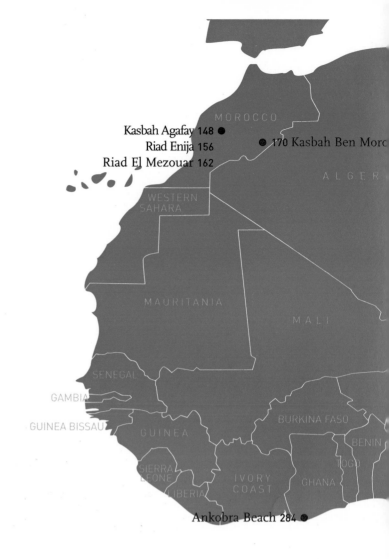

"Travel is fatal to prejudice, bigotry, and narrow-mindedness."
Mark Twain

Hotel Marsam 176 ●
Hotel Al Moudira 182

Hippo Point House 190 ●
● 198 Ngong House

● 206 Mnemba Island Lodge
Tarangire Treetops 202 ● ● 216 Zanzibar Serena Inn

● 222 Frégate Island Private

● 234 Matetsi Water Lodge

● 242 Sandibe Safari Lodge
250 Mombo Camp

Le Prince Maurice 228 ●

● 270 Makalali Private Game Reserve

Sabi Sabi Earth Lodge 262 ●

Kensington Place 278 ●

Fort Marrakech

Kasbah Agafay, near Marrakech

Kasbah Agafay, near Marrakech

Fort Marrakech

Once a derelict hilltop fort owned by a holy man, this landmark building is now in the hands of a visionary designer. In a dramatic tribute to Morocco's architectural heritage, the traditional Berber mud fort has been transformed into a stunning and exclusive retreat, with panoramic views over olive groves, desert hills and the snow-capped Atlas Mountains.

Inside the massive terraced ramparts of the Kasbah Agafay are spacious suites, decorated in contemporary style and surrounded by terraced gardens and traditional courtyards – riads. A traditional hammam – steam bath – and meditation cave are pleasurable elements of this serene haven. You can choose to spend a night or more in a Berber tent, sumptuously furnished with antiques and traditional textiles, enjoying a candlelit supper under the starry sky, amidst palm groves. Daylight excursions include tours of Marrakech palaces and the souk, camel and horse treks, and visits to local Berber villages to learn about their traditional cooking, music and culture.

Outside the city in a unique desert setting, away from the noise and bustle of the marketplace, but close enough to visit, this idyllic bolthole offers an authentic Kasbah experience.

Book to pack: "Mother Comes of Age" by Driss Chraïbi

Kasbah Agafay		
Route de l'Airport BP 226		
40000 Marrakech Medina		
Morocco		
Tel: + 212 (44) 42 09 60		
Fax: + 212 (44) 42 09 70		
E-mail: info@kasbahagfay.com		
Website: www.kasbahagafay.com		
Booking: www.great-escapes-hotels.com		

DIRECTIONS	15 km/9 m west from Marrakech's Menara airport, 20 km/12 m from the city centre.
RATES	US$380 per suite, US$426 per luxury tented suite and US$471 per luxury family tented suite, including breakfast and transfers.
ROOMS	14 suites, 4 luxury tented suites.
FOOD	Moroccan, Berber and international cuisine.
HISTORY	Re-opened in December 2000 after an intensive three year restoration programme.
X-FACTOR	Stunning desert setting and style and a large mosaic tiled swimming pool.

Fort Marrakesch

Während dieses charakteristische Gebäude einst eine heruntergekommene Festung und im Besitz eines heiligen Mannes war, gehört es heute einem visionären Designer. Auf eindrucksvolle Weise wurde dem marokkanischen Architekturerbe Tribut gezollt, als diese traditionelle Berber-Lehmfestung in einen überwältigend schönen und exklusiven Zufluchtsort mit Panoramablick über Olivenhaine, Wüstenhügel und das Atlas Gebirge mit seinen schneebedeckten Gipfeln umgewandelt wurde.

In den massiven terrassenartigen Wällen der Kasbah Agafay verbergen sich geräumige Suiten – ausgestattet in zeitgenössischem Stil und umgeben von Terrassengärten und landestypischen Höfen – riads. Ein traditionelles Hammam – Dampfbad – und eine Meditationshöhle sind angenehme Elemente in dieser unbeschwerten Oase. Auf Wunsch können Sie eine oder mehrere Nächte in einem mit kostbaren Antiquitäten und Textilien ausgestatteten Berberzelt zubringen und bei Kerzenschein ein Abendessen unter Sternenhimmel in einem Palmenhain genießen. Zu den möglichen Tagesexkursionen gehören Touren zu Palästen und dem Souk (Markt) in Marrakesch, Kamelund Pferdeausritte, sowie Besuche in nahegelegenen Berberdörfern, wo man Wissenswertes über deren Kochgewohnheiten, Musik und Kultur erfahren kann. Außerhalb der Stadt und weit entfernt vom Lärm und der Betriebsamkeit des Marktes, und dennoch nah genug für einen Besuch, bietet dieses idyllische Versteck ein authentisches Kasbah Erlebnis.

Buchtipp: »Die Zivilisation, Mutter!« von Driss Chraïbi

Fort Marrakech

La Kasbah Agafay, remarquable construction érigée au sommet d'une colline, appartenait autrefois à un religieux. Jadis en ruine, ce fort berbère traditionnel est passé aux mains d'un créateur visionnaire. Aujourd'hui retraite spectaculaire et luxueuse rendant hommage à l'héritage architectural marocain, il domine un paysage d'oliveraies et de collines désertiques et permet d'admirer les sommets enneigés de l'Atlas.

À l'intérieur, les immenses remparts en terrasses accueillent des suites spacieuses de style contemporain cernées de jardins également en terrasses et de cours typiques, les *riads*. Le *hammam* (bain de vapeur) traditionnel et la grotte de méditation sont deux agréables composants de ce havre de paix. Vous pourrez passer une nuit ou plus sous une tente berbère somptueusement décorée d'antiquités et d'étoffes traditionnelles. Le dîner, éclairé aux chandelles sous un ciel étoilé, est servi au milieu des palmeraies. Les excursions de jour comprennent des randonnées à dos de chameau et de cheval. Vous pourrez également visiter les palais et le *souk* de Marrakech ainsi que les villages berbères dont vous découvrirez la cuisine, la musique et la culture traditionnelles.

Situé en dehors de la ville dans un paysage désertique unique, loin du bruit et de l'effervescence de la place du marché, mais assez près pour visiter, ce refuge idyllique vous permettra de faire l'expérience de la vie dans une authentique casbah.

Livre à emporter : « La civilisation, ma Mère ! » de Driss Chraïbi

ANREISE	15 km westlich vom Menara Flughafen bei Marrakesch entfernt, 20 km von der Stadtmitte.
PREIS	380 US$ für die Suite, 426 US$ für die Luxus-Zeltsuite und 471 US$ für Familien-Luxus-Zeltsuite, inklusive Frühstück und Transfers.
ZIMMER	14 Suiten, 4 Luxus-Zeltsuiten.
KÜCHE	Marokkanisch, Berberspezialitäten und internationale Küche.
GESCHICHTE	Nach aufwändiger, dreijährige Restaurierung, im Dezember 2000 wiedereröffnet.
X-FAKTOR	Umwerfende Wüstenatmosphäre und ein großer mit Mosaiken ausgelegter Swimming Pool.

ACCÈS	À 15 km à l'ouest de l'aéroport de Menara près de Marrakech, à 20 km du centre-ville.
PRIX	380 $ US par suite, 426 $ US par tente aménagée en suite de luxe et 471 $ US par tente familiale aménagée en suite de luxe, petits-déjeuners et transferts compris.
CHAMBRES	14 suites, 4 tentes aménagées en suites luxueuses.
RESTAURATION	Cuisine marocaine, berbère et internationale.
HISTOIRE	Rouvert en décembre 2000 après une restauration intensive de trois ans.
LES « PLUS »	Style et cadre désertique impressionnants ainsi qu'une grande piscine carrelée en mosaïque.

Inner sanctum...
Riad Enija, Marrakech

Riad Enija, Marrakech

Inner sanctum

It is usual to escape the bustle of the city by going to the country, to spend time in some quiet retreat. Here in the red-walled city of Marrakech you can have the best of both worlds in one place. Out of sight down a maze of narrow alleys in the medina is Riad Enija, once the town house – riad – of a silk trader. Now it is a small hotel, one that has been restored in a style faithful to its Islamic origin. Seclusion is key to the design.

Typically, riads have thick walls that insulate from the heat of the sun or the cold and most of the outside noise. Indoor and outdoor living space has always merged in the traditional Moroccan house. With an inner courtyard, the house centres on a walled garden. In the middle of the courtyard is a tiled fountain, often strewn with rose petals. It is a place of tranquillity for its residents, who are cloistered away from the outside world.

The colourful guesthouse is only a few minutes walk from the old city's huge main square, the Djemaa el Fna. From morning to night it teems with life. Orange and date sellers ply their trade; snake charmers, musicians, acrobats and storytellers amuse the crowds.

Book to pack: "Dreams of Trespass: Tales of a Harem Girlhood" by Fatima Mernissi

Riad Enija
Rahba Lakdima
9 Derb Mesfioui
Marrakech, Morocco
Tel: + 212 (44) 44 09 26/44 00 14
Fax: + 212 (44) 44 27 00
E-mail: riadenija@iam.net.ma;
riadenija@riadenija.com
Website: www.riadenija.com
Booking: www.great-escapes-hotels.com

DIRECTIONS	Only at a 5-minute walk from the Djemaa el Fna, Marrakech's central square.
RATES	US$230 to US$320 per double room, including breakfast.
ROOMS	4 rooms, 4 suites and 1 deluxe suite.
FOOD	Good simple fare – light pastas, salads and grilled meats.
HISTORY	Made up from two adjoining Riad houses, one being about 450 years old and the other 380 years old.
X-FACTOR	Secret garden and charming authentic character.

Im Innern Frieden

Normalerweise flieht man vor der hektischen Betriebsamkeit
der Stadt, indem man sich aufs Land zurückzieht, um etwas
Zeit in einem ruhigen Refugium zu verbringen. Hier, in der
rotwandigen Stadt Marrakesch kann man die Vorteile beider
Welten gleichzeitig genießen. Verborgen in einem Labyrinth
enger Gässchen, inmitten der Altstadt, liegt Riad Enija, einst
das Stadthaus – Riad – eines Seidenhändlers. Nun ist es ein
kleines Hotel – eines, das ganz im Stile seines islamischen
Ursprungs restauriert wurde. Abgeschiedenheit lautet dabei
das Geheimnis seiner Bauart.

Dicke Wände, die als Isolation gegen die Hitze der Sonne und
gegen Kälte dienen und den Großteil der Straßengeräusche
verschlucken, sind typisch für Riads. Immer schon sind Innen-
und Außenwohnräume in traditionellen Marokkanischen
Häusern miteinander verschmolzen. Im Zentrum des Hauses
liegt ein Innenhof mit einem von Mauern umrandeten Garten.
In dessen Mitte steht ein gekachelter Springbrunnen, oftmals
bestreut mit Rosenblüten. Für seine Bewohner, abgeschieden
von der Außenwelt, ist dies ein Ort der Ruhe.

Die farbenprächtige Unterkunft liegt nur wenige Gehminuten
vom großen Hauptplatz der Altstadt, dem Djemaa el Fna,
entfernt, wo von morgens bis abends das Leben pulsiert.
Orangen- und Dattelhändler betreiben ihr Gewerbe, Schlan-
genbeschwörer, Musikanten, Akrobaten und Geschichten-
erzähler unterhalten das Volk.

**Buchtipp: »Der Harem in uns. Die Furcht vor dem anderen
und die Sehnsucht der Frauen« von Fatima Mernissi**

Le saint des saints

On échappe généralement au tumulte et à l'agitation de la
ville en allant passer quelque temps à la campagne dans une
retraite paisible. Marrakech, la cité aux murs rouges, réunit
tous les avantages. Caché dans la médina, derrière un dédale
de ruelles étroites, se trouve Riad Enija. Cet ancien hôtel
particulier *(riad)* qui appartenait à un marchand de soie est
aujourd'hui un petit hôtel, restauré dans un style fidèle à ses
origines islamiques, avec une architecture qui préserve
l'intimité de ceux qui l'occupent.

Les riads ont généralement des murs épais qui les isolent
de la chaleur du soleil ou du froid et du bruit extérieur.
L'espace intérieur et l'espace extérieur ont toujours formé
un tout dans les maisons marocaines traditionnelles.
Le centre de l'hôtel Riad Enija est formé par une cour
intérieure et un jardin clos. Au milieu de cette cour se
trouve une fontaine carrelée, fréquemment parsemée de
pétales de rose. Dans ce lieu serein, les hôtes sont isolés
du monde extérieur.

Cette pension colorée se trouve à quelques minutes de
marche seulement de l'immense place principale de la
vieille ville, Djemaa el Fna, qui déborde de vie du matin au
soir avec ses vendeurs d'oranges et de dattes, ses charmeurs
de serpents, ses musiciens, ses acrobates et ses conteurs
qui amusent les badauds.

**Livre à emporter : « Rêves de femmes : Une enfance au harem »
de Fatima Mernissi**

ANREISE	Nur 5-minütiger Fußmarsch vom Djemaa el Fna, Marrakeschs Hauptplatz.	ACCÈS	À 5 minutes à pied de Djemaa el Fna, la place centrale de Marrakech.
PREIS	Von 230 US$ bis 320 US$ für ein Doppelzimmer, inklusive Frühstück.	PRIX	De 230 à 320 $ US par chambre double, petit-déjeuner compris.
ZIMMER	4 Zimmer, 4 Suiten und 1 Luxussuite.	CHAMBRES	4 chambres, 4 suites et 1 suite de luxe.
KÜCHE	Gute, einfache Kost – leichte Nudelgerichte, Salate und gegrilltes Fleisch.	RESTAURATION	Cuisine simple et savoureuse : pâtes, salades et grillades.
GESCHICHTE	Entstanden durch den Zusammenschluss zweier angrenzender Riads, von welchen eines etwa 450 Jahre alt ist, das andere 380 Jahre.	HISTOIRE	L'hôtel est formé par la réunion de deux hôtels particuliers mitoyens dont l'un a environ 450 ans et l'autre 380 ans.
X-FAKTOR	Geheimnisvoller Garten und bezaubernd authentischer Charakter.	LES « PLUS »	Jardin secret et charme authentique.

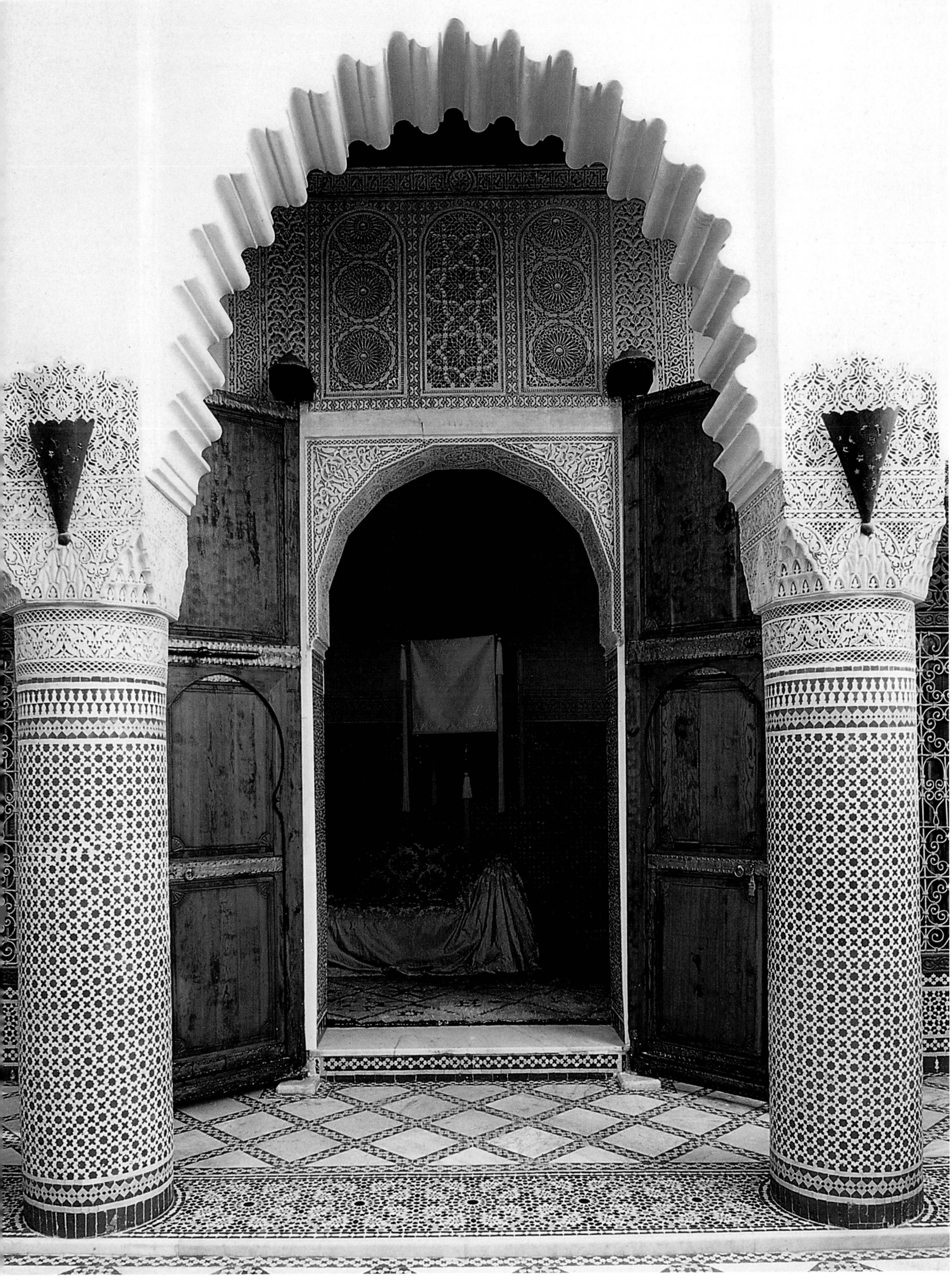

Five lantern luxury...

Riad El Mezouar, Marrakech

Riad El Mezouar, Marrakech

Five lantern luxury

Judgment has been passed on the merit of many places to stay. Worldwide, there are a variety of methods employed to indicate quality, from stars to numbers. Here in Morocco, some of the riads are rated on a scale of lanterns.

This seems rather an apt measure in a realm well known for its beautiful lamps. Decorative lanterns are widely used here; very much a part of the style that is Morocco. More often than not, they are what visitors take home with them. Riad El Mezouar has attained the top lantern rank; and it has a glow that is all of its own. From the bustling street outside, a door opens into a world where there is at once a sense of calm. This sudden feeling of peace is a planned effect. The pleasing symmetry of the columns and the garden are like an antidote to the disorder of life in the souk beyond the thick walls. At first sight, it may look simple: a courtyard with a large square-cut emerald pool, bounded on all sides by the classic galleries of this skilfully restored old house.

But there is inner decoration, done with a light yet sure hand. There are sumptuous touches here; rich velvet that is the colour of Moroccan merlot, old portraits, and filigree metal sconces that cast patterns of light on the wall. A covetous eye will look for their twins in the market. Such a lantern would be a radiant reminder of days and nights spent here.

Book to pack: "This Blinding Absence of Light" by Tahar Ben Jelloun

Riad El Mezouar

28, derb el Hammam, Issebtinne

40000 Marrakech Medina

Morocco

Tel: + 212 (44) 38 09 49

Fax: + 212 (44) 38 09 43

E-mail: info@mezouar.com

Website: www.mezouar.com

Booking: www.great-escapes-hotels.com

DIRECTIONS	A 10-minute walk from the Djemaa el Fna, Marrakech's central square.
RATES	From US$145 per night, including breakfast.
ROOMS	3 suites, 2 double rooms.
FOOD	Moroccan cuisine with French and Asian influences.
HISTORY	The building dates from the eighteenth century.
X-FACTOR	Hint of opulence, and the swimming pool.

Fünf-Lanternen-Luxus

Viele Hotels und Restaurants müssen Beurteilungen über sich ergehen lassen. Von Sternen bis zu Nummern – weltweit hat man verschiedene Methoden entwickelt, mit denen man diverse Qualitätsstandards zu bewerten versucht. In Marokko werden einige der Riads nach einer Skala von Laternen eingestuft, was in einer Gegend, die berühmt für ihre wundevollen Lampen ist, durchaus eine angebrachte Idee zu sein scheint. Überall werden hier dekorative Laternen benutzt. Sie gehören unabdingbar zum marokkanischen Stil, weshalb sie auch häufig von Besuchern als Souvenir mit nach Hause genommen werden.

Mit seinem ihm eigenen Glühen hat Riad El Mezouar die Spitze der Laternenskala erreicht. Von dem Trubel der Straße aus öffnet sich eine Türe zu einer Welt, in der urplötzlich eine ruhige Stille herrscht. Dieses überraschende Gefühl des Friedens ist ein erwünschter und geplanter Effekt.

Die angenehme Symmetrie, die sich in der Anordnung der Säulen und des Gartens zeigt, wirkt wie ein Gegengift zu dem chaotischen Durcheinander, das jenseits dieser dicken Steinmauern auf dem Souk herrscht. Auf den ersten Blick mag hier alles sehr einfach erscheinen – ein Innenhof mit einem großen, eckigen, smaragdgrünen Becken, auf allen Seiten umrahmt von den klassischen Galerien dieses kunstvoll restaurierten alten Gebäudes.

Doch es gibt Verzierungen im Innenbereich, die auf einen dezenten, und dabei stilsicheren Geschmack schließen lassen. Samt in der Farbe von marokkanischem Merlot, alte Gemälde und filigrane, metallene Wandleuchter, die Lichtfiguren an die Wände werfen, lassen einen Hauch von Opulenz durch die Räume wehen. Und möglicherweise werden Ihre Augen begehrlich nach ähnlichen Gegenständen suchen, wenn Sie über die Märkte streifen. Eine solche Laterne könnte als strahlende Erinnerung an die hier verbrachten Tage und Nächte dienen.

Buchtipp: »Das Schweigen des Lichts« von Tahar Ben Jelloun

Cinq lanternes, la marque du luxe

Des jugements ont été portés sur la valeur de nombreuses destinations. Il existe dans le monde diverses méthodes visant à indiquer leur qualité, par exemple les étoiles ou les chiffres. Ici, au Maroc, certains riads sont classés à l'aide d'un système de lanternes.

Ce système d'évaluation semble tout à fait approprié dans un pays réputé pour la beauté de ses lampes. Les lanternes décoratives, très répandues ici, sont une partie intégrante du style marocain. Très souvent, ce sont ces lampes que les visiteurs ramènent de leur voyage.

Riad El Mezouar a obtenu le nombre maximum de lanternes et brille d'un éclat tout à fait particulier. De la rue débordante d'activité, une porte s'ouvre sur un univers où l'on éprouve immédiatement une impression de calme. Ce sentiment de quiétude soudain n'est pas dû au hasard : l'harmonieuse symétrie des colonnes et du jardin fait l'effet d'un antidote au désordre qui règne dans le souk, de l'autre côté des murs épais. À première vue, cette vieille maison habilement restaurée semble d'une grande simplicité : une cour avec un grand bassin carré couleur émeraude, bordée de tous côtés par des galeries classiques.

Toutefois, la décoration intérieure somptueuse, discrète mais réalisée de main de maître, contredit quelque peu cette impression : riches velours de la couleur du merlot marocain, vieux portraits et appliques métalliques en filigrane dessinant des motifs lumineux sur les murs. Ces dernières sont d'ailleurs si jolies qu'à n'en pas douter, les plus passionnés tenteront de dénicher leur réplique sur le marché. Des lanternes d'une beauté éclatante en souvenir des jours et des nuits passés ici.

Livre à emporter : « Cette aveuglante absence de lumière » de Tahar Ben Jelloun

ANREISE	10-minütiger Fußmarsch vom Djemaa el Fna, dem zentralen Platz in Marrakesch.
PREIS	Ab 145 US$ pro Nacht, inklusive Frühstück.
ZIMMER	3 Suiten, 2 Doppelzimmer.
KÜCHE	Lokale Restaurants oder auf Anfrage Abendessen im Hotel.
GESCHICHTE	Das Gebäude stammt aus dem 18. Jahrhundert.
X-FAKTOR	Ein Hauch von Opulenz und der Swimming pool.

ACCÈS	À 10 minutes à pied de Djemaa el Fna, la place centrale de Marrakech.
PRIX	À partir de 145 $ US par nuit, petit-déjeuner compris.
CHAMBRES	3 suites, 2 chambres doubles.
RESTAURATION	Possibilité de dîner à l'hôtel sur demande ou dans les restaurants alentour.
HISTOIRE	Le bâtiment date du XVIIIe siècle.
LES « PLUS »	Un soupçon d'opulence et la piscine.

Deserted castle
Kasbah Ben Moro, near Ouarzazate

Kasbah Ben Moro, near Ouarzazate

Deserted castle

Slavery is still rife in this place; but don't make a fuss, it's only in the movies.

For the 'dream weavers' of Hollywood, the desert sands and vibrant cities of North Africa have long been preferred locations. It is in part the quality of the light, dry, clear and bright, that draws filmmakers. Additionally, the stunning landscape of great sand dunes, lush, palm-filled oases, and snow-capped mountains helps create a whole range of film backdrops, from the epic "Lawrence of Arabia" to "Gladiator".

Kasbah Ben Moro is no film set. It is an authentic old castle, now acting in a new role; being a hotel. Built in the 17th Century, it gives guests a feel of old Morocco. The stylish yet simple rooms are on all three levels of the Kasbah's towers. Scenes of the High Atlas Mountains, and the ruins of the old Amerhidil Kasbah are spread out below; the rich green palm grove in this stark desert landscape is quite a theatrical contrast. The kasbah is in the quiet little village of Skoura. At night, it is very still, and the stars shine bright above. It is not far from here to the much busier resort town of Ouarzazate, which is the focus of the Moroccan film industry. You can tour the sets built for "Asterix & Obelix 2", Timothy Dalton's "Cleopatra" and "Kundun", and more. Some of the guides will tell you they have been slaves, but it was only on screen.

Book to pack: "A Life Full of Holes" by Driss Ben Hamed Charhadi

Kasbah Ben Moro

Skoura

Morocco

Tel: + 212 (44) 85 21 16

Fax: + 212 (44) 85 20 26

E-mail: hotelbenmoro@yahoo.fr

Website: www.passionmaroc.com

Booking: www.great-escapes-hotels.com

DIRECTIONS	30 minutes south of Ouarzazate; four and a half hours drive southeast from Marrakech.
RATES	From US$45 per person per night, including half board.
ROOMS	13 double rooms.
FOOD	Simple but good.
HISTORY	17th Century fort, restored and recently converted to a hotel.
X-FACTOR	Dramatic landscape, with fields of roses.

Ein Palast in der Wüste

Hier ist die Sklaverei noch weit verbreitet, doch keine
Aufregung, – natürlich nur in Filmen. Seit langem schon
gehören der Wüstensand und die pulsierenden Städte Nord-
afrikas zu den beliebtesten Drehorten von Hollywoods
Traumfabrikanten. Was die Filmemacher hierher zieht, ist
zum Teil die Lichtqualität, trocken, klar und hell. Außerdem
kann die überwältigende Landschaft aus großen Sanddünen,
grünen Palmenoasen und schneebedeckten Berggipfeln
als Kulisse für die verschiedensten Filme dienen, vom
Epos »Lawrence von Arabien«, bis hin zu »Gladiator«.
Kasbah Ben Moro ist kein Drehort, sondern ein authen-
tischer alter Palast, der nun in eine neue Rolle als Hotel
geschlüpft ist. Im 17. Jahrhundert erbaut, vermittelt er den
Gästen ein Gefühl für das Marokko der alten Zeit. Die stilvollen, doch einfachen Räume befinden sich auf allen drei
Etagen des Turms der Kashbah. Darunter erstreckt sich das
Panorama über das hohe Atlasgebirge und die Ruinen der
alten Kashbah Amerhidil. Der dichte, grüne Palmenhain
bildet einen geradezu theatralischen Kontrastpunkt in dieser
vollkommenen Wüstenlandschaft. Die Kashbah befindet
sich in dem kleinen, ruhigen Dorf Skoura, wo des Nachts
eine vollkommene Stille herrscht und die Sterne hell am
Himmel glitzern.

Von hier aus ist es nicht mehr weit nach Ouarzazate, einem
Urlaubsort, in dem weitaus mehr Trubel herrscht; es ist die
Hauptstadt der marokkanischen Filmindustrie. Hier können
Sie die Drehorte von »Asterix und Obelix 2«, Timothy
Daltons »Kleopatra«, sowie »Kundun« und einige andere
besuchen. Manche Führer werden Ihnen erklären, dass sie
Sklaven waren, aber nur auf der Leinwand.

**Buchtipp: »Ein Leben voller Fallgruben« von Driss Ben Hamed
Charhadi**

La forteresse des sables

Ici, l'esclavage reste chose commune, mais rassurez-vous,
uniquement dans les films.
Les sables du désert et les villes hautes en couleur d'Afrique
du Nord font partie depuis longtemps des lieux de tournage
favoris des « faiseurs de rêve » d'Hollywood. C'est
notamment la qualité de la lumière, nette, pure et éclatante,
qui attire les cinéastes. Par ailleurs, le superbe paysage
d'immenses dunes de sable, de montagnes enneigées et
d'oasis luxuriantes où poussent de nombreux palmiers a
servi et sert encore aujourd'hui de toile de fond à toutes
sortes de longs-métrages, de « Lawrence d'Arabie » à
« Gladiator ».
La Kasbah Ben Moro n'est pas un décor de cinéma. Il s'agit
d'un vieux château authentique qui interprète aujourd'hui
un nouveau rôle, celui d'un hôtel. Construit au XVIIᵉ siècle,
il permet aux hôtes de retrouver l'atmosphère du Maroc
d'autrefois. Les chambres au style étudié mais simple sont
réparties sur les trois niveaux des tours de la casbah. Vous
verrez en contrebas le Haut Atlas et les ruines de l'ancienne
casbah d'Amerhidil. Le contraste entre la désolation du
paysage désertique et la luxuriance de la palmeraie
verdoyante est assez spectaculaire. La casbah se trouve dans
le petit village de Skoura. La nuit, une grande tranquillité y
règne et les étoiles brillent dans le ciel.
La Kasbah Ben Moro est situé à proximité d'Ouarzazate,
ville touristique beaucoup plus animée et centre de l'industrie cinématographique du pays. Vous pourrez visiter les
décors construits pour le tournage d' « Astérix & Obélix 2 »,
de « Cléopâtre » par Timothy Dalton, de « Kundun », etc.
Certains guides vous diront qu'ils ont un jour été esclaves,
mais seulement le temps d'un film.

**Livre à emporter : « Une vie pleine de trous » de Driss Ben
Hamed Charhadi**

ANREISE	30 Minuten südlich von Ouarzazate; viereinhalb-stündige Fahrt südöstlich von Marrakesch.	ACCÈS	À 30 minutes d'Ouarzazate par le sud et à 4H30 en voiture de Marrakech par le sud-est.
PREIS	Ab 45 US$ pro Person und pro Nacht, inklusiv Halbpension.	PRIX	À partir de 45 $ US par personne et par nuit, comprend la demi-pension.
ZIMMER	13 Doppelzimmer.	CHAMBRES	13 chambres doubles.
KÜCHE	Einfach aber gut.	RESTAURATION	Simple mais savoureuse.
GESCHICHTE	Burg aus dem 17. Jahrhundert, kürzlich renoviert und zum Hotel umgebaut.	HISTOIRE	Fort datant du XVIIᵉ siècle, restauré et récemment transformé en hôtel.
X-FAKTOR	Spektakuläre Landschaft mit Rosenfeldern.	LES « PLUS »	Paysage spectaculaire où l'on peut admirer des champs de roses.

A painterly retreat...

Hotel Marsam, Luxor West Bank

Hotel Marsam, Luxor West Bank

A painterly retreat

This is the place where the nobility of the country stayed. Well, if the truth must be told, not exactly right here, but very close – and they never left. 'They' are the long dead. Preserved forever, people come here to see them in their tombs.

The ancient village of Qurna, on the west bank of the Nile at Luxor, is perched on hills, rock honeycombed with tombs. It's here in the midst of this great open-air museum that the Hotel Marsam stands. It's no wonder then that it is one of the most preferred 'digs' of archaeologists. This is the closest you can get to being in ruins, and by choice. Artists come here too, for the wealth of subjects. In fact, the word Marsam is Arabic for "a painter's studio." From 1941, graduate fine art students lived in part of the hotel. For the next three decades, it was like Montmartre in Paris. The art students are long gone but the hotel art gallery installed next door carries on the tradition.

The simple mud brick building sits alongside waving date palms and fields of sugar cane. It is typical of the adobe style once common but now rare in Nubia and Upper Egypt. Most of the life of the hotel is centred in the lush garden. It opens to the east with a view over the fields towards the Nile and the Colossi of Memnon. The twin statues are almost all that is left of the once vast mortuary temple of Amenhotep III.

Book to pack: "An Egyptian Journal" by William Golding

Hotel Marsam	
Qurna	
Luxor West Bank	
Egypt	
Tel: + 20 (95) 372 403	
E-mail: marsam@africamail.com	
Booking: www.great-escapes-hotels.com	
DIRECTIONS	Beside the Ticket Office, Luxor West Bank.
RATES	Renovated rooms US$9 per night per person, including breakfast, standard rooms US$6 per night per person, including breakfast.
ROOMS	4 renovated rooms, 20 standard rooms.
FOOD	Popular Egyptian and European dishes; authentic "solar" bread served with every meal.
HISTORY	Some of the buildings of the hotel were built in 1920 to house archaeologists. The rest were built between 1940 and 1970 by Ali Abdul Rasoul, who was the owner of the hotel at that time.
X-FACTOR	Simple living in the dead centre of history.

Ein malerisches Versteck

Hier ist es, wo die Adeligen des Landes verweilten. Um exakt zu sein, nicht genau hier, aber ganz in der Nähe – und sie haben diesen Ort niemals verlassen. »Sie« sind seit langer Zeit tot. Menschen kommen hierher, um sie in ihren Gräbern zu sehen, wo sie, für die Ewigkeit konserviert, liegen. Das antike Dorf Qurna liegt auf Hügeln am westlichen Nil-ufer in Luxor – Felsgestein, bienenwabenartig mit Gräbern gespickt. Hier, in der Mitte dieses großartigen Freilichtmu-seums, steht das Hotel Marsam. Dass dies eine der begehrte-sten Ausgrabungsstätten für Archäologen ist, überrascht daher kaum. Nirgendwo sonst kann man so nah an Ruinen (nicht am Ruin) sein, wie hier. Auch Künstler kommen hier-her, wegen der Fülle an Motiven. Der Begriff Marsam steht im Arabischen für »Malerwerkstatt«. Ab 1941 lebten Studien-absolventen der bildenden Künste in einem Teil dieses Hotels. Für die darauffolgenden drei Jahrzehnte war es das, was Mont-martre für Paris ist. Zwar sind die Kunststudenten längst ver-schwunden, doch in der hoteleigenen Kunstgalerie, die gleich nebenan eingerichtet wurde, besteht diese Tradition fort. Das einfache Schlamm- und Ziegelgebäude grenzt an wogende Dattelpalmen und Zuckerrohrfelder an und entspricht ganz dem Stil der luftgetrockneten Lehmhäuser, die in Nubien und Oberägypten einst weit verbreitet waren, nun aber sehr selten geworden sind. Das Hotelleben spielt sich hauptsächlich in dem sattgrünen Garten ab. Nach Osten hin eröffnet sich von hier der Blick über die Felder in Richtung Nil und den Mem-non-Koloss. Die Zwillingsstatuen sind beinahe das Einzige, was von dem einst mächtigen Grabtempel Amenhoteps II noch übrig ist.

Buchtipp: »Ein ägyptisches Tagebuch. Reisen, um glücklich zu sein« von William Golding

Le refuge des peintres

C'est ici, ou pour être exact, tout près d'ici, que résidaient les nobles du pays. Et ils n'en sont jamais partis. Disparus depuis longtemps, préservés pour l'éternité, c'est à leurs tombeaux que l'on rend aujourd'hui visite.
Le village antique de Qurna, sur la rive ouest du Nil, à Louxor, est perché sur des collines truffées de tombeaux. C'est au cœur de cet immense musée en plein air que se dresse l'hôtel Marsam. Alentour, tout n'est que ruine, par choix. Rien d'étonnant à ce que ce site soit l'un des lieux de fouille préférés des archéologues. Les artistes y viennent également en nombre, attirés par la richesse des sujets à disposition. De fait, « Marsam » signifie « atelier de peintre » en arabe. En 1941, les étudiants diplômés des Beaux-Arts commencèrent à venir s'installer dans une partie de l'hôtel, et pendant les trois décennies suivantes, l'endroit ressem-blait à Montmartre. Les étudiants en art sont partis depuis longtemps, mais la galerie d'art de l'hôtel, qui jouxte celui-ci, perpétue la tradition.
L'édifice simple, construit avec des briques d'argile séchées au soleil, côtoie des dattiers et des champs de canne à sucre qui se balancent sous le vent. Ces constructions en adobe, autrefois courantes en Nubie et en Haute Égypte, y sont rares de nos jours. La plus grande partie de l'activité de l'hôtel a lieu dans son jardin luxuriant. Celui-ci s'ouvre vers l'est et offre une vue sur un paysage de champs puis, à l'horizon, sur le Nil et les Colosses de Memnon. Ces deux statues jumelles sont les uniques vestiges du vaste temple funéraire d'Amhénotep III.

Livre à emporter : « Journal égyptien » de William Golding

ANREISE	Neben dem Ticketschalter, in Luxor West Bank.	ACCÈS	À côté du bureau de vente de billets, rive ouest du Nil.
PREIS	Renovierte Räume für 9 US$ pro Nacht und Person, inklusive Frühstück, Standardzimmer 6 US$ pro Nacht und Person, inklusive Frühstück.	PRIX	9 $ US par nuit et par personne pour les chambres rénovées ; 6 $ US par nuit et par personne pour les chambres standard, petit-déjeuner compris.
ZIMMER	4 renovierte Räume, 20 Standardzimmer.	CHAMBRES	4 chambres rénovées, 20 chambres standard.
KÜCHE	Bekannte ägyptische und europäische Gerichte; zu jedem Essen wird echtes »Sonnenbrot« gereicht.	RESTAURATION	Cuisine populaire égyptienne et européenne. Chaque repas est accompagné d'authentique pain « solaire ».
GESCHICHTE	Einige Teile des Hotels wurden 1920 für die Unterbrin-gung von Archäologen gebaut. Die übrigen errichtete Ali Abdul Rasoul, der damalige Hotelbesitzer, zwischen 1940 und 1970.	HISTOIRE	Certains bâtiments de l'hôtel datent des années 20. Ils étaient destinés à accueillir les archéologues. Le reste a été construit entre les années 40 et les années 70 par Ali Abdul Rasoul, propriétaire de l'hôtel à l'époque.
X-FAKTOR	Einfach leben, im Totenzentrum der Geschichte.	LES « PLUS »	Vie simple au centre funéraire de l'Histoire.

A palace fit for Cleopatra...
Hotel Al Moudira, Luxor

Hotel Al Moudira, Luxor

A palace fit for Cleopatra

Do you fancy the life of a pharaoh? Or to live like a queen, such as the lovely Cleopatra?

Of course you are too late; those dynasties are long in their tombs, but you can be a slave to luxury staying here in this modern temple. You will be given the royal treatment in a setting that is duly lavish.

Al Moudira Hotel has just risen up on the West bank of the Nile, where the most splendid ancient sites are to be found. This latter-day palace is no more than a few minutes away from the Valley of the Kings. It was there that the most famous of the pharaohs – Seti I, Ramses II, and Tutankhamen – were laid to rest. Until they were dug up, that is, and all their grandeur revealed – then plundered. The hotel has been built on the edge of where fields end and the desert begins. Sugar cane growers tend their land just as their ancestors have done for thousands of years. In contrast to this simplicity, as has always been the custom, there is this grand hotel, a work of art in a realm full of them. Its walls enclose a lush garden; the air is fragrant with jasmine and henna. Maybe these photographs might serve you and me both as a modern kind of hieroglyphics; those ancient images that showed the viewer how others lived once they could, at last, be read.

So, as I am in charge, I will let this 'dazzling mosaic' of images tell their own tale.

Book to pack: "Antony and Cleopatra" by William Shakespeare

Hotel Al Moudira	DIRECTIONS	20 minutes from Luxor airport.
Luxor	RATES	US$180 to US$250 for deluxe rooms and junior suites. The prices are by room.
Egypt		
Tel: + 20 (12) 393 83 32 / 325 13 07	ROOMS	54.
Fax: + 20 (12) 322 05 28	FOOD	Mediterranean inspired, with Levantine and oriental flavours.
E-mail: moudirahotel@yahoo.com	HISTORY	Opened in 2002, designed by owner Zeina Aboukheir together with architect Olivier Sednaoui, and integrating pieces saved from old Egyptian buildings.
Website: www.moudira.com		
Booking: www.great-escapes-hotels.com	X-FACTOR	Living like Cleopatra now.

Ein Palast wie für Cleopatra

Würden Sie gerne leben wie ein Pharao? Oder wie eine Königin, beispielsweise die bezaubernde Cleopatra? Dafür sind Sie freilich zu spät dran, längst ruhen diese Dynastien in ihren Gräbern. Aber wenn Sie sich für einen Aufenthalt in diesem modernen Tempel entscheiden sollten, können Sie einem Luxus frönen, der dem ihren gleichkommt. In einer entsprechend prachtvollen Umgebung können Sie sich wahrhaft königlich verwöhnen lassen. Das Al Moudira Hotel wurde erst kürzlich am westlichen Nilufer errichtet, also dort, wo sich der größte Teil der großartigen alten Sehenswürdigkeiten befindet. Dieser neuzeitliche Palast liegt nur einige Minuten vom Tal der Könige entfernt. Hier wurden Seti I, Ramses II, sowie Tutenchamun in ihre letzte Ruhestätte gelegt – zumindest bis man sie wieder ausgrub, das Geheimnis ihrer ganzen Größe aufdeckte und ihre Gräber schließlich ausplünderte.

Das Hotel wurde dort errichtet, wo bewirtschaftete Felder und Wüste ineinander übergehen. Zuckerrohrbauern bestellen ihre Felder noch genauso, wie es ihre Vorfahren seit Tausenden von Jahren getan haben. Dieses Grand Hotel steht in unmittelbarem Gegensatz zu einer solchen Einfachheit. Ein Kontrast, wie er hier immer üblich war. Es ist ein Kunstwerk in einem Königreich voll Kunstwerken. Seine Mauern umschließen einen üppigen Garten und die Luft duftet nach Jasmin und Henna. Vielleicht können diese Abbildungen Ihnen ja als eine Art moderner Hieroglyphen dienen, jene altertümlichen Bilder, die dem Betrachter Aufschluss über die Lebensweise vergangener Kulturen gaben, als man sie schließlich entziffern konnte. Da es nun an mir ist, Ihnen einen Eindruck zu vermitteln, werde ich einfach dieses wundervolle Mosaik von Bildern für sich selbst sprechen lassen.

Buchtipp: »Antonius und Cleopatra« von William Shakespeare

Un palais pour Cléopâtre

Vous rêvez de vivre la vie d'un pharaon ? Ou la vie d'une reine, peut-être, par exemple celle de la délicieuse Cléopâtre ? Bien sûr, vous arrivez un peu tard. Ces dynasties sont depuis bien longtemps enfouies dans la tombe. Cependant, Al Moudira vous donne aujourd'hui la possibilité de faire un séjour dans le luxe d'un temple moderne et d'être traité comme un roi dans un cadre forcément fastueux.

De construction récente, l'hôtel Al Moudira s'élève sur la rive ouest du Nil, où se trouvent les plus beaux sites antiques. Ce palace des temps modernes n'est qu'à quelques minutes de la Vallée des Rois où reposaient les pharaons les plus célèbres, Séti Ier, Ramsès II et Toutankhamon, jusqu'à l'exhumation et le pillage de leurs sarcophages qui révélèrent leur magnificence.

L'hôtel est situé à la limite entre les champs et le désert. Les cultivateurs de canne à sucre travaillent la terre de la même manière que leurs ancêtres depuis des milliers d'années. Cette simplicité, habituelle ici, contraste avec ce grand hôtel, véritable œuvre d'art dans une contrée où on ne compte plus les merveilles. Ses murs renferment un jardin luxuriant, où jasmins et hennés embaument l'air. Nous pouvons peut-être utiliser ces photos comme un genre nouveau de hiéroglyphes, ces dessins antiques qui, une fois déchiffrés, révélèrent le mode de vie d'une autre civilisation.

Laissons donc cette extraordinaire mosaïque d'images parler d'elle-même.

Livre à emporter : « Antoine et Cléopâtre » de William Shakespeare

ANREISE	20 Minuten vom Flughafen Luxor.
PREIS	Von 180 US$ bis 250 US$ für Luxuszimmer und Juniorsuite. Die Preise sind pro Zimmer.
ZIMMER	54.
KÜCHE	Mediterran mit levantinischen und orientalischen Geschmäckern.
GESCHICHTE	Entworfen vom Besitzer Zeina Aboukheir und dem Architekten Olivier Sednaoui, wurde das Hotel im Jahr 2002 eröffnet; Bauteile die aus alten ägyptischen Gebäuden stammen und erhalten werden konnten, wurden dabei integriert.
X-FAKTOR	In unserer Zeit wie Cleopatra leben.

ACCÈS	À 20 minutes de l'aéroport de Louxor.
PRIX	De 180 à 250 $ US pour une chambre de luxe ou une chambre-salon. Les tarifs s'appliquent par chambre.
CHAMBRES	54.
RESTAURATION	D'inspiration méditerranéenne. Saveurs levantines et orientales.
HISTOIRE	Ouvert en 2002, conçu par le propriétaire, Zeina Aboukheir, en collaboration avec l'architecte Olivier Sednaoui, cet hôtel réunit des objets provenant dans d'anciennes constructions égyptiennes.
LES « PLUS »	Vivre comme Cléopâtre à notre époque.

Vestiges of England...
Hippo Point House, Lake Naivasha

Hippo Point House, Lake Naivasha

Vestiges of England

There are no fairies at the bottom of this English garden. Instead, the real reverse of those fantasy and lighter-than-air creatures lives here. Hundreds of "river horses", as the Greeks once called them, or hippopotami, as we know them now, are just outside the fence. They like to eat the flowers, so they must be kept out.

Hippo Point House is set in a garden of fragrant roses and verdant lawns; a mock-Tudor manor in classic grounds leading down to a pretty lake.

So far, it is a scene typical in an English landscape, but it is in the heart of Kenya's Great Rift Valley. That makes the livestock to be seen here even more of a contrast to the house. The lovely old home was built in the 1930s in the romantic style popular in England then. Its original owners had been transplanted to 'deepest darkest Africa'; to them, this house and garden was a token of their native land thousands of miles away. Years later it was found in ruins, but reinvented as a fine guesthouse. Under its gabled roof, the elegant rooms are furnished with antiques, more memories of a distant Europe. Inside, it could still be a corner of England. Once outside, the difference is of course clear. This is a sanctuary; giraffe, hippo, antelope, zebra, and leopards, and hundreds of different sorts of birds live here. The sounds, and scents, of Africa and England are worlds apart.

Books to pack: "White Mischief" by James Fox "The Hippopotamus" by Stephen Fry

Hippo Point House

P. O. Box 1852

Naivasha

Kenya

Tel: + 254 (311) 30124 / 20098

Fax: + 254 (311) 21295

E-mail: hippo-pt@africaonline.co.ke

Website: www.hippopointkenya.com

Booking: www.great-escapes-hotels.com

DIRECTIONS	By air, a 20-minute charter from Nairobi to Naivasha airstrip, and then a 40-minute drive to the estate. By road, a 1.5-hour drive north west from Nairobi.
RATES	US$500 per person per night, inclusive full board and estate activities.
ROOMS	8 rooms for up to 14 people.
FOOD	French influenced.
HISTORY	Built in the 1930s, and much later Dodo's Tower, the folly, was built on the same property by the present owners.
X-FACTOR	Seeming to have a foot in two countries.

Englische Reminiszenzen

Elfen, die ja angeblich in jedem echten englischen Garten zu
finden sind, gibt es hier zwar keine, dafür aber das genaue
Gegenteil dieser zarten Fantasiegestalten, die leichter sind als
Luft. Direkt hinter dem Zaun leben Hunderte von Flusspferden
oder Hippopotami, wie sie schon die alten Griechen nannten.
Der Zaun soll sie davon abhalten die Blumen zu fressen.
Hippo Point House liegt inmitten eines duftenden, grünen
Rosengartens. Es wurde einem Tudorgut nachempfunden, und
seine klassische Parkanlage führt zu einem kleinen See hinab.
Bis hierher klingt dies alles nach einem typisch englischen
Schauplatz, doch er liegt im Herzen von Kenias Great Rift
Valley. Die Tiere, die man hier beobachten kann, bilden
dadurch einen umso stärkeren Kontrast zu dem Haus.
Das bezaubernde alte Gebäude wurde in den 1930er Jahren
erbaut – gemäß dem romantischen Stil, der zu jener Zeit in
England so beliebt war. Seine ursprünglichen Besitzer waren
gezwungen gewesen, in das »tiefste, schwärzeste Afrika« zu
ziehen, deshalb stellten für sie dieses Haus und der Garten
eine Art Verbindungsglied dar zu ihrer Tausende von Meilen
weit entfernten Heimat. Jahre später, das Haus war mittlerwei-
le eine Ruine, entdeckte man es neu und baute es zu einem
Hotel um. Unter seinem Giebeldach befinden sich elegante
Räume, die – ausgestattet mit Antiquitäten – Erinnerungen
an das ferne Europa wachrufen.
Die Innenräume könnten tatsächlich in irgendeinem Winkel
Englands liegen. Doch sobald man aus dem Gebäude heraus-
tritt, wird der Unterschied selbstverständlich sofort offen-
sichtlich: Dies ist ein unberührtes Wildreservat in welchem
Giraffen, Flusspferde, Antilopen, Zebras, Leoparden, sowie
Hunderte verschiedener Vogelarten leben. Zwischen den
Geräuschen und Gerüchen Afrikas und Englands liegen
wahrhaftig Welten.

**Buchtipps: »Weißes Verhängnis« von James Fox
»Das Nilpferd« von Stephen Fry**

Vestiges d'Angleterre

Au fond de ce jardin anglais, tout droit sorties d'un conte de
fées, évoluent des créatures aux antipodes de ces êtres
fantastiques et gracieux. Des centaines d'hippopotames,
ou « chevaux de rivière » comme les appelaient les Grecs,
vivent en effet juste de l'autre côté de la clôture. Étant donné
leur goût prononcé pour les fleurs, l'entrée du site leur est
interdite.
Hippo Point House, imitation d'un manoir Tudor, est installé sur un domaine d'agencement classique descendant jusqu'à un lac charmant, au milieu d'un jardin de roses odorantes et de pelouses verdoyantes.
Ce cadre, qui s'apparente à un paysage anglais typique,
se trouve en réalité au cœur de la grande vallée du Rift, au
Kenya, d'où le fort contraste entre la propriété et la faune
alentour. Cette jolie vieille demeure fut construite dans les
années trente dans le style romantique alors en vogue en
Angleterre. Pour ses premiers propriétaires, transplantés
« au plus profond de l'Afrique noire », la maison et son jardin symbolisaient leur pays natal, à des milliers de kilomètres
de là. Des années plus tard, la bâtisse, alors en ruine, fut restaurée et retrouva une nouvelle vie en tant que pension de
famille raffinée. Protégées par un toit à double pente, les
chambres élégantes sont meublées d'antiquités, autres souvenirs d'une Europe lointaine. Encore aujourd'hui, une fois à
l'intérieur, on pourrait se croire en Angleterre. Mais dès que
l'on met le pied dehors, la différence saute aux yeux : des
girafes, des hippopotames, des antilopes, des zèbres, des léopards et des centaines d'espèces d'oiseaux vivent dans cette
réserve naturelle. Et les sons et les parfums de l'Afrique n'ont
rien à voir avec ceux de l'Angleterre.

**Livres à emporter : « Je rêvais de l'Afrique » de Kuki Gallmann
« L'hippopotame » de Stephen Fry**

ANREISE	Ein etwa 20-minütiger Flug mit einer privaten Charter-maschine von Nairobi nach Naivasha. Von dort aus 40-minütige Fahrt zum Anwesen. Mit dem Wagen 1,5- stündige Fahrt nordwestlich von Nairobi.
PREIS	500 US$ pro Person pro Nacht, inklusive Vollpension und Unterhaltungsangebot.
ZIMMER	8 Zimmer für bis zu 14 Personen.
KÜCHE	Französisch angehaucht.
GESCHICHTE	Erbaut in den 1930er Jahren; auf dem selben Grundstück errichteten die heutigen Besitzer viel später Dodo's Tower.
X-FAKTOR	Zwei Kulturen an einem Ort.

ACCÈS	Trajet de 20 minutes en avion de Nairobi jusqu'à la piste d'atterrissage de Naivasha, puis 40 minutes en voiture jusqu'à la propriété. À 1H30 au nord-ouest de Nairobi en voiture.
PRIX	500 $ US par personne et par nuit en pension complète avec animations.
CHAMBRES	8 chambres pouvant accueillir jusqu'à 14 personnes.
RESTAURATION	Influences françaises.
HISTOIRE	Construit dans les années 30. Bien plus tard, les propriétaires actuels firent édifier une folie, la Tour de Dodo, sur le même domaine.
LES « PLUS »	Impression d'être dans deux pays différents à la fois.

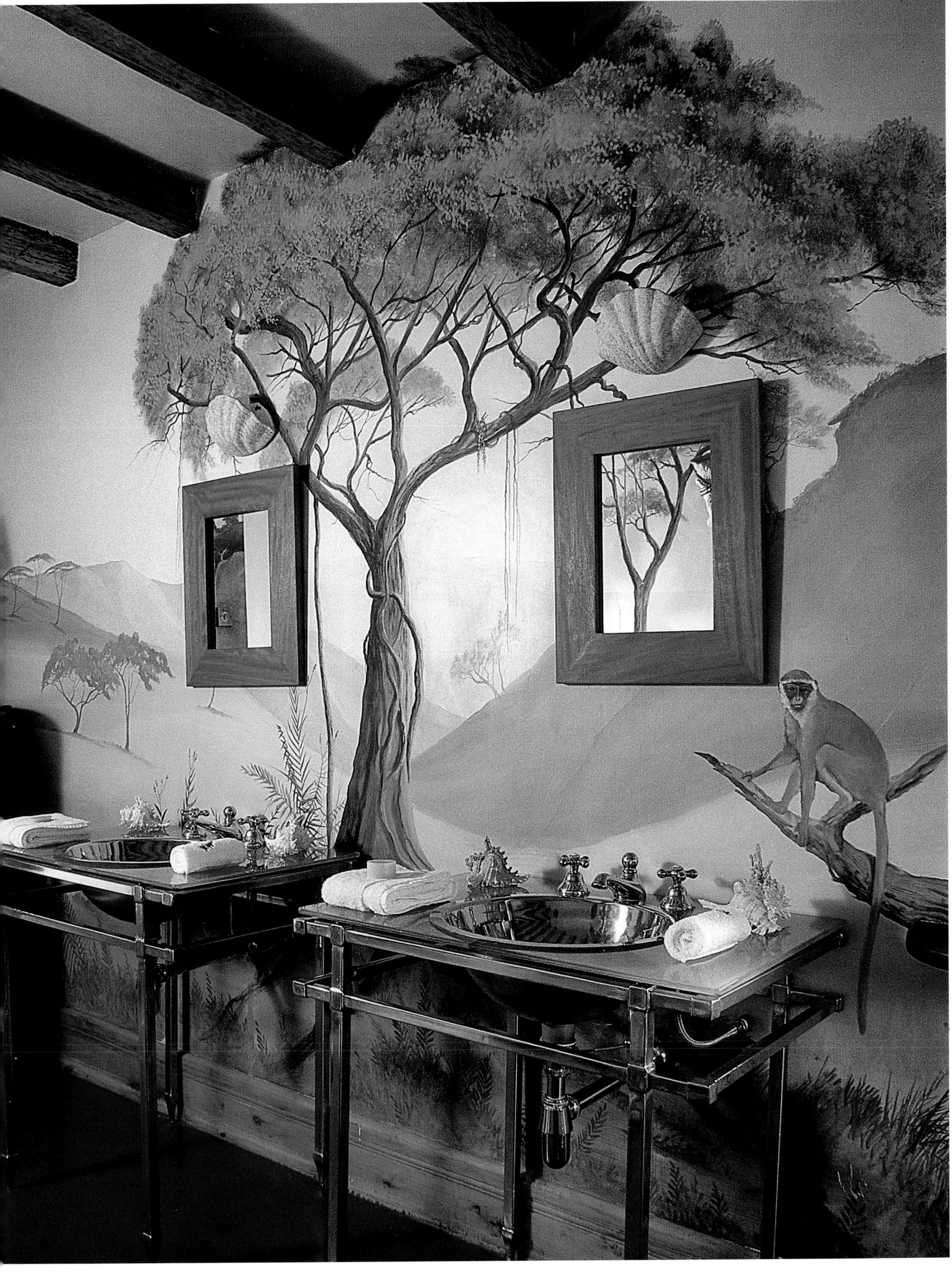

Smell the coffee...
Ngong House, near Nairobi

Ngong House, near Nairobi

Smell the coffee

Those with a sharp sense of smell might detect a lingering aroma here: the rich scent of coffee. Or perhaps only those with a keen mind's eye may think it so. It would be a reminder of the past owner and a use this land was once put to: as a coffee farm, whose mistress was Tania Blixen. Ngong House is on what was the famous writer's estate.

"I had a farm in Africa, at the foot of the Ngong Hills." This opening line from her book is a spare prologue to the story of the land she grew to love and describe so expressively. "The Equator runs across these highlands, in the daytime you felt as though you had got high up, near to the sun, but the early mornings and evenings were limpid and restful, and the nights were cold."

There is height here indeed, in the landscape and in the lodgings. Tree houses are the rooms with a view at Ngong House; not the usual style though. These are more whimsical, on two levels, with plump four-poster beds, doors made from old Arab ships, stained glass windows, a fireplace, bar, even a kitchen. Each one has its own character. The furniture might be made of camphor wood, or of old railway hardwood sleepers, or the intricate hand-carved chairs of the island of Lamu. The verandah is a place to bask in the sun, drink gin, tea, or coffee, and watch the bird life fly by or gaze at the misty Ngong Hills.

"The Mountain of Ngong stretches in a long ridge from north to south, and is crowned with four noble peaks like immovable darker blue waves against the sky."

Book to pack: "Out of Africa" by Tania Blixen

Ngong House	
Karen District	
Nairobi	
Kenya	
Tel: + 254 (20) 891-856 / 890 140 / 891 296	
Fax: + 254 (20) 890 674	
E-mail: enquiries@roveafrica.com	
Website:	
www.roveafrica.com/properties/ngong.htm	
Booking: www.great-escapes-hotels.com	

DIRECTIONS	A 20-minute drive south from the centre of Nairobi.
RATES	US$560 per night for two persons; includes all meals, excursions and transfers.
ROOMS	5 tree houses, 2 rooms in the main house.
FOOD	High quality to go with the lofty location.
HISTORY	Opened in 1995.
X-FACTOR	The feeling of a remote African outpost, not far from the city.

Kaffeeduft liegt in der Luft

Wer über einen ausgeprägten Geruchssinn verfügt, mag hier ein feines Aroma in der Luft bemerken: den Geruch von Kaffee. Vielleicht bilden sich das aber auch nur diejenigen ein, die eine starke Vorstellungskraft haben. Der Geruch erinnert daran, wer hier einst die Besitzerin war, und wofür das Land zu jener Zeit genutzt wurde: dies ist die Kaffeeplantage, über die einst Tania Blixen Herrin war.

Ngong House wurde auf dem Grund erbaut, der damals der berühmten Schriftstellerin gehörte. »Ich hatte eine Farm in Afrika am Fuß der Ngong Hügel.« Dieser erste Satz ihres Romans ist eine recht spärlich klingende Einleitung zu der Geschichte des Landes, das sie so lieben lernte und später so eindrucksvoll beschrieb. »Der Äquator verläuft durch dieses Hochland. Tagsüber fühlte man sich, als wäre man hoch hinaufgekommen, in die Nähe der Sonne, aber die frühe Morgenzeit und die Abende waren klar und friedlich und die Nächte waren kalt«.

Hoch hinaus geht es hier tatsächlich, sowohl was die Landschaft, als auch was die Unterkunft betrifft. Zimmer mit Ausblick, damit sind hier, in Ngong House, Baumhäuser gemeint, wenn auch keine gewöhnlichen. Die zweistöckigen Baumhäuser sind skurrile Bauwerke mit mächtigen 4-pfostigen Betten, Türen, die aus arabischem Schiffsholz gefertigt sind, bunten Glasfenstern, einer offenen Feuerstelle, einer Bar und sogar einer Küche. Jede Hütte hat ihren eigenen Charakter. Die Einrichtung besteht zum Teil aus Kampferholz, wie die Hartholzbetten aus alten Eisenbahnschlafwagen oder die aufwändig handgeschnitzten Stühle von der Insel Lamu.

Auf der Veranda kann man in der Sonne liegen, während man einen Gin, Tee oder Kaffee zu sich nimmt und dabei die Vögel beobachtet, oder auf die in leichtem Nebel liegenden Ngong Hügel blickt.

»Der Ngong Berg erstreckt sich in einem langen Rücken von Nord nach Süd und ist mit vier edlen Gipfeln gekrönt, die sich wie unbewegliche, dunkle blaue Wellen vom Himmel abheben.«

Buchtipp: »Out of Africa« von Tania Blixen

L'ivresse de café

Ceux qui ont un odorat développé seront peut-être capables de détecter ici un arôme persistant : le parfum enivrant du café. Ou peut-être seules les personnes douées d'une imagination fertile seront-elles en mesure de percevoir ces effluves qui évoquent l'ancienne propriétaire, Tania Blixen, et l'usage que l'on faisait autrefois de cette terre : une plantation de café.

Ngong House se trouve sur un domaine qui appartenait au célèbre écrivain. « J'avais une ferme en Afrique, au pied des montagnes Ngong. » La première phrase de son livre est une introduction laconique à l'histoire de cette terre que Tania Blixen apprit à aimer et qu'elle décrivit de façon si expressive. « L'Équateur s'étend le long de ces montagnes. Pendant la journée, on avait l'impression de s'élever très haut et de toucher le soleil, mais l'aube et le soir étaient limpides et paisibles, et les nuits étaient froides. »

La hauteur est en effet bien présente ici, dans le paysage comme dans les habitations. À Ngong House, les chambres avec vue sont des maisonnettes perchées dans les arbres. Leur style est unique et insolite. Elles s'étendent sur deux niveaux et sont dotées de lits à baldaquin moelleux, de portes fabriquées à partir d'anciens vaisseaux arabes, de fenêtres à vitraux, d'une cheminée, d'un bar et même d'une cuisine. Chaque chambre a son caractère propre. Le mobilier est en bois de camphrier ou fabriqué à partir de traverses en bois dur d'anciennes voies de chemin de fer ou de chaises provenant de l'île de Lamu dont les gravures complexes ont été exécutées à la main.

La véranda est idéale pour se prélasser au soleil, boire un verre de gin, une tasse de thé ou de café en regardant les oiseaux dans le ciel ou les montagnes Ngong couvertes de brume.

« La longue chaîne des montagnes Ngong s'étend du nord au sud. Elle est couronnée de quatre nobles pics formant autant de vagues bleu sombre contre le ciel. »

Livre à emporter : « La ferme africaine » de Tania Blixen

ANREISE	20-minütige Autofahrt südlich vom Zentrum in Nairobi entfernt.
PREIS	560 US$ pro Nacht für zwei Personen, inklusive aller Mahlzeiten, Getränke, Exkursionen und Transfers.
ZIMMER	5 Baumhäuser, 2 Zimmer im Haupthaus.
KÜCHE	«Hohe» Küche, passend zur hohen Behausung.
GESCHICHTE	Eröffnet im Jahre 1995.
X-FAKTOR	Atmosphäre wie in einem weit abgelegenen Außenposten Afrikas, nicht weit von der Stadt entfernt.

ACCÈS	À 20 minutes en voiture du centre de Nairobi, par le sud.
PRIX	560 $ US la nuit pour deux personnes. Le prix comprend tous les repas, les excursions et les transports locaux.
CHAMBRES	5 maisonnettes dans les arbres, 2 chambres dans le bâtiment principal.
RESTAURATION	Excellente, en accord avec la noblesse du lieu.
HISTOIRE	Ouvert en 1995.
LES « PLUS »	Atmosphère d'un avant-poste africain isolé, tout près de la ville.

Baobab bungalows...
Tarangire Treetops, Tarangire Conservation Area

Tarangire Treetops, Tarangire Conservation Area

Baobab bungalows

The baobab tree is one of the most stunning sights in Africa. It can grow to a massive size; some are hundreds of years old. In many parts of the continent it is thought to be sacred. Legend has it that the tree so angered the gods that they tore it up then flung it back to earth, upside down, so it landed with its roots in the air.

The chalets that make up Tarangire Treetops Lodge are built on platforms high up in the canopy of these extraordinary trees. When we were children many of us fell in love with tree houses; sometimes we fell head over heels out of them. We had to give them up when we grew up. The 'huts' here are far more sophisticated than our childish kind; they may be in trees but that is where the resemblance ends – and all for the better. These are definitely a step up, and more.

A bar is set among the eaves of a massive baobab, where drinks are served before dinner. Even the dining 'room' is in a tree. And the creators of the Lodge really 'branched out' in their design of the chalets; each has a living room as well as a large bedroom. Of course a deluxe bathroom is part of this more adult version. The décor is stylish too, a skilful mix of local fabrics, Maasai craftsmanship and Swahili opulence. Down at ground level are the neighbours. Leopard, cheetah, lion, greater kudu and huge herds of elephant are at home here.

Book to pack: "The Flame Trees of Thika: Memories of an African Childhood" by Elspeth Huxley

Tarangire Treetops

Tarangire Conservation Area
Tanzania
Tel: + 225 (27) 254 45 74
Fax: + 225 (27) 250 92 77-81
E-mail: res@halcyontz.com
Website: www.halcyonafrica.com
Booking: www.great-escapes-hotels.com

DIRECTIONS	120 km/75 m south west of Arusha, or by plane to the Tarangire airstrip, 32 km/20 m away.
RATES	Drive in rate: US$145 to US$225 per person in a double room, including lunch and dinner. Fly in rate: US$240 to US$385 per person in a double room, including lunch, dinner, transfers and game drives.
ROOMS	28 chalets built on top giant Baobab and Maroela trees.
FOOD	Old world cuisine simmered in the African melting pot.
HISTORY	The lodge was built with the local Maasai community. For every guest US$20 is contributed to the village improvement.
X-FACTOR	A chance to re-live childhood days.

Baobab Bungalows

Der Affenbrotbaum gehört zu den verblüffendsten Sehenswürdigkeiten Afrikas. Er kann zu einer enormen Größe
heranwachsen und manche Exemplare sind mehrere hundert
Jahre alt. In vielen Teilen des Kontinents gilt der Baobab
als heilig. Eine Legende besagt, dass der Baum die Götter
so sehr ärgerte, dass sie ihn zerfetzten und ihn mit der
Krone nach unten zurück auf die Erde warfen, so dass
er mit den Wurzeln nach oben landete.

Die Hütten aus denen sich Tarangire Lodge zusammensetzt,
wurden auf Plattformen gebaut, die hoch oben auf diesen
Bäumen thronen. Kopfüber haben sich viele von uns als Kinder in die Idee verliebt, ein Baumhaus zu haben, kopfüber
ist so mancher hinuntergefallen, und als wir älter wurden,
mussten wir sie aufgeben. Diese Hütten hier sind von tech-
nisch viel raffinierterer Art, als es unsere »kindlichen«
Baumhäuser waren. Zwar befinden sie sich auf Bäumen,
doch damit endet die Ähnlichkeit auch schon, denn sie
sind definitiv viel ausgeklügelter. Wer möchte, kann vor dem
Abendessen einen Drink an der Bar einnehmen, die zwischen
die Stämme eines riesigen Affenbrotbaumes gebaut wurde.
Selbst der »Speisesaal« ist auf einem Baum gelegen. Und
was die Inneneinrichtung der Hütten angeht, kann man nur
sagen, dass die Gestalter der Lodge »astrein« geplant haben.
Jede Hütte hat sowohl ein Wohnzimmer, als auch ein Schlafzimmer. Selbstverständlich sind auch Luxusbadezimmer Teil
dieser Erwachsenenversion eines Baumhauses. Der Dekor ist
ebenfalls stilvoll – eine gekonnte Mischung aus einheimischen Materialien, Massai-Handwerkskunst und opulenter
Swahili-Kunst.

Unten am Grund leben die Nachbarn. Hier sind Leopard,
Gepard, Löwe, die große Kuduantilope und riesige Elefan-
tenherden zu Hause.

**Buchtipp: »Die Flammenbäume von Thika. Erinnerungen an
eine Kindheit in Afrika« von Elspeth Huxley**

Baobab bungalows

Le baobab est l'un des arbres les plus fascinants d'Afrique.
Considéré comme sacré dans de nombreuses régions du
continent, il peut atteindre des hauteurs vertigineuses et
certains spécimens sont plusieurs fois centenaires. La
légende dit que son aspect vient de ce que les dieux, cour-
roucés par son gigantisme, le déracinèrent et le renvoyèrent
sur terre, tête en bas et racines en l'air.

Les bungalows de Tarangire Treetops Lodge sont érigés sur
des plates-formes installées dans la voûte de ces arbres extraordinaires. Enfants, nombre d'entre nous étaient friands des
cabanes construites dans les arbres. Certains même les trou-
vaient si bien qu'ils en tombaient parfois à la renverse. En
grandissant, nous avons dû y renoncer. Les « cabanes » de
Tarangire Treetops sont bien plus sophistiquées que celles
de notre enfance. Elles sont installées dans les arbres, soit,
mais la ressemblance s'arrête là, ce qui est tout à votre avantage. Ces cabanes sont d'une catégorie bien supérieure.

Un bar installé entre les feuilles d'un énorme baobab vous
attend pour un apéritif avant le dîner et même la salle du
restaurant est perchée dans un arbre. Par ailleurs, les créa-
teurs de l'hôtel ont exploré une branche réellement originale
de la conception de bungalows. En effet, chacun de ces derniers se compose d'un salon et d'une grande chambre, et
bien sûr, cette version adulte de la cabane est équipée d'une
salle de bain luxueuse. La décoration, tout aussi élégante,
est une habile combinaison d'étoffes locales, d'artisanat
massaï et d'opulence swahili.

Les voisins habitent au rez-de-chaussée : léopards, guépards,
lions, grands kudus et énormes troupeaux d'éléphants sont
ici chez eux.

Livre à emporter : « Le lion » de Joseph Kessel

ANREISE	Mit dem Auto 120 km südwestlich von Arusha; mit dem Flugzeug zum 32 km entfernten Flugplatz in Tarangire.
PREIS	Drive in Rate: von 145 US$ bis 225 US$ pro Person im Doppelzimmer, inklusive Mahlzeiten. Fly in Rate: von 240 US$ bis 385 US$ pro Person im Doppelzimmer, inklusive Mahlzeiten, Transfers und Safaris.
ZIMMER	28 Hütten, die hoch oben in riesigen Affenbrot- und Maroelabäumen errichtet wurden.
KÜCHE	Europäische Küche mit afrikanischem Einschlag.
GESCHICHTE	Die Lodge wurde zusammen mit den einheimischen Massai gebaut. Pro Gast fließen 20 US$ in ein Hilfsprojekt.
X-FAKTOR	Lassen Sie sich in ihre Kindheit zurückversetzen.

ACCÈS	En voiture, à 120 km au sud-ouest d'Arusha, ou par avion jusqu'à Tarangire, distant de 32 km.
PRIX	Drive in Rate: de 145 $ US à 225 $ US par personne en chambre partagée. Fly in Rate: de 240 $ US à 385 $ US avec pension complète et safaris.
CHAMBRES	28 bungalows construits en haut de baobabs et de maroelas géants.
RESTAURATION	Cuisine européenne aux saveurs africaines.
HISTOIRE	Hôtel construit avec les Massaï. Pour chaque résident, 20 $ US sont investis dans l'aide à la population locale.
LES « PLUS »	L'occasion de redevenir enfant.

Spiritual therapy...
Mnemba Island Lodge, near Zanzibar

Mnemba Island Lodge, Zanzibar

Spiritual therapy

If you had spent a week creating heaven and earth, this would be the place to rest on the seventh day. You could reflect on your work, and pat yourself on the back for creating such an idyllic place.

A few days at Mnemba Lodge, on a heart-shaped atoll off the coast of Zanzibar, is sure therapy for the spirit. This is one of the islands that are home to fragrant spices like nutmeg, cloves and cinnamon. Their stimulating scent, the sound of soft sea breezes rustling through the fronds of coconut palms and the lush plant life, all combine to make this an especially tempting place. Famed as being one of the most romantic spots in the world, Mnemba is a totally private island. Set in the turquoise Indian Ocean and surrounded by coral reefs, its pure white sand beaches are swathed around it like a halo. As suits an earthly paradise, it has a climate that is nearly perfect. Life is centred on the beach. Dinner is often served seated under the stars, at the edge of the water, with the guests' bare feet in the sea.

So, when you are feeling stressed enough to try the patience of a saint, this is the place to retreat to. A cloud nine is at hand.

Book to pack: "How I found Livingstone" by Henry Morton Stanley

Mnemba Island Lodge	
P.O. Box 2055	
Zanzibar	
Tanzania	
Tel: + 255 (24) 223 31 10	
Fax: + 255 (24) 223 31 17	
E-mail: webenquiries@ccafrica.com	
Website: www.mnemba-island.com	
Booking: www.great-escapes-hotels.com	

DIRECTIONS	Mnemba lies 2 km/1.2 m north-east of the island of Zanzibar, a 20-minute cruise in a traditional boat.
RATES	US$625 per person in a double room, including all meals, drinks, wind surfing, snorkelling and scuba diving.
ROOMS	10 secluded bungalows for up to 20 guests.
FOOD	Pan-African cuisine with Mediterranean and Moroccan influences.
X-FACTOR	Tropical paradise.

Balsam für die Seele

Hätten Sie eine Woche damit zugebracht, Himmel und Erde zu erschaffen, so wäre dies der Ort, um am siebten Tage zu ruhen. Hier könnten Sie über Ihr Werk nachsinnen und sich selbst dafür auf die Schulter klopfen, dass Sie einen solch idyllischen Ort geschaffen haben.

Ein paar Tage in der Mnemba Lodge auf einem herzförmigen Atoll vor der Küste Sansibars zu verbringen ist sicherer Balsam für die Seele. Dies ist eine jener Inseln, die nach Muskat, Gewürzelken und Zimt riechen. Jener anregende Duft und das leichte Rascheln, wenn eine sanfte Meeresbrise zart durch die Wedel der Kokospalmen streicht, machen diese Insel zusammen mit der üppigen Vegetation zu einem besonders verführerischen Ort. Mnemba, dafür bekannt einer der romantischsten Flecken der Erde zu sein, ist eine vollkommen private Insel im türkisfarbenen Indischen Ozean, umgeben von Korallenriffen und gesäumt von weißen Sandstränden, wie von einem Heiligenschein. Wie es sich für das Paradies auf Erden gehört, weist die Insel zudem ein beinahe perfektes Klima auf. Das Leben spielt sich am Strand ab, und das Abendessen wird oftmals direkt am Strand unter dem Sternenhimmel serviert, während das Wasser die Füße sanft umspült.

Sollten Sie sich also gestresst genug fühlen, es einmal mit Engelsgeduld zu versuchen, so ist dies der Ort, an den Sie sich zurückziehen sollten. Wolke Sieben ist noch frei.

Buchtipp: »Wie ich Livingstone fand« von Henry Morton Stanley

Ressourcer l'âme et l'esprit

Si vous aviez passé une semaine à créer le ciel et la terre, c'est ici que vous vous reposeriez le septième jour. Vous pourriez alors méditer sur le travail accompli et vous féliciter d'avoir donné vie à un lieu aussi idyllique.

Quelques jours au Mnemba Lodge, situé sur un atoll en forme de cœur au large de la côte de Zanzibar, est la meilleure des thérapies de l'âme. Cette île est l'une de celles qui produisent des épices odorantes telles que la noix de muscade, le clou de girofle et la cannelle. Leur parfum stimulant et le souffle de la douce brise de mer qui fait bruisser les feuilles des cocotiers et la végétation exubérante en font un lieu particulièrement attrayant. Tenue pour l'un des endroits les plus romantiques au monde, Mnemba est une île où l'intimité est complète. Située au milieu de l'Océan Indien couleur turquoise, elle est entourée de barrières de corail et ses plages de pur sable blanc l'enveloppent tel un halo. Comme il se doit dans ce paradis terrestre, le climat est proche de la perfection. La vie s'organise autour de la plage : il vous arrivera souvent de dîner sous les étoiles, au bord de l'océan, les pieds dans l'eau.

Si votre stress est tel que vous ne savez plus à quel saint vous vouer, venez vous réfugier sur cette île. Le septième ciel vous attend.

Livre à emporter : « Comment j'ai retrouvé Livingstone » d'Henry Morton Stanley

---

ANREISE	Mnemba liegt 2 km nordöstlich der Insel Sansibar, eine 20-minütige Fahrt in einem traditionellen Boot.
PREIS	625 US$ pro Person im Doppelzimmer, inklusive aller Speisen und Getränke, Windsurfing, Schnorcheln und Flaschentauchen.
ZIMMER	10 abgeschiedene Bungalows für maximal 20 Gäste.
KÜCHE	Panafrikanische Küche mit mediterraner und marokkanischer Note.
X-FAKTOR	Tropisches Paradies.

ACCÈS	Mnemba se trouve à 2 km au nord-est de Zanzibar, soit un trajet de 20 minutes à bord d'une embarcation traditionnelle.
PRIX	625 $ US par personne en chambre double. Le prix comprend tous les repas, les boissons, la location de planches à voile, la plongée avec tuba et la plongée sous-marine.
CHAMBRES	10 bungalows isolés. Le nombre d'hôtes est limité à 20.
RESTAURATION	Cuisine panafricaine aux influences méditerranéennes et marocaines.
LES « PLUS »	Un paradis dans les tropiques.

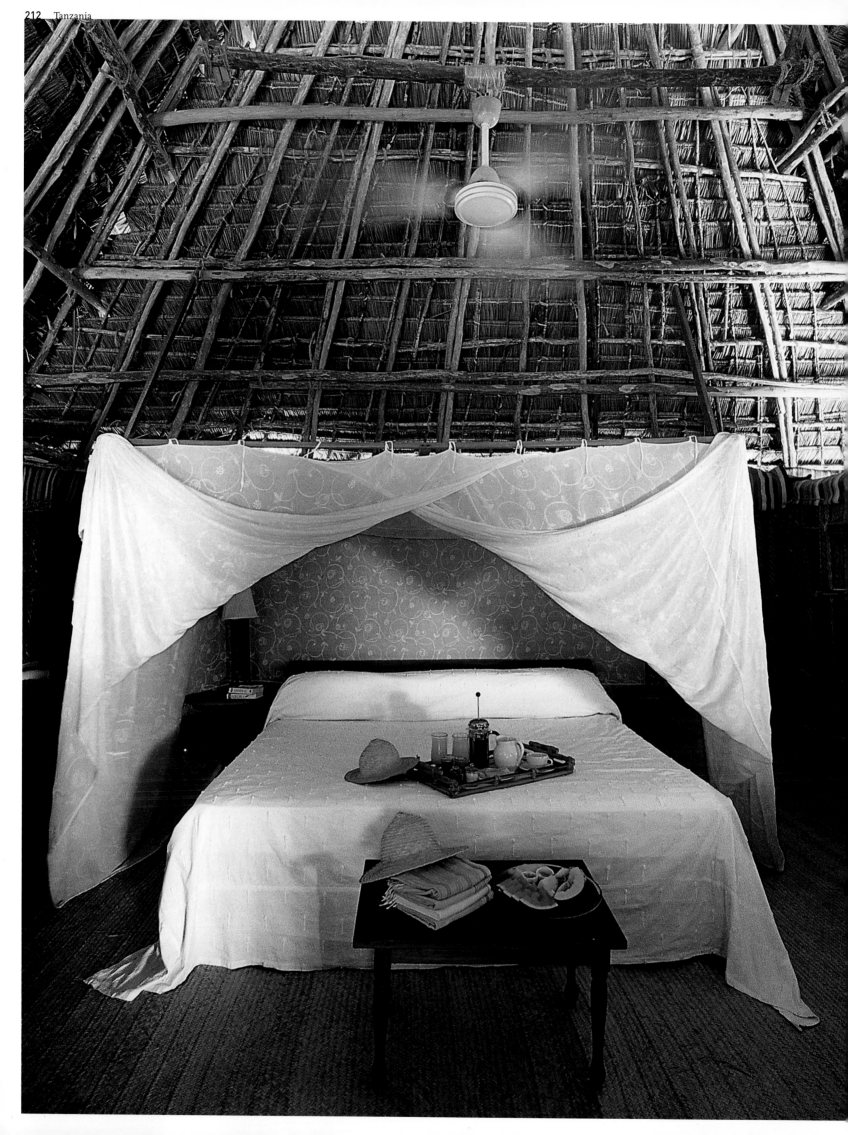

Sunset terrace...
Zanzibar Serena Inn, Zanzibar

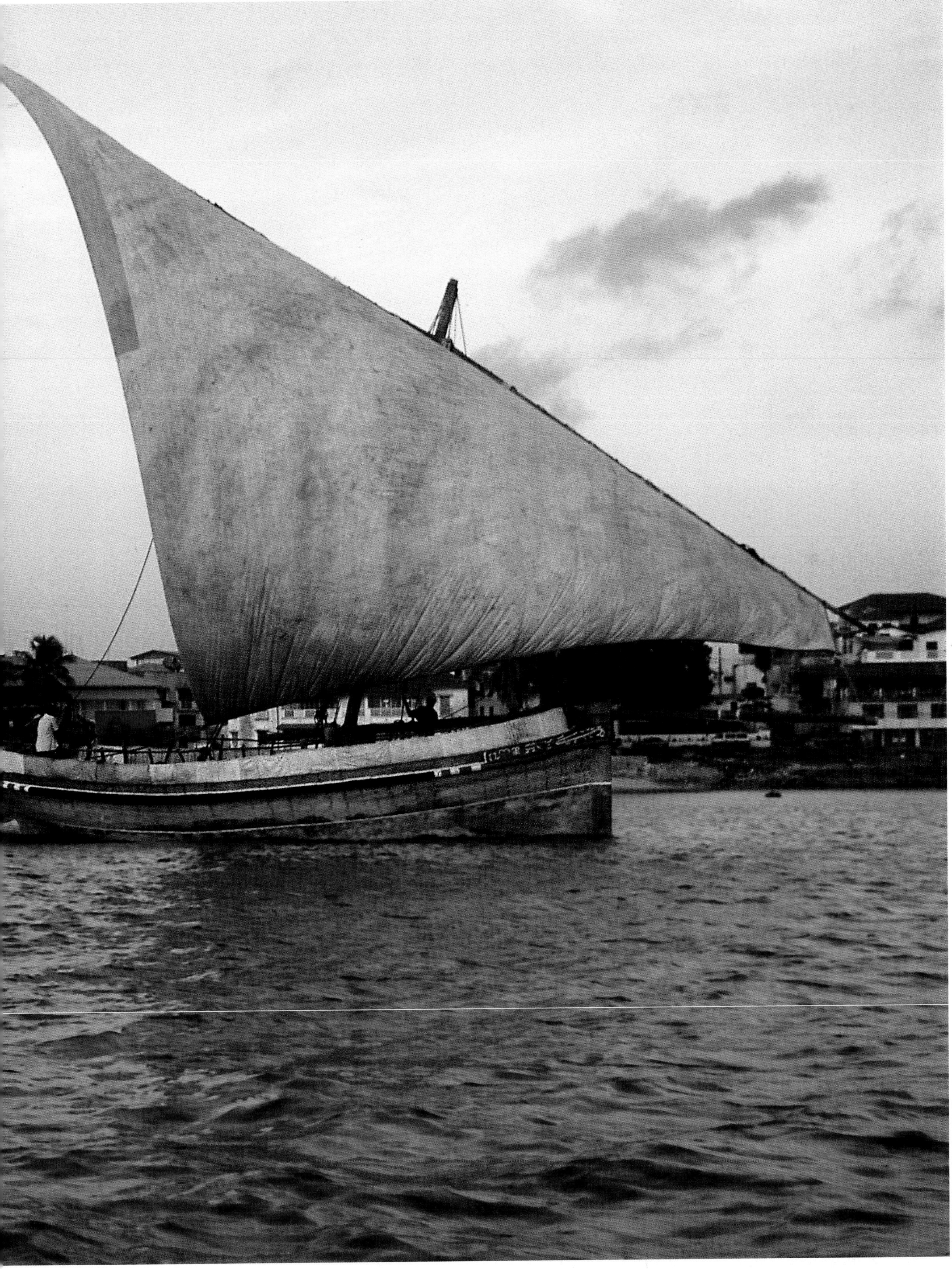

Zanzibar Serena Inn, Zanzibar

Sunset terrace

This place has long been one of the world's busiest intersections. For centuries, the island has been a virtual crossroads; traffic from all corners of the globe has passed by here. Traders of spices or slaves, travellers from one land to others, all have left their mark on Zanzibar.

The architecture is one proof of that: much of the island's heritage is marked out in its buildings. Many of them have been given a new purpose. The Zanzibar Serena Inn is one of those. Two old houses on the seafront of historic Stone Town have been combined and restored to their earlier grandeur to form the hotel. Inside the design refers to the island's rich Arabian influences as well as its African lineage. It makes the most of its grandstand view of the Indian Ocean, too. The terrace is the prime place to see the stunning sunsets that light up the water as far as the mainland. The hotel offers day trips to its own private beach; a tranquil scene that is close to the infamous "slave caves" used for illegal slave trading after it was abolished. By the mid-19th century, Zanzibar was the world's largest producer of cloves, and it had the largest slaving centre on the east coast. Some fifty thousand slaves were put up for sale in its market each year. Few, if any, saw this place again.

Book to pack: "Trade Wind" by Mary Margaret Kaye

Zanzibar Serena Inn	
Kelele Square	
Stone Town	
Zanzibar	
Tel: + 255 24 (2) 23 10 15	
Fax: + 255 24 (2) 23 30 19	
E-mail: serena@slh.com	
Website: www.serenahotels.com	
Booking: www.great-escapes-hotels.com	

DIRECTIONS	Daily flights from Nairobi or Mombasa. Daily high speed ferries from Dar es Salaam c. 1.5 hours. On the sea front of the historic Stone Town on the western side of Zanzibar Island.
RATES	US$240 per double room and US$600 per suite, including breakfast.
ROOMS	47 double rooms, 4 suites.
FOOD	Local seafood a speciality; the menu reflects the many cultural influences that have passed this way.
HISTORY	Opened in 1997.
X-FACTOR	Prime sea front position.

Ein Platz an der Sonne

Lange Zeit stellte dieser Ort einen der wichtigsten Verkehrsknotenpunkte der Welt dar. Diese Insel war gewissermaßen über Jahrhunderte hinweg eine Art Kreuzung, durch welche der Verkehr aus allen erdenklichen Ecken der Erde floss. Gewürz- und Sklavenhändler, Weltreisende, alle haben sie ihre Spuren in Sansibar hinterlassen.

Ein Beweis dafür liegt nicht zuletzt in der Architektur, ein Großteil des kulturellen Erbes der Insel manifestiert sich sichtbar in den Gebäuden. Viele von ihnen erfüllen heute einen neuen Zweck. Dies ist auch der Fall beim Zanzibar Serena Inn: Zwei alte, direkt am Meer gelegene Häuser der historischen Stadt Stone Town wurden miteinander zu diesem Hotel zusammengeschlossen und erstrahlen, frisch renoviert, nun in ihrem altem Glanz. Die Innenausstattung bezieht sich deutlich auf die arabischen Einflüsse sowie die afrikanische Abstammung, welche die Insel so nachhaltig geprägt haben. Den bühnenartigen Ausblick auf den Indischen Ozean hätte sich das Hotel nicht besser zu Nutze machen können. Die Terrasse ist ein optimaler Ort, um die atemberaubenden Sonnenuntergänge zu beobachten, die das Wasser bis zum Festland hin aufleuchten lassen.

Das Hotel bietet Tagestouren zu seinem Privatstrand an, einem ruhigen Schauplatz, nahe bei den berüchtigten Sklavenhöhlen, die nach Abschaffung der Sklaverei zum illegalen Sklavenhandel genutzt wurden. In der Mitte des 19. Jahrhunderts war Sansibar weltweit führend im Gewürznelkenanbau und galt außerdem als der größte Sklavenmarktplatz an der Ostküste. Jedes Jahr wurden hier etwa 50.000 Sklaven verkauft. Nur wenige, wenn überhaupt irgendeiner von ihnen, sah diesen Ort je wieder.

Buchtipp: »Tod in Sansibar« von Mary Margaret Kaye

La terrasse aux mille couchers de soleil

Cet endroit a longtemps été l'un des lieux de passge les plus fréquentés de la planète. Pendant des siècles, l'île fut un véritable carrefour où se croisaient des gens venus des quatre coins du monde. Marchands d'épices et d'esclaves, voyageurs, tous ont laissé une marque de leur passage à Zanzibar.

L'architecture en est une preuve puisqu'une grande partie du patrimoine de l'île se manifeste dans ses bâtiments. Nombre d'entre eux servent aujourd'hui de nouveaux objectifs. Ainsi, l'hôtel Zanzibar Serena Inn est formé par la réunion de deux vieilles maisons du front de mer de Stone Town, la ville de pierre historique, auxquelles on a rendu leur splendeur passée. À l'intérieur, le décor témoigne des riches influences arabes de l'île et de son lignage africain. Zanzibar Serena Inn a également su tirer le meilleur parti d'une vue incomparable sur l'Océan Indien. Sa terrasse est l'emplacement rêvé pour assister aux couchers de soleil époustouflants qui illuminent la mer jusqu'au continent. L'hôtel vous propose de passer la journée sur sa plage privée, lieu paisible situé à proximité des « grottes aux esclaves », tristement célèbres pour le commerce illégal des esclaves qui s'y tenait après l'abolition. Au milieu du XIXᵉ siècle, Zanzibar était le premier producteur de clous de girofle au monde et abritait le plus grand marché d'esclaves de la côte est. Chaque année, quelque cinquante mille personnes y étaient mises en vente. Rares furent celles qui revirent un jour ce lieu.

Livre à emporter : « Zanzibar » de Mary Margaret Kaye

ANREISE	Mit dem Flugzeug (täglich) von Nairobi oder Mombasa. Oder ca. 1,5-stündige Fahrt mit dem Schnellboot (täglich) von Dar es Salaam. Das Hotel liegt an der dem Meer zugewandten Seite des historischen Stone Town.	ACCÈS	Vols quotidiens depuis Nairobi ou Mombasa. Traversées quotidiennes en ferry depuis Dar es Salaam d'environ 1H30. L'hôtel est situé sur le front de mer de Stone Town, la ville historique située à l'ouest de l'île de Zanzibar.
PREIS	240 US$ pro Doppelzimmer und 600 US$ pro Suite, Frühstück inklusive.	PRIX	240 $ US la chambre double et 600 $ US la suite, petit-déjeuner compris.
ZIMMER	47 Doppelzimmer, 4 Suiten.	CHAMBRES	47 chambres doubles, 4 suites.
KÜCHE	Fisch und Meeresfrüchte aus der Gegend. In der Speisekarte spiegeln sich die verschiedenen Einflüsse diverser Kulturen wider.	RESTAURATION	Les fruits de mer de l'île sont la spécialité locale. Le menu reflète les nombreuses influences culturelles qui ont marqué l'île.
GESCHICHTE	Eröffnet im Jahre 1997.	HISTOIRE	Ouvert en 1997.
X-FAKTOR	Direkt am Meer.	LES « PLUS »	Front de mer incomparable.

Treasure trove...
Frégate Island Private, Frégate Island

Frégate Island Private, Frégate Island

Treasure trove

Long ago, pirates came in search of the treasure they thought was to be found here. They were looking for gold on this remote island, but their spades struck only rock. The real treasure was not buried, but clearly able to be seen, in the rich green landscape and hoard of bird-life. High on the cliffs, hidden amongst cashew and almond trees, is some more fortune: the villas of Frégate Island Resort. Each villa is set apart, and blends into its lush background.

The spectacular sea views, secluded beaches, and coral reef protected waters are just some of the spoils for those who are privileged to stay here.

Privacy is one more of the riches here. Giant tortoises might cross your path in this elite hideaway, but you will see few people. Even fewer sightings will be made of the world's rarest bird, the magpie robin. But you may hear its song, one thought so beautiful that the bird was sought for a life of captivity in gilded cages. Now it has found refuge on one of the most unspoiled places on earth.

A safe haven that it shares, with others who seek to turn their backs on the outside world for a while.

Book to pack: "Treasure Island" by Robert Louis Stevenson

Frégate Island Private

Frégate Island

Tel: + 248 22 47 89

Fax: + 248 32 44 99

E-mail: fregate@seychelles.net

Website: www.fregate.com

Booking: www.great-escapes-hotels.com

DIRECTIONS	A 20 minute flight from the international airport at Mahé by a private chartered aircraft.
RATES	US$1,700 to US$2,000 per night per villa for two persons plus taxes, all-inclusive, five nights minimum stay.
ROOMS	16 villas.
FOOD	Gourmet, much of it grown on the island.
X-FACTOR	Seclusion and luxury faraway in exotic surroundings.

Eine Schatzinsel

Vor langer Zeit kamen Piraten hierher, um den Schatz zu heben, den sie hier vermuteten. Es war Gold, wonach sie auf dieser abgelegenen Insel suchten, doch ihre Spaten stießen nur auf Felsgestein.

Der wahre Schatz der Insel lag nirgendwo vergraben, sondern deutlich sichtbar in der üppigen grünen Landschaft und dem Reichtum der Vogelwelt. Hoch oben auf den Klippen verbirgt sich eine weitere Kostbarkeit: die Villen des Frégate Island Resort. Jede der Villen steht für sich allein und fügt sich harmonisch in den sattgrünen Hintergrund ein. Der Meeresblick, die Strände und die geschützten Korallenriffgewässer sind nur einige der Annehmlichkeiten, die sich jenen bieten, die das Glück haben hier verweilen zu dürfen. Ein weiterer Reichtum der Insel ist die Ungestörtheit, die man hier genießt. Und während einem an diesem exklusiven Zufluchtsort durchaus einige Riesenschildkröten begegnen können, trifft man Menschen hier eher selten. Noch weniger oft wird es einem gelingen, einen Blick auf die Seychellen-Schamadrossel zu erhaschen, den seltensten Vogel der Welt. Doch man kann sie singen hören und ihr Gesang galt lange Zeit als so betörend schön, dass diese Vögel gejagt wurden, um ihr Leben in goldenen Käfigen gefangen zu fristen. Heute haben sie einen geschützten Zufluchtsort in einem der unberührtesten Flecken der Erde gefunden – ein sicherer Hafen, den sie mit anderen teilen, die sich danach sehnen, dem Rest der Welt für eine Weile den Rücken zuzukehren.

Buchtipp: »Die Schatzinsel« von Robert Louis Stevenson

L'île aux trésors

Il y a de cela bien longtemps, des pirates débarquèrent sur cette île isolée, pensant y trouver un trésor. À la recherche d'or, leurs pelles ne rencontrèrent que du roc.

Le véritable trésor, un luxuriant paysage verdoyant et une multitude d'oiseaux, n'était pas enfoui mais exposé à la vue de tous. Le sommet des falaises recèle d'autres joyaux, tapis à l'ombre des anacardiers et des amandiers : les villas de la station balnéaire de l'île Frégate. Chacune d'entre elles a un style unique et se fond dans un paysage exubérant.

Les vues spectaculaires sur la mer, les plages retirées et les eaux protégées par des barrières de corail ne sont que quelques exemples des trésors découverts par ceux qui ont le privilège de séjourner dans ce lieu.

L'intimité et la solitude font partie des grandes richesses de cette retraite fastueuse, où votre chemin croisera peut-être celui de tortues géantes, mais plus difficilement celui de l'oiseau le plus rare du monde, le merle dyal. Toutefois, vous aurez peut-être la chance d'entendre son chant, si merveilleux que cet oiseau fut longtemps chassé puis gardé en captivité dans une cage dorée. Il a aujourd'hui trouvé refuge dans l'un des endroits les mieux préservés de la Terre, un havre de paix qu'il partage avec ceux qui souhaitent pour un temps oublier le monde extérieur.

Livre à emporter : « L'Île au trésor » de Robert Louis Stevenson

ANREISE	20-minütiger Flug mit einer privaten Chartermaschine vom internationalen Flughafen in Mahé.
PREIS	Von 1.700 US$ bis 2.000 US$ pro Nacht pro Villa für zwei Personen, zuzüglich Steuer, alles inklusive, Mindestaufenthaltsdauer 5 Nächte.
ZIMMER	16 Villen.
KÜCHE	Gourmet, viele der Zutaten stammen aus inseleigenem Anbau.
X-FAKTOR	Abgeschiedenheit und Luxus, entfernt vom Rest der Welt in exotischer Umgebung.

ACCÈS	À 20 minutes de l'aéroport international de Mahé en avion-charter privé.
PRIX	1.700 à 2.000 $ US hors taxes par nuit et par villa pour deux personnes, tout compris. Séjour de 5 nuits minimum.
CHAMBRES	16 villas.
RESTAURATION	Gastronomique, essentiellement élaborée à partir des produits locaux.
LES « PLUS »	Cadre exotique et luxueux, à l'écart du reste du monde.

Ocean bliss...
Le Prince Maurice, Mauritius

Le Prince Maurice, Mauritius

Ocean bliss

Like Oscar Wilde, Mark Twain had a great deal to say on most topics. And he seems to have journeyed to most continents; his writings pass judgement on where he had been. His verdict on this place was that God had copied the idea of heaven from Mauritius.

This could be taken to mean that it was created first, and heaven was an afterthought. Whatever the right order might be, it is true that this is one of the most naturally endowed islands on earth. It has all the basics said to be ideal for an island: white sands, aquamarine waters, palm trees and the bluest of blue skies. But there is more to these essentials in Mauritius. It has a style that comes from the influence of quite a few different cultures. A mélange of African and French, plus Muslim, Chinese and Hindu traditions make up the end product.

All this has been distilled to a stylish simplicity at Le Prince Maurice Hotel. A perfect calm seems to have settled under the soaring timber entrance vault. It is the gateway to a lush 'Garden of Eden' set between it and a private lagoon, rimmed of course by a dazzling beach. There is an understated glamour here, too, both in the surroundings and the suites. Each of the suites has a colour theme that has been inspired by the shades of spices, in a tribute to the condiments that have flavoured the island's history.

Book to pack: "Following the Equator: A Journey Around the World" by Mark Twain

Le Prince Maurice	DIRECTIONS	On the north east coast of the island, 35 km/22 m east from the capital Port-Louis, 15 minutes from the International Airport SSR of Mauritius by helicopter.
Choisy Road		
Poste de Flacq	RATES	US$263 to US$5,700 per person per night, including breakfast, service and tax.
Mauritius		
Tel: + 230 413 91 00/26	ROOMS	76 junior suites, 12 senior suites and 1 princely suite.
Fax: + 230 413 91 29/30	FOOD	Aromatic and often spicy, from a range of restaurants, including one that floats on water.
E-mail: resa@princemaurice.com		
Website: www.princemaurice.com	HISTORY	Opened in 1998, named after Prince Maurice Van Nassau of Holland.
www.ccafrica.com		
Booking: www.great-escapes-hotels.com	X-FACTOR	A "Guerlain" spa, more bliss from the inspired creator of Shalimar.

Perle im Ozean

Wie Oscar Wilde hatte auch Mark Twain zu den meisten
Dingen etwas zu erzählen und seinen literarischen Werken
entnehmen wir, dass er, die meisten Kontinente bereist hat.
Die Insel Mauritius erschien ihm als hätte sie Gott als
Vorlage für den Himmel gedient. Das würde allerdings
bedeuten, dass die Insel zuerst entstanden und der Himmel
ein nachträglicher Einfall sei.

Wie auch immer die Reihenfolge sein mag, es ist zweifellos
wahr, dass es kaum eine andere Insel auf der Welt gibt, die
so mit den Schönheiten der Natur gesegnet ist, wie diese.
Sie weist wirklich alle Eigenschaften einer idealen Trauminsel
auf: weiße Sandstrände, aquamarinblaues Wasser, Palmen und
einen strahlend blauen Himmel. Doch Mauritius bietet noch
weitaus mehr: Einflüsse verschiedenster Kulturen haben ihren
besonderen Stil geprägt, der aus einer Vermischung
afrikanischer, französischer, sowie muslimischer, chinesischer
und hinduistischer Traditionen resultiert. Diese Elemente ver-
schmelzen im Le Prince Maurice Hotel zu einer stilvollen
Einfachheit. Unter dem hohen hölzernen Eingangsgewölbe
breitet sich eine wohl tuende Ruhe aus. Es ist das Tor zu
einem üppigen Garten Eden, der zwischen dem Haus und
einer privaten Lagune liegt, die von einem wunderschönen
Strand umrahmt ist. Sowohl die Umgebung, als auch die
Räumlichkeiten haben etwas dezent Glamouröses an sich. Jede
der Suiten ist nach einem Farbthema dekoriert, in Anlehnung
an die Gewürze und Aromen, welche die Geschichte der Insel
bestimmen.

Buchtipps: »Reise durch die alte Welt« von Mark Twain
»Die Wellen von Mauritius« von Lindsey Collen

Félicité au bord de l'océan

Tout comme Oscar Wilde, Mark Twain avait beaucoup de
choses à dire sur la plupart des sujets. Il semble que l'écrivain ait séjourné sur la plupart des continents. Dans ses
écrits, il porte un jugement sur les endroits où il s'est rendu.
Son verdict en ce qui concerne l'île Maurice est que Dieu
s'en est inspiré pour créer le paradis, ce qui laisserait penser
que l'île a été créée en premier et que le paradis n'en est
qu'une copie.

Quoi qu'il en soit, il s'agit à n'en pas douter de l'une des
îles les plus paradisiaques de la planète. Elle réunit tous les
ingrédients de base que l'on considère généralement comme
formant l'essence de l'île idéale : sable blanc, eau oscillant
entre le bleu et le vert, palmiers et ciel d'un bleu pur. Mais
l'île Maurice, c'est bien plus que cela. Héritière d'un style
marqué par plusieurs cultures différentes, elle est un creuset
de traditions africaines, françaises, musulmanes, chinoises
et hindoues.

L'hôtel Prince Maurice, véritable concentré de simplicité
et d'élégance, témoigne de ces influences. Un calme parfait
règne sous sa haute voûte d'entrée en bois. À l'intérieur,
vous découvrez un « jardin d'Éden » luxuriant attenant à un
lagon privé, bordé cela va sans dire d'une plage d'une beauté
éblouissante. Un charme discret et raffiné émane tant du
paysage que des suites. La couleur de chacune de ces dernières s'inspire d'une nuance d'épice, en hommage aux
condiments qui ont pimenté l'histoire de l'île.

Livres à emporter : « Les jours Kaya » de Carl de Souza
« Les voyages des innocents » de Mark Twain

ANREISE	An der nordöstlichen Küste gelegen, 35 km östlich von der Hauptstadt Port-Louis entfernt; 15-minütiger Flug mit dem Hubschrauber von Mauritius internationalen Flughafen SSR.	ACCÈS	Situé sur la côte, au nord-est de l'île, à 15 minutes en hélicoptère de l'aéroport international de l'île Maurice et à 35 km à l'est de la capitale Port-Louis.
PREIS	Von 263 US$ bis 5.700 US$ pro Person pro Nacht, inklusive Frühstück, Service und Steuern.	PRIX	263 à 5.700 $ US par nuit et par personne, petit-déjeuner, services et taxes compris.
ZIMMER	76 Standardsuiten. 12 Luxussuiten und 1 Fürstensuite.	CHAMBRES	76 chambres-salons, 12 suites doubles et 1 suite royale.
KÜCHE	Aromatisch und oft scharf; es gibt verschiedene Restaurants, darunter auch ein schwimmendes.	RESTAURATION	Cuisine aux aromates, assez épicée.
GESCHICHTE	Eröffnet im Jahr 1998, benannt nach Prinz Maurice Van Nassau zu Holland.	HISTOIRE	Ouvert en 1998, l'hôtel tire son nom du Prince Maurice de Nassau.
X-FAKTOR	Ein »Guerlain«-Spa, Entspannung à la Shalimar.	LES « PLUS »	Centre de mise en forme Guerlain, l'ivresse des sens par le créateur inspiré de Shalimar.

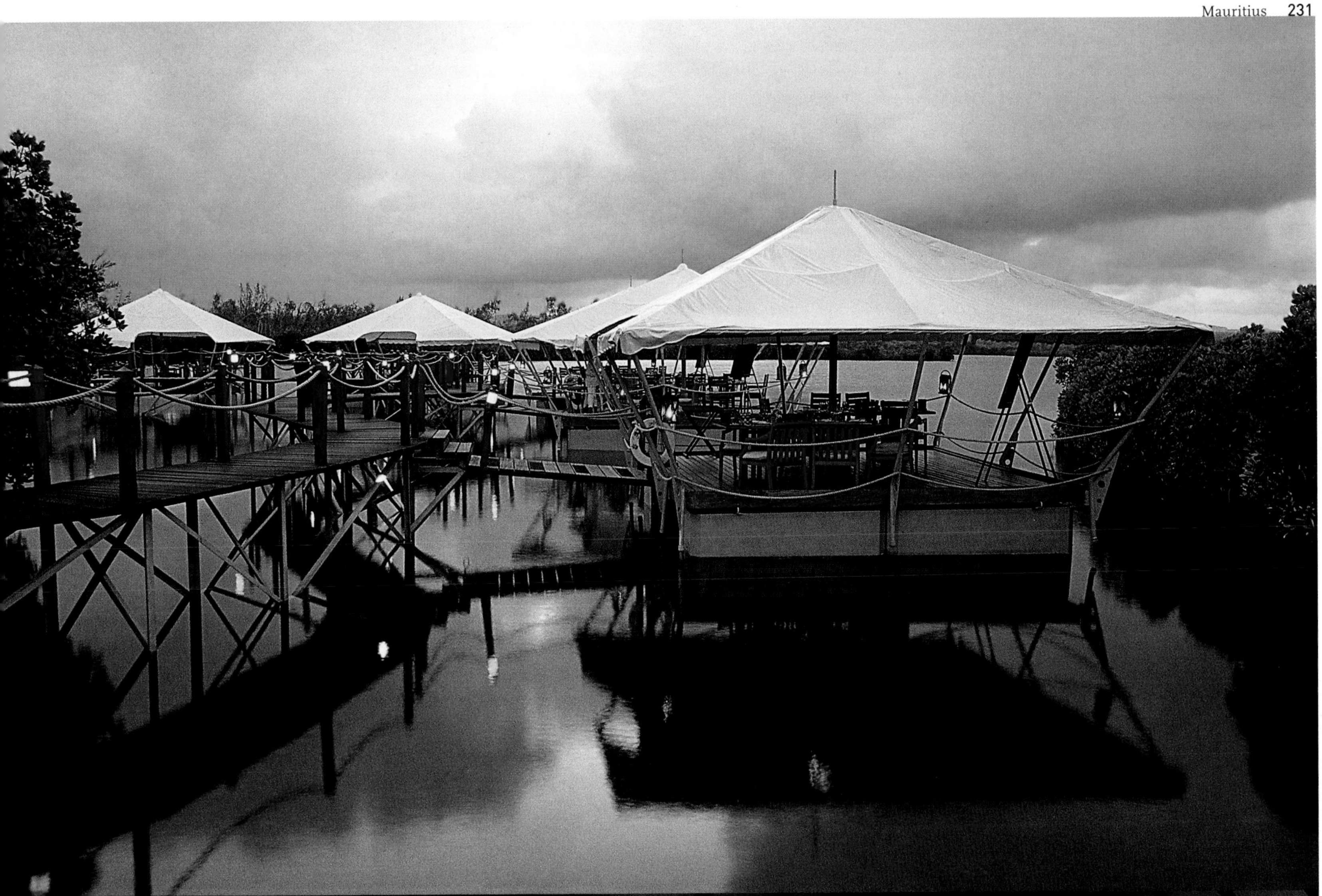

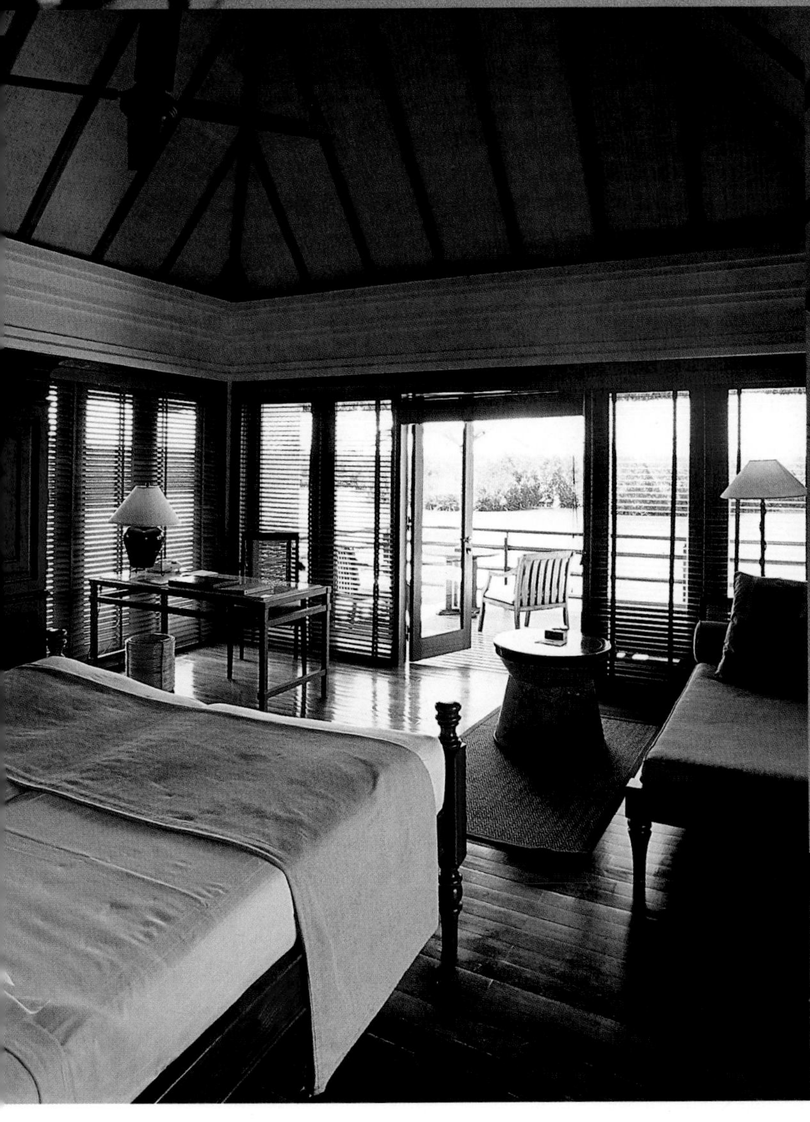

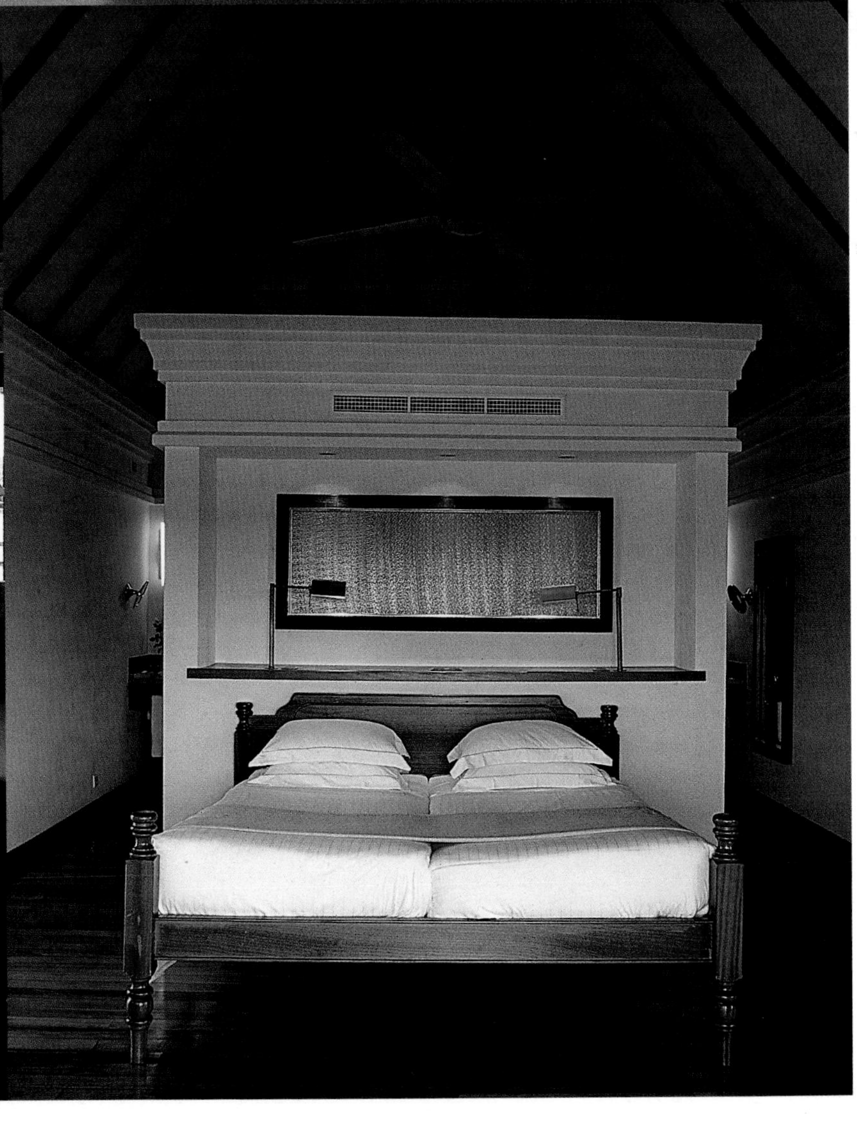

Going with the flow...

Matetsi Water Lodge, Matetsi Safari Area

Matetsi Water Lodge, Matetsi Safari Area

Going with the flow

An old Swahili proverb warns that appearances may well be deceptive. "Nyumba njema si mlango"; a good house is not judged by its door.

The entrance is not deceptive here. At Matetsi Water Lodge, the vast teak doors swing wide open to reveal true inner style and the sight of one of Africa's great rivers. The mighty Zambesi flows by the camp; boats and canoes will carry you on it. The lodge design is a polished blend of textures and colours. And from the canopied bed or the plunge pool on the tree-sheltered deck, the views are superb.

This game reserve is part of a huge wildlife paradise that spans two countries. Up to fifty thousand elephants, 'nature's great masterpiece', roam it – the greatest mass anywhere on earth. Lion calls can often be heard at night. It's best not to answer them. You can hear as well as see that the bird life is teeming. The Zambezi is home to the largest and most dangerous of African reptiles, the Nile crocodile. Its mean appearance is real; it has earned its rank as a killer. Large mammals are part of its diet.

Hippo too are often seen and heard along the river's edge. The loudest noise in these parts though is the rumbling of the Victoria Falls, just a short distance away. "Mosi oa tunya, the smoke that thunders" is the local name for the stunning cascade. It is a sight so impressive that many deem it one of the top wonders of our world.

Books to pack: "Livingstone's River: A History of the Zambezi Expedition, 1858–1864" by George Martelli
"Don't Let's Go to the Dogs Tonight" by Alexandra Fuller
"Butterfly Burning" by Yvonne Vera

Matetsi Water Lodge

Matetsi Safari Area

Victoria Falls

Zimbabwe

Tel: + 263 (13) 45949

Fax: + 263 (13) 42128

E-mail: information@ccafrica.com

Website: www.ccafrica.com

Booking: www.great-escapes-hotels.com

DIRECTIONS	Matetsi Water Lodge is accessible by scheduled flights to Victoria Falls Airport, followed by a 45-minute road transfer.
RATES	US$275 to US$325 per person, inclusive of all meals, drinks and scheduled safari activities.
ROOMS	3 separate camps each with 6 suites.
FOOD	Cooked by a chef named Comfort – comfort food!
HISTORY	Opened in 1996.
X-FACTOR	Life on the river, and near the stunning Victoria Falls.

Sich treiben lassen

Ein altes Swahili Sprichwort warnt vor dem trügerischen Schein: »Nyumba njema si mlango«, ein gutes Haus erkennt man nicht an seiner Türe. In diesem Fall ist der Eingang nicht trügerisch. Wenn in der Matetsi Water Lodge die breiten Teakholztüren aufschwingen, geben sie nicht nur den Blick auf ein stilvolles Interieur, sondern auch auf einen von Afrikas beeindruckenden Flüssen frei. Der mächtige Sambesi, den Sie mit Booten und Kanus befahren können, fließt direkt am Camp vorbei. Die Innengestaltung der Lodge ist eine ausgefeilte Zusammenstellung von Materialien und Farben. Und der Ausblick, den man vom Schlafsofa oder vom Tauchbecken aus genießen kann, das sich unter dem Schutz von Bäumen auf der Terrasse befindet, ist fantastisch.

Dieses Wildreservat gehört zu einem riesigen Naturschutzparadies, das sich über zwei Länder erstreckt. Hier leben bis zu 50 000 Elefanten – so viele wie nirgendwo sonst auf der Welt. Des Nachts hört man oft Löwen, denen man besser keine Beachtung schenkt. Die vielen Vögel kann man sowohl hören, als auch sehen. Ebenfalls im Sambesi beheimatet ist das größte und gefährlichste aller afrikanischen Reptilien, das Nilkrokodil. Sein bedrohliches Aussehen täuscht keineswegs, denn es hat sich einen Namen als Killer gemacht. Und auf seinem Speiseplan stehen auch große Säugetiere.

Entlang des Flusses kann man die Nilpferde hören und sehen. Das lauteste Geräusch in dieser Gegend ist jedoch das Donnern der Victoria Falls, die nur wenige Meilen entfernt sind. »Mosi oa tunya«, den donnernden Rauch, nennen die Einheimischen die atemberaubenden Wasserfälle. Ihr Anblick ist derart spektakulär, dass viele Leute sie zu den größten Weltwundern zählen.

Buchtipp: »Schmetterling in Flammen« von Yvonne Vera

Au fil de l'eau

Un vieux proverbe swahili dit que les apparences sont parfois trompeuses : « *Nyumba njema si mlango* », « on ne juge pas la qualité d'une maison à sa porte ».

La porte d'entrée de Matetsi Water Lodge, elle, n'a rien de trompeur : les énormes battants en teck s'ouvrent en grand sur un intérieur véritablement luxueux d'où l'on peut admirer l'un des plus grands fleuves d'Afrique, le formidable Zambèze, qui coule près du camp et sur lequel vous pourrez naviguer en bateau ou en canoë. Le design de l'hôtel est un mélange sophistiqué de textures et de couleurs. La vue est toujours superbe, que vous l'admiriez de votre lit à baldaquin ou depuis le bassin de la terrasse protégée par les arbres. Cette réserve naturelle fait partie d'un vaste paradis pour les animaux qui s'étend sur deux pays. Cinquante mille éléphants, ce « grand chef-d'œuvre de la nature » et la plus grande espèce terrestre, le parcourent en tous sens. La nuit, le rugissement des lions se fait souvent entendre. Mieux vaut ne pas y répondre. Et il suffit d'ouvrir les yeux et les oreilles pour se rendre compte que les oiseaux sont ici extrêmement nombreux. Le Zambèze abrite également le plus gros et le plus dangereux des reptiles africains : le crocodile du Nil. Son apparence sanguinaire reflète la réalité. En effet, sa réputation de tueur n'est pas usurpée, et les gros mammifères figurent parfois à son menu.

Souvent, vous verrez et entendrez également les hippopotames le long des rives du fleuve. Toutefois, le bruit le plus imposant dans cette partie de la Zambie est le grondement des stupéfiantes Chutes Victoria toutes proches, que les autochtones appellent *Mosi oa tunya*, « la fumée qui tonne ». Le spectacle est tellement impressionnant que nombreux sont ceux qui les considèrent comme l'une des plus belles merveilles du monde.

Livre à emporter : « Larmes de pierre : Une enfance africaine » d'Alexandra Fuller

ANREISE	Anreise mit dem Linienflug zum Victoria Falls Flughafen mit anschließender 45-minütiger Autofahrt.
PREIS	Von 275 US$ bis 325 US$ pro Person, inklusive allen Mahlzeiten, Getränken und Safaritrips.
ZIMMER	3 einzelne Camps, jedes mit 6 Suiten.
KÜCHE	Die Gerichte werden zubereitet von einem Koch, der Comfort heißt – Komfort(abel) speisen!
GESCHICHTE	Eröffnet im Jahre 1996.
X-FAKTOR	Leben am Fluss und in der Nähe der großartigen Victoria Wasserfälle.

ACCÈS	Un vol régulier jusqu'à l'aéroport Victoria Falls, suivi d'un transfert en voiture de 45 minutes.
PRIX	De 275 $ US à 325 $ US par personne. Le prix comprend les repas, les boissons et les activités de safari planifiées.
CHAMBRES	3 camps distincts, disposant chacun de 6 suites.
RESTAURATION	Le chef cuisinier s'appelle Comfort, et les plats qu'il élabore font honneur à son nom !
HISTOIRE	Ouvert en 1996.
LES « PLUS »	La vie au bord du fleuve ; proximité des Victoria Falls, chutes d'eau époustouflantes.

Studying the tracks...
Sandibe Safari Lodge, Okavango Delta

Sandibe Safari Lodge, Okavango Delta

Studying the tracks

You never know when you might need a few basic skills. Here at Sandibe Lodge, you can apply yourself to gaining some.

Interpretive bush walks are in the care of a local San – Bushman – guide. This is your chance to learn traditional bush skills; like making rope from grasses, how to construct traps, light fires with friction sticks, and how to track animals. Or you can just sit and watch them.

Elephants have walked the meandering paths by the camp for hundreds of years. Perhaps moved by this, the lodge has been built with a commitment to "treading lightly on the earth." No trees were felled in its construction; instead, the cottages were built in a natural clearing. Their roofs are thatched, but that is where the resemblance to a usual cottage ends.

These are far removed from the sort that this English word often means. Their airy rooms are styled with a rich fusion of colour and texture, and of tactile fabrics like silk and leather, woven mats, copper and rough-hewn wood. An exotic landscape surrounds them, a forest of wild palms and twisting trees, flanked by channels of a delta that contains 95 per cent of all the surface water in Botswana. The mud spires of giant termite mounds and great baobab trees stand out in the scenery. Sandibe is set in a backwater, and all the better for it. A wealth of wildlife, birds, and plants thrive in the grass-wept floodplains of the Okavango Delta.

"The art of moving gently, without suddenness, is the first to be studied by the hunter, and more so by the hunter with the camera." Karen Blixen

Books to pack: "Among the Elephants" by Iain & Oria Douglas-Hamilton

"The White Bone" by Barbara Gowdy

Sandibe Safari Lodge

Adjacent to Moremi Wildlife Reserve

Okavango Delta

Botswana

Tel: + 267 686 19 79

Fax:+ 267 686 19 72

E-mail: webinquiries@ccafrica.com

Website: www.sandibe.com

www.ccafrica.com

Booking: www.great-escapes-hotels.com

DIRECTIONS	Accessible only by scheduled flights from Johannesburg to Maun or Kasane, followed by a 30-minute flight from Maun, or a 1.5-hour flight from Kasane and a short drive to the camp.
RATES	US$380 to 475 per person, including all meals, drinks, scheduled safari activities and other extras.
ROOMS	8 double-room cottages.
FOOD	Pan-African cuisine.
HISTORY	Opened in 1998.
X-FACTOR	Unique cottages in an idyllic environment.

Auf Spurensuche

Man kann nie wissen, wann man einmal ein paar grundlegende Fertigkeiten gebrauchen kann. Hier, in der Sandibe Lodge, können Sie bei Kulturwanderungen durch die Buschlandschaft unter der Führung eines einheimischen San, eines Buschmannes, einige davon erwerben.

Dies ist Ihre Chance, die Fertigkeiten zu erlernen, die ein Buschmann traditionellerweise beherrscht, zum Beispiel ein Seil aus Gräsern zu flechten, Fallen zu bauen, Feuer durch das Aneinanderreiben zweier Stöckchen zu entflammen und die Fährten der Tiere zu lesen. Oder aber Sie bleiben einfach sitzen und beobachten die Tiere nur. Seit Hunderten von Jahren schon ziehen die Elefanten entlang der Pfade, die sich am Camp vorbeischlängeln. Vielleicht war dies der ausschlaggebende Grund, warum man sich beim Bau der Lodge dazu verpflichtet hat, sanft vorzugehen, es wurde kein Baum für ihre Errichtung gefällt. Stattdessen baute man die Hütten in eine natürliche Lichtung hinein. Ihre Dächer sind strohgedeckt, doch damit endet auch schon jedwede Ähnlichkeit mit einer gewöhnlichen Hütte. Die Hütten, von denen hier die Rede ist, sind weit entfernt von dem, was dieses Wort im Deutschen oft impliziert. Eine luxuriöse Verbindung von Farben und Materialien verleiht den luftigen Räumen Stil: sinnliche Stoffe wie Seide und Leder, gewebte Matten und Kupfer kombiniert mit grob behauenem Holz. Umgeben sind die Hütten von einer exotischen Landschaft, einem Wald aus wilden Palmen und gekrümmten Bäumen, an dem die Kanäle eines Flussdeltas vorbeilaufen, das 95 Prozent des gesamten Oberflächenwassers in Botswana enthält. Gegen den Horizont zeichnen sich die Schlammspitzen der riesigen Termitenhügel und beeindruckende Affenbrotbäume ab. Ein großer Vorteil von Sandibe ist, dass es in einem Stauwasserbereich gelegen ist. Im Gras- und Schwemmland des Okavango Deltas tummelt sich eine reiche Artenvielfalt von Tieren, Vögeln und Pflanzen.

Buchtipps: »Unter Elefanten« von Iain und Oria Douglas-Hamilton
»Der weiße Knochen« von Barbara Gowdy

Repérer les empreintes

Qui sait si certaines techniques de survie ne vous seront pas un jour utiles ? Pour en apprendre quelques-unes, venez à Sandibe Lodge.

Un guide local *San,* un bushman, vous y attend pour vous entraîner dans des excursions explicatives à travers la brousse. Vous aurez la possibilité d'apprendre les techniques traditionnelles de la brousse, notamment comment élaborer une corde avec de l'herbe, construire des pièges, faire démarrer un feu à l'aide de morceaux de bois et suivre la trace des animaux. Vous pourrez également vous contenter d'observer le guide. Les éléphants qui arpentent les chemins sinueux du camp depuis des centaines d'années sont peut-être à l'origine de l'engagement des constructeurs de l'hôtel, « fouler la terre d'un pas léger ». Aucun arbre n'a été abattu pour la construction de l'établissement et les chaumières ont été érigées dans une clairière naturelle. Leurs toits sont recouverts de chaume, mais la ressemblance avec des chaumières traditionnelles s'arrête là.

Ces chaumières-là n'ont pratiquement rien à voir avec la définition habituelle du mot : les chambres, claires et spacieuses, présentent une riche association de couleurs et de textures, des étoffes qui invitent à la caresse, par exemple la soie et le cuir, des tapis tissés, du cuivre et du bois équarri. Un environnement exotique entoure les pavillons : une forêt de palmiers sauvages et d'arbres volubiles bordée des canaux d'un delta qui contient 95 % de la totalité de l'eau de surface du Botswana. Les flèches de boue des monticules des termites géantes et les immenses baobabs tranchent sur le paysage. Sandibe est situé au cœur des eaux mortes, ce qui est tout à son avantage. Une profusion d'animaux sauvages, d'oiseaux et de plantes s'épanouit dans les plaines inondables du delta d'Okavango balayées par les herbes.

Livres à emporter : « Les éléphants et nous » de Iain et Oria Douglas-Hamilton
« Un lien sûr » de Barbara Gowdy

ANREISE	Nur per Linienflug von Johannesburg nach Maun oder Kasane mit anschließendem 30-minütigen Flug von Maun, oder 1,5-stündigen Flug von Kasane und kurzer Autofahrt zum Camp erreichbar.	ACCÈS	Accessible uniquement par vol régulier de Johannesburg à Maun ou à Kasane, puis 30 minutes d'avion depuis Maun ou d'1H30 depuis Kasane, suivier d'un trajet de 10 minutes en voiture jusqu'au camp.
PREIS	Von 380 US$ bis 475 US$ pro Person, inklusive aller Mahlzeiten, Getränke, festgelegte Safari-Unternehmungen und anderer Extras.	PRIX	De 380 à 475 $ US par personne. Le prix comprend les repas, les boissons, les activités de safari planifiées et autres extras.
ZIMMER	8 Hütten für 2 Personen.	CHAMBRES	8 pavillons pour 2 personnes.
KÜCHE	Panafrikanisch.	RESTAURATION	Cuisine pan-africaine.
GESCHICHTE	Eröffnet im Jahre 1998.	HISTOIRE	Ouvert en 1998.
X-FAKTOR	Einzigartige Hütten in idyllischer Umgebung.	LES « PLUS »	Des pavillons au style unique au cœur d'un cadre idyllique.

Pavilions in the wild...

Mombo Camp, Okavango Delta

Mombo Camp, Okavango Delta

Pavilions in the wild

This is where the sound of cameras might just be louder than the noises of nature. On safari now, most of the wildlife is seen through a lens, rather than down the sights of a rifle. Just who or what is the hunter here is pleasantly confused. Mombo Camp is most famous for the number of predators on show– the animal kind that is. Close to the camp is the home territory of many prides of lions, cheetahs, leopards and African painted wolves. The game viewing here is so good that this is where many documentary filmmakers and photographers choose to lie in wait for their quarry. As well as the great variety and mass of wildlife, the game reserve where Mombo is situated is endowed with a matchless diversity of landscape. Marshes and floodplains, acacia bushveld, grassland and mopane forests provide a habitat that suits and shelters many creatures.

The habitat on offer to humans is under canvas, in tents that are a far cry from the usual. These are more like luxury pavilions, each one raised off the ground by wooden decks, with great views across the Delta. The scene inside is also a very fine one.

Book to pack: "Dangerous Beauty. Life and death in Africa: True Stories from a Safari Guide" by Mark C. Ross

Mombo Camp

Moremi Game Reserve

Okavango Delta

Botswana

Tel: + 27 (11) 807 18 00

Fax: + 27 (11) 807 21 00

E-mail: enquiry@wilderness.co.za

Website: www.wilderness-safaris.com

Booking: www.great-escapes-hotels.com

DIRECTIONS	Accessible only by scheduled flights from Johannesburg to Maun or Kasane, followed by a 30-minute flight from Maun, or a 1.5-hour flight from Kasane and a short drive to the camp.
RATES	US$500 to US$1,220, including all meals, activities, park fees and drinks.
ROOMS	12, in two independent camps, Mombo with 9 rooms and Little Mombo with 3.
FOOD	Gourmet African and Western style.
HISTORY	Mombo Lodge has been completely rebuilt and the new camps opened in June 2000.
X-FACTOR	Prolific wildlife observed from a luxurious setting.

Pavillons in der Wildnis

Hier ist das Klicken der Kameraauslöser teilweise lauter als die Geräusche der Natur selbst. Wer heute auf Safari geht, betrachtet die wilden Tiere eben eher durch die Linse einer Kamera, als durch das Zielfernrohr eines Gewehres.
Wer oder was der Jäger ist, scheint hier auf angenehme Weise vertauscht zu sein. Mombo Camp ist berühmt dafür, dass man eine Unmenge an wilden Raubtieren – und Raubtiere sind sie nun einmal – zu Gesicht bekommt. Nahe beim Camp liegt das Heimatgebiet von Löwen, Geparden, Leoparden und Steppenwölfen. Die Gegend eignet sich so hervorragend zur Wildbeobachtung, dass viele Dokumentarfilmer und Fotografen hierher kommen, um sich auf die Lauer zu legen. Das Wildreservat in welchem Mombo liegt, besticht jedoch nicht nur durch die großartige Vielfalt seiner Tierwelt, sondern ist auch mit einer beispiellos abwechslungsreichen Landschaft gesegnet. Marsch- und Schwemmland, Akazienwälder, Graslandschaften und Mopanewälder stellen für viele Tiere einen idealen Lebensraum dar.
Der unmittelbare Lebensraum der menschlichen Besucher liegt unter Segeltuchplanen, in Zelten, die alles andere als gewöhnlich sind. Sie erinnern vielmehr an Luxuspavillons; jedes Einzelne steht auf einem hölzernen Deck über dem Grund und bietet einen großartigen Ausblick über das Delta. Auch innen herrscht eine sehr gehobene Atmosphäre.
Buchtipp: »Afrika. Das letzte Abenteuer. Die Geschichte eines Safariführers« von Mark C. Ross

Pavillons sauvages

Ici, seul le crépitement des appareils photo est susceptible de couvrir les bruits de la nature. De nos jours, lors d'un safari, la plupart des animaux sont observés à travers un objectif plutôt qu'à travers la lunette d'un fusil.
Il est difficile en ces lieux de distinguer le chasseur du chassé, ce qui s'avère tout à fait plaisant. Mombo Camp est en partie célèbre pour son grand nombre de prédateurs. (Nous parlons bien sûr des animaux !) Nombreuses sont les troupes de lions, de guépards, de léopards et les meutes de chiens sauvages africains qui ont établi leur territoire à proximité du camp. L'endroit est tellement idéal pour l'observation des animaux que de nombreux réalisateurs de documentaires et photographes ont choisi ce site pour guetter leur proie. Outre sa faune extrêmement variée et abondante, la réserve naturelle qui accueille Mombo est dotée d'un paysage à la diversité incomparable. Les marécages et les plaines inondables, les steppes à acacia, les prairies et les forêts de mopani sont des habitats parfaitement adaptés aux multiples créatures qu'ils abritent.
L'habitat proposé aux visiteurs est fait de toile, mais les tentes qui les accueilleront n'ont rien à voir avec les tentes habituelles. Comparables à des pavillons de luxe, montées sur pilotis et pontons en bois, elles donnent sur les superbes paysages du delta. Et l'intérieur est tout aussi beau.
Livre à emporter : « Grands chasseurs sous la lune : Les lions du Savuti » de Beverly Joubert et Dereck Joubert

ANREISE	Nur per Linienflug von Johannesburg nach Maun oder Kasane mit anschließendem 30-minütigen Flug von Maun, oder 1,5-stündigen Flug von Kasane.
PREIS	500 US$ bis 1.220 US$, inklusive aller Mahlzeiten, Unternehmungen, Eintrittsgelder und Getränke.
ZIMMER	12, in zwei voneinander unabhängigen Camps, 9 Zimmer in Mombo und 3 in Little Mombo.
KÜCHE	Afrikanische Feinkost und Westlicher Stil.
GESCHICHTE	Mombo Camp und Little Mombo wurden neu aufgebaut und im Juni 2000 wurden die neuen Camps 800 m von der alten Stelle entfernt eröffnet.
X-FAKTOR	Luxuriöse Ausstattung im Schoß von Mutter Natur.

ACCÈS	Accessible uniquement par vol régulier de Johannesburg à Maun ou à Kasane, suivi d'un vol de 30 minutes de Maun ou d'1H30 de Kasane et d'un court trajet en voiture jusqu'au camp.
PRIX	500 à 1.220 $ US tout compris. Le prix comprend les repas, les boissons, les billets d'entrée et les activités.
CHAMBRES	12, situées dans deux camps séparés : Mombo (9 chambres) et Little Mombo (3 chambres).
RESTAURATION	Cuisine gastronomique africaine et occidentale.
HISTOIRE	Mombo Camp et Little Mombo ont été entièrement reconstruits et de nouveaux camps ont ouvert en juin 2000 sur un nouveau site situé à 800 m de l'ancien.
LES « PLUS »	Observation de la faune depuis un cadre luxueux.

Earthly pleasures...
Sabi Sabi Earth Lodge, Skukuza

Sabi Sabi Earth Lodge, Skukuza

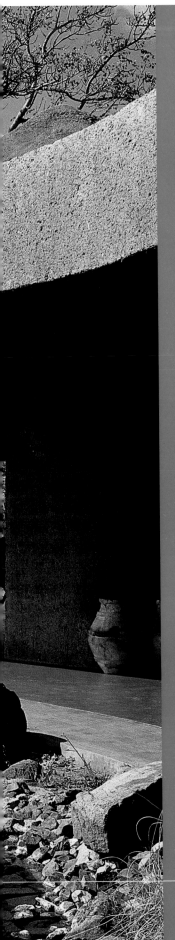

Earthly pleasures

If you feel that you are overly 'wired', this is a place where you can 're-earth' yourself.

You can go to ground, in both the factual and symbolic sense. But, save for the cost, there is nothing you must give up. No forfeit is needed. This is a cocoon of sheer luxury sculpted deep into the earth. The ultimate shelter, where you are insulated from the outside world, yet still open to it.

At first glance, this sumptuous lodge seems quite austere. Sabi Sabi Earth Lodge follows the contours of the landscape, so well that it is all but hidden. The buildings are kept low in the environment. Within the lodge, the colours echo the earth shades of the outside walls. It was built in an organic style with all natural resources, as far as was possible. The result is a quite distinctive place that makes a strong visual impact. Tree trunks have been creatively used; crafted as bars, benches, and just decorative forms. But the plain look is deceptive. There is a double standard of sorts at play here. Simple materials are used, but only the best has been chosen. Each suite is minimalist, yet it has its own butler, and pool. One has its own exercise room, steam room, study, and kitchen. There is a spa, a vast wine cellar, and a meditation garden.

Of course, Africa is the real star here. A vast bushveld panorama lies in wait; wild creatures are just a walk or drive away.

Books to pack: "Rare Earth" by Peter D. Ward and Donald Brownlee

"Letters from the Earth" by Mark Twain

Sabi Sabi Earth Lodge	
Sabi Sand Private Game Reserve	
P.O. Box 16	
Skukuza 1350	
South Africa	
Tel: + 27 (13) 735 52 61	
Fax: + 27 (13) 735 52 60	
E-mail reservations: res@sabisabi.com	
Website: www.sabisabi.com	
Booking: www.great-escapes-hotels.com	

DIRECTIONS	A 5-hour drive from Johannesburg, or a 2-hour scenic drive from Nelspruit; daily flights from Johannesburg International Airport to Skukuza Airport.
RATES	Suites US$495 (ZAR5,000), Amber Presidential Suite for US$990 (ZAR10,000) per person in a double room, inclusive of all meals, drinks, night and day safaris, shuttle.
ROOMS	12 suites, 1 presidential suite.
FOOD	Fusion of African, French and Italian cuisine.
HISTORY	Sabi Sabi Earth Lodge was opened in 2001.
X-FACTOR	The most stylish 'bunker' in existence.

Irdische Vergnügen

Wenn Sie vollkommen abgespannt sein sollten und sozusagen knapp vor einem Kurzschluss stehen, so ist hier der richtige Ort, um sich wieder zu »erden«. Hier kann man im wörtlichen wie im übertragenen Sinn auf den Boden zurückkehren. Dabei müssen Sie jedoch auf nichts verzichten und keinerlei Abstriche machen. Dies ist ein Kokon des puren Luxus, der tief in die Erde hinein geformt wurde, ein ultimativer Unterschlupf, in dem man von der Außenwelt geschützt, aber dennoch nicht von ihr abgeschnitten ist.

Auf den ersten Blick erscheint diese opulente Lodge eher asketisch. Sabi Sabi Earth Lodge passt sich den Konturen der Landschaft so gut an, dass sie schwer zu erkennen ist. Die Gebäude sind niedrig gehalten. In den Innenräumen der Lodge werden die Erdschattierungen der Außenwände farblich wieder aufgegriffen. Beim Bau hat man versucht, so viele organische Baumaterialien zu verwenden wie nur irgend möglich. Das Ergebnis dieser Bauweise ist ein ganz besonderer Ort, der einen recht ungewöhnlichen Anblick bietet. Baumstämme wurden auf kreative Art und Weise integriert und funktionieren als Bar, Bänke oder dienen einfach dekorativen Zwecken. Doch das schlichte Erscheinungsbild trügt. Zwar wurden einfache Materialien verarbeitet, doch nur qualitative hochwertige. Jede der Suiten wirkt minimalistisch, hat aber einen eigenen Diener und einen Pool. Eine davon verfügt über einen eigenen Trainingsraum, Dampfbad, Arbeitszimmer und Küche. Außerdem gibt es ein Heilbad, einen gut sortierten Weinkeller und einen Meditationsgarten. Die eigentliche Sehenswürdigkeit ist auch hier natürlich Afrika selbst und der herrliche Ausblick über die weite Buschlandschaft. Wildtiere sind nur einen Fußmarsch oder eine kurze Fahrt weit entfernt.

Buchtipps: »Unsere einsame Erde« von Peter D. Ward und Donald Brownlee
»Briefe von der Erde« von Mark Twain

Plaisirs terrestres

Si vous vous sentez trop stressé, voici l'endroit idéal pour vous ressourcer.

Il vous permettra de retourner à la terre, au sens propre comme au sens figuré, sans devoir renoncer à quoi que ce soit. Si ce n'est le coût de votre séjour, vous n'aurez pas à en payer le prix. Sabi Sabi Earth Lodge est un cocon de luxe absolu sculpté profondément dans la terre, l'abri suprême où vous serez isolé du monde extérieur sans toutefois lui tourner le dos.

À première vue, cet hôtel somptueux semble assez austère. Sabi Sabi Earth Lodge épouse les contours du paysage ; si bien d'ailleurs qu'il s'en trouve presque dissimulé. Ses bâtiments peu élevés ne déparent pas l'environnement. Les couleurs de l'intérieur évoquent les nuances des murs extérieurs qui sont de couleur terre. Pour la construction de l'hôtel, de style organique, des matériaux entièrement naturels ont été utilisés chaque fois que cela était possible. Le résultat est un édifice original qui fait forte impression. Les troncs d'arbre y sont utilisés de façon créative ; ils ont en effet été travaillés pour devenir des bancs, des bars ou tout simplement des formes décoratives. Mais l'apparence simple et dépouillée de l'hôtel est trompeuse. Il existe ici deux mesures. Les matériaux de construction sont basiques mais de la plus haute qualité. Les suites sont minimalistes, mais chacune a son propre majordome et sa piscine. L'une d'elles compte même une salle de sport, un sauna, un bureau et une cuisine. L'hôtel dispose également d'installations de cure thermale, d'une grande cave à vins et d'un jardin de méditation.

Bien sûr, la véritable star reste l'Afrique : une vue panoramique sur la vaste steppe vous attend, et les animaux sauvages ne sont qu'à quelques minutes de marche ou de voiture.

Livre à emporter : « La plus belle histoire de la terre » d'André Brahic et al.

ANREISE	Eine etwa 5-stündige Fahrt von Johannesburg oder 2-stündige Panoramafahrt von Nelspruit aus. Täglich Flüge von Johannesburg International Airport zum Skukuza Airport.
PREIS	Suiten 495 US$ (5.000 ZAR), die Bernstein- Präsidentensuite 990 US$ (10.000 ZAR) pro Person im Doppelzimmer, inklusive aller Mahlzeiten, Getränke und Tag- bzw. Nachtsafaris, Shuttle.
ZIMMER	12 Suiten, 1 Präsidentensuite.
KÜCHE	Mischung afrikanischer, französischer un italiescher Speisen.
GESCHICHTE	Die Sabi Sabi Earth Lodge wurde im Jahre 2001 eröffnet.
X-FAKTOR	Der stilvollste »Bunker« der Welt.

ACCÈS	À 5 heures de Johannesburg en voiture ou à 2 heures de Nelspruit le long d'une route touristique. Vols quotidiens en partance de Johannesburg jusqu'à l'aéroport de Skukuza.
PRIX	Suites à partir de 495 $ US (5.000 R), suite présidentielle ambrée à partir de 990 $ US (10.000 R) Prix par personne en chambre double, pension complète, boissons et safaris diurnes et nocturnes compris.
CHAMBRES	12 suites, plus une suite présidentielle.
RESTAURATION	Cuisine fusion africaine, française et italienne.
HISTOIRE	Sabi Sabi Earth Lodge a ouvert ses portes en 2001.
LES « PLUS »	Le « bunker » le plus élégant du monde.

A sense of place...
Makalali Private Game Reserve, Limpopo Province

Makalali Private Game Reserve, Limpopo Province

A sense of place

It is said that the best architecture is that which reflects a real sense of place.

The red clay structures at Makalali are a potent mix of modern and ethnic style. Their thatched roofs rise up through towering jackalberry trees, roofs that have been crowned with straw to look like a traditional village. Inside the luxury bush camp is where the resemblance ends. Natural textures blend with African craftsmanship, to create a look that is at once both rustic and opulent. The surrounds may be cultured, but just beyond the camp there is plenty of wild and beastly behaviour going on.

The camp lies on shady riverbanks, in a private game reserve within thousands of acres of open savannah grassland. Lion, leopard, cheetah, elephant, giraffe, white rhino, zebra, antelope and an array of small mammals make their home in these grasslands.

This is the new safari age, one where the aim is to protect the environment and the stunning local animal life. Here, visitors can experience a sense of close connection with nature, yet live at a safe distance from it, guarded from curious wildlife coming too near.

Book to pack: "The White Lioness: A Mystery" by Henning Mankell

Makalali Private Game Reserve	
P.O. Box 809	
Hoedspruit 1380	
Limpopo Province	
South Africa	
Tel: + 27 (15) 793 17 20	
Fax: + 27 (15) 793 17 39	
E-mail: makalali@mweb.co.za	
Website: www.makalali.com	
Booking: www.great-escapes-hotels.com	

DIRECTIONS	Daily flights from Johannesburg to Hoedspruit and Phalaborwa. By road about a 4.5-hour drive from Johannesburg, or arrive in a small aircraft at the private airstrip.
RATES	US$267 (ZAR2,700) to US$400 (ZAR4,050) fully inclusive of all meals and two game drives per day.
ROOMS	Four separate 12-bed camps.
FOOD	Award-winning cuisine.
HISTORY	Opened in July 1996.
X-FACTOR	Stunning architecture and animal life.

Ein Ort mit Seele

Man sagt, dass die beste Architektur diejenige ist, welche den wahren Geist eines Ortes widerspiegelt.

Die roten Lehmelemente in Makalali stellen eine ausdrucksstarke Verbindung zwischen modernem und ethnischem Stil dar. Strohgedeckte Dächer ragen durch gewaltige »Schakalbeerenbäume« empor, ihre Spitzen wurden mit Stroh verziert, damit sie wie ein traditionelles Dorf wirken. Betritt man das luxuriöse Buschcamp, wird man jedoch schnell feststellen, dass das so ziemlich die einzige Ähnlichkeit ist. Die Verbindung natürlicher Stoffe mit afrikanischen Kunsthandwerke erzeugt eine rustikale, aber zugleich opulente Atmosphäre. Die unmittelbare Umgebung ist kultiviert, doch direkt hinter den Grenzen des Camps spielt sich das raue und wilde Leben der Tierwelt ab. Das Camp liegt auf schattigen Flussbänken in einem privaten Wildpark und ist umgeben von Tausenden von Morgen weiter Graslandschaft. In dieser Savanne sind Löwen, Leoparden, Geparden, Elefanten, Giraffen, weiße Nashörner, Zebras, Antilopen und eine Reihe kleiner Säugetiere zu Hause.

Eine neue Ära des Safaritourismus ist angebrochen, eine Ära, die sich den Schutz der Natur und den Erhalt der beeindruckenden Tierwelt, die dort lebt, zum Ziel gesetzt hat. Besucher können hier ein Gefühl der engen Verbundenheit mit der Natur erfahren und dabei doch in sicherer Entfernung bleiben, sodass ihnen neugierige Tiere trotzdem nicht allzu nah kommen.

Buchtipp: »Die weiße Löwin« von Henning Mankell

Le bon goût sauvage

On dit d'une architecture réussie qu'elle reflète le véritable esprit d'un lieu.

Les structures en argile rouge de Makalali sont un puissant mélange de modernité et d'ethnicité. Leurs toits de chaume, qui pointent çà et là au travers d'imposants arbres jackalberry, sont couronnés de paille pour évoquer un village traditionnel. Cependant, la ressemblance se limite à l'aspect extérieur. C'est en effet dans un camp de brousse luxueux que vous entrerez, où les textures naturelles associées à l'art africain créent une ambiance à la fois rustique et opulente. Les environs du camp sont cultivés, mais un peu plus loin le territoire appartient aux animaux sauvages et la loi de la jungle prévaut.

Le camp est situé sur les berges ombragées d'une rivière, dans une réserve naturelle privée qui s'étend sur des milliers d'hectares de savane où vivent des lions, des léopards, des guépards, des éléphants, des girafes, des rhinocéros blancs, des zèbres, des antilopes et toutes sortes de petits mammifères.

Nous sommes entrés dans une ère où safari rime avec protection de l'environnement et de l'extraordinaire faune locale. Ici, les visiteurs se sentiront très proches de la nature tout en restant à une distance respectueuse garantissant leur sécurité face à des animaux qui, curieux, pourraient s'approcher trop près.

Livre à emporter : « Silences africains » de Peter Matthiessen

ANREISE	Tägliche Flüge von Johannesburg nach Hoedspruit und Phalaborwa. Mit dem Wagen etwa viereinhalbstündige Fahrt von Johannesburg aus. Anreise im kleinen Flugzeug zum privaten Flugplatz möglich.
PREIS	Von 267 US$ (2.700 ZAR) bis 400 US$ (4.050 ZAR) inklusive aller Mahlzeiten und zwei Wildbeobachtungsfahrten pro Tag.
ZIMMER	Vier separate 12-Betten Camps.
KÜCHE	Preisgekrönt!
GESCHICHTE	Eröffnet im Juli 1996.
X-FAKTOR	Betörende Architektur und Tierwelt.

ACCÈS	Vols quotidiens en partance de Johannesburg jusqu'à Hoedspruit et Phalaborwa. À 4H30 en voiture de Johannesburg. Possibilité d'emprunter une avionnette jusqu'à la piste d'atterrissage privée.
PRIX	De 267 $ US (2.700 R) à 400 $ US (4.050 R). Le prix comprend tous les repas et deux promenades par jour en voiture à la recherche d'animaux.
CHAMBRES	Quatre camps séparés comptant chacun 12 lits.
RESTAURATION	Cuisine récompensée par plusieurs prix.
HISTOIRE	Ouvert en juillet 1996.
LES « PLUS »	Architecture et faune exceptionnelles.

Town and country...
Kensington Place, Cape Town

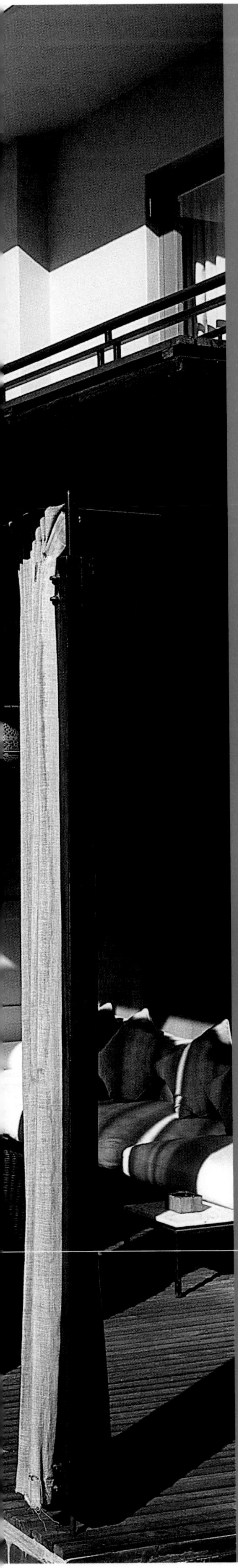

Kensington Place, Cape Town

Town and country

Only two of Henry VIII's six wives lost their heads in the real sense. The other four were able to avoid such a blunt end to their unions. All of them are recalled here, for the rooms at Kensington Place are each named after one of the monarch's wives or his daughters. And it seems a fitting response to their varied characters that each room should have a distinct style. There are, of course, some common themes. One is the choice of materials. Suede, silk and leather are featured, just some of the rich fabrics long favoured by royalty – and those who are at home with luxury. And plush colours like whisky, chocolate and cinnamon mixed with cream please the eye as much as those flavours please the taste. The design is a blend of Africa and Europe, a fusion of textures and fabrics to great effect.

A lush garden surrounds the hotel, which is in a quiet residential area of Capetown, deemed to be one of the most prestigious in the city. The views from here are duly majestic too. Although its setting is an urban one, the outlook from the terrace is more of a stately vista than might be expected; scenes of the harbour and the mountains meet the eye. If guests wish to venture forth to the world outside the gates, beaches, gardens and wineries are within reach. And although not visible from here, quite close by a great animal kingdom lies in wait.

Book to pack: "July's People" by Nadine Gordimer

Kensington Place

38 Kensington Crescent

Higgovale

Cape Town 8001

South Africa

Tel: + 27 (21) 424 47 44

Fax: + 27 (21) 424 18 10

E-mail: kplace@mweb.co.za

Website: www.kensingtonplace.co.za

Booking: www.great-escapes-hotels.com

DIRECTIONS	Approximately 24 km/15 m from Cape Town International Airport.
RATES	US$130 (ZAR1,300) to US$210 (ZAR2,100) including breakfast.
ROOMS	8 double rooms with private terraces.
FOOD	A menu fit for monarchs and other crowned heads.
HISTORY	Opened in 1997, far too late for Henry VIII to visit in person.
X-FACTOR	A perfect match between town and country.

Stadt und Land

Nur zwei der sechs Frauen von Henry VIII. verloren ihren Kopf im wörtlichen Sinne. Den anderen vier Gemahlinnen gelang es, ein solch stumpfes Ende ihrer ehelichen Verbindung zu umgehen. Die Räume des Kensington Place sind benannt nach den Frauen des Monarchen beziehungsweise nach seinen Töchtern und es scheint eine angemessene Antwort auf deren unterschiedliche Charaktere zu sein, dass jeder der Räume in einem anderen Stil eingerichtet ist. Dennoch gibt es einige Gemeinsamkeiten, zum Beispiel in der Verwendung von Wildleder, Seide und Leder, solch prächtige Stoffe wurden schon immer von Königen und solchen, die im Luxus leben, favorisiert. Und die edlen mit Cremetönen versetzten Whisky-, Schokoladen- und Zimtfarbenen gefallen dem Auge ebenso wie sie betörende Düfte hervorrufen. Die Inneneinrichtung mischt afrikanische und europäische Elemente, eine äußerst effektvolle Verbindung von Stoffen und Geweben. Ein üppiger Garten umgibt das Hotel, das sich in einer ruhigen Wohngegend, einer der privilegiertesten von Kapstadt, befindet. Dementsprechend majestätisch ist auch der Ausblick, den man von hier aus genießen kann. Obwohl das Hotel in der Stadt liegt, ist der Blick von der Terrasse beeindruckender, als man zunächst glauben möchte, wenn man das Auge weit über Hafenbuchten und Bergketten hinwegschweifen lässt. Gäste, welche die Welt außerhalb der Tore kennen lernen möchten, können dies tun: Strände, Gärten und Weinberge liegen ebenso wie eine großartige Tierwelt, ganz in der Nähe.

Buchtipp: »July's Leute« von Nadine Gordimer

La ville verdure

Seules deux des six épouses d'Henry VIII perdirent la tête, au sens propre. Les quatre autres surent échapper à cette façon quelque peu abrupte de mettre fin à leur union. Kensington Place a souhaité toutes les évoquer en donnant le nom des femmes ou des filles du roi aux chambres de l'hôtel. À l'image de ces dames, chaque chambre a un caractère bien particulier. Certains éléments sont bien sûr communs à toutes : les matières somptueuses par exemple, avec le daim, la soie et le cuir, pour lesquelles les familles royales et ceux qui aiment le luxe ont toujours eu une préférence ; les superbes couleurs, avec de riches tons whisky, chocolat et cannelle qui, associés à la couleur crème, flattent le regard tout autant que les parfums qu'ils évoquent ravissent le palais. Le décor est un mélange d'Afrique et d'Europe, une fusion de textures et d'étoffes du plus bel effet.
L'hôtel, situé dans une zone résidentielle tranquille du Cap, l'une des plus prestigieuses de la ville, se trouve au centre d'un jardin luxuriant. Le spectacle qui s'offre aux yeux des résidents de l'hôtel est majestueux : le cadre est urbain, mais la vue depuis la terrasse, sur le port et les montagnes proches, est plus impressionnante qu'on pourrait le croire. Vous souhaitez vous aventurer à l'extérieur de l'enceinte ? Les plages, les jardins et les établissements vinicoles ne sont qu'à un jet de pierre.
Vous pouvez par ailleurs admirer une faune extraordinaire et variée, invisible depuis l'hôtel mais pourtant toute proche.

Livre à emporter : « Ceux de July » de Nadine Gordimer

ANREISE	Etwa 24 km vom Cape Town International Airport.	ACCÈS	À environ 24 Km de l'aéroport international du Cap.
PREIS	Von 130 US$ (1.300 ZAR) bis 210 US$ (2.100 ZAR) inklusive Frühstück.	PRIX	De 130 $ US (1.300 R) à 210 $ US (2.100 R), petit-déjeuner compris.
ZIMMER	8 Doppelzimmer mit eigener Terrasse.	CHAMBRES	8 chambres doubles avec terrasse privée.
KÜCHE	Eine Speisekarte für Könige und andere gekrönte Häupter.	RESTAURATION	Menu digne des monarques et autres têtes couronnées.
GESCHICHTE	Eröffnet im Jahr 1997 und somit viel zu spät, um von Henry VIII. persönlich besucht worden zu sein.	HISTOIRE	Ouvert en 1997, bien trop tard pour qu'Henry VIII puisse le visiter.
X-FAKTOR	Eine perfektes Zusammenspiel von Stadt und Land.	LES « PLUS »	Alliance parfaite entre ville et campagne.

The beat goes on...

Ankobra Beach, Axim

Ankobra Beach, Axim

The beat goes on

Most people are not keen on neighbours who play the drums. The sound travels; a learner can drive listeners 'round the bend'.

At Ankobra Beach Resort drumming is encouraged; in fact, they teach it to the guests here. Free lessons in drumming, and in dancing, are to hand. It is in the age-old African kind. It was from this continent that percussion came; Africa is the source of the beat. But this is also a quiet place; there are no amplifiers. Lessons are short and during the day. The sound of the sea, and the sigh of the coconut palms stroked by the breeze, muffle most noise.

The group of round bungalows is much like an African village. Clustered amongst coconut trees, on the edge of a sandy beach, at first glance they appear to be quite small. Looks can be deceptive. As if by magic, they are larger inside than they seem from outside. As the river meets the ocean here, Ankobra Beach has a broad motto; "where Africa meets the world." This guides the resort owners and the staff. They want time spent here to give an insight to African culture and current life; a life led outside the cities. The focus is on the beauty and grace that Africa still offers. Beauty also abounds in the nature here.

Some of the history is not so lovely. Many people left Ghana from this Atlantic coast, forced aboard slave ships; but they took their rhythms with them.

Books to pack: "Search Sweet Country" by B. Kojo Laing
"The Beautiful Ones Are Not Yet Born" by Ayi Kwei Armah

Ankobra Beach
P.O. Box 79
Axim
Ghana
Tel: + 233 342 22349/22400
Email: ankobrabeach@hotmail.com
Website: www.ankobrabeach.de
Booking: www.great-escapes-hotels.com

DIRECTIONS	A 4-hour drive west from Accra Airport.
RATES	Rooms from US$25, bungalows from US$35, including breakfast.
ROOMS	10 rooms, 6 bungalows.
FOOD	African and international cooking.
HISTORY	Opened in 1996.
X-FACTOR	The slower, simpler, and gentle pace of life.

Im Rhythmus der Wellen

Auf Trommelspielende Nachbarn sind die Wenigsten erpicht.
Den Klang von Trommeln hört man durch Wände, und schon
so mancher Trommelschüler mag seine unfreiwilligen
Zuhörer in den Wahnsinn getrieben haben.

Im Ankobra Beach Resort hingegen ist Trommeln erwünscht,
um genauer zu sein, lehrt man hier die Gäste das Trommel-
spielen. Es besteht die Möglichkeit, an kostenlosen Trommel-
und Tanzstunden nach altafrikanischer Tradition teilzuneh-
men. Auf diesem Kontinent ist die Perkussion zu Hause,
Afrika ist sozusagen die Mutter des Rhythmus. Gleichzeitig
ist dies jedoch auch ein ruhiger Ort und es gibt keine Verstär-
ker. Die Übungsstunden dauern nur kurz und werden tagsüber abgehalten. Das Geräusch des Meeres und das Rascheln
der Kokosnusspalmen im Wind verschlucken den Großteil
der Klänge.

Die Gruppe runder Bungalows erinnert stark an ein afrikani-
sches Dorf. Geduckt zwischen Kokosnussbäumen und am
Rande eines Sandstrandes, wirken sie auf den ersten Blick
relativ klein. Umso erstaunter ist man, wenn man beim Betre-
ten ihre stattliche Größe erfährt. Da der Fluss hier ins Meer
mündet gibt es in Ankobra Beach ein Motto: »Wo Afrika und
die Welt zusammentreffen«. Das ist der Leitspruch für die
Besitzer der Anlage und das Personal. Sie wollen, dass die
Zeit, die man hier verbringt, einen Einblick in die afrikanische Kultur und das jetzige Leben vermittelt; ein Leben außerhalb der Städte. Im Mittelpunkt stehen die Schönheit und
Anmut, die Afrika immer noch bietet. Schönheit findet man
hier in der natürlichen Umgebung überall.

Aber dieser Teil Afrikas hat im Lauf der Geschichte auch weniger schöne Zeiten erlebt. Auf Sklavenschiffe verfrachtet mussten viele Menschen Ghana von dieser Küste aus verlassen,
doch ihre Rhythmen nahmen sie mit.

Buchtipps: »Die Sonnensucher« von B. Kojo Laing
»Die Schönen sind noch nicht geboren« von Ayi Kwei Armah

Au rythme des vagues

La plupart d'entre nous n'apprécieraient pas d'avoir pour
voisin un joueur de tambour. Le son se propage, et un
joueur débutant peut rendre complètement fous des audi-
teurs non consentants.

À Ankobra Beach Resort, la pratique de cet instrument est
encouragée. De fait, des cours de percussion et de danse
gratuits sont proposés. Bien sûr, ces cours portent sur les
percussions africaines traditionnelles. C'est sur ce continent
en effet que sont nés ces instruments. C'est en Afrique que
se trouve l'origine du rythme. Mais ne vous inquiétez pas.
L'endroit peut aussi être silencieux. Il n'y a pas d'amplifica-
teurs, et les leçons sont courtes et ont lieu pendant la journée. Pour le reste, le bruit de la mer et le murmure des
cocotiers caressés par la brise couvrent la plupart des bruits.
L'ensemble formé par les bungalows circulaires ressemble
beaucoup à un village africain. Regroupés à l'ombre des
cocotiers, au bord de la plage, ceux-ci paraissent de taille
relativement réduite à première vue. Mais les apparences
sont parfois trompeuses. Il suffit d'y entrer et, comme par
enchantement, on découvre un intérieur plus spacieux que
ce à quoi l'on pouvait s'attendre. Ankobra Beach se trouve à
jonction d'un fleuve et de l'océan. De là peut-être sa devise,
« là où l'Afrique rencontre le monde », qui guide à tout
moment les propriétaires de l'hôtel et le personnel.

Pour eux, un séjour à Ankobra Beach doit être l'occasion de
découvrir la culture et le mode de vie actuel en Afrique, loin
de la ville. L'accent est mis sur la beauté et la grâce qui sont,
encore de nos jours, caractéristiques de l'Afrique. Et cette
beauté est partout présente dans le paysage environnant.
L'Histoire, elle, est moins reluisante. Cette côte de l'Atlantique a vu de nombreuses personnes quitter le Ghana à bord de
négriers. Les percussions faisaient elles aussi partie du voyage.

Livre à emporter : « L'âge d'or n'est pas pour demain » d'Ayi
Kwei Armah

ANREISE	4-stündige Fahrt westlich von Accra Airport.
PREIS	Zimmer ab 25 US$, Bungalows ab 35 US$, inklusive Frühstück.
ZIMMER	10 Zimmer, 6 Bungalows.
KÜCHE	Afrikanische und internationale Gerichte.
GESCHICHTE	Eröffnet im Jahre 1996..
X-FAKTOR	Die einfache und geruhsame Art zu leben.

ACCÈS	À 4 heures en voiture de l'aéroport d'Accra, à l'ouest.
PRIX	Chambres à partir de 25 $ US, bungalows à partir de 35 $ US, petit-déjeuner compris.
CHAMBRES	10 chambres, 6 bungalows.
RESTAURATION	Cuisine africaine et internationale.
HISTOIRE	Ouvert en 1996.
LES « PLUS »	Un rythme de vie simple et tranquille.

Asia

India • Sri Lanka • Cambodia
Malaysia • Indonesia • The Philippines
Vietnam • China • Japan

Text by Christiane Reiter   *Edited by* Angelika Taschen

"For my part, I travel not to go anywhere, but to go.
I travel for travel's sake. The great affair is to move."
Robert Louis Stevenson

● 402 Red Capital Club & Residence

NORTH
KOREA

SOUTH
KOREA

JAPAN

● 410 Asaba

TAIWAN

PHILIPPINES

VIETNAM

● 398 Whale Island Resort

● 392 The Barceló Pearl Farm Island Resort

INDONESIA

● 368 Amankila
380 Begawan Giri Estate

Desert Life...
Royal Desert Camp, Pushkar, Rajasthan

Royal Desert Camp, Pushkar, Rajasthan

Desert Life

When at the start of the seventeenth century, the Indian ruler Jahangir embarked on a pleasure trip to Kashmir, he was a bit worried that the palaces there would not be up to his standards. He decided to travel with a complete entourage and his own tent city – and resided in luxurious marquees with soft beds and pillows, beautiful carpets and fabrics, sparkling glass and porcelain, a mobile kitchen and evening entertainment. The "Royal Desert Camp" was invented and from then on became a fixed part of the nobility's family parties, hunting excursions or wedding celebrations. In the meantime, normal mortals also get the chance to camp in royal style – at the Pushkar Fair, the most colourful and perhaps most beautiful event that Rajastan has to offer. To refer to it as a "folklore show" would almost be an insult – the Pushkar Fair is the largest camel trade fair in the world. It is also a place of pilgrimage for the Hindus, who wash away all their worries in the holy waters of the Pushkar Lake; a fashion show where India's women show themselves at their most beautiful and where they even newly dress and perfume the camels. In short, the Pushkar Fair is the distillation of tradition and joie de vivre for an entire region.

Book to pack: "A Son of the Circus" by John Irving

Royal Desert Camp	
c/o Pushkar Palace	
Chhoti Basti, Pushkar – 305022	
District Ajmer, Rajasthan, India	
Tel. +91 (145) 277 20 01 and 277 24 01	
Fax +91 (145) 277 22 26	
Email: hppalace@datainfosys.net	
Website: www.hotelpushkarpalace.com/rdc.htm	
Booking: www.great-escapes-hotels.com	

DIRECTIONS	Pushkar is situated in the desert between Jodhpur and Jaipur, 140 km/225 miles east of Jaipur Airport. Nearest train station is Ajmer (13 km/8 miles).
RATES	Tents starting at US$125 per night (2 people).
TENTS	234 comfortable tents with connected bathrooms (running water, toilet), beds, fan heater.
FOOD	Restaurant tent with specialties from India and Rajastan, coffee shop.
HISTORY	Every November at the Pushkar Fair, the seventeenth century notion of the tent-city springs back to life.
X-FACTOR	The most luxurious camp site in the world.

Die Wüste lebt

Als der indische Herrscher Jahangir zu Beginn des 17. Jahrhunderts eine Vergnügungsfahrt nach Kaschmir unternahm, war er etwas in Sorge, dass die dortigen Paläste seinen Ansprüchen nicht genügen könnten. Er beschloss daher, mit kompletter Entourage und seiner eigenen Zeltstadt zu reisen – und residierte unter Luxusplanen mit weichen Betten und Kissen, traumhaften Teppichen und Stoffen, blinkendem Glas und Porzellan, einer mobile Küche und abendlichem Entertainment. Das »Royal Desert Camp« war erfunden und wurde fortan zum festen Bestandteil von adligen Familienfesten, Jagdausflügen oder Hochzeitspartys des Adels. Inzwischen haben auch Normalsterbliche die Möglichkeit, königlich zu campen – anlässlich der Pushkar Fair, dem farbenprächtigsten und vielleicht schönsten Event, das Rajasthan zu bieten hat. Es mit dem Begriff »Folkloreshow« zu umschreiben, wäre fast eine Beleidigung – die Pushkar Fair ist die größte Kamelmesse der Welt, eine Pilgerstätte für die Hindus, die in den heiligen Wassern des Pushkar Lake die Sorgen ihres ganzen Lebens wegwaschen, eine Modenschau, bei der sich Indiens Frauen von ihrer schönsten Seite zeigen und sogar die Kamele neu eingekleidet und parfümiert werden, kurz: die Pushkar Fair ist das Destillat der Traditionen und der Lebensfreude einer ganzen Region.

Buchtipp: »Zirkuskind« von John Irving

La vie du désert

Alors qu'il était sur le point d'entreprendre, au début du 17e siècle, un voyage d'agrément au Cachemire, le seigneur indien Jahangir se demanda soudain si les palais de cette région lui offriraient le confort auquel il était habitué. Il décida donc d'installer, pour lui et sa cour, un véritable campement. C'est ainsi que le prince résida dans des tentes somptueuses équipées de lits et de coussins moelleux, de tapis et d'étoffes de rêves, de porcelaines et de verres étincelants, d'une cuisine roulante, et permettant d'organiser le soir les divertissements les plus splendides. Le « Royal Desert Camp » était né et la noblesse du pays s'accoutuma bien vite à ce mode de résidence pour ses fêtes de famille, ses parties de chasse et ses mariages. Aujourd'hui, le commun des mortels a lui aussi la possibilité de camper comme un seigneur indien – et ce, à l'occasion de la foire de Pushkar, l'une des manifestations les plus colorées et peut-être les plus belles qui se déroulent au Rajasthan. La décrire comme un « spectacle folklorique » serait presque lui faire injure. La foire de Pushkar est la plus grande foire aux chameaux du monde et un lieu de pèlerinage pour les Hindous qui viennent se laver de leurs péchés dans les eaux du lac Pushkar. Mais elle est aussi un défilé de mode où les femmes indiennes se présentent parées de leurs plus beaux atours et où l'on habille même de neuf les chameaux que l'on a parfumés. En bref, la foire de Pushkar est un condensé des traditions et de la joie de vivre de toute une région.

Livre à emporter : « Un enfant de la balle » de John Irving

ANREISE	Pushkar liegt in der Wüste zwischen Jodhpur und Jaipur, 140 km östlich des Flughafens Jaipur. Nächster Bahnhof ist Ajmer (13 km).	ACCÈS	Situé dans le désert entre Jodhpur et Jaipur, à 140 km à l'est de l'aéroport de Jaipur et à 13 km de la gare d'Ajmer.
PREIS	Zelt ab 125 US$ pro Nacht (2 Personen).	PRIX	Tente à partir de 125 $ US la nuit (2 personnes).
ZELTE	234 komfortable Zelte mit angeschlossenem Bad (fließendes Wasser, Toilette), Betten, Heizlüfter.	TENTES	234 tentes confortables avec salle de bains attenante (eau courante, toilettes), lits, chauffage électrique.
KÜCHE	Restaurantzelt mit Spezialitäten aus Indien und Rajasthan, Coffee Shop.	RESTAURATION	Tente-restaurant proposant des spécialités de l'Inde et du Rajasthan, Coffee Shop.
GESCHICHTE	Die Idee der Zeltstadt aus dem 17. Jahrhundert lebt jedes Jahr im November bei der Pushkar Fair neu auf.	HISTOIRE	L'idée de campement née au 17e siècle revit chaque année en novembre pendant la foire de Pushkar.
X-FAKTOR	Der luxuriöseste Campingplatz der Welt.	LE « PETIT PLUS »	Le camping le plus luxueux du monde.

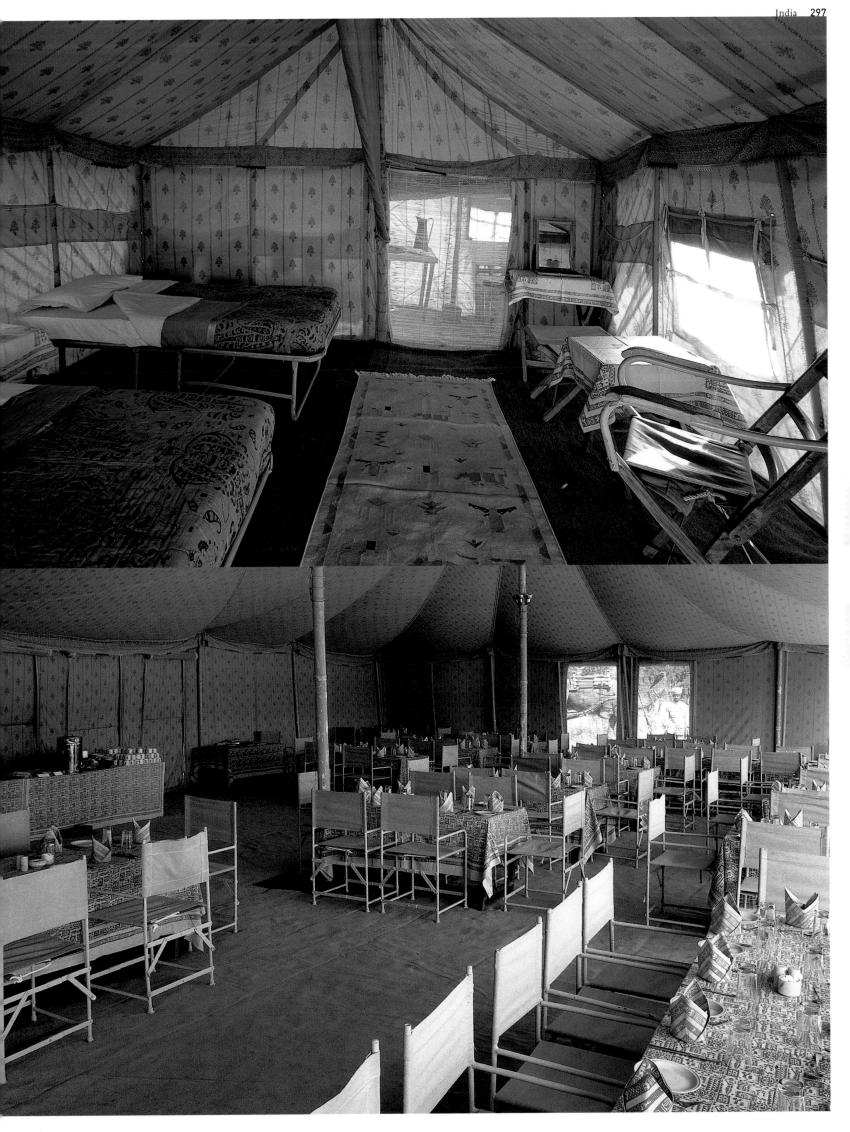

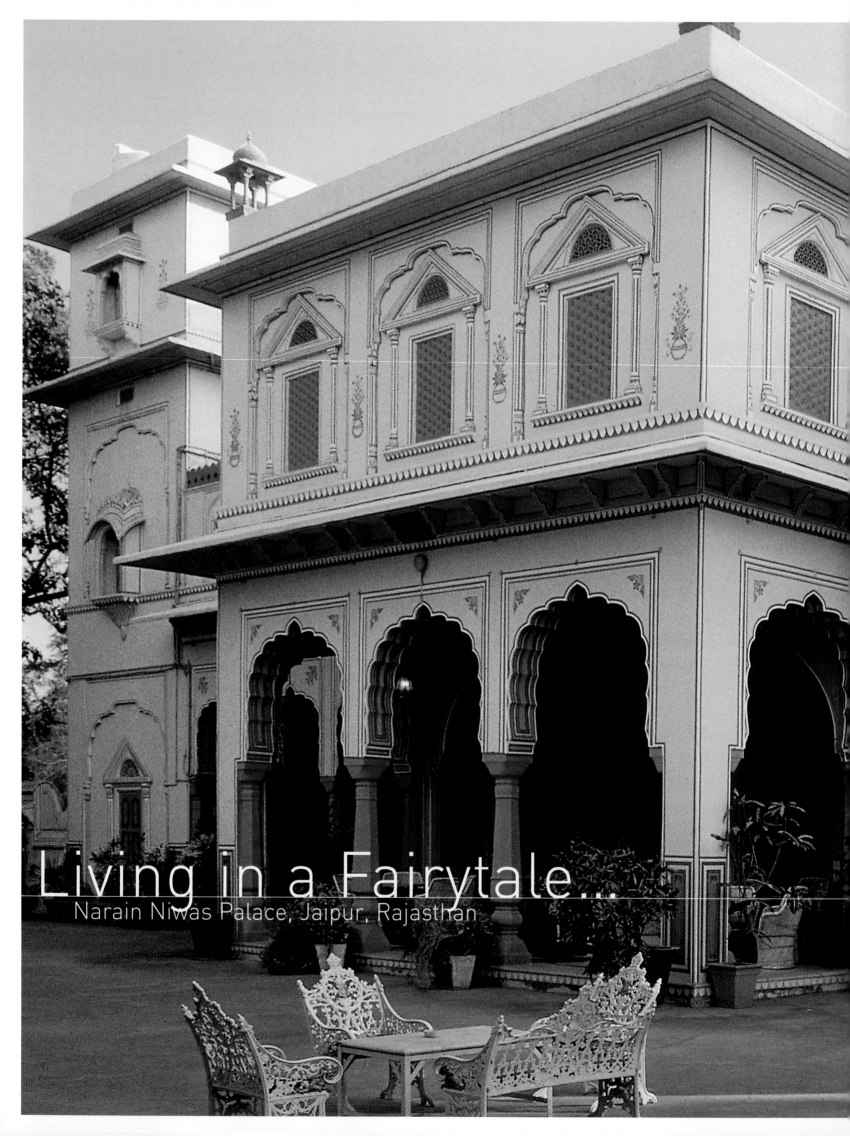

Living in a Fairytale...

Narain Niwas Palace, Jaipur, Rajasthan

Narain Niwas Palace, Jaipur, Rajasthan

Living in a Fairytale

Amar Singh Ji was one of the most influential men in Rajasthan during the early twentieth century. He was Thakur of Kanota, General of the Jaipur Armed Forces and close confidant of the Maharaja. A 24-hour job, one might think – but despite all of his responsibilities Amar Singh Ji still had time for his most important hobby: keeping a journal. He recorded his life on several thousand pages and also told of the construction of his country estate, which he had built in 1928 and which was named after his father Narain, former police chief of Jaipur. He spent his free time at his desk in this house, walking through the park or riding in the nearby jungle to shoot birds, wild pigs and even the occasional panther. Today the estate has been turned into a beautiful and relatively unknown palace hotel in which the Anglo-Indian style of the Victorian era lives on. While the exterior is cream coloured, strong yellow and ochre tones prevail inside, from the antique furnishings to the dashes of colour here and there – from a colourful pane of glass to a painted archway. And even if the leisure activities are not as exciting as they were during the times of the passionate hunter Amar Singh Ji, in the mango garden or at the pool one does experience the typical atmosphere and hospitality of ancient Rajasthan.

Book to pack: "May You Be the Mother of a Hundred Sons: A Journey Among the Women of India" by Elisabeth Bumiller

Narain Niwas Palace		
Kanota Bagh, Narain Singh Road	DIRECTIONS	Situated in the centre of Jaipur, 11 km / 7 miles from the airport and 5 km / 3 miles from the train station.
Jaipur – 302004, Rajasthan, India	RATES	Double rooms starting at US$ 45 per night, suites starting at US$ 55 per night.
Tel. +91 (141) 256 12 91	ROOMS	24 standard rooms, 7 suites.
Fax +91 (141) 256 10 45	FOOD	Indian and Chinese specialties as well as western menus.
Email: info@hotelnarainniwas.com	HISTORY	Built in 1928 as the Thakur's country estate, later converted to a hotel.
Website: www.hotelnarainniwas.com		
Booking: www.great-escapes-hotels.com	X-FACTOR	Luxurious country estate – and right in the middle of the city.

Wohnen wie im Märchen

Amar Singh Ji war einer der einflussreichsten Männer im Rajasthan des frühen 20. Jahrhunderts – Thakur von Kanota, General der Streitkräfte von Jaipur und enger Vertrauter des Maharadschas. Ein 24-Stunden-Job, so könnte man meinen, doch Amar Singh Ji hatte trotz all seiner Verpflichtungen Zeit für sein wichtigstes Hobby, das Tagebuchschreiben. Auf mehreren tausend Seiten hielt er sein Leben fest und erzählte auch vom Bau seines Landsitzes, den er anno 1928 errichten und nach seinem Vater Narain, einst der Polizeichef von Jaipur, benennen ließ. In diesem Haus saß er in seiner Freizeit am Schreibtisch, spazierte durch den Park oder ritt in den nahen Dschungel, um einen Vogel, ein Wildschwein oder vielleicht sogar einen Panther zu schießen. Heute ist aus dem Anwesen ein schönes und vergleichsweise unbekanntes Palasthotel geworden, in dem der angloindische Stil der viktorianischen Ära fortlebt. Außen cremefarben wird Narain Niwas innen von kräftigen Gelb- und Ockertönen beherrscht, von antikem Mobiliar und dem ein oder anderen Farbtupfer – sei es eine bunte Glasscheibe oder ein bemalter Torbogen. Und sind auch die Freizeitaktivitäten nicht mehr ganz so aufregend wie zu Zeiten des passionierten Jägers Amar Singh Ji, so erlebt man im Mangogarten oder am Pool doch die typische Atmosphäre und Gastfreundschaft des alten Rajasthan.

Buchtipp: »Hundert Söhne sollst Du haben. Frauenleben in Indien« von Elisabeth Bumiller

Habiter un palais de conte de fées

Amar Singh Ji, qui fut thakur de Kanota, général des armées de Jaipur et intime du maharadjah, a été l'un des hommes les plus influents du Rajasthan au début du 20ᵉ siècle. Malgré cet emploi du temps chargé, Amar Singh Ji réussissait à trouver des moments libres pour s'adonner à son occupation favorite, écrire son journal. Sur plusieurs milliers de pages, il a noté ses faits et gestes quotidiens et raconte aussi la construction de la résidence de campagne qu'il fit réaliser en 1928 et nommer d'après son père Narain, ex-chef de la police de Jaipur.

C'est ici qu'il passait ses loisirs à écrire, à se promener dans le parc ou à se rendre à cheval dans la jungle toute proche pour chasser un oiseau, un sanglier, peut-être même une panthère. Aujourd'hui, la propriété est devenue un hôtel superbe et relativement peu connu dans lequel le style anglo-indien de l'ère victorienne continue de déployer son élégance teintée d'exotisme.

Derrière une façade couleur crème, Narain Niwas est dominé à l'intérieur par des tons jaune vif et ocre, un mobilier ancien et, ici et là, un accent de couleur vive, une vitre multicolore ou une arcade peinte, par exemple. Et si les activités proposées ne sont plus aussi excitantes que du temps du chasseur passionné Amar Singh Ji, l'hôte qui se promène dans le jardin planté de manguiers ou se détend près de la piscine fait l'expérience de l'atmosphère caractéristique et de la convivialité de l'ancien Rajasthan.

Livre à emporter : « Compartiment pour dames » d'Anita Nair

ANREISE	Im Zentrum von Jaipur gelegen, 11 km vom Flughafen und 5 km vom Bahnhof entfernt.	ACCÈS	Situé au centre de Jaipur, à 11 km de l'aéroport et à 5 km de la gare.
PREIS	Doppelzimmer ab 45 US$ pro Nacht, Suite ab 55 US$ pro Nacht.	PRIX	Chambre double à partir de 45 $ US la nuit, suite à partir de 55 $ US la nuit.
ZIMMER	24 Standardzimmer, 7 Suiten.	CHAMBRES	24 chambres standard, 7 suites.
KÜCHE	Indische und chinesische Spezialitäten, außerdem westliche Menüs.	RESTAURATION	Spécialités indiennes et chinoises, menus occidentaux.
GESCHICHTE	1928 als Landsitz des Thakurs erbaut, später zum Hotel umgebaut.	HISTOIRE	Construit en 1928 pour servir de maison de campagne au thakur, transformé plus tard en hôtel.
X-FAKTOR	Luxuriöses Landhaus – und das mitten in der Stadt.	LE « PETIT PLUS »	Une luxueuse maison de campagne – au cœur de la ville.

Gone Hunting...
Sardar Samand Palace, Jodhpur, Rajasthan

Sardar Samand Palace, Jodhpur, Rajasthan

Gone Hunting

The Maharaja did not think much of huge palaces with thousands of turrets and arcades. He was a down-to-earth type of person; he liked nature and hunting – and Art Deco. In 1933, Umaid Singh had a weekend residence built in a style quite unique in India. His lodge reigns high above an artificial lake whose water is speckled pink with flamingos; its grey-brown stone seems to have merged with the surrounding rock, and it sports a kind of lookout tower with a white domed roof and turquoise-coloured balustrades. Inside one is amazed at the number of ways that sage green and salmon pink can be combined and at how successful the Maharaja was at hunting. A gazelle peers out from the wall; a buffalo watches over the door; a hollowed horn serves as an ashtray; books are stacked on elephant feet that are covered in leopard skin. Much of the decor also carries the trademark of Polish artist Stefan Norblin, who gave the Sardar Samand a complete facelift in the 1940s, turning it into an eccentric but extremely amusing lady. Not much has changed since; the descendents of the Maharaja only allow for small repairs if the original building material is preserved. The hotel comprises only 19 rooms; the owners themselves live in the others – because even today, the family still does not think much of huge palaces with thousands of turrets and arcades.

Book to pack: "Freedom at Midnight" by Larry Collins & Dominique Lapierre

Sardar Samand Palace	
Sardar Samand, District Pali	
Jodhpur – 306103	
Rajasthan, India	
Tel. +91 (2960) 24 50 01	
Fax +91 (291) 257 12 40	
Email: marwar@del3.vsnl.net.in	
Booking: www.great-escapes-hotels.com	

DIRECTIONS	Situated 60 km/37 miles southeast of Jodhpur Airport, on the shore of Sardar Samand Lake.
RATES	Double rooms starting at US$100.
ROOMS	19 deluxe rooms in Art-Deco style.
FOOD	Restaurant with specialities from India and Rajasthan as well as continental cuisine.
HISTORY	Built in 1933 as a hunting lodge; enlarged and renovated in the 1940s.
X-FACTOR	Highly unusual – but very agreeable.

Auf der Jagd

Von riesigen Palästen mit tausenden von Türmchen und Arkaden hielt der Maharadscha nicht viel. Er war ein bodenständiger Typ, mochte die Natur und die Jagd – und Art déco. 1933 ließ Umaid Singh eine Wochenendresidenz bauen, deren Stil in Indien wohl einmalig ist. Hoch über einem Stausee mit von Flamingos rosa gesprenkeltem Wasser thront eine Lodge, deren grau-brauner Stein mit dem Fels verwachsen scheint und die eine Art Aussichtsturm mit weißem Kuppeldach und türkisfarbene Balustraden besitzt. Im Inneren staunt man, auf wie viele Arten sich Schilfgrün und Lachsfarben kombinieren lassen – und wie viel Erfolg der Maharadscha beim Jagen hatte. Hier schaut eine Gemse aus der Wand, dort bewacht ein Büffel die Tür; Zigarettenasche landet in ausgehöhltem Horn, Bücher stapeln sich auf mit Leopardenfell bezogenen Elefantenfüßen. Vieles trägt auch die Handschrift des polnischen Künstlers Stefan Norblin, der Sardar Samand in den vierziger Jahren einem Facelifting unterzog und es zu einer exzentrischen, aber ungeheuer amüsanten Lady machte. Seitdem hat sich hier nicht mehr viel verändert; die Nachfahren des Maharadschas erlauben selbst kleine Reparaturen nur dann, wenn die ursprüngliche Bausubstanz erhalten bleibt. Als Hotel dienen übrigens nur 19 Zimmer. In den anderen Räumen wohnen die Eigentümer selbst – denn von riesigen Palästen mit tausenden von Türmchen und Arkaden hält die Familie auch heute noch nicht viel.

Buchtipp: »Gandhi. Um Mitternacht die Freiheit«
von Larry Collins und Dominique Lapierre

Les plaisirs de la chasse

Le maharadjah n'affectionnait guère les palais aux multiples tours et arcades. Homme aux goûts simples, il aimait la chasse et la nature – ainsi que l'art Déco. En 1933, Umaid Singh se fit construire une résidence secondaire dont le style est certainement unique en Inde. Dominant un barrage dont les eaux sont colorées ici et là par les flamants roses, le bâtiment a été construit avec des pierres d'un gris brunâtre qui semblent se fondre avec la falaise. Il se distingue surtout par sa tour coiffée d'une coupole blanche et par ses balustrades turquoises. A l'intérieur, les multiples combinaisons de vert et de saumon ainsi que les nombreux trophées de chasse du maharadjah attirent le regard. Ici, une gazelle nous observe accrochée au mur, là un buffle garde la porte. Les cendres de cigarette sont déposées dans une corne évidée et les livres s'empilent sur des pieds d'éléphant recouverts d'une peau de léopard. Beaucoup de choses portent aussi la signature de l'artiste polonais Stefan Norblin qui, dans les années quarante, fit subir un lifting à Sardar Samand le transformant ainsi en lady excentrique mais incroyablement amusante. Depuis cette époque, rien n'a changé ou presque. Même pour les petites réparations, les héritiers du maharadjah veillent à ce que la substance du bâtiment ne soit pas modifiée. D'ailleurs l'hôtel ne compte que 19 chambres, les autres pièces sont occupées par les propriétaires – aujourd'hui encore la famille n'affectionne guère les palais aux multiples tours et arcades.

Livre à emporter : « Cette nuit la liberté » de Larry Collins
et Dominique Lapierre

ANREISE	60 km südöstlich vom Flughafen Jodhpur gelegen, am Ufer des Sardar Samand Lake.	ACCÈS	Situé à 60 km au sud-est de l'aéroport de Jodhpur, sur les rives du lac Sardar Samand.
PREIS	Doppelzimmer ab 100 US$.	PRIX	Chambre double à partir de 100 $ US.
ZIMMER	19 Deluxe-Zimmer im Art-déco-Stil.	CHAMBRES	19 chambres de luxe décorées dans le style art Déco.
KÜCHE	Restaurant mit Spezialitäten aus Indien und Rajasthan, außerdem kontinentale Küche.	RESTAURATION	Restaurant proposant des spécialités indiennes et du Rajasthan, ainsi qu'une cuisine continentale.
GESCHICHTE	1933 als Jagdhaus erbaut, in den vierziger Jahren erweitert und renoviert.	HISTOIRE	Construit en 1933 comme pavillon de chasse, agrandi et rénové dans les années quarante.
X-FAKTOR	Ganz schön schräg – aber sehr sympathisch.	LE « PETIT PLUS »	Plutôt bizarre – mais très sympathique.

On Cloud Nine...
Nilaya Hermitage, Goa

Nilaya Hermitage, Goa

On Cloud Nine

"Goa Dourada" is what the natives affectionately call it, "Golden Goa". And anyone who has lain even once on that famous beach – golden sand below, golden sun above – would agree with them. But this island on the west coast of India has an even broader palette of colours to offer – the most beautiful proof of which is the hotel Nilaya Hermitage. It opens up like a paintbox in the hills of Arpora with its bold and perfectly harmonised colours. Turquoise blue, yellow-green and bright orange are not generally considered to be the best of friends, but when you set eyes on them together in the lobby of the Nilaya you become instantly convinced that exactly this combination is just perfection itself. With a lot of colour and typical accessories, Claudia Derain and Hari Ajwani have conjured a Portuguese flair into the rooms which recall Goa's colonial past. Also, thanks to the predomination of rounded forms in the design, one has the pleasant feeling that even the odd hard edge won't cause any problems. The rooms have been named after cosmic elements like the sun, moon and fire – and the name "Nilaya" itself translates as nothing less than "heaven". By the way, many guests find their cloud nine by the pool, where east-meets-west specialties are served in the evenings.

Book to pack: "Voyage of Discovery" by Vasco da Gama

Nilaya Hermitage		
Arpora Bhati	DIRECTIONS	Situated 350 km / 217 miles south of Mumbai (the transfer from/to the airport is organized).
Goa 403518, India	RATES	Double rooms starting at US$ 140 per night (including breakfast and dinner).
Tel. +91 (832) 27 67 93 and 27 67 94		
Fax +91 (832) 27 67 92	ROOMS	12 double rooms.
Email: nilaya@goatelecom.com	FOOD	Combines flavours from Goa, India, China and the Mediterranean area.
Website: www.nilayahermitage.com	HISTORY	Opened in 1994 as an alternative to the classic beach resorts on Goa.
Booking: www.great-escapes-hotels.com	X-FACTOR	Multicultural vacation – Portugal meets India.

Auf Wolke sieben

»Goa Dourada« nennen es die Einheimischen liebevoll,
»Goldenes Goa«. Und wer auch nur einmal an einem der
berühmten Strände gelegen hat – goldenen Sand unter sich,
die goldene Sonne über sich –, wird ihnen zustimmen. Doch
die Insel an der Westküste Indiens hat noch eine breitere
Farbpalette zu bieten – der hübscheste Beweis dafür ist das
Hotel Nilaya Hermitage. In den Hügeln von Arpora öffnet
es sich wie ein Malkasten mit mutigen, aber perfekt auf-
einander abgestimmten Tönen. Türkisblau, Gelbgrün und
leuchtendes Orange sind nicht immer die besten Freunde;
doch wer sie in der Lobby des Nilaya sieht, ist innerhalb von
Sekunden davon überzeugt, dass genau diese Kombination
die einzig richtige und mögliche ist. Mit viel Farbe und typischen Accessoires zaubern Claudia Derain und Hari Ajwani
auch in die Zimmer portugiesisches Flair und erinnern an
die koloniale Vergangenheit Goas; und dank der überwie-
gend runden Formen hat man das gute Gefühl, sich auch an
den wenigen echten Ecken gar nicht richtig stoßen zu können. Benannt sind die Räume nach kosmischen Elementen
wie Sonne, Mond und Feuer – und »Nilaya« selbst bedeutet
nichts Geringeres als »Himmel«. Wolke sieben ist für viele
Gäste übrigens der Pool, an dem abends East-meets-West-
Spezialitäten serviert werden.
**Buchtipp: »Die Entdeckung des Seewegs nach Indien«
von Vasco da Gama**

Le septième ciel

Les habitants l'appellent amoureusement « Goa Dourada »,
Goa la dorée. Et celui qui s'est déjà allongé sur l'une de ses
célèbres plages, où l'or du sable joue avec l'or du soleil, ne
pourra que partager ce sentiment. Pourtant l'île de la côte
occidentale de l'Inde propose une gamme de couleurs encore
plus vaste et le plus bel exemple en est assurément l'hôtel
Nilaya Hermitage. Dans les collines d'Arpora il se présente
comme la palette d'un peintre, avec des coloris audacieux
mais qui s'harmonisent entre eux. D'habitude le bleu turquoise, le vertjaune et l'orange vif ne font pas toujours bon
ménage mais lorsqu'on les voit dans le hall de réception du
Nilaya, on est tout de suite convaincu que cette combinaison
de tons est la seule possible. En s'aidant de la couleur et
d'accessoires typiques Claudia Derain et Hari Ajwani ont
aussi donné aux chambres une atmosphère portugaise qui
rappelle le passé colonial de Goa. Et grâce aux formes arrondies qui prédominent dans les pièces, il est possible de se
déplacer librement sans craindre de se cogner à tout
moment. Les chambres ont été baptisées d'après les éléments cosmiques, comme le soleil, la lune et le feu – et
« Niyala » signifie le ciel. D'ailleurs pour beaucoup de clients
le septième nuage est la piscine, au bord de laquelle des spé-
cialités dites « East-meets-West » sont servies le soir.
**Livre à emporter : « La Découverte de la route des Indes »
de Vasco de Gama**

ANREISE	350 km südlich von Mumbai gelegen (Transfer ab/zum Flughafen wird organisiert).	ACCÈS	Situé à 350 km au sud de Mumbai (le transfert entre l'aéroport et l'hôtel est organisé).
PREIS	Doppelzimmer ab 140 US$ pro Nacht (inklusive Frühstück und Dinner).	PRIX	Chambre double à partir de 140 $ US la nuit (petit-déjeuner et dîner compris).
ZIMMER	12 Doppelzimmer.	CHAMBRES	12 chambres doubles.
KÜCHE	Verbindet Aromen aus Goa, Indien, China und dem Mittel-meerraum.	RESTAURATION	Associe les arômes de Goa, de l'Inde, de la Chine et du bassin méditerranéen.
GESCHICHTE	1994 als Alternative zu den klassischen Strandresorts auf Goa eröffnet.	HISTOIRE	Ouvert en 1994 comme alternative aux hôtels de la plage classiques de Goa.
X-FAKTOR	Multikultureller Urlaub – hier liegt Portugal in Indien.	LE « PETIT PLUS »	Vacances multiculturelles – ici le Portugal se trouve en Inde.

Seeing Green...
Green Magic Nature Resort, Kerala

Green Magic Nature Resort, Kerala

Seeing Green

Those summers in the tree house were unique: Days spent in the woods behind my grandparents' house with my best friends and scratches on our legs, filled with secrets and giddiness and the nights spent between the sky and earth. Are these happy times all over and relegated to the past? No, these summers still exist: In the tropical rainforest of Kerala, three houses seem to sway in the treetops. They are suspended 25 meters above the ground and rather luxuriously equipped with a bedroom, a bathroom with shower and toilet, a covered veranda and outdoor seating. Hydraulic lifts, somewhat reminiscent of the cages used in mines, transport visitors and luggage right up into the heart of the jungle. What does the rustling of the foliage and the cries of the animals sound like? How does the light morning fog and the first rays of sun feel on one's skin? How fast is one's pulse during a thunderstorm or monsoon? Anyone preferring to experience the whims of nature with solid ground under their feet can move to one of the six eco-cottages instead. They too have been constructed by native craftsmen using only natural materials. Further proximity to nature is brought by walks along the Periyar Tiger Trail and even at mealtimes as well: Fruit and vegetables are from the resort's own farm and meals are prepared with the help of solar energy and served on banana leaves – this is the taste of Kerala.

Book to pack: "The Jungle Book" by Rudyard Kipling

Green Magic Nature Resort

c/o Tourindia
Post Box No. 163
Mahatma Gandhi Road
Trivandrum – 695001, Kerala, India
Tel. +91 (471) 233 04 37 and 233 15 07
Fax +91 (471) 233 14 07
Email: tourindia@vsnl.com
Website: www.tourindiakerala.com
Booking: www.great-escapes-hotels.com

DIRECTIONS	Situated 250 km/155 miles southwest of Bangalore, 65 km/40 miles from Calicut Airport.
RATES	Tree houses US$180 per night, cottages starting at US$110 per night (including breakfast, lunch and dinner).
ROOMS	3 tree houses, 6 cottages.
FOOD	Local dishes consisting of fruit and vegetables (organic farming), served on banana leaves.
HISTORY	Eco-lodge that works together with the Kerala Forest Authority. In 1998 it received the International Environment Award.
X-FACTOR	Adventure holiday – right in the middle of the rainforest.

Alles im grünen Bereich

Diese Sommer im Baumhaus waren einzigartig. Damals, in Wäldchen hinter dem Haus der Großeltern – mit den besten Freunden und Schrammen an den Beinen, voller Geheimnisse und Schwindelgefühle und mit Nächten zwischen Himmel und Erde. Vorbei und zu Ende? Nein, diese Sommer gibt es noch: Im tropischen Regenwald von Kerala scheinen drei Häuser in den Baumkronen zu schweben.
25 Meter über dem Boden und geradezu luxuriös mit Schlafzimmer, Bad inklusive Dusche und Toilette, überdachter Veranda und Freisitz ausgestattet. Mit hydraulisch betriebenen Aufzügen, die ein bisschen an die Förderkörbe im Bergbau erinnern, kommen Bewohner und Gepäck nach oben, mitten ins Herz des Dschungels. Wie klingen das Rauschen der Blätter und die Schreie der Tiere? Wie fühlen sich der leichte Morgennebel und die ersten Sonnenstrahlen auf der Haut an? Wie schnell geht der Puls bei einem Gewitterregen oder Monsun? Wer die Launen der Natur lieber mit festem Boden unter den Füßen erlebt, kann in eines von sechs Eco-Cottages ziehen; sie sind ebenfalls mit natürlichen Materialien und von einheimischen Handwerkern gebaut. Auf Tuchfühlung mit der Natur geht man auch bei Wanderungen auf dem Periyar Tiger Trail und sogar beim Essen: Obst und Gemüse stammen aus eigenem Anbau, gekocht wird mit Hilfe von Solarenergie und serviert auf Bananenblättern – so schmeckt Kerala.

Buchtipp: »Das Dschungelbuch« von Rudyard Kipling

Dans la verdure

Ces étés étaient uniques. Avec mes meilleurs copains, nous avions construit une cabane perchée dans les arbres, dans le bois qui se trouvait derrière chez mes grands-parents – je me souviens des jambes toutes griffées, du trop-plein de secrets et de sentiments vertigineux et des nuits entre le ciel et la terre. On peut retrouver ces étés-là au Kerala, dans la forêt vierge, où trois cabanes semblent planer en haut des arbres.
Elles se situent à 25 mètres au-dessus du sol et sont dotées de chambres à coucher, d'une salle de bains avec douche et d'un W.-C., d'une véranda couverte et d'un siège en plein air – le luxe. Dans des ascenseurs hydrauliques qui évoquent les cages des mineurs, les habitants et leurs bagages sont hissés dans la cime des arbres, au cœur de la jungle, en union directe avec la nature : écouter le bruissement des feuilles et les cris d'animaux ; sentir la légère brume matinale et les premiers rayons du soleil sur la peau ; trembler quand l'orage gronde et que la pluie se déverse sur le toit... Celui qui ne veut pas vivre à ce point dans l'intimité de la forêt peut s'installer dans un des six cottages, également construits avec des matériaux naturels par des artisans locaux.
La nature n'est jamais loin lorsqu'on suit le Periyar Tiger Trail et même pendant les repas : les fruits et les légumes sont produits ici, ils sont cuits à l'aide de l'énergie solaire et servis sur des feuilles de bananier – c'est le goût du Kerala.

Livre à emporter : « Le livre de la jungle » de Rudyard Kipling

ANREISE	250 km südwestlich von Bangalore gelegen, 65 km vom Flughafen Calicut entfernt.
PREIS	Baumhaus 180 US$ pro Nacht, Cottage ab 110 US$ pro Nacht (inklusive Frühstück, Lunch und Dinner).
ZIMMER	3 Baumhäuser, 6 Cottages.
KÜCHE	Einheimische Gerichte aus Obst und Gemüse (biologischer Anbau), serviert auf Bananenblättern.
GESCHICHTE	Eco-Lodge, die mit der Kerala Forest Authority zusammenarbeitet. 1998 mit dem International Environment Award ausgezeichnet.
X-FAKTOR	Abenteuerurlaub – mitten im Regenwald.

ACCÈS	Situé à 250 km au sud-ouest de Bangalore, à 65 km de l'aéroport de Calicut.
PRIX	Cabane dans un arbre 180 $ US la nuit, cottage à partir de 110 $ US la nuit (repas compris).
CHAMBRES	3 cabanes, 6 cottages.
RESTAURATION	Plats régionaux à base de fruits et de légumes (agriculture biologique), servis sur des feuilles de bananier.
HISTOIRE	Hôtel écologique qui collabore avec la Kerala Forest Authority. Le prix International Environment Award lui a été décerné en 1998.
LE « PETIT PLUS »	Les plaisirs de l'enfance au cœur de la forêt vierge.

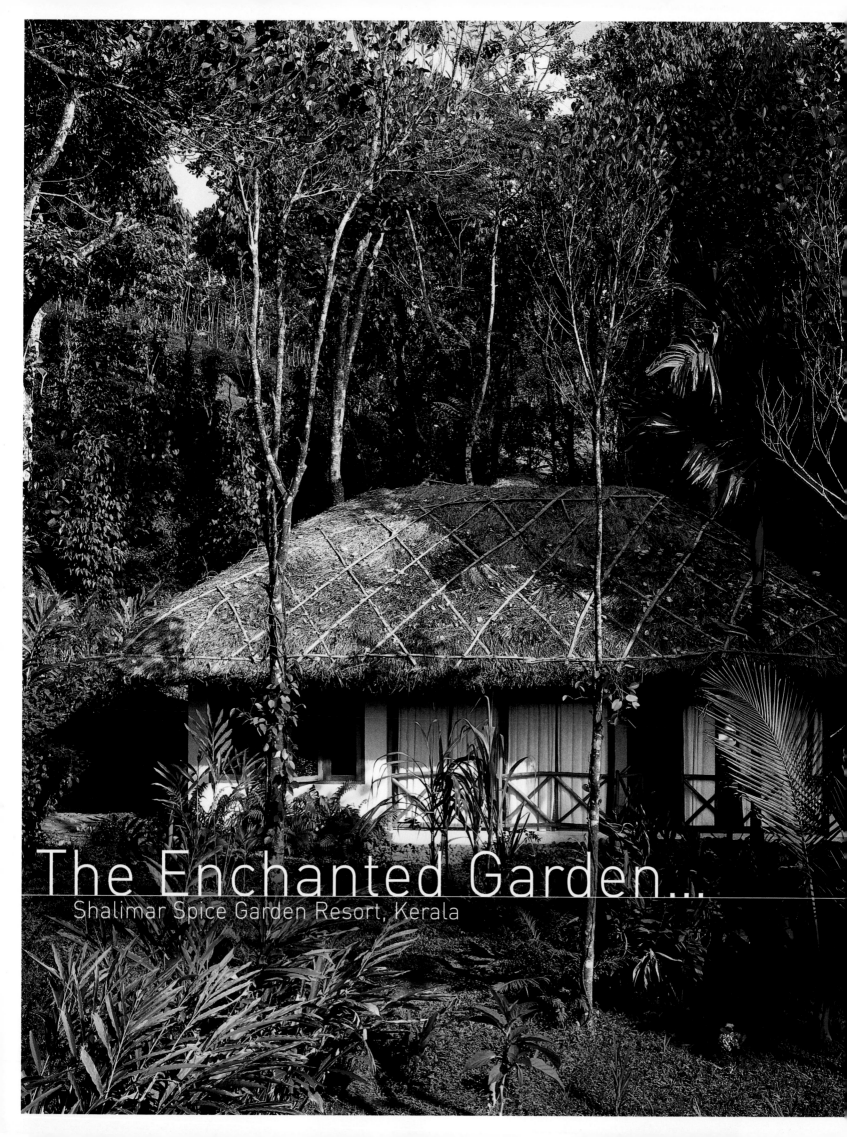

The Enchanted Garden...
Shalimar Spice Garden Resort, Kerala

Shalimar Spice Garden Resort, Kerala

The Enchanted Garden

There is a simple remedy for the heat and humidity of the plains of Kerala: a trip to the mountains where, at the edge of the Periyar Tiger Reserve, the Shalimar Spice Garden Resort is located. At a height of 800 metres, where the air is relatively cool, the Italian Maria Angela Fernhof and the Indian Shaji Antony have created their own personal paradise and given it a name which is a combination of their own two first names. Life is simple up here, yet there also seems to be an excess of everything: The straw-covered cottages stand in the midst of bright green palm groves and amongst trees and plants where mangos, nutmeg and cardamom flourish – for hobby biologists, the tropical flora is even explained on small signs. The kitchen refines the Indian dishes by adding precisely the right amount of Italian flavouring (and vice versa). If after yoga and a massage in distant Europe or the United States, you wanted to wake up feeling as relaxed as you do here, it would require a lot of money and a lot of patience. Lovers of solitude will enjoy staying longer – everyone else should plan a safari in the nearby reserve and follow the tracks of wild elephants, leopards and deer.

Book to pack: "The God of Small Things" by Arundhati Roy

Shalimar Spice Garden Resort	
Thekkady	
Idukki District – 685535	
Kerala, India	
Tel. +91 (484) 238 10 38	
Fax +91 (486) 236 44 85	
Email: reservation@shalimarkerala.com	
Website: www.shalimarkerala.com	
Booking: www.great-escapes-hotels.com	

DIRECTIONS	Situated 150 km/93 miles southwest of Madurai Airport at the edge of the Periyar Tiger Reserve.
RATES	Double rooms starting at US$120 per night, cottages starting at US$150 per night.
ROOMS	7 cottages and 8 double rooms, all individually furnished.
FOOD	Indian-Italian dishes are served in the glass restaurant.
HISTORY	Constructed in 1996 as a comfortable resort which is close to nature and connects eastern and western elements.
X-FACTOR	A dream in an enchanted garden – a perfect hideaway.

Ein Haus im Grünen

Es gibt ein einfaches Rezept gegen die Hitze und Schwüle der Ebenen von Kerala: eine Fahrt in die Berge, wo am Rand des Periyar Tiger Reservats das Shalimar Spice Garden Resort steht. In 800 Metern Höhe und in vergleichsweise kühler Luft haben die Italienerin Maria Angela Fernhof und der Inder Shaji Antony ihr persönliches Paradies geschaffen und ihm einen aus ihren beiden Vornamen kombinierten Titel verliehen. Es ist ein einfaches Leben hier oben, das aber gleichzeitig alles im Überfluss zu haben scheint: Die strohgedeckten Cottages stehen inmitten leuchtend grüner Palmenhaine und unter Bäumen und Stauden, an denen Mango, Muskatnuss oder Kardamom gedeihen – für Hobby-biologen wird die Tropenflora sogar auf kleinen Schildern erklärt. Die Küche verfeinert indische Gerichte mit genau dem richtigen Hauch Italienaroma (und umgekehrt), und wollte man nach Yogastunden und Massagen im fernen Europa oder Amerika genauso entspannt aufstehen wie hier, man müsste viel Geld und Geduld aufbringen. Wer länger bleiben möchte, muss die Einsamkeit lieben – alle anderen sollten eine Safari im nahen Reservat planen und den Spuren wilder Elefanten, Leoparden und Hirsche folgen.

Buchtipp: »Der Gott der kleinen Dinge« von Arundhati Roy

Le jardin enchanté

Il existe une recette toute simple pour fuir la chaleur accablante de la vallée de Kerala : il suffit de se réfugier dans les montagnes où se trouve le Shalimar Spice Garden Resort, situé près de la réserve de tigres de Periyar. C'est ici, à 800 mètres d'altitude, là où l'air est plus frais, que l'Italienne Maria Angela Fernhof et l'Indien Shaji Antony ont créé leur petit paradis, qu'ils ont nommé en mariant leurs deux prénoms. La vie dans ce lieu est à la fois simple et abondante. Les cottages aux toits recouverts de paille se trouvent au milieu d'une végétation éclatante d'arbres et d'arbustes ployant sous le poids des mangues et des noix de muscade. Cette flore tropicale est expliquée sur de petits panneaux à l'attention des biologistes amateurs. La cuisine combine avec bonheur les influences indiennes et italiennes des propriétaires, et il faudrait certainement débourser beaucoup d'argent en Amérique ou en Europe pour éprouver le même sentiment de détente après les massages ou les cours de yoga dispensés à l'hôtel. Le client qui désire prolonger son séjour doit aimer la solitude – sinon il a la possibilité de faire un safari dans la réserve toute proche où il pourra partir sur les traces des éléphants sauvages, des léopards et des cerfs.

Livre à emporter : « Le Dieu des petits riens » de Arundhati Roy

ANREISE	150 km südwestlich des Flughafens Madurai gelegen, am Rand des Periyar Tiger Reservats.	ACCÈS	Situé à 150 km au sud-ouest de l'aéroport de Madurai, près de la réserve de tigres de Periyar.
PREIS	Doppelzimmer ab 120 US$ pro Nacht, Cottage ab 150 US$ pro Nacht.	PRIX	Chambre double à partir de 120 $ US la nuit, cottage à partir de 150 $ US la nuit.
ZIMMER	7 Cottages und 8 Doppelzimmer, alle individuell eingerichtet.	CHAMBRES	7 cottages et 8 chambres doubles, tous aménagés de façon individuelle.
KÜCHE	Im gläsernen Restaurant werden indisch-italienische Gerichte serviert.	RESTAURATION	Cuisine italo-indienne servie dans le restaurant de verre.
GESCHICHTE	1996 als naturnahes und doch komfortables Resort erbaut, das östliche und westliche Elemente verbindet.	HISTOIRE	Construit en 1996, l'hôtel à la fois proche de la nature et confortable, allie les éléments orientaux et occidentaux.
X-FAKTOR	Träumen im verwunschenen Garten – ein perfektes Hideaway.	LE « PETIT PLUS »	Rêver dans un jardin enchanté – la retraite idéale.

The White House...
Sun House, Galle

Sun House, Galle

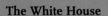

The White House

In Galle time seems to have stood still sometime during the colonial period. The slowly beating heart of the little city on Sri Lanka's south coast is a Dutch fort whose thick city walls conceal old merchants' houses and aged cars rattle through the narrow streets. It is where you can take evening strolls to Star Bastion and experience one of the kitschiest and most beautiful sunsets in the Indian Ocean. Another destination for a trip to the island's colonial past is the Sun House, with its pillar-lined covered veranda, which reigns high upon a hill. Up here, a Scottish spice trader, for whom the house was built in the mid-nineteenth century, found the best spot to watch for ships from his homeland. Today you can enjoy the knee-tremblingly beautiful view of the harbour but without the business worries. The six rooms in the Sun House are also simply beautiful; decorated entirely in white with a few dark accents. They have a wonderful way of making you feel like you are in your own living room – not in a hotel where there were guests before you and will be guests after you. In the gardens full of frangipanis and mango trees or at the pool, the days in the tropics drift past in a dream. But a word of warning: In the evening, the menus do full justice to the name "Spice Island of Sri Lanka" and the bottle of water always stands within easy reach.

Book to pack: "Cinnamon Gardens" by Shyam Selvadurai

The Sun House	
18 Upper Dickson Road	
Galle, Sri Lanka	
Tel. +94 (74) 38 02 75	
Tel. and Fax +94 (9) 226 24	
Email: sunhouse@sri.lanka.net	
Website: www.thesunhouse.com	
Booking: www.great-escapes-hotels.com	

DIRECTIONS	Situated 100 km/62 miles south of Colombo (travel time: 1.5 hr.) on the south coast of the island.
RATES	Small double rooms starting at US$99 per night, large double rooms starting at US$160 per night, suites starting at US$245 per night.
ROOMS	4 small double rooms, 1 large double room, 1 Cinnamon Suite.
FOOD	"Cuisine of the Sun" – with influences from India, Malaysia, Portugal and Holland.
HISTORY	Built in the nineteenth century as a Scottish spice trader's residence, today it is a small boutique hotel.
X-FACTOR	Vacation of the best quality in colonial ambience.

Das weiße Haus

In Galle scheinen die Uhren in der Kolonialzeit stehengeblieben zu sein. Das langsam schlagende Herz des Städtchens an der Südküste von Sri Lanka ist das holländische Fort, wo hinter dicken Stadtmauern alte Kaufmannshäuser stehen, Oldtimer durch enge Straße knattern und man abends zur Star Bastion spaziert, um einen der kitschigschönsten Sonnenuntergänge im Indischen Ozean zu erleben. Ziel einer Reise in die koloniale Vergangenheit der Insel ist auch das Sun House, das mit seinen säulengesäumten und überdachten Veranden auf einem Hügel thront. Hier oben hatte der schottische Gewürzhändler, der das Haus Mitte des 19. Jahrhunderts bauen ließ, den besten Platz gefunden, um nach Schiffen aus seiner Heimat Ausschau zu halten – heute genießt man den zum Niederknien schönen Blick auf den Hafen aber eher ohne geschäftliche Verpflichtungen. Schlicht schön sind auch die sechs Zimmer des Sun House; ganz in Weiß gehalten und mit sparsamen dunklen Akzenten. Sie lassen einen auf wundersame Weise glauben, im eigenen Wohnzimmer zu sein – nicht in einem Hotel, in dem schon vorher Gäste da waren und auch nachher welche kommen werden. In den Gärten voller Frangipanis und Mangobäume oder am Pool plätschern die Tropentage traumhaft dahin. Aber Vorsicht: Abends machen die Menüs der Gewürzinsel Sri Lanka alle Ehre – die Flasche Wasser steht stets in Reichweite.

Buchtipp: »Die Zimtgärten« von Shyam Selvadurai

La maison blanche

A Galle, les pendules semblent s'être arrêtées à l'époque coloniale. Le cœur tranquille de la petite ville méridionale du Sri Lanka est le fort hollandais qui dissimule derrière ses murs d'enceinte d'anciennes maisons de négociants. Ici, on peut encore voir de vieilles automobiles pétarader dans les étroites ruelles et le soir on va se promener au Star Bastion afin d'admirer l'un des plus beaux couchers de soleil sur l'océan Indien. Ce voyage dans le passé colonial de l'île conduit aussi à la Sun House qui trône sur une colline, avec sa véranda entourée de colonnes. La maison a été construite au 19e siècle par un marchand d'épices écossais qui avait ainsi trouvé l'endroit idéal pour voir arriver ses bateaux venant d'Ecosse. Aujourd'hui, on jouit de la vue splendide sur le port sans arrière-pensée commerciale. Les six chambres de la Sun House sont aussi belles et sobres avec leur décoration blanche ponctuée seulement ici et là de touches sombres. Elles donnent au visiteur l'étonnante impression de se croire dans sa salle à manger et non pas dans une chambre d'hôtel où les clients se succèdent. Dans les jardins regorgeant de frangipaniers et de manguiers ou près de la piscine les journées sous les tropiques s'écoulent comme en rêve ; mais attention, le soir les menus de « l'île aux épices » font honneur à son nom. Mieux vaut avoir une bouteille d'eau à portée de main.

Livre à emporter : « Jardins de cannelle » de Shyam Selvadurai

ANREISE	100 km südlich von Colombo gelegen (Fahrtzeit: 1,5 h), an der Südküste der Insel.	ACCÈS	Situé à 100 km au sud de Colombo (1 heure et demie de trajet), sur la côte méridionale de l'île.
PREIS	Kleines Doppelzimmer ab 99 US$ pro Nacht, großes Doppelzimmer ab 160 US$ pro Nacht, Suite ab 245 US$ pro Nacht.	PRIX	Petite chambre double à partir de 99 $ US la nuit, grande chambre double à partir de 160 $ US la nuit, suite à partir de 245 $ US la nuit.
ZIMMER	4 kleine Doppelzimmer, 1 großes Doppelzimmer, 1 Cinnamon-Suite.	CHAMBRES	4 petites chambres doubles, 1 grande chambre double, 1 suite Cinnamon.
KÜCHE	»Cuisine of the Sun« – gut gewürzt und mit Einflüssen aus Indien, Malaysia, Portugal und Holland.	RESTAURATION	« Cuisine of the Sun » – avec des influences de l'Inde, de la Malaisie, du Portugal et de Hollande.
GESCHICHTE	Im 19. Jahrhundert als Residenz eines schottischen Gewürzhändlers erbaut, heute ein kleines Boutique-Hotel.	HISTOIRE	Construite au 19e siècle pour un marchand d'épices écossais, la maison est aujourd'hui un petit hôtel.
X-FAKTOR	Ferien vom Feinsten im Kolonialambiente.	LE « PETIT PLUS »	Un séjour de qualité dans une atmosphère coloniale.

Luxury Can Be This Simple...
Pansea Angkor, Siem Reap

Pansea Angkor, Siem Reap

Luxury Can Be This Simple

Luxury can be that simple: A pool lined with 45 000 tiles – each reflecting a different shade of green – that has the same proportions as the artificial lakes of Cambodian temple complexes. A room with furniture made of local wood and bamboo, soft cotton materials and bright, colourful pillows. And a balcony that seems custom-made for a private break-fast or a game of draughts. The Pansea Angkor, situated on the river in the heart of Siem Reap and just a short walk from Angkor Wat, does not let itself be intimidated by the grandeur of its environment and shows its own version of Cambodia – a quiet, warm-hearted and obliging country. In the building itself, materials and skills from other lands only play tiny, minor roles; the predominant wood, bamboo, stone and fabrics come from the immediate vicinity and are processed in local workshops as well as in workshops for the disabled. Food is cooked according to traditional recipes and with fresh ingredients; used water is not just poured into the ground but used to irrigate the garden; you don't cruise around the neighbourhood in a car but ride a bicycle. It sounds a bit like eco-tourism and Spartan living – but is worlds away from that, because, like we said: Luxury really can be this simple.

Book to pack: "The Royal Way" by André Malraux

Pansea Angkor	
River Road	
Siem Reap, Cambodia	
Tel. +855 (63) 96 33 90	
Fax +855 (63) 96 33 91	
Email: angkor@pansea.com	
Website: www.pansea.com	
Booking: www.great-escapes-hotels.com	

DIRECTIONS	Situated in the centre of Siem Reap, 7 km/4 miles southeast of the airport and 10 minutes from the temple grounds.
RATES	Rooms starting at US$180 per night, suites starting at US$480 per night (including breakfast).
ROOMS	54 rooms and 1 suite.
FOOD	Traditional Asian specialities, French Haute Cuisine with Khmer flavors, as well as snacks in the bar with a beautiful view of the river.
HISTORY	Opened in February 2002.
X-FACTOR	Khmer flair and the comfort of modern Cambodia.

So schlicht kann Luxus sein

Ein Pool, der mit 45 000 Kacheln ausgelegt ist, von denen jede in einem anderen Grünton schimmert, und der dieselben Proportionen besitzt wie die künstlichen Seen kambodschanischer Tempelanlagen. Ein Zimmer mit Möbeln aus einheimischem Holz und Bambus, weichen Baumwollstoffen und leuchtend bunte Kissen. Ein Balkon wie geschaffen für ein privates Frühstück oder eine Partie Dame. Das Pansea Angkor, am Fluss mitten in Siem Reap gelegen und nur einen Spaziergang von Angkor Wat entfernt, lässt sich von der Grandezza seiner Umgebung nicht einschüchtern und zeigt sein eigenes Kambodscha – ein ruhiges, warmherziges und zuvorkommendes Land. Materialien und Fähigkeiten aus fremden Nationen sollten beim Bau nur winzige Nebenrollen spielen; Holz, Bambus, Stein und Stoffe stammen aus der unmittelbaren Umgebung und wurden in lokalen Handwerksbetrieben und Behindertenwerkstätten verarbeitet. Gekocht wird nach überlieferten Rezepten aus frischen Zutaten, einmal verwendetes Wasser versickert nicht nutzlos im Boden, sondern dient zur Gartenbewässerung. Man rollt nicht ständig mit dem Auto durch die Gegend, sondern setzt sich aufs Fahrrad. Es klingt ein wenig nach Ökotourismus und mangelndem Komfort – und ist doch Welten davon entfernt. Denn wie gesagt: So schlicht kann Luxus sein.

Buchtipp: »Der Königsweg« von André Malraux

Le luxe est dans la sobriété

Une piscine aux innombrables carreaux dont chacun jette des lueurs d'un vert différent et qui présente les mêmes proportions que les lacs artificiels des temples cambodgiens. Une chambre aux meubles en bois et en bambou décorée de douces étoffes en coton et de coussins aux couleurs vives. Un balcon qui donne envie de prendre le petit-déjeuner en tête à tête ou de faire une partie de dames. Le Pansea Angkor, situé près du fleuve en plein cœur de Siem Reap et à quelques kilomètres d'Angkor Wat, ne se laisse pas intimider par le décor grandiose et montre son propre Cambodge – un pays tranquille où les habitants sont accueillants et pleins d'attentions. Lors de la construction de l'hôtel, les matériaux et le savoir-faire étrangers n'ont joué qu'un petit rôle. Le bois, le bambou, la pierre et les étoffes proviennent des environs et ont été travaillés dans les entreprises artisanales et les centres pour handicapés de la région. La cuisine est préparée avec des produits frais selon des recettes traditionnelles. Les eaux usées ne sont pas jetées inconsidérément mais servent à arroser le jardin, on enfourche son vélo pour sillonner les environs au lieu de prendre constamment la voiture. Tout cela peut donner l'impression d'un tourisme écologique et d'un manque de confort, mais ce n'est absolument pas le cas, car le véritable luxe est dans la simplicité des choses.

Livre à emporter : « La Voie royale » d'André Malraux

ANREISE	Im Zentrum von Siem Reap gelegen, 7 km südöstlich des Flughafens und zehn Minuten von den Tempelanlagen entfernt.
PREIS	Zimmer ab 180 US$ pro Nacht, Suite ab 480 US$ pro Nacht (inklusive Frühstück).
ZIMMER	54 Zimmer und 1 Suite.
KÜCHE	Traditionelle asiatische Spezialitäten und französische Haute Cuisine mit Khmer-Aromen. Außerdem Snacks in der Bar mit traumhaftem Flussblick.
GESCHICHTE	Im Februar 2002 eröffnet.
X-FAKTOR	Khmer-Flair und der Komfort des modernen Kambodscha.

ACCÈS	Situé dans le centre de Siem Reap à 7 km au sud-est de l'aéroport et à 10 min des temples.
PRIX	Chambre à partir de 180 $ US la nuit, suite à partir de 480 $ US la nuit (petit-déjeuner compris).
CHAMBRES	54 chambres et 1 suite.
RESTAURATION	Spécialités asiatiques traditionnelles et Haute Cuisine française aux arômes Khmer. Le bar propose des snacks et une vue magnifique sur le fleuve.
HISTOIRE	Ouvert en février 2002.
LE « PETIT PLUS »	Allie ambiance khmère et confort du Cambodge moderne.

Tropical Magic...
The Datai, Langkawi

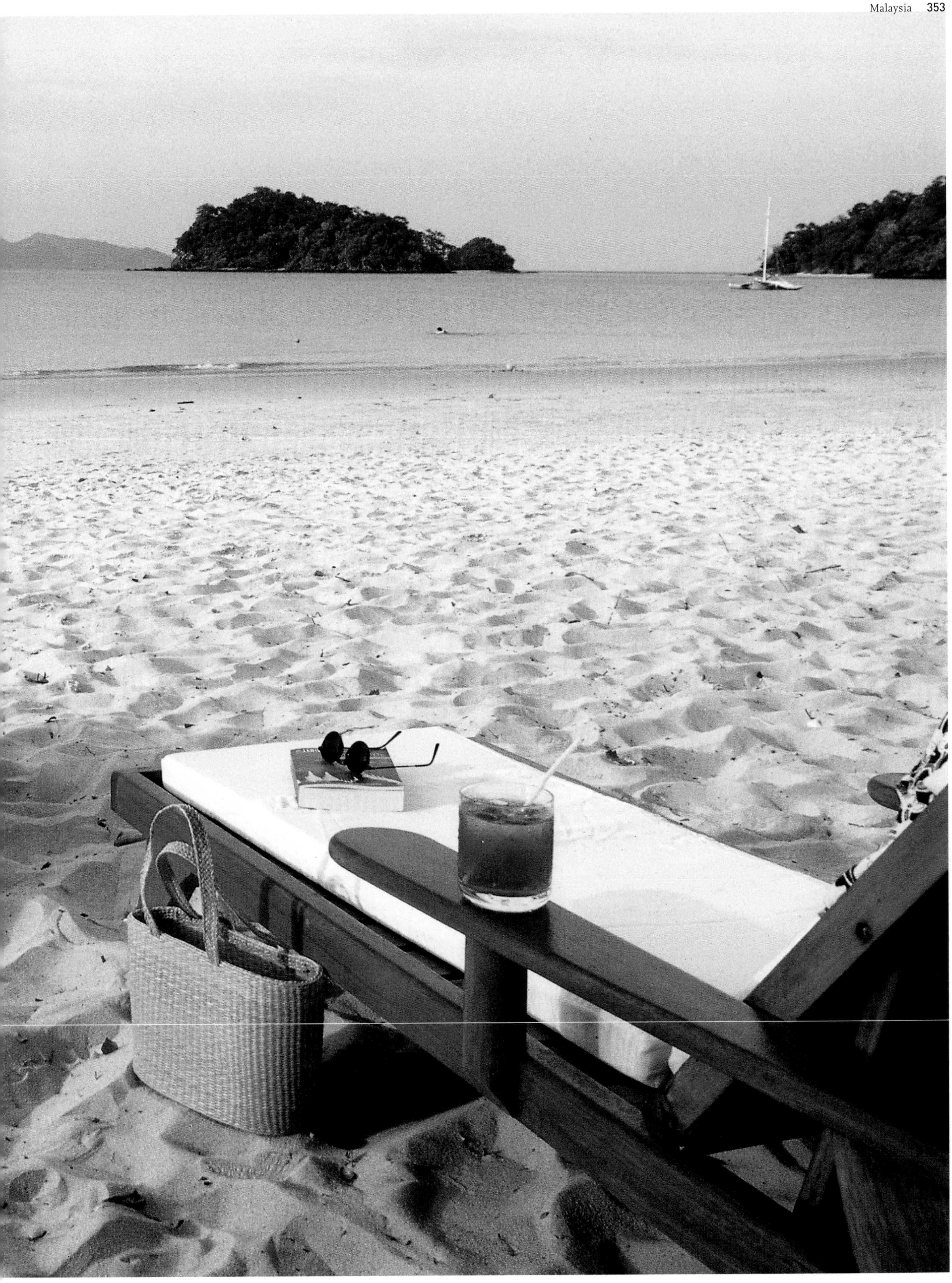

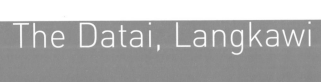

The Datai, Langkawi

Tropical Magic

God must have personally placed this island in the ocean
after he had finished with the rest of the world – carefully,
like a floating candle, after having touched up the rainforest
again with a gentle brush. Ever since, Langkawi has lain
like a pearl before Malaysia's west coast – with beaches too
beautiful for any advertisement. The tropical heat is forgotten at the sight of the green-mantled hills and waterfalls.
Wouldn't it be wonderful to own a house here, to stroll during the day along winding paths through the jungle and in
the evening to watch the setting sun illuminate the Anda-
man Sea? Well, The Datai makes it possible, if not for a whole
lifetime, then for a whole holiday at least. On slopes leading
down to the icing sugar beach, there are villas linked by a
labyrinth of paths, decked with cool stone or such shiny polished wood that they could easily pass for a mirror. Natural
beige and brown tones and clear lines determine the design
of the rooms – in the correct understanding that more splen-
dour and glamour would have been a futile attempt to com-
pete with mother nature outside the door. Dashes of colour
are only allowed in "Mandara Spa" where you can lie in bath-
tubs filled with colourful flowers and look out across *God's
own country*.

Book to pack: "Love and Vertigo" by Hsu-Ming Teo

The Datai	
Jalan Teluk Datai,	
07000 Pulau Langkawi	
Kedah Darul Aman, Malaysia	
Tel. +60 (4) 959 25 00	
Fax +60 (4) 959 26 00	
Email: datai@ghmhotels.com	
Website: www.ghmhotels.com	
Booking: www.great-escapes-hotels.com	

DIRECTIONS	Situated on the northwest coast of Langkawi, a 30-minute drive from the airport (the transfer is organized).
RATES	Deluxe rooms starting at US$ 350 per night, villas starting at US$ 400 per night, suites starting at US$ 550 per night.
ROOMS	54 deluxe rooms, 40 villas, 18 suites.
FOOD	Malaysian, Thai and western specialities, most beautifully at the open-air restaurant "The Pavilion" or in "The Beach Club" directly on the beach.
HISTORY	Opened in 1994.
X-FACTOR	A paradise – thankfully without apple trees.

Tropischer Zauber

Diese Insel muss Gott persönlich ins Meer gesetzt haben, als er mit dem Rest der Welt fertig war – vorsichtig wie eine Schwimmkerze und erst, nachdem er den Regenwald mit einem weichen Pinsel noch einmal abgestaubt hatte. Seither liegt Langkawi perlengleich vor Malaysias Westküste; mit Stränden zu schön für jeden Werbespot, grün überzogenen Hügeln und mit Wasserfällen, bei deren Anblick man alle Tropenhitze vergisst. Wäre es nicht wunderbar, hier ein Haus zu besitzen, tagsüber auf gewundenen Pfaden durch den Dschungel zu spazieren und abends zu sehen, wie die untergehende Sonne die Andamanische See aufglühen lässt? Wenn nicht für ein ganzes Leben – für einen ganzen Urlaub macht The Datai das möglich. An Hängen und bis zum Puderzuckerstrand hinunter stehen Villen, die ein Labyrinth von Wegen verbindet; ausgelegt mit kühlem Stein oder so blank poliertem Holz, dass es ohne weiteres als Spiegel durchgehen könnte. Beige und braune Naturtöne und klare Linien bestimmen das Design der Zimmer – im richtigen Bewusstsein, dass mehr Glanz und Glamour ein vergeblicher Versuch gewesen wären, mit der Natur draußen vor der Tür zu konkurrieren. Farbtupfer sind nur im »Mandara Spa« erlaubt, wo man in mit bunten Blüten gefüllten Badewannen liegt und hinausblickt auf *gods own country*.

Buchtipp: »Jadetöchter« von Hsu-Ming Teo

Des Tropiques de rêve

Dieu lui-même a dû créer cette île après s'être accordé un repos bien mérité – il l'a posée avec précaution sur les flots, ayant pris soin d'épousseter la forêt vierge avec un doux pinceau. Depuis, Langkawi repose telle une perle devant la côte ouest de la Malaisie. Ses plages sont trop belles pour les spots publicitaires, ses collines verdoyantes et ses cascades font oublier les températures tropicales.

Ne serait-il pas merveilleux de posséder une maison ici, d'explorer durant la journée les chemins sinueux qui traversent la jungle et de regarder le soir le soleil embraser le lac Andamini ? The Datai peut exaucer ce rêve – au moins le temps des vacances. Sur les pentes des collines et jusqu'à la plage de sable fin se dressent des villas que relie un labyrinthe de chemins. Elles sont en pierre ou en bois si poli que l'on pourrait s'y mirer. Des tons naturels beige et ocre et des lignes claires déterminent le design des pièces. Les aménager avec plus d'éclat et de glamour ne serait en effet qu'une vaine tentative d'entrer en compétition avec la nature environnante.

Des accents de couleur ne sont autorisés qu'au « Mandara Spa ». Ici, on peut s'allonger dans des baignoires où flottent des fleurs multicolores et regarder au dehors « gods own country ».

Livre à emporter : « Salina » d'Abdul Samad Said

ANREISE	An der Nordwestküste von Langkawi gelegen, 30 Fahrtminuten vom Flughafen entfernt (Transfer wird organisiert).
PREIS	Deluxe-Zimmer ab 350 US$ pro Nacht, Villa ab 400 US$ pro Nacht, Suite ab 550 US$ pro Nacht.
ZIMMER	54 Deluxe-Zimmer, 40 Villen, 18 Suiten.
KÜCHE	Malaysische, thailändische und westliche Spezialitäten, am schönsten im Open-air-Restaurant »The Pavillion« oder im »The Beach Club« direkt am Strand.
GESCHICHTE	1994 eröffnet.
X-FAKTOR	Ein Paradies – zum Glück ohne Apfelbäume.

ACCÈS	Situé sur la côte nord-ouest de l'île de Langkawi, à 30 min de voiture de l'aéroport (le transfert est organisé).
PRIX	Chambre de luxe à partir de 350 $ US la nuit, villa à partir de 400 $ US la nuit, suite à partir de 550 $ US la nuit.
CHAMBRES	54 chambres de luxe, 40 villas, 18 suites.
RESTAURATION	Spécialités malaisiennes, thaï et occidentales, le plus beau cadre est le restaurant en plein air « The Pavillion » ou « The Beach Club » sur la plage.
HISTOIRE	Ouvert en 1994.
LE « PETIT PLUS »	Un paradis – mais ne cherchez pas le pommier.

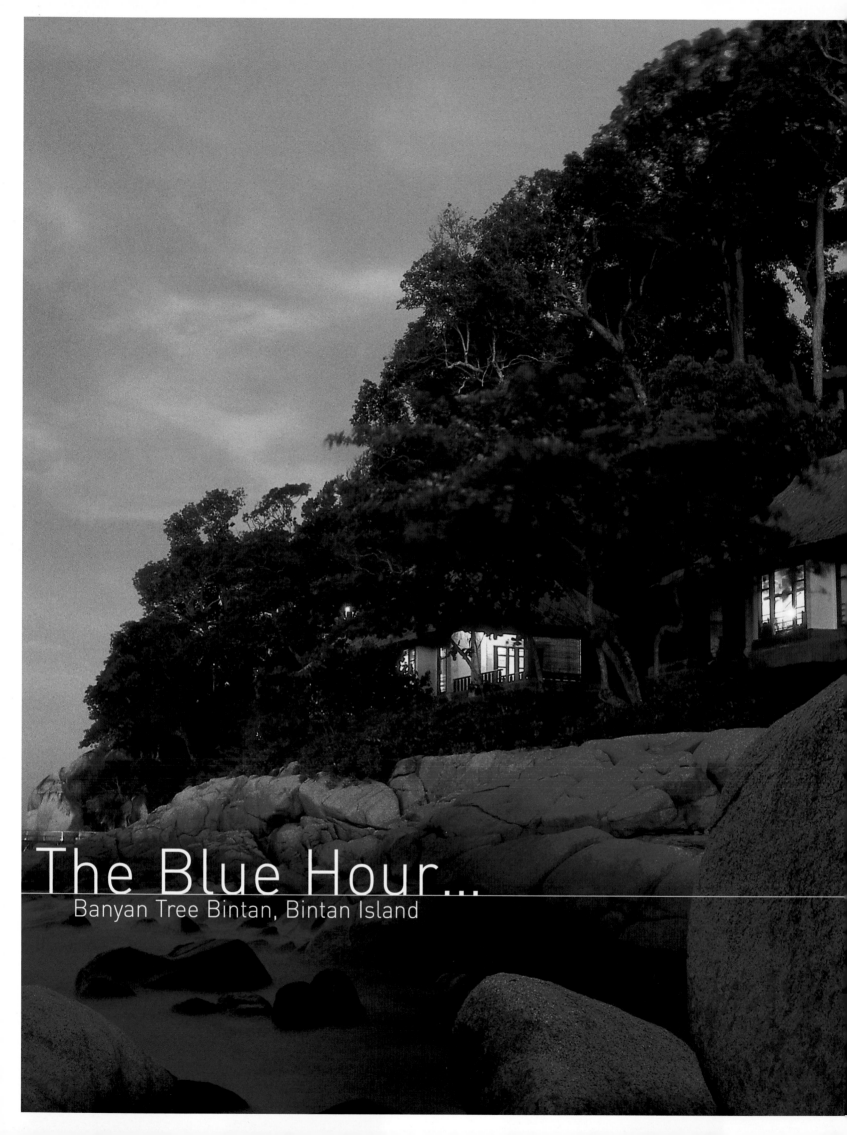

The Blue Hour...
Banyan Tree Bintan, Bintan Island

Banyan Tree Bintan, Bintan Island

The Blue Hour

Singapore was once closer to the tropics than any other city. You were almost completely surrounded by greenery; your skin was lightly coated with a film of moisture and you could hear the birds singing and smell the rain long before it drummed on the ground. Today Singapore primarily tends to keep the tropics at a distance: With houses whose air conditioning systems generate an ice age regardless of the real climate outside. Windows can no longer be opened and shopping centres are always sealed in glass – there are days when you only move in the artificial world between underground car park, office, supermarket and apartment, never once encountering a single breath of fresh air. But not to worry, if you are missing contact with nature then you don't have to look far. A 45-minute crossing from Singapore to Bintan Island should do the trick, because here the Banyan tree brings back all the long-forgotten charm of the region to Bintan. Villas stand on the outskirts of the jungle and by the ocean like little packages of paradise. They are sparingly designed with a limited palette and clear lines, but each features a personal touch lent by a bright blossom in a glass, a patterned pillow or an unusual stone on the shelf. One villa serves as a private spa and has all of the splendours of Asia in oil and cream form. Others are truly *on the rocks,* balancing high above the sea, and yet more are to be found completely encircled by forest. A promise: This is a place to rediscover the tropics – and oneself at the same time.

Book to pack: "Sinister Twilight. The fall of Singapore "
by Noel Barber

Banyan Tree Bintan	
Site A4, Lagoi	
Tanjong Said	
Bintan, Indonesia	
Tel. +62 (770) 69 31 00	
Fax +62 (770) 69 32 00	
Email: bintan@banyantree.com	
Website: www.banyantree.com	
Booking: www.great-escapes-hotels.com	
DIRECTIONS	Situated on the northwest point of Bintan Island, southeast of Singapore (45-minute crossing in a high-speed catamaran).
RATES	Jacuzzi villas starting at US$ 470 per night, bay front pool villas starting at US$ 950, sea-view pool villas starting at US$ 1250, spa pool villas starting at US$ 1300.
ROOMS	55 Jacuzzi villas, 6 sea-view pool villas, 8 bay front pool villas, 1 spa pool villa.
FOOD	Southeast Asian cuisine in the "Saffron" and Mediterranean food in "The Cove".
HISTORY	Opened in 1995.
X-FACTOR	A sigh of relief in old Asia.

Blaue Stunde

Singapur war einst den Tropen so nah wie kaum eine zweite Stadt. Man saß fast überall im Grünen, hatte einen leichten Feuchtigkeitsfilm auf der Haut, hörte die Vögel singen und roch den Regen, lange bevor er auf die Erde prasselte. Heute hält Singapur die Tropen meist auf Distanz: Mit Häusern, in denen Klimaanlagen ohne Rücksicht aufs Wetter eine Eiszeit produzieren, mit Fenstern, die sich nicht mehr öffnen lassen, und rundum verglasten Einkaufszentren – es gibt Tage, an denen man auf frische Luft verzichten und sich nur in der künstlichen Welt zwischen Tiefgarage, Büro, Supermarkt und Apartment bewegen kann. Doch keine Sorge: Wer das Naturgefühl vermisst, braucht nicht lange zu suchen. Eine 45-minütige Überfahrt von Singapur zur Insel Bintan genügt, denn dort verströmt das Banyan Tree Bintan all den vergessen geglaubten Charme der Region. Am Rand des Dschungels und am Ozean stehen Villen wie kleine Paradiese; mit wenigen Farben und klaren Linien sparsam designt und zugleich mit persönlichem Touch – dank einer leuchtenden Blüte im Glas, einem gemusterten Kissen oder einem seltenen Stein auf dem Regal. Es gibt eine Villa, die zugleich als privates Spa dient und alle Herrlichkeiten Asiens in Öl- und Cremeform besitzt, andere Häuser, die *on the rocks* hoch über dem Meer balancieren, und dritte, die auf allen Seiten von Wald umschlossen sind. Es ist ein Versprechen: Hier findet man die Tropen wieder – und sich selbst noch dazu.

Buchtipp: »Tanamera. Der Roman Singapurs« von Noel Barber

L'heure bleue

Singapour a probablement été autrefois plus proche des Tropiques qu'aucune autre ville. La végétation était quasi omniprésente, l'humidité ambiante recouvrait la peau d'un léger voile de sueur, les oiseaux chantaient et on sentait la pluie bien avant que l'averse n'arrive.

Aujourd'hui, Singapour aurait plutôt tendance à tenir les Tropiques à distance, avec des maisons climatisées sans souci des températures environnantes, des fenêtres hermétiquement closes et des centres d'achats sous verre – on peut se déplacer dans ce monde artificiel entre le parking souterrain, le bureau, le supermarché et l'appartement sans jamais se rendre à l'air libre.

Mais les amoureux de la nature ne doivent pas chercher longtemps. Situé à trois quarts d'heures de bateau de Singapour, sur l'île Bintan, le Banyan Tree Bintan émane tout ce charme que l'on croyait oublié. A l'orée de la jungle et au bord de la mer de Chine, se dressent des villas paradisiaques aux teintes sobres et aux lignes simples et claires, avec en même temps une touche personnelle – une fleur éclatante dans un vase, un coussin aux beaux motifs ou une pierre rare sur une étagère.

Une villa fait office de centre de remise en forme privé et possède ce que l'Asie a de meilleur sous forme d'onguents et d'huiles, d'autres maisons sont posées en équilibre sur les falaises qui surplombent la mer, et d'autres encore sont entourées de végétation luxuriante. Ici, on retrouve les Tropiques – et en plus, on se retrouve soi-même.

**Livres à emporter : « La vie n'est pas une foire nocturne » de Pramoedya Anata Toer
« L'étreinte de Singapour » de J. G. Farrell**

ANREISE	An der nordwestlichen Spitze der Insel Bintan gelegen, südöstlich von Singapur (45-minütige Überfahrt im High-speed-Katamaran).
PREIS	Jacuzzi-Villa ab 470 US$, Bayfront-Pool-Villa ab 950 US$, Seaview-Pool-Villa ab 1250 US$, Spa-Pool-Villa ab 1300 US$.
ZIMMER	55 Jacuzzi-Villen, 6 Seaview-Pool-Villen, 8 Bayfront-Pool-Villen, 1 Spa-Pool-Villa.
KÜCHE	Südostasiatisches im Restaurant »Saffron«, Mediterranes im »The Cove«.
GESCHICHTE	1995 eröffnet.
X-FAKTOR	Aufatmen im alten Asien.

ACCÈS	Situé au nord-ouest de la pointe de l'île Bintan, au sud-est de Singapour (traversée en 45 min dans un catamaran à grande vitesse).
PRIX	Jacuzzi Villa à partir de 470 $ US la nuit, Bayfront Pool Villa à partir de 950 $ US la nuit, Seaview Pool Villa à partir de 1250 $ US la nuit, Spa Pool Villa à partir de 1300 $ US la nuit.
CHAMBRES	55 Jacuzzi Villas, 6 Seaview Pool Villas, 8 Bayfront Pool Villas, 1 Spa Pool Villa.
RESTAURATION	Extrême-orientale au « Saffron », méridionale à « The Cove ».
HISTOIRE	Ouvert en 1995.
LE « PETIT PLUS »	Un grand moment de détente dans l'Asie ancienne.

A Private Paradise...
Amankila, Manggis, Bali

Amankila, Manggis, Bali

A Private Paradise

Slowly descending stairs can have something very majestic and glamorous about it – just think of a curved stairwell in a castle garden, the sparkling show steps on a Hollywood stage or simply a gangway high above a runway. If you dream of experiencing this feeling but do not want to wait for your rich prince or famous president, you can try your luck in Amankila. Stairs are the symbol of this exclusive resort on Bali's east coast. Narrow steps, for instance, link all suites to the reception and restaurant area; small steps in a wall lead to canals full of lotus blossoms, and even a pool extends cascade-like down three large terraces to the sea. "Step by step" one also discovers the other details on this "peaceful hill", which is what the term Amankila means. There is the fairytale-like view of the coast and ocean, a play of light and shade in the elegant suites and a figure of a deity adorning a wall in the living room. Two of the island's most important temples – Lempuyang and Besakih – can be found within the hotel's immediate vicinity. After an excursion, a picnic in the hills above the Amankila awaits you, where you can get even closer to heaven.

Book to pack: "Lord Jim" by Joseph Conrad

Amankila	
P. O. Box 33	
80871 Klungkung, Karangasem	
Bali, Indonesia	
Tel. +62 (363) 413 33	
Fax +62 (363) 415 55	
Email: reservations@amanresorts.com	
Website: www.amanresorts.com	
Booking: www.great-escapes-hotels.com	

DIRECTIONS	Situated on Bali's east coast, 1.5 hours or 15 minutes by helicopter from Denpasar Airport.
RATES	Suites starting at US$625 per night, Deluxe Pool Suites starting at US$1000 per night, Amankila Suites starting at US$2400 per night.
ROOMS	34 individual suites, including 9 Deluxe Pool Suites and 1 Amankila Suite, which contains two pavilions.
FOOD	Indonesian, Asian and Western. Particularly lovely is tea time in the library with ginger tea and Balinese cake.
HISTORY	Opened in 1992.
X-FACTOR	Privacy pure by fabulous pools.

Ein privates Paradies

Langsam eine Treppe hinunter zu steigen, kann etwas sehr Majestätisches und Glamouröses haben – man denke nur an eine geschwungene Freitreppe in einen Schlossgarten, eine funkelnde Showtreppe oder einfach eine Gangway hoch über dem Rollfeld. Wer von diesem Gefühl träumt, aber nicht auf den reichen Prinzen oder berühmten Präsidenten warten will, kann im Amankila sein Glück versuchen. Das exklusive Resort an der Ostküste Balis hat Stufen zu seinem Symbol erkoren. So sind zum Beispiel alle Suiten über schmale Treppen mit Rezeption und Restaurantbereich verbunden, kleine Mauertritte führen zu Kanälen voller Lotusblüten, und sogar ein Pool zieht sich kaskadenartig über drei große Terrassen zum Meer hinab. Wie in Schichten entdeckt man auch die weiteren Details auf dem »friedlichen Hügel«, wie Amankila übersetzt heißt. Da ist der märchenhafte Blick über die Küste und den Ozean, das Spiel von Licht und Schatten in den eleganten Suiten und die Götterfigur, die eine Wand im Wohnzimmer ziert. Ganz in der Nähe des Hotels stehen übrigens zwei der wichtigsten Tempel der Insel – Lempuyang und Besakih. Nach einem Ausflug wartet ein Picknick in den Hügeln über dem Amankila, wo man dem Himmel noch ein Stück näher kommt.

Buchtipp: »Lord Jim« von Joseph Conrad

Un paradis pour soi

On peut descendre lentement un escalier avec majesté et glamour – il suffit de penser à l'escalier monumental d'un château, à celui brillant de tous ses feux que nous montre le show-biz ou tout simplement à la passerelle d'un avion. Celui qui rêve d'éprouver cette sensation, tout en sachant pertinemment qu'il ne sera jamais ni un prince fortuné ni un président célèbre, peut tenter sa chance à Amankila. Le très sélect hôtel sur la côte est de Bali a élevé l'escalier au rang de symbole. Ainsi toutes les suites sont-elles reliées par de petits escaliers à la réception et à la salle de restaurant, des marches ménagées dans les murets conduisent aux bassins remplis de fleurs de lotus et l'une des piscines, étagée sur trois terrasses, descend même en cascade jusqu'à la mer. A Amankila, dont le nom signifie « la colline paisible », les autres détails se découvrent successivement : la vue merveilleuse sur la côte et l'océan, le jeu d'ombre et de lumière dans les suites élégantes et les dieux qui ornent un mur de la salle à manger. D'ailleurs deux des temples les plus importants de l'île se trouvent à proximité – Lempuyang et Besakih. Et l'une des excursions prévoit un pique-nique dans les collines au-dessus d'Amankila, pour se rapprocher encore un peu plus des cieux.

Livre à emporter : « Lord Jim » de Joseph Conrad

ANREISE	An der Ostküste von Bali gelegen, 1,5 Fahrtstunden oder 15 Helikopterminuten vom Flughafen Denpasar entfernt.
PREIS	Suite ab 625 US$ pro Nacht, Deluxe-Pool-Suite ab 1000 US$ pro Nacht, Amankila-Suite ab 2400 US$ pro Nacht.
ZIMMER	34 freistehende Suiten, darunter 9 Deluxe Pool Suiten und 1 Amankila Suite, die zwei Pavillons umfasst.
KÜCHE	Indonesisch, asiatisch und westlich. Besonders schön: die Teestunde in der Bibliothek mit Ingwertee und balinesischen Kuchen.
GESCHICHTE	1992 eröffnet.
X-FAKTOR	Privatsphäre pur an herrlichen Pools.

ACCÈS	Situé sur la côte est de Bali, à 1 h ½ en voiture ou 15 min en hélicoptère de l'aéroport de Denpasar.
PRIX	Suite à partir de 625 $ US la nuit, suite de luxe avec piscine à partir de 1000 $ US la nuit, suite Amankila à partir de 2400 $ US la nuit.
CHAMBRES	34 suites indépendantes, dont 9 suites de luxe avec piscine et 1 suite Amankila Suite, qui comprend 2 pavillons.
RESTAURATION	Cuisine asiatique et européenne. Thé au gingembre et gâteaux balinais dans la bibliothèque.
HISTOIRE	Ouvert en 1992.
LE « PETIT PLUS »	Intimité totale près des magnifiques piscines.

The Four Elements...
Begawan Giri Estate, Bali

Begawan Giri Estate, Bali

The Four Elements

This is one of those "once in a lifetime" hotels – and one which you have to visit with all your heart. The five buildings that are hidden in the jungle behind Ubud between rice terraces and waterfalls at first seem a bit sinister and like a mirage, which threatens to dissolve the moment you extend your hand or breathe too heavily. But never fear, the wood from Bali, the stone from Sumba, the silk from Thailand and the porcelain from China are solid enough, turning the five buildings into deluxe jungle residences. And also into places where the four elements are always present: for example, as a cool breeze that drifts across the veranda, as a private campfire site, as untreated stone or a pool that seems to have no edge. If you travel to Begawan Giri Estate, you will rediscover nature and yourself – and not only during solitary yoga hours or meditation. The estate is surrounded by some of the most beautiful jogging paths on the island; three sacred springs are just a stroll away, and then in the spa "The Source" you can have a foot massage with Balinese oil. And who knows? Perhaps you will not leave it at just "once in a lifetime"...

Book to pack: "Bali: A Paradise Created" by Adrian Vickers

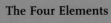

Begawan Giri Estate

P. O. Box 54, Ubud – 80571
Bali, Indonesia
Tel. +62 (361) 97 88 88
Fax +62 (361) 97 88 89
Email: reservations@begawan.com
Website: www.begawangiri.com
Booking: www.great-escapes-hotels.com

DIRECTIONS	Situated 20 minutes north of Ubud, 1 hour from Denpasar Airport (40 km/25 miles, transfer upon request).
RATES	Suites starting at US$ 475 per night, complete residences starting at US$ 2375 per night (including breakfast).
ROOMS	22 individually furnished suites in 5 residences (one private butler per house).
FOOD	International, with an Indonesian touch. Served in the residences or in "Biji" restaurant.
HISTORY	Built in 1999 by Debbie and Bradley Gardner.
X-FACTOR	Superlative hotel and spa with just a hint of spiritual.

Die vier Elemente

Es ist ein Hotel der Kategorie »Einmal im Leben« – und eines, auf das man sich mit ganzem Herzen einlassen muss. Die fünf Häuser, die im Dschungel hinter Ubud verborgen stehen, zwischen Reisterrassen und Wasserfällen, wirken auf den ersten Blick ein wenig unheimlich und wie eine Fata Morgana, die sich aufzulösen droht, sobald man die Hand nach ihr ausstreckt oder auch nur zu heftig ausatmet. Doch keine Sorge, das Holz aus Bali, der Stein aus Sumba, die Seide aus Thailand und das Porzellan aus China halten der Berührung durchaus stand und machen die fünf Gebäude zu Dschungelresidenzen de luxe. Und zu Orten, an denen die vier Elemente allgegenwärtig sind; als kühle Brise über der Veranda zum Beispiel, als private Feuerstelle, unbearbeiteter Stein oder scheinbar randloser Pool. Wer nach Begawan Giri Estate kommt, soll die Natur und sich selbst wiederfinden – und das nicht nur bei einsamen Yogastunden oder Meditationen. Ringsum das Anwesen verlaufen einige der schönsten Joggingstrecken der Insel, drei heilige Quellen liegen nur eine Wanderung entfernt, und im Spa »The Source« werden die Füße anschließend mit balinesischen Ölen massiert. Und wer weiß? Vielleicht belässt man es ja dann doch nicht bei »Einmal im Leben«...

Buchtipp: »Bali. Ein Paradies wird erfunden« von Adrian Vickers

Les quatre éléments

Cet hôtel fait partie de ceux dont on sait qu'on n'y séjournera qu'une fois dans sa vie et dont il faut savourer pleinement les journées. Les cinq bâtiments, cachés dans la jungle derrière la ville d'Ubud, entre les rizières et les cascades, suscitent au premier abord une impression bizarre, on dirait un mirage que l'on craint de voir s'évanouir si l'on a le malheur de tendre la main vers lui ou de respirer un peu trop fort. Mais n'ayez crainte le bois de Bali, la pierre de Sumba, la soie de Thaïlande et la porcelaine de Chine sont bien réels, transformant les cinq constructions en résidences de luxe. Et en lieux où les quatre éléments sont omniprésents : que ce soit sous la forme d'une légère brise soufflant sur la véranda, d'un feu de camp, de la pierre laissée à l'état brut ou de la piscine semblant dépourvue de bord. Celui qui vient à Begawan Giri Estate, doit redécouvrir la nature et se redécouvrir lui-même. Il y parviendra pendant les cours de yoga et de méditation, mais aussi par le biais du footing car quelques-unes des plus belles pistes de l'île entourent le complexe hôtelier. Trois sources sacrées se trouvent à quelques heures de marche seulement et dans le centre de remise en forme « The Source », les pieds bénéficieront d'un délicieux massage avec des huiles balinaises. Et qui sait ? peut-être reviendrons-nous...

Livre à emporter : « Bali et les petites îles de la Sonde » de Liz Capaldi, Joshua Eliot.

ANREISE	20 Fahrtminuten nördlich von Ubud gelegen, 1 Fahrtstunde vom Flughafen Denpasar entfernt (40 km, Transfer auf Wunsch).
PREIS	Suite ab 475 US$ pro Nacht, komplette Residenz ab 2375 US$ pro Nacht (inklusive Frühstück).
ZIMMER	22 individuell ausgestattete Suiten in 5 Residenzen (ein Privatbutler pro Haus).
KÜCHE	International, mit indonesischen Akzenten. Serviert in den Residenzen oder im Restaurant »Biji«.
GESCHICHTE	Von Debbie und Bradley Gardner 1999 gebaut.
X-FAKTOR	Hotel und Spa der Superlative; spirituell angehaucht.

ACCÈS	Situé à 20 min en voiture au nord d'Ubud, à 1 h en voiture de l'aéroport de Denpasar (40 km, transfert sur demande).
PRIX	Suite à partir de 475 $ US la nuit, résidence complète à partir de 2375 $ US la nuit (petit-déjeuner compris).
CHAMBRES	22 suites aménagées individuellement dans 5 résidences (un majordome par maison).
RESTAURATION	Internationale, teintée d'influences indonésiennes. Plats servis dans les résidences ou au restaurant « Biji ».
HISTOIRE	Construit en 1999 par Debbie et Bradley Gardner.
LE « PETIT PLUS »	Hôtel et centre de remise en forme pour lesquels on ne peut employer que des superlatifs.

A Living Room by the Sea...

The Barceló Pearl Farm Island Resort, Samal Island

The Barceló Pearl Farm Island Resort, Samal Island

A Living Room by the Sea

If you travel to the tropics and step from a propeller-driven plane onto a runway the size of a towel or step outside after having been in a thoroughly air-conditioned room, the blast of heat is often like a concrete wall. For seconds your air supply seems to have been shut off and if you close your eyes you feel like you are in a sauna where some eager punter has just poured more water onto the stones. Unless, that is, the trip happens to takes you to Samal Island. Here in the Gulf of Davao you immerse yourself in the warmth like in a large tub filled with gentle water and you inhale the scent of sea salt, exotic fruits and plants so green that the chlorophyll almost colours the air. The Barceló Pearl Farm Beach Resort is situated in this world of wonders and its most beautiful rooms can be found in the Samal House directly by the ocean. The houses were built based on the traditional stilt houses of the Samal seafarers. One glimpse of the colourful swarms of fish swimming through the crystal-clear water is enough to easily convince you that you will have no need for the television in the back room. On Samal Island, modern technology is just a concession to modern times; the rooms with their slight ethnic touch are intended primarily to reflect the beauty of their surroundings. Homes and nature are mostly linked by wooden footbridges and even by rope ladders – a more beautiful way of getting from the living room to the beach does not exist!

Book to pack: "Playing with Water" by James Hamilton-Paterson

The Barceló Pearl Farm Island Resort	
Kaputian, Island Garden City of Samal	
Davao del Norte, Philippines	
Tel. +63 (82) 221 99 70	
Fax +63 (82) 221 99 79	
Email: pearlfarm@barcelo-asia.com	
Website: www.barcelo-asia.com	
Booking: www.great-escapes-hotels.com	

DIRECTIONS	Samal Island is situated south of Manila at the Gulf of Davao, 1.5 hours by air and then 45 minutes by boat.
RATES	Double rooms starting at US$ 100 per night, Samal Suites starting at US$ 330 per night, Malipano Villas starting at US$ 560 per night (for 6 to 8 people).
ROOMS	19 Samal Houses with a total of 22 rooms, 6 Samal Suites, 41 rooms in the Balay, Mandaya and Hilltop Houses, 7 Malipano Villas.
FOOD	Typical Filipino, the seafood is particularly good.
HISTORY	Opened in December 1992. The spa "Ylang-Ylang Soothing Lounge" was added recently.
X-FACTOR	Experience the unspoilt Philippines and modern luxury.

Ein Wohnzimmer am Wasser

Wenn man in die Tropen reist und auf einem handtuch-
großen Rollfeld aus der Propellermaschine steigt oder aus
einem gut klimatisierten Hotelzimmer ins Freie tritt, trifft
einen die Hitze oft wie eine Betonwand. Für Sekunden
scheint die Luft zum Atmen abgedreht, und wer die Augen
schließt, fühlt sich in eine Sauna versetzt, in der ein besonders Schwitzbedürftiger eben erst einen Aufguss über die
Steine geschüttet hat. Es sei denn, die Reise führt nach
Samal Island. Hier, im Golf von Davao, versinkt man in der
Wärme wie in einer großen, mit weichem Wasser gefüllten
Wanne und atmet den Duft nach Meersalz, exotischen
Früchten und Pflanzen, die so sattgrün sind, dass das Chlo-
rophyll beinahe die Luft färbt. In dieser Wunderwelt steht
das Barceló Pearl Farm Beach Resort, dessen schönste
Unterkünfte, die Samal Houses, direkt am Ozean stehen.
Sie wurden den traditionellen Stelzenhäusern des Seefahrer-
stammes der Samal nachempfunden – wer den Blick auf
die bunten Fischschwärme, die durchs kristallklare Wasser
ziehen, einmal erlebt hat, könnte ohne weiteres auf den
Fernseher im rückwärtigen Zimmer verzichten. Moderne
Technik ist auf Samal Island ohnehin nur ein Zugeständnis
an moderne Zeiten, die Räume mit leichtem Ethno-Touch
sollen in erster Linie die Schönheit ihrer Umgebung wider-
spiegeln. Verbunden sind Häuser und Natur übrigens meist
über hölzerne Stege und sogar über Strickleitern – eine
schönere Art, vom Wohnzimmer zum Strand zu gelangen,
gibt es nicht!

Buchtipp: »Wasserspiele« von James Hamilton-Paterson

Un salon dans l'eau

Sous les Tropiques, le voyageur qui descend de l'avion à
hélices et se retrouve sur une piste grande comme un mou-
choir de poche ou qui sort de son hôtel climatisé se heurte
à la chaleur comme à un mur en béton. Pendant quelques
secondes, il a l'impression qu'il n'a plus d'air pour respirer,
et en fermant les yeux il lui semble se trouver dans un bain
de vapeur dont la température aurait été forcée par un visiteur trop bien intentionné. Celui qui se rend à Samal Island
ne connaît pas ces vicissitudes. Ici, dans le golfe de Davao,
la chaleur vous enveloppe comme l'eau tiède et douce dans
une grande baignoire, l'air marin est chargé de senteurs de
fruits exotiques et de plantes si vertes que la chlorophylle
semble colorer l'atmosphère.

Le Barceló Pearl Farm Resort est situé dans ce monde merveilleux, dont les plus belles résidences, les Samal Houses,
sont placées au bord de l'océan. Elles imitent les traditionnelles maisons sur pilotis des Samal, un peuple de naviga-
teurs. Celui qui a vu les bancs de poissons multicolores se
déplacer dans l'eau limpide peut renoncer sans regret au
téléviseur dont sa maison est équipée.

De toute façon, à Samal Island, la technologie moderne
n'est qu'une concession à l'époque actuelle, les pièces qui
montrent une légère touche ethno doivent avant tout refléter
la beauté de leur environnement. Du reste, les maisons et
la nature sont reliées le plus souvent par des passerelles en
bois et même en corde – il n'y a pas de plus belle manière
de passer du salon à la plage.

**Livre à emporter : « Le dieu volé et autres nouvelles »
de José Francisco Sionil**

ANREISE	Samal Island liegt im Golf von Davao, 1,5 Flugstunden und weitere 45 Bootsminuten südlich von Manila.
PREIS	Doppelzimmer ab 100 US$, Samal-Suite ab 330 US$, Malipano-Villa (diese für 6 bis 8 Personen) ab 560 US$.
ZIMMER	19 Samal Houses mit insgesamt 22 Zimmern, 6 Samal-Suiten, 41 Zimmer in den Balay, Mandaya und Hilltop Houses, 7 Malipano-Villen.
KÜCHE	Typisch philippinisch, besonders gut ist das Seafood.
GESCHICHTE	Im Dezember 1992 eröffnet. Seit kurzem auch mit dem Spa »Ylang-Ylang Soothing Lounge«.
X-FAKTOR	Die ursprünglichen Philippinen und modernen Luxus erleben.

ACCÈS	Samal Island est située dans le golfe de Davao, à 1 h ½ de vol et 45 min de bateau du sud de Manille.
PRIX	Chambre double à partir de 100 $ US, suite Samal à partir de 330 $ US, villa Malipano (6 à 8 pers), à par- tir de 560 $ US.
CHAMBRES	19 Samal Houses abritant 22 chambres, 6 suites Samal, 41 chambres dans les Balay, Mandaya et Hill- top Houses, 7 villas Malipano.
RESTAURATION	Cuisine traditionnelle philippine, les plats de poisson.
HISTOIRE	Ouvert en décembre 1992. Il abrite depuis peu de temps un centre de remise en forme « Ylang-Ylang Soothing Lounge ».
LE « PETIT PLUS »	Les Philippines traditionnelles avec le luxe moderne.

In the Shade of the Palms...

Whale Island Resort, Ile de la Baleine

Whale Island Resort,
Ile de la Baleine

In the Shade of the Palms

The Frenchman Michel Galey and his wife had just completed a taxing trekking tour through the highlands of Vietnam and were in need of a little peace and relaxation on level ground. They chartered a boat at Van Phong Bay, sailed through the bay northeast of Nha Trang and discovered their own personal paradise: Whale Island, a small private island with the best of what the tropics have to offer. Bays with white sandy beaches, palm trees whose leaves rustle in the wind and swimming in crystal-clear waters accompanied by swarms of tiny shining fish. As of 1997 visitors have been able to share this picture-book island with the couple: Whale Island has become an enchanting refuge in the truest sense of the word. The route through the coastal landscape would challenge even the most adept boy scout, which is why every new arrival is picked up in Nha Trang and brought to the pier in Dam Mon, where the boats depart for the brief final leg of the journey. On Whale Island you live in simple bungalows, whose apparent lack of comfort is more than made up for by an unforgettable view of the beach, the warm-heartedness of the hosts and the seafood cuisine – a vacation at your best friend's could not be better. Between mid-January and mid-October, divers in particular are in their watery element. The maritime life around the bay's reef is a dazzling display of colour. Jacques Cousteau is said to have discovered his love of diving here.

Book to pack: "The Girl in the Picture: The Story of Kim Phuc" by Denise Chong

Whale Island Resort	
Ile de la Baleine, Vietnam	
Tel. +84 (58) 84 05 01	
Fax +84 (58) 84 05 01	
Email: decouvrir@dng.vnn.vn or	
info@whaleislandresort.com	
Website: www.whaleislandresort.com	
Booking: www.great-escapes-hotels.com	

DIRECTIONS	Situated about 140 km/87 miles northeast of Nha Trang (the two-and-a-half hour transfer from the airport).
RATES	Double rooms US$110 per night (2 people, including full board). 3 nights cost US$245, 5 nights US$360 and 7 nights US$455. Group rates are available upon request.
ROOMS	20 bungalows directly on the beach, 5 budget rooms.
FOOD	Daily changing Vietnamese specialities; primarily seafood.
HISTORY	Opened in 1997 as a prime example of peaceful tourism.
X-FACTOR	Pure nature in an entirely private paradise.

Im Schatten der Palmen

Der Franzose Michel Galey und seine Frau hatten eine
anstrengende Trekkingtour durchs Hochland Vietnams hinter sich und wollten nur noch Ruhe und Erholung auf mög-
lichst ebener Fläche. An der Van Phong Bay charterten sie
ein Boot, segelten durch die Bucht nordöstlich von Nha
Trang – und entdeckten ihr ganz persönliches Paradies:
Whale Island, eine kleine Privatinsel mit dem Besten, was
die Tropen zu bieten haben. Buchten mit weißen Sandstränden, Palmen, deren Blätter im Wind rascheln, und kristall-
klares Wasser, in dem man beim Schwimmen von Schwär-
men winziger, leuchtend bunter Fische begleitet wird. Seit
1997 können Besucher diese Bilderbuchinsel mit den beiden
teilen: Whale Island ist ein zauberhaftes Refugium geworden – und das im wahrsten Sinne des Wortes. Die Anfahrt
durch die Küstenlandschaft überfordert selbst versierte
Pfadfinder, deshalb wird jeder Neuankömmling in Nha
Trang abgeholt und zum Pier von Dam Mon gebracht, wo
die Boote für die kurze Passage ablegen. Auf Whale Island
wohnt man in schlichten Bungalows, deren vermeintlich
fehlender Komfort durch einen unvergesslichen Blick über
den Strand, die Herzlichkeit der Gastgeber und die Seafood-
Küche mehr als wettgemacht wird – Ferien bei den besten
Freunden könnten nicht besser gelingen. Zwischen Mitte
Januar und Mitte Oktober sind hier vor allem Taucher im
nassen Element. Das maritime Leben rund um die Riffe der
Bucht ist ein Feuerwerk der Farben, schon Jacques Cousteau
soll hier seine Leidenschaft fürs Tauchen entdeckt haben.
**Buchtipp: »Das Mädchen hinter dem Foto. Die Geschichte der
Kim Phuc« von Denise Chong**

A l'ombre des palmiers

Le Français Michel Galey et sa femme ayant terminé leur
épuisant trekking à travers les hauts plateaux du Viêt-nam,
ne souhaitaient plus qu'une chose, trouver calme et détente,
dans un endroit plat si possible. Ils louèrent un bateau sur
la baie Van Phong, naviguèrent au nord-est de Nha Trang et
découvrirent leur paradis : l'Ile de la Baleine, une petite île
privée, qui offraient tous les charmes des tropiques. Criques
aux plages de sable blanc, cocotiers crissant sous le vent et
des eaux limpides dans lesquelles des multitudes de poissons minuscules et multicolores accompagnent le nageur.
Depuis 1997, les deux Français partagent leur île de carte
postale avec les visiteurs. L'Ile de la Baleine est devenue un
véritable refuge car il faut dire que l'accès par la côte décou-
ragerait même des randonneurs chevronnés. Les nouveaux
venus sont attendus à Nha Trang et conduits jusqu'à la jetée
de Dam Mon où sont ancrés les bateaux qui effectuent la tra-
versée. A l'Ile de la Baleine, le client habite dans de simples
bungalows dont l'apparente rusticité est compensée au cen-
tuple par une vue inoubliable sur la plage, l'accueil chaleu-
reux des hôtes et la cuisine de fruits de mer. Des vacances
chez des amis ne se passeraient pas dans de meilleures
conditions. Entre la mi-janvier et la mi-octobre, les plon-
geurs peuvent s'en donner à cœur joie. Les fonds marins
autour des récifs offrent un feu d'artifice de couleurs, et
c'est ici que Jacques Cousteau aurait découvert sa passion
pour la plongée sous-marine.
Livre à emporter : « La fille de la photo » de Denise Chong

ANREISE	Rund 140 km nordöstlich von Nha Trang gelegen (zwei-einhalbstündiger Transfer ab dem Flughafen).
PREIS	Doppelzimmer 110 US$ pro Nacht (2 Personen, inklusive Vollpension). 3 Nächte kosten 245 US$, 5 Nächte 360 US$ und 7 Nächte 455 US$. Gruppenpreise auf Anfrage.
ZIMMER	20 Bungalows direkt am Strand, 5 Economy Rooms.
KÜCHE	Täglich wechselnde vietnamesische Spezialitäten, vor allem Seafood.
GESCHICHTE	1997 als Musterbeispiel für sanften Tourismus eröffnet.
X-FAKTOR	Natur pur im ganz privaten Paradies.

ACCÈS	Situé à 140 km environ au nord-est de Nha Trang (le transfert de deux heures et demie depuis l'aéroport).
PRIX	Chambre double 110 $ US la nuit (2 personnes en pension complète). 3 nuits coûtent 245 $ US, 5 nuits 360 $ US et 7 nuits 455 $ US. Prix de groupe sur demande.
CHAMBRES	20 bungalows donnant directement sur la plage, 5 Economic Rooms.
RESTAURATION	Tous les jours différentes spécialités vietnamiennes, en particulier fruits de mer.
HISTOIRE	Construit en 1997, l'hôtel est un exemple de tourisme modéré.
LE « PETIT PLUS »	Un petit paradis privé où la nature est reine.

On Mao's Trail...
Red Capital Club & Residence, Beijing

Red Capital Club & Residence, Beijing

On Mao's Trail

The impression you get in the Chairman's Suite is that Mao has only just left the building. Black-and-white photos of his family hang on the wall; his favourite books fill the shelves and an Art Deco lamp from his house in Zhongnanhai adorns one corner. It is almost a disappointment when the doors open and the man who was once China's most powerful leader does not walk back into the room. But despite his absence, the Red Capital Club still exudes the complete communist flair of the 1950s. The house in Beijing's Dongsi quarter is in the style of the private residences which were sought after by leading politicians after 1949 as their pieds-à-terre of choice, and the five suites are furnished in impressive detail. The concubines' rooms are to the right and left of the Chairman's Suite; they seem to consist almost entirely of beds and are furnished with antiques from the Qing Dynasty. Two other suites are dedicated to the Chinese writer Han Suiyin and Edgar Snow respectively. The former political elite of the country also makes an appearance in the restaurant whose "Zhongnanhai cuisine" includes Mao's favourite dishes. Even when embarking on excursions into the city, you follow in Mao's tracks. Or to put it more accurately, in his tracks – because the stretch-limousine that once used to chauffeur Madame Mao and which is the only existing car of this type left, is today available for the exclusive use of hotel guests. All seven metres of it including red flags, champagne and Russian caviar.

Book to pack: "The Private Life of Chairman Mao: The Memoirs of Mao's Personal Physician" by Li Zhi-Sui

Red Capital Club & Residence	
No. 9 Dongsi Liutiao	
Dongcheng District	
Beijing 100007, China	
Tel. +86 (10) 64 02 71 50	
Fax +86 (10) 64 02 71 53	
Email: info@redcapitalclub.com.cn	
Website: www.redcapitalclub.com	
Booking: www.great-escapes-hotels.com	

DIRECTIONS	Situated in Beijing's Dongsi quarter, 30 minutes from the airport.
RATES	Author's Suites starting at US$138 per night, Concubine's Suites and Chairman's Suites starting at US$175 per night.
ROOMS	2 Author's Suites, 2 Concubine's Suites, 1 Chairman's Suite.
FOOD	"Zhongnanhai cuisine". In other words: Mao's favourite foods and everything that was once served up at state banquets.
HISTORY	This former residence for leading politicians has been a small hotel since 1 July 2001.
X-FACTOR	Living like the socialist political elite.

Auf Maos Spuren

Die Chairman's Suite wirkt, als hätte Mao nur eben kurz den Raum verlassen – an der Wand hängen Schwarz-Weiß-Aufnahmen seiner Familie, im Regal stehen seine Lieblingsbücher und eine Ecke ziert eine Art-déco-Lampe aus seinem Haus in Zhongnanhai. Man ist fast enttäuscht, wenn die Türe aufgeht und nicht der einst mächtigste Mann Chinas ins Zimmer zurückkehrt; doch der Red Capital Club verbreitet auch ohne ihn das vollendet kommunistische Flair der fünfziger Jahre. Das Haus im Dongsi-Viertel von Peking knüpft an die Tradition der Privatresidenzen an, die sich führende Politiker nach 1949 als bevorzugte Adressen aussuchten, und hat fünf Suiten, die mit unvorstellbarer Liebe zum Detail eingerichtet sind. Rechts und links der Chairman's Suite liegen die Zimmer der Konkubinen, die fast nur aus Betten zu bestehen scheinen und für die man Antiquitäten aus der Qing-Dynastie auftrieb. Zwei weitere Suiten wurden dem chinesischen Schriftsteller Han Suiyin sowie Edgar Snow gewidmet. Präsent ist die einstige politische Elite des Landes auch im Restaurant, hinter dessen »Zhongnanhai Cuisine« sich die Lieblingsgerichte Maos verbergen, und selbst Ausflüge durch die Stadt unternimmt man auf Maos Spuren. Besser gesagt, in seiner Spur – denn die sieben Meter lange Stretch-Limousine, in der sich Madame Mao chauffieren ließ und die der einzige noch existierende Wagen dieses Typs ist, steht heute exklusiv den Gästen des Hauses zur Verfügung. Inklusive roter Flagge, Champagner und russischem Kaviar.

Buchtipp: »Ich war Maos Leibarzt« von Zhi-Sui Li

Sur les traces de Mao

En pénétrant dans la suite présidentielle, on a l'impression que Mao vient juste de quitter la pièce : des photographies en noir et blanc de sa famille sont encore accrochées au mur, ses livres préférés reposent sur l'étagère et une lampe Art déco provenant de sa maison à Zhongnanhai orne un coin de la salle. Quand la porte s'ouvre, on est presque déçu de ne pas se retrouver face à l'homme qui fut, à son époque, le plus puissant de la Chine. Pourtant, même en l'absence de celui-ci, l'atmosphère du communisme des années cinquante plane encore sur le Red Capital Club. La maison située dans le quartier Dongsi de Pékin se rattache à la tradition des résidences privées, particulièrement prisées des hommes politiques à partir de 1949. Ses cinq suites sont aménagées avec un amour du détail particulièrement étonnant. A droite et à gauche de la suite présidentielle se trouvent les chambres des concubines qui semblent n'être composées que de lits et pour lesquelles on dénicha des antiquités de la dynastie des Qing. Deux autres suites ont été dédiées à l'écrivain chinois Han Suiyin et à Edgar Snow. Le grand timonier est également présent dans la salle de restaurant puisque la « Zhongnanhai Cuisine » propose ses plats préférés. Même lors des excursions à travers la ville, il convient de partir sur les traces de Mao. Ou à la place de ce dernier, devrait-on dire, car la longue limousine de sept mètres, qui servait jadis aussi à Madame Mao et qui est la seule automobile de ce type à exister encore, se tient exclusivement à la disposition des clients de la maison. Petit drapeau rouge, champagne et caviar russe compris.

Livre à emporter : « La vie privée du président Mao » de Zhi-Sui Li

ANREISE	Im Dongsi-Viertel Pekings gelegen, 30 Fahrtminuten vom Flughafen entfernt.
PREIS	Author's-Suite ab 138 US$ pro Nacht, Concubine's-Suite und Chairman's-Suite ab 175 US$ pro Nacht.
ZIMMER	2 Author's-Suiten, 2 Concubine's-Suiten, 1 Chairman's-Suite.
KÜCHE	»Zhongnanhai Cuisine«. Übersetzt: Maos Leibspeisen und alles, was einst bei Staatsbanketten auf den Tisch kam.
GESCHICHTE	Die ehemalige Residenz führender Politiker ist seit 1. Juli 2001 ein kleines Hotel.
X-FAKTOR	Wohnen wie die politische Elite des Sozialismus.

ACCÈS	Situé dans le quartier Dongsi de Pékin à 30 min en voiture de l'aéroport.
PRIX	Author's suite à partir de 138 $ US la nuit, Concubine's suite et Chairman's suite à partir de 175 $ US la nuit.
CHAMBRES	2 Author's suites, 2 Concubine's suites, 1 Chairman's suite.
RESTAURATION	« Zhongnanhai Cuisine » : les plats préférés de Mao et tous les plats servis lors des banquets de l'Etat.
HISTOIRE	Depuis le 1er juillet 2001, l'ancienne résidence des personnalités politiques est devenue un petit hôtel.
LE « PETIT PLUS »	Résider comme l'élite politique à l'époque du communisme.

The Fount of Knowledge...
Asaba, Shizuoka-ken

Asaba, Shizuoka-ken

The Fount of Knowledge

There are these photos with three or four men sitting in a steaming Japanese pool and somehow they manage to look both bored and extremely pleased. Since they are mostly somewhat advanced in years, you get the impression that you would have to spend your entire life training for such a facial expression – but sometimes just a few days are all you need. For example, on the peninsula of Izu where Japan's oldest thermal springs bubble and the Hotel Asaba was already accommodating spa guests long before the term "wellness oasis" was invented. In 1675 the Asaba family opened their small house in the midst of a bamboo forest and on the banks of a pool upon whose surface the building almost seems to float. Today, as in the past, what counts here are clear design, simple forms and colours – they supplement the surrounding nature which looks like it has been softly sketched and bring out its mysticism perfectly. Rugged rocks from the region surround the outer pool; the rooms and baths are also furnished with local materials, and from every room you have a view of the surrounding vegetation. If the natural spectacle is not enough for you, then attend a theatre evening on the floating stage – the traditional dances and lyrical dramas beneath a star-studded sky are magical. And after a few days you will have attained that pleasant, celestial state – as proof, a single photo is all that you will need. The photo will show a person who looks both bored and extremely pleased.

Book to pack: "The Dancing Girl of Izu" by Yasunari Kawabata, "Memoirs of a Geisha" by Arthur Golden

Asaba	
3450–1 Shuzenji-Machi	
Shizuoka-ken 410–2416	
Japan	
Tel. +81 (558) 72 70 00	
Fax +81 (558) 72 70 77	
Email: asaba@relaischateaux.com	
Website: www.relaischateaux.com	
Booking: www.great-escapes-hotels.com	

DIRECTIONS	Situated in the north of the peninsula of Izu, 200 km/124 miles southwest of Tokyo-Narita Airport.
RATES	Rooms starting at US$ 800 per night (2 people, including breakfast and dinner).
ROOMS	15 rooms, 4 suites.
FOOD	Traditional Japanese dishes prepared from regional ingredients.
HISTORY	Opened in 1675 as a small inn and has been one of the most beautiful thermal hotels in Japan ever since.
X-FACTOR	Where simple hot water equals happiness.

Die Quelle der Erkenntnis

Es gibt diese Bilder, auf denen drei oder vier Männer in einem dampfenden japanischen Becken sitzen und es irgendwie schaffen, zugleich gelangweilt und ungeheuer zufrieden dreinzuschauen. Ihr meist etwas höheres Alter lässt den Eindruck entstehen, man müsse für diesen Gesichtsausdruck ein Leben lang trainieren – dabei genügen manchmal wenige Tage. Zum Beispiel auf der Halbinsel Izu, wo die ältesten Thermalquellen Japans sprudeln und das Hotel Asaba schon Kurgäste empfing, als der Begriff Wellness-Oase noch gar nicht erfunden war: 1675 eröffnete die Familie Asaba das kleine Haus inmitten eines Bambuswaldes und am Ufer eines Teichs, über dessen Wasserfläche die Gebäude fast zu schweben scheinen. Damals wie heute zählen hier klares Design, einfache Formen und Farben – sie ergänzen die umliegende Natur, die stets wie weichgezeichnet wirkt, und bringen ihre Mystik perfekt zur Geltung. Unbearbeitete Felsen aus der Gegend umrahmen die Außenbecken, auch die Zimmer und Bäder sind mit einheimischen Materialien ausgestattet, und man blickt von jedem Raum aus ins Grüne. Wem das natürliche Schauspiel nicht genügt, der besucht einen Theaterabend auf der schwimmenden Bühne – die traditionellen Tänze und Singspiele unterm Sternenhimmel sind Magie. Und nach ein paar Tagen hat man dann jenen angenehmen, gleichsam sphärischen Zustand erreicht, für dessen Beweis ein einziges Foto genügt: Das Bild zeigt einen Menschen, der zugleich gelangweilt und ungeheuer zufrieden dreinschaut.

Buchtipps: »Die Tänzerin von Izu« von Yasunari Kawabata, »Die Geisha« von Arthur Golden

Aux sources de la félicité

Qui ne connaît pas ces photos sur lesquelles on peut voir, assis dans un bain de vapeur japonais, trois ou quatre hommes, dont les visages expriment à la fois l'ennui et un contentement suprême ? Puisqu'ils sont en général d'un grand âge, on peut être amené à penser qu'ils ont dû s'exercer toute leur vie pour obtenir cette expression particulière – mais parfois quelques jours seulement suffisent. Par exemple sur l'archipel d'Izu où jaillissent les plus anciennes sources thermales du Japon et où l'hôtel Asaba accueillait déjà des curistes alors que le mot « wellness » n'existait pas encore. C'est en 1675 que la famille Asaba ouvrit la petite maison située au milieu d'une forêt de bambous et au bord d'un étang au-dessus duquel les bâtiments paraissent presque flotter. Aujourd'hui comme hier le design sobre, les formes simples et les couleurs sont de la plus haute importance – ils complètent la nature environnante, dont les contours semblent toujours quelque peu estompés, et mettent parfaitement en valeur son côté mystique. Des rochers non travaillés provenant des environs encadrent les bassins extérieurs, les chambres et les salles de bains sont décorées avec des matériaux de la région, et chaque pièce offre une vue sur la verdure. Celui qui ne peut se contenter de ce spectacle de la nature, ira à une soirée théâtrale donnée sur la scène flottante – les danses et les pièces chantées traditionnelles sont magiques sous le ciel étoilé. Au bout de quelques jours, on atteint alors cet état de félicité et la photo prise à ce moment montre un visage à la fois ennuyé et extrêmement satisfait.

Livres à emporter : « La Danseuse d'Izu » de Yasunari Kawabata, « Geisha » de Arthur Golden

ANREISE	Im Norden der Halbinsel Izu gelegen, 200 km südwestlich des Flughafens Tokio-Narita.
PREIS	Zimmer ab 800 US$ pro Nacht (2 Personen, inklusive Frühstück und Dinner).
ZIMMER	15 Zimmer, 4 Suiten.
KÜCHE	Klassische japanische Gerichte aus regionalen Zutaten.
GESCHICHTE	1675 als kleines Gasthaus eröffnet und seitdem eines der schönsten Thermenhotels in Japan.
X-FAKTOR	Wo einfaches heißes Wasser glücklich macht.

ACCÈS	Situé au nord de l'archipel d'Izu, à 200 km au sud-ouest de l'aéroport de Tokyo-Narita.
PRIX	Chambre à partir de 800 $ US la nuit (2 personnes, petit-déjeuner et dîner compris).
CHAMBRES	15 chambres, 4 suites.
RESTAURATION	Plats japonais classiques préparés avec des produits de la région.
HISTOIRE	Petite auberge ouverte en 1675, elle est devenue l'un des plus beaux hôtels thermaux du Japon.
LE « PETIT PLUS »	Incroyable comme un peu d'eau chaude peut rendre heureux.

South America

Brazil • Uruguay
Argentina • Chile

Photos by Tuca Reinés   *Text by* Christiane Reiter   *Edited by* Angelika Taschen

"There are no foreign lands. It is the traveler only who is foreign."
Robert Louis Stevenson

Pousada Maravilha **420**

Pousada do Quadrado **430**
Estrela d'Água **440**

explora en Atacama **534**

Bodega El Esteco de Cafayate **464**

Hotel Casa Real **522**

456 Posada La Bonita

472 Dos Lunas

Estancia Ancón **480**

448 La Posada Aguaverde

La Pascuala Delta Lodge **484**

492 Estancia La Candelaria

500 Ten Rivers & Ten Lakes Lodge

Estancia Arroyo Verde **504**

514 Los Notros

The play of light...
Pousada Maravilha, Fernando de Noronha

Pousada Maravilha,
Fernando de Noronha

The play of light

When Portuguese merchant Fernando de Noronha discovered the 21-island archipelago off the north-eastern coast of
Brazil in 1503, he took little interest in it – after a cursory
inspection of the bizarre formations of volcanic rock, he took
to the ocean again, looking for greater adventures. Others
who followed him stayed longer, though not always of their
own free will – in the 18th century the main island was
made a penal colony, and around 1930 a gaol for political
prisoners was established. In the Second World War it was
an air base, and in the Sixties a NASA satellite observation
post. Tourism did not take off till Fernando de Noronha was
declared a nature reserve in 1988. Since then, it has earned
a name as one of Brazil's best diving areas, celebrated for
its dolphins and turtles in particular. Those who aren't so
interested in the underwater world, but are happy to enjoy a
unique experience on dry land, will relish a stay at the Pousada Maravilha. The eight bungalows blend in naturally with
their setting by a magical bay – the wood replicates the hues
of the rocks, the pool picks up the blue of the sky and the
ocean. Relax on cream futons or gently swaying hammocks.
The occasional strong notes of colour – cushions or crockery
– are the only added extras the design permits itself; otherwise, a purist tone is dominant, showing in the most appea-
ling of ways just how well the simple life and luxury can go
together.
Book to pack: "The Lizard's Smile" by João Ubaldo Ribeiro

Pousada Maravilha

BR 363, S/N – Sueste
Fernando de Noronha, PE
Brazil
CEP 53990 000
Tel. (55) 8136191290
Fax (55) 8136190028
E-mail: pousadamaravilha@hotmail.com
Website: www.pousadamaravilha.com.br
Booking: www.great-escapes-hotels.com

DIRECTIONS	350 km/225 miles off the north-east coast of Brazil, with daily flights from Natal and Recife.
RATES	Bungalow US$ 420 for 2 persons, apartment from US$ 360 for 2 persons (US$ 560 for 4). Breakfast included.
ROOMS	5 bungalows for 2 people, 3 apartments for 4 people max.
FOOD	A delightful restaurant serving Mediterranean speciali-ties. Room service is available.
HISTORY	The first luxury hideaway on Fernando de Noronha.
X-FACTOR	Purist design hotel affording plenty of privacy.

Lichterspiele

Als der portugiesische Kaufmann Fernando de Noronha das Archipel mit 21 Inseln vor der Nordostküste Brasiliens 1503 entdeckte, interessierte es ihn kaum – nach wenigen Blicken auf das bizarr geformte Vulkangestein stach er wieder in See und segelte vermeintlich größeren Abenteuern entgegen. Andere, die nach ihm kamen, hielten es länger aus – wenn auch nicht immer ganz freiwillig: Im 18. Jahrhundert wurde die Hauptinsel zur Strafkolonie, um 1930 richtete man hier ein politisches Gefängnis ein. Im Zweiten Weltkrieg diente sie als Luftwaffenstützpunkt und in den sechziger Jahren als Satellitenbeobachtungsposten der NASA. Der Tourismus begann erst, als Fernando de Noronha 1988 zum Naturschutzgebiet erklärt wurde – seitdem gilt es als eines der besten Tauchreviere Brasiliens und ist vor allem für seine Delfine und Meeresschildkröten berühmt. Wer sich nicht nur für die Unterwasserwelt interessiert, sondern auch an Land Einzigartiges erleben möchte, zieht am besten in die Pousada Maravilha. An einer zauberhaften Bucht passen sich die acht Bungalows wie selbstverständlich ihrer Umgebung an – das Holz nimmt den Farbton der Felsen auf, der Pool scheint direkt ins Blau von Himmel und Meer zu fließen, man entspannt auf cremefarbenen Futons oder in sanft schwingenden Hängematten. Ein paar Farbtupfer – Kissen oder Geschirr – sind die einzigen Extras, die sich das Design gönnt; ansonsten dominiert hier der Purismus und zeigt auf angenehmste Weise, wie gut *simple life* und Luxus zusammenpassen können.

Buchtipp: »Das Lächeln der Eidechse« von João Ubaldo Ribeiro

Jeux de lumière

Lorsque le marchand portugais Fernando de Noronha a découvert en 1503 cet archipel qui fait face à la côte nord-est du Brésil, on ne peut pas dire que les 21 îles l'aient captivé. Après avoir jeté quelques coups d'œil sur les roches volcaniques aux formes bizarres, il leva l'ancre et s'en alla vers de nouvelles aventures. D'autres sont venus après lui, mais ceux-là sont restés plus longtemps, et pas toujours de leur plein gré : au 18e siècle, en effet, l'île principale devint un pénitencier, en 1930 on y construisit une prison politique. Au cours de la Deuxième Guerre mondiale, elle a servi de base aérienne et dans les années 60, la N.A.S.A. y a installé un poste d'observation de satellites. Et puis Fernando de Norhona a été déclaré site naturel protégé, et le tourisme a fait son apparition. Aujourd'hui, l'endroit est considéré comme l'une des meilleures zones de plongée du Brésil et il est renommé pour ses dauphins et ses tortues de mer. La Pousada Maravilha est faite pour ceux qui non seulement s'intéressent au monde sous-marin mais aussi aux richesses uniques de la terre ferme. Les huit bungalows s'harmonisent tout naturellement avec le paysage de la baie superbe qui les entoure – le bois prend la couleur des rochers, la piscine semble couler dans le bleu du ciel et de la mer ; les futons couleur crème et les hamacs qui oscillent doucement sont propices à la détente. Les quelques accents de couleur des coussins et de la vaisselle sont les seuls « manquements » au design délibérément puriste qui montre avec beaucoup de charme combien la simplicité et le luxe font bon ménage.

Livre à emporter : « Le sourire du lézard » de João Ubaldo Ribeiro

ANREISE	350 Kilometer vor Brasiliens Nordostküste gelegen, tägliche Flüge ab Natal und Recife.	ACCÈS	Situé à 350 kilomètres de la côte nord-est du Brésil, vols journaliers à partir de Natal et Recife.
PREISE	Bungalow US$ 420 für 2 Personen, Apartment ab US$ 360 für 2 Personen (bei Belegung mit 4 Personen US$ 560). Mit Frühstück.	PRIX	Bungalow US$ 420 pour 2 personnes, appartement à partir de US$ 360 pour 2 personnes (pour 4 personnes US$ 560). Petit-déjeuner inclus.
ZIMMER	5 Bungalows für 2 Personen, 3 Apartments für maximal 4 Personen.	CHAMBRES	5 bungalows pour 2 personnes, 3 appartements pour 4 personnes maximum.
KUCHE	Schönes Restaurant mit mediterranen Spezialitäten, Zimmerservice möglich.	RESTAURATION	Le beau restaurant offre des spécialités méditerranéennes, service de chambre possible.
GESCHICHTE	Das erste Luxus-Hideaway auf Fernando de Noronha.	HISTOIRE	Le premier « refuge » de luxe sur Fernando de Noronha.
X-FAKTOR	Puristisches Designhotel mit viel Privatsphäre.	LE « PETIT PLUS »	Le goût de la simplicité et beaucoup d'intimité.

A hideaway in the greenery...
Pousada do Quadrado, Bahia

Pousada do Quadrado, Bahia

A hideaway in the greenery

"Architects are advisors, not dictators," says Sig Bergamin, who in recent years has made himself a name as a designer far beyond São Paolo and Brazil. To hire him is to look forward not to some cool and impersonal work of art but to a house tailored to an individual personality – with a European influence here, or an Asian quotation there, but always familiar. So too with what was formerly the Hotel do Praça in Trancoso, which Sig Bergamin transformed into the Pousada do Quadrado in December 2001. Close to the centre of what was once a Jesuit settlement, the architect has created a retreat brimful of all Bahia's charm – two apartments and eleven suites, no two of them alike. You can relax on beds made in white and red, or on cheerfully striped cushions, and admire the finely woven table runner, wooden or straw artwork, or immense baskets of fruit. For all the arresting details, the rooms are so spacious and airy that you feel you hardly need go out – if it weren't that the tropical wonderland and inviting terraces had stolen a special place in your heart. The easy-going style of Bahia is also in evidence in the restaurant, chef Letícia Pimenta may have cooked in celebrated restaurants around the world, but her international menus always have a local touch and the wines served are South American. The best way to conclude the evening is with music and drinks in the bar – both similarly from Brazil's loveliest state, of course.

**Book to pack: "Dona Flor and her Two Husbands"
by Jorge Amado**

Pousada do Quadrado	
Trancoso	
Bahia	
Brazil	
Tel. (55) 73 6681808 and 6681811	
E-mail: infopousadadoquadrado@ pousadadoquadrado.com.br	
Website: www.pousadadoquadrado.com.br	
Booking: www.great-escapes-hotels.com	
DIRECTIONS	Situated 40 km/25 miles south of Porto Seguro international airport. Transfer by road, or by ferry (Porto Seguro-Arraial d'Ajuda) and road.
RATES	Apartments from US$ 50 for 2 persons, suites from US$ 70 for 2.
ROOMS	2 apartments, 11 suites.
FOOD	International cuisine with a Brazilian touch in the Restaurant do Jacaré.
HISTORY	The former Hotel do Praça was transformed into the Pousada do Quadrado in 2001.
X-FACTOR	Living in the new old style of Bahia.

Ein Versteck im Grünen

»Architekten sind Berater, keine Diktatoren«, sagt Sig Bergamin, der sich in den vergangenen Jahren weit über die Grenzen São Paolos und Brasiliens einen Namen als Designer gemacht hat. Wer ihn engagiert, bekommt kein kühles und fremd wirkendes Kunstwerk, sondern ein Haus, das seiner Persönlichkeit entspricht – vielleicht mit europäischem Einfluss hier, vielleicht mit einem asiatischen Zitat dort, aber immer vertraut. So auch das ehemalige Hotel do Praça in Trancoso, das Sig Bergamin im Dezember 2001 in die Pousada do Quadrado verwandelte. Nahe des Zentrums der einstigen Jesuitensiedlung hat der Architekt eine Adresse mit dem ganzen Charme Bahias geschaffen – zwei Apartments und elf Suiten, von denen keine der anderen gleicht. Man entspannt zum Beispiel auf weiß-rot bezogenen Betten oder Kissen im fröhlichen Streifenlook, bewundert fein gewebte Tischläufer, Kunst aus Holz und Stroh oder riesige Obstkörbe. Bei allen Details sind die Räume so voller Luft und Weite, dass man fast darauf verzichten könnte, ins Freie zu gehen – würden draußen nicht ein tropisches Wunderland und große Terrassen warten, die zu echten Lieblingsplätzen avancieren. Der unbeschwerte Stil von Bahia lässt sich auch im Restaurant nicht verleugnen: Küchenchefin Letícia Pimenta stand zwar schon in berühmten Lokalen in fernen Ländern am Herd, verbindet ihre internationalen Menüs aber immer mit einheimischem Touch und serviert südamerikanische Weine dazu. Am schönsten klingt der Abend dann in der Bar aus, bei Musik und Drinks – beides selbstverständlich ebenfalls aus Brasiliens schönstem Bundesstaat.

Buchtipp: »Dona Flor und ihre zwei Ehemänner« von Jorge Amado

Bahia de tous les sens

« Les architectes sont des conseillers, pas des dictateurs », dit le designer pauliste Sig Bergamin qui s'est fait un nom bien au-delà des frontières du Brésil ces dernières années. Celui qui l'engage n'obtient pas une œuvre d'art froide, étrangère à son propriétaire, mais une maison correspondant à sa personnalité – avec peut-être une influence européenne ici, une citation asiatique là, mais toujours familière. L'ancien Hotel do Praça à Trancoso que Sig Benjamin a transformé en Pousada do Quadrado en décembre 2001 ne fait pas exception à la règle.

L'architecte a créé à proximité du cœur de l'ancienne cité jésuite une maison qui possède tout le charme de Bahia – deux appartements et onze suites toutes différentes les unes des autres. On se détend par exemple sur des lits habillés de rouge et de blanc ou sur des coussins joyeusement rayés, on admire des nappes de toile fine, des objets d'art en bois et en paille ou des corbeilles de fruits gigantesques. Les pièces sont si spacieuses et si aérées qu'on est presque tenté de rester à l'intérieur – mais des merveilles tropicales attendent dehors et de vastes terrasses, rapidement devenues des endroits de repos privilégiés.

Le restaurant subit lui aussi avec bonheur l'influence insouciante de Bahia : le chef Letícia Pimenta a été formée à la gastronomie dans les restaurants les plus fameux du monde, mais ses menus internationaux ne renient pas les saveurs brésiliennes et les plats sont accompagnés de vins sud-américains. La soirée s'achève au bar, à écouter de la musique bahianaise en dégustant des boissons régionales, cela va de soit.

Livre à emporter : « Dona Flor et ses deux maris » de Jorge Amado

ANREISE	40 Kilometer südlich des Internationalen Flughafens Porto Seguro gelegen. Transfer per Fähre (Porto Seguro-Arraial d'Ajuda) und Auto oder nur per Auto.
PREISE	Apartment ab US$ 50 für 2 Personen, Suite ab US$ 70 für 2 Personen.
ZIMMER	2 Apartments, 11 Suiten.
KÜCHE	Internationale Gerichte mit brasilianischem Touch im Restaurant do Jacaré.
GESCHICHTE	Aus dem ehemaligen Hotel do Praça wurde 2001 die Pousada do Quadrado.
X-FAKTOR	Wohnen im neuen alten Stil Bahias.

ACCÈS	Situé à 40 kilomètres au sud de l'aéroport international de Porto Seguro. Transfert par ferry (Porto Seguro-Arraial d'Ajuda) et voiture ou seulement par voiture.
PRIX	Appartement à partir de US$ 50 pour 2 personnes, suite à partir de US$ 70 pour 2 personnes.
CHAMBRES	2 appartements, 11 suites.
RESTAURATION	Cuisine internationale avec un accent brésilien au Restaurant do Jacaré.
HISTOIRE	L'ancien Hotel do Praça est devenu la Pousada do Quadrado en 2001.
LE « PETIT PLUS »	Le charme du vieux Bahia.

Blue peace and tranquillity...
Estrela d'Água, Bahia

Estrela d'Água, Bahia

Blue peace and tranquillity

Trancoso has always been a place of refuge. The small town was founded in the mid-16th century by Jesuits wanting to afford the indigenous peoples some protection from the colonial conquerors. In the Seventies the hippies and drop-outs discovered it, finding in this tranquil settlement between the ocean and the rain forest the perfect antidote to the bustle of São Paulo. And then there were the artists, seeking inspiration in the light and magic of this coast. Travellers can find happiness here too. Trancoso has miles of perfect beaches, among the finest in all Brazil, and it also has the Estrela d'Água – a Pousada that is virtually paradise. Right on the famous Praia dos Nativos in grounds of 23,000 square metres (247,500 square feet) studded with palms and pink hibiscus, it has suites and chalets with all the cheery charm of the Bahia. To gaze at the pool and the ocean is to discover whole new unguessed-at shades of blue. You stroll down steps with gleaming red or blue rails, relax on turquoise sofas, and recline on cushions patterned with sun-yellow flowers. But there's no risk of colour overkill, thanks to the quiet tonalities of the understated interiors – dark parquet and dark wood, plain lines and plain materials, lots of room and plenty of space. If anywhere could possibly be better to relax than the hammock, it can only be the spacious veranda, dappled by sunlight through the roof that leaves magical patterns of stripes on the seats and recliners. And if you really do need movement, there are fitness or yoga classes, a tennis court close by, or of course the blue Atlantic to go diving in.

Book to pack: "The Brazilians" by Joseph A. Page

Estrela d'Água	
Estrada Arraial d'Ajuda-Trancoso	
Trancoso – Porto Seguro	
Bahia	
Brazil	
CEP 45 818 000	
Tel. and fax (55) 73 6681030	
E-mail: estreladagua@uol.com.br	
Website: www.estreladagua.com.br	
Booking: www.great-escapes-hotels.com	

DIRECTIONS	Situated 40 km/25 miles south of Porto Seguro international airport. Transfer by ferry (Porto Seguro-Arrial d'Ajuda) and road or by road only. There is a heliport 10 km/6 miles from the hotel.
RATES	Suite for 2 from US$ 120. Breakfast included. The "Hibisco" chalet sleeps up to 6 persons, from US$ 195.
ROOMS	14 suites, 2 master suites, 2 chalets.
FOOD	The restaurant has a dream veranda and serves mainly regional cuisine.
HISTORY	A beach resort in a former drop-out heaven.
X-FACTOR	The colours are simply unbelievable!

Blaue Pause

Ein Fluchtpunkt war Trancoso schon immer: Mitte des
16. Jahrhunderts gründeten Jesuiten den kleinen Ort am
Atlantik, um den Indianern Schutz vor den Kolonialherren
zu bieten, in den 70ern kamen die Aussteiger und Hippies,
die in der Kolonie zwischen Meer und Regenwald Abstand
zum lauten Leben von São Paulo suchten, und schließlich
die Künstler, die sich von Licht und Magie der Küste Inspiration erhofften. Auch Reisende können hier ihr Glück finden: Trancoso besitzt kilometerlange Traumstrände, die zu
den schönsten Brasiliens gehören, und die Estrela d'Água –
eine Pousada wie ein Paradies. Direkt an der berühmten
Praia dos Nativos und auf 23.000m² voller Palmen und
pink leuchtendem Hibiskus gelegen, besitzt sie Suiten und
Chalets mit dem fröhlichen Charme von Bahia. Der Blick
auf Pool und Meer erweitert die Farbpalette »blau« um nie
geahnte Nuancen, man läuft Treppen mit strahlend rot
oder blau gestrichenem Geländer hinauf, entspannt auf türkisfarbenen Sofas und lehnt in Kissen mit sonnengelben
Blumenmotiven. Dafür, dass die vielen Farbtupfer keine
Farbblindheit verursachen, sorgt das ansonsten reduzierte
Interiordesign – dunkles Parkett und Holz, einfache Linien
und einfache Materialien, viel Raum und viel Weite. Schöner
als in der Hängematte lässt es sich vielleicht nur noch auf
der großen Veranda entspannen, durch deren Dach die Sonnenstrahlen fallen und Streifenmuster auf Sitzgruppen und
Liegen zaubern. Wer sich unter allen Umständen bewegen
will, nimmt Fitness- oder Yogastunden, spielt eine Runde
Tennis auf dem nahen Court oder taucht einfach im Blau
des Atlantiks ab.

Buchtipp: »Brasilien, Brasilien« von João Ubaldo Ribeiro

L'heure bleue

Transoco a été fondé par les jésuites au milieu du 16ᵉ siècle
pour recueillir les Indiens persécutés par les coloniaux. Des
amoureux de la nature et de la paix qui cherchaient entre
l'océan et la forêt tropicale un endroit à l'écart de São Paulo
la trépidante, l'ont redécouvert au cours des années 70, et
finalement des artistes en quête d'inspiration et attirés par
la lumière et la magie de la côte sont venus s'y installer.
Trancoso possède aussi, pour le plus grand bonheur des
voyageurs, des kilomètres de fin sable blanc et de cocotiers,
les plus belles plages du Brésil, et une pousada paradisiaque.
L'Estrela d'Água, c'est son nom, est située sur la célèbre
Praia dos Nativos. Sur 23.000 mètres carrés plantés de palmiers et d'hibiscus flamboyants, elle propose des suites et
des chalets qui possèdent le charme enjoué et nonchalant
de Bahia. La plage et l'océan offrent des tons de bleus incon-
nus, les rampes des escaliers sont peintes en bleu ou rouge
vif, les canapés turquoise et des coussins aux motifs de tour-
nesols ensoleillés invitent à la détente. L'œil peut se reposer
de ces splendeurs bariolées dans les intérieurs au design
plus sobre – parquets et bois sombres, lignes et matériaux
simples, beaucoup d'espace et de place. On peut aussi
délaisser le hamac pour la grande véranda et regarder les
rayons du soleil dessiner des rayures sur les fauteuils et les
divans. Celui qui veut vraiment faire de l'exercice peut
s'adonner au programme de remise en forme ou prendre
des cours de yoga, jouer un moment au tennis sur le court
tout proche ou plonger tête première dans le grand bleu.

Livre à emporter : « Vive le peuple brésilien »
de João Ubaldo Ribeiro

ANREISE	40 Kilometer südlich des Internationalen Flughafens Porto Seguro gelegen, Transfer per Fähre (Porto Seguro-Arrial d'Ajuda) und Auto oder nur per Auto. Ein Heliport ist 10 Kilometer vom Hotel entfernt.
PREISE	Suite für 2 Personen ab US$ 120. Mit Frühstück. Chalet »Hibisco« für bis zu 6 Personen ab US$ 195.
ZIMMER	14 Suiten, 2 Master Suiten, 2 Chalets.
KÜCHE	Im Restaurant mit Traumveranda wird vor allem regionale Küche serviert.
GESCHICHTE	Strandresort im ehemaligen Aussteigerparadies.
X-FAKTOR	Alles so schön bunt hier!

ACCÈS	Situé à 40 kilomètres au sud de l'aéroport internatio-nal de Porto Seguro, transfert par ferry (Porto Seguro-Arrial d'Ajuda) et par voiture. Un héliport se trouve à 10 kilomètres de l'hôtel.
PRIX	Suite pour 2 personnes à partir de US$ 120. Petit déjeuner inclus. Chalet « Hibisco » jusqu'à 6 per-sonnes, à partir de US$ 195.
CHAMBRES	14 suites, 2 Master Suites, 2 chalets.
RESTAURATION	Le restaurant propose des spécialités régionales.
HISTOIRE	Hôtel de plage, autrefois le paradis de ceux qui avaient tout laissé derrière eux.
LE « PETIT PLUS »	Des couleurs enchanteresses !

Green spaces...
La Posada Aguaverde, Maldonado

La Posada Aguaverde, Maldonado

Green spaces

Everyone should at least have seen **Punta del Este**, the cosmopolitan ocean resort on a peninsula between the River Plate and the Atlantic, where the rich and famous (and of course the wannabes) settle hotel bills as high as the cost of a family saloon, dally the hours away on the beach or at night-long parties in exclusive clubs, and are tracked each and every summer by the press and TV reporters of Uruguay and Argentina, anxious not to miss a moment. But spending an entire vacation at South America's Monte Carlo is not for everyone – nor, thank goodness, need it be. Just a mile or so from Punta del Este there are magical country residences awaiting guests who are out to discover the real Uruguay. La Posada Aguaverde is one such, a horseshoe-shaped farmhouse built in the late 18th century and now converted into a hotel, set amidst an enchanted garden full of chasing light and shadows. The suites and family apartment are furnished in a sturdy country style. Proprietress Blanca Alvarez de Toledo breeds not only cattle and sheep but also magnificent Arab horses – and a horseback ride is the ideal way to get to know the gentle countryside all around. (No need to worry about aching muscles when you return – the hotel offers miraculous massages!). And it's the perfect end to the day when the fragrances of genuine country cooking prepared in the open on a charcoal burner are wafted upon the evening air.

Book to pack: "Let the Wind Speak" by Juan Carlos Onetti

La Posada Aguaverde		
Camino Eguzquiza, km 7.5	DIRECTIONS	7.5 km/5 miles from Punta del Este (airport transfer is organised).
La Barra de Maldonado	RATES	Double room in apartment from US$ 110 for 2, suite from US$ 125 for double occupancy. Includes breakfast, airport transfer, and all leisure activities.
Punta del Este		
Uruguay		
Tel. (598) 42 669941	ROOMS	5 suites (each with en suite bath), 1 apartment with 2 double rooms and bath.
Mobile: (598) 94 205336		
E-mail: aguaverde@vivapunta.com	FOOD	Genuine Uruguayan home cooking.
Website: www.vivapunta.com/aguaverde	HISTORY	A late 18th-century country house converted to an appealing country inn.
Booking: www.great-escapes-hotels.com	X-FACTOR	A farmstead vacation.

Ganz im Grünen

Punta del Este muss man ein Mal gesehen haben – das mondäne Seebad auf einer Halbinsel zwischen Río de la Plata und Atlantik, wo die Schönen und Reichen (und solche, die es gerne wären) Hotelrechnungen im Gegenwert eines Mittelklassewagens begleichen, zwischen süßem Nichtstun am Strand und nächtelangen Partys in Edelclubs pendeln und Sommer für Sommer von Gazetten sowie Fernsehsendern aus ganz Uruguay und Argentinien auf Schritt und Tritt beobachtet werden. Doch ein ganzer Urlaub im Sylt Südamerikas ist nicht jedermanns Sache – und muss es zum Glück auch gar nicht sein. Denn nur wenige Kilometer von Punta del Este entfernt warten zauberhafte Landsitze auf Gäste, die das ursprüngliche Uruguay kennenlernen wollen – zum Beispiel La Posada Aguaverde. Das U-förmige Farmhaus, das Ende des 18. Jahrhunderts gebaut und inzwischen zum Hotel umfunktioniert wurde, liegt inmitten eines verwunschenen Gartens voller Licht-und-Schattenspiele und besitzt im robusten Countrystil eingerichtete Suiten und ein Apartment für Familien. Besitzerin Blanca Alvarez de Toledo züchtet neben Kühen und Schafen auch prachtvolle Araberpferde, auf deren Rücken man die sanfte Natur ringsum am besten erkundet (um eventuell verspannte Muskeln muss sich niemand Sorgen machen, denn im Hotel wirken Masseure Wunder!). Und der Tag endet perfekt, wenn unter freiem Himmel und mit Hilfe eines Holzkohleofens echte Landhausküche zubereitet wird.

Buchtipp: »So traurig wie sie. Erzählungen« von Juan Carlos Onetti

Noyés dans la verdure

Punta del Este, située sur une presqu'île entre le Rio de La Plata et l'Atlantique, est une station balnéaire réputée. Ici, les gens les plus huppés, tous beaux et riches (ou qui voudraient l'être), paient des factures d'hôtel dont le montant équivaut au prix d'une voiture de classe moyenne, passent leurs journées à se dorer sur la plage et leurs nuits à faire la fête dans des clubs privés et les casinos – et l'œil de la presse et de la télévision uruguayenne et argentine à qui rien n'échappe les observe été après été. On conviendra que passer ses vacances ici n'est pas du goût de tout le monde. Heureusement, à quelques kilomètres de Punta del Este, des résidences enchanteresses attendent des hôtes qui s'intéressent à l'Uruguay authentique, celui des origines. La Posada Aguaverde est l'une d'elles.

Cette ferme en U, construite à la fin du 18e siècle et transformée depuis en hôtel, se dresse au milieu d'un jardin à la végétation exubérante où l'ombre joue avec la lumière. Elle possède des suites et un appartement réservé aux familles, le tout aménagé dans un style rustique robuste. La propriétaire, Blanca Alvarez de Toledo, élève des vaches et des moutons mais aussi de magnifiques chevaux arabes. Ils sont à la disposition de ceux qui veulent explorer les paysages environnants, et si les muscles des cavaliers sont endoloris par le manque d'exercice, les masseurs de l'hôtel font des miracles. Et la journée s'achève dans une douce quiétude quand la cuisine traditionnelle du Rio de La Plata est préparée en plein air sur un feu de charbon de bois.

Livre à emporter : « Les bas-fonds du rêve » de Juan Carlos Onetti

ANREISE	7,5 Kilometer von Punta del Este entfernt (Transfer ab/an Flughafen wird organisiert).
PREISE	Doppelzimmer im Apartment ab US$ 110 für 2 Personen, Suite ab US$ 125 für 2 Personen. Mit Frühstück, Flughafentransfer und allen Freizeitaktivitäten.
ZIMMER	5 Suiten (je mit privatem Bad), 1 Apartment mit 2 Doppelzimmern und einem Bad.
KÜCHE	Echte Hausmannskost aus Uruguay.
GESCHICHTE	Landhaus aus dem späten 18. Jahrhundert, zum hübschen *Country Inn* umgebaut.
X-FAKTOR	Ferien auf dem Bauernhof.

ACCÈS	Situé à 7,5 kilomètres de Punta del Este (transfert organisé).
PRIX	Chambre double en appartement à partir de US$ 110 pour 2 personnes, suite à partir de US$ 125 pour 2 personnes. Petit-déjeuner, transfert de l'aéroport et activités de loisir inclus.
CHAMBRES	5 suites (avec salle de bains), 1 appartement avec 2 chambres doubles et une salle de bains.
RESTAURATION	Authentique cuisine régionale uruguayenne.
HISTOIRE	Villa de la fin du 18e siècle transformée en jolie auberge de campagne.
LE « PETIT PLUS »	Des vacances à la ferme.

A jungle lodge...
Posada La Bonita, Misiones

Posada La Bonita, Misiones

A jungle lodge

This jungle is more like an enchanted forest in a fairy tale. The green of the twined plants is so rich you almost think it's dripping from the leaves. A faint veil seems always to be drifting upon the air, and a tremendous waterfall is tumbling into the depths. Never has it been so easy to achieve a state resembling that of meditation – the Posada La Bonita grants the soul the very best, from the very first moment. A jungle lodge in the extreme northeastern of Argentina, it is entirely one with its natural setting. The rooms are done in an abundance of wood and hand-woven fabrics, and with greenery visible from every room and veranda you won't miss the high-tech environment of the world you've left behind for a single second. The perfect day in La Bonita begins with the dawn chorus and breakfast in the open, and then it's time to explore the labyrinthine river system and forests in a kayak or hand-carved canoe, or get to know the country on horseback. After a candlelight dinner with lounge music in the background you can idle for a while in a hammock before turning in – no need to worry about mosquitoes, since they rarely make an appearance at this altitude. At this hour, the soothing splash of the waterfall is better than any sleeping pill. And if you find the sheer fascination of water is getting to you, try visiting the nearby Saltos del Moconá, where the Uruguay River races down three kilometres (1.8 miles) of breathtaking cascades.

Book to pack: "What the Night Tells the Day"
by Hector Bianciotti

Posada La Bonita	
Moconá, El Soberbio	
Misiones	
Argentina	
Tel. (54) 3755 680380 and (54) 11 47474745	
E-mail: posadalabonita@hotmail.com	
Website: www.posadalabonita.com.ar	
Booking: www.great-escapes-hotels.com	

DIRECTIONS	Situated 300 km/188 miles southeast of Iguazú airport. The transfer is organised.
RATES	Double rooms US$ 80 for 2 people. Includes full board.
ROOMS	6 double rooms.
FOOD	Regional and Italian cuisine, with a substantial range of vegetarian fare.
HISTORY	Opened in March 1999.
X-FACTOR	The full glorious spectacle of nature.

Dschungellodge

Dieser Urwald ist ein Märchenwald: Die ineinander verschlungenen Pflanzen sind so sattgrün, dass man glaubt, die Farbe von den Blättern tropfen zu sehen, in der Luft scheint immer ein leichter Schleier zu schweben, und ein mächtiger Wasserfall stürzt in die Tiefe. Nie war es so einfach, sich in einen meditationsähnlichen Zustand zu versetzen – wer in die Posada La Bonita zieht, gönnt seiner Seele vom ersten Moment an nur das Beste. Die Dschungellodge im äußersten Nordosten Argentiniens ist mit der Natur verwachsen, hier wohnt man in mit viel Holz und handgewebten Stoffen ausgestatteten Zimmern, blickt von jedem Raum und jeder Veranda aus ins Grüne und vermisst die High-Tech-Errungenschaften der restlichen Welt keine Sekunde lang. Der perfekte Tag in La Bonita beginnt mit einem Konzert der Vögel und einem Frühstück im Freien, anschließend spürt man vom Kajak oder handgeschnitzten Kanu aus die Geheimnisse der Flusslabyrinthe und des Waldes auf oder entdeckt die Umgebung per Pferd. Nach einem Abendessen bei Kerzenschein und mit Loungemusik im Hintergrund schaukelt man in der Hängematte der Nacht entgegen und muss sich dabei nicht vor Mückenstichen fürchten – dank der Höhenlage kommen die angriffslustigen Insekten hier so gut wie gar nicht vor. Das Plätschern des Wasserfalls wirkt zu später Stunde dann besser als jede Baldriantablette – wen während des Urlaubs die Faszination des nassen Elements nicht mehr loslässt, der sollte auch zu den nahen Saltos del Moconá fahren, wo der Fluss Uruguay auf einer Länge von drei Kilometern eine rauschende Kaskade bildet.
**Buchtipp: »Wie die Spur des Vogels in der Luft«
von Hector Bianciotti**

Lodge de la jungle

Cette forêt semble sortie tout droit d'un conte de fées : les plantes qui s'entrelacent sont d'un vert si intense que l'on croit voir la couleur goutter de leurs feuilles, un voile léger de condensation flotte dans l'air et une imposante cascade se jette dans les profondeurs. Jamais il n'a été aussi facile qu'ici de se retrouver dans un état proche de la méditation – celui qui réside à la Posada La Bonita peut choyer son âme dès le premier moment. Situé à l'extrême nord-est de l'Argentine, ce lodge est intimement lié à la nature environnante. Le bois et les étoffes tissées à la main abondent dans les chambres qui offrent toutes, ainsi que les vérandas, une vue sur la verdure. Ici, on ne regrette pas une seconde les progrès technologiques du reste du monde. À La Bonita, la journée commence avec le chant des oiseaux au réveil et un petit-déjeuner en plein air. Ensuite, on part en kayak ou dans un canoë gravé à la main, à la découverte des mystères du fleuve et de la forêt ou bien on fait une randonnée à cheval. Après un dîner aux chandelles avec une musique douce en fond sonore, on peut savourer la tombée de la nuit dans un hamac. Nulle crainte à avoir des moustiques, il n'y en a pratiquement pas à cette altitude. Le murmure au loin de la cascade fait plus d'effet que n'importe quelle pilule pour dormir. Et si pendant ces vacances, la fascination de l'eau ne vous quitte plus, allez donc visiter les chutes Saltos del Moconá, là où le fleuve Uruguay forme sur trois kilomètres une cascade impressionnante.
**Livre à emporter : « Comme la trace de l'oiseau dans l'air »
de Hector Bianciotti**

ANREISE	300 Kilometer südöstlich des Flughafens Iguazú gelegen. Transfer wird organisiert.
PREISE	Doppelzimmer US$ 80 für 2 Personen. Mit Vollpension.
ZIMMER	6 Doppelzimmer.
KÜCHE	Regionale und italienische Menüs, großes Angebot für Vegetarier.
GESCHICHTE	Im März 1999 eröffnet.
X-FAKTOR	Ein Naturschauspiel.

ACCÈS	Situé à 300 kilomètres au sud-est de l'aéroport d'Iguazú. Le transfert est organisé.
PRIX	Chambre double US$ 80 pour 2 personnes En pension complète.
CHAMBRES	6 chambres doubles.
RESTAURATION	Menus régionaux et italiens. Grand choix de plats végétariens.
HISTOIRE	Ouvert en mars 1999.
LE « PETIT PLUS »	Un spectacle de la nature.

Homage to fine wine...
Bodega El Esteco de Cafayate, Salta

Bodega El Esteco de Cafayate, Salta

Homage to fine wine

It's almost like being in the old heart of a Spanish town. Through the imposing arched gateways you come upon whitewashed buildings with rounded arches, bell towers and patios, with geraniums and roses to fill the scene with colour and fragrance. And that first impression is absolutely right: the colonial-inspired architecture of the Bodega El Esteco de Cafayate was modelled on the Barrio de la Santa Cruz, the historic centre of Seville. Still, the surroundings quickly remind you that you're in South America. All around the estate are vineyards, stretching as far as the horizon, it seems, or at least to the Andean Cordilleras. The grapes that grow in the Valles Calchaquíes are first class, thanks to the 340 days of sunshine per annum, the cool nights, and an ideal high-lying location some 1,700 metres (about 5,300 feet) above sea level – and the local wine-growers export their vintages all over the world. The Bodega El Esteco de Cafayate (hitherto also known to aficionados as the Bodega La Rosa) was established in 1892 by two brothers, David and Salvador Michel, who haled from Catalonia. Currently it is being re-structured as a kind of boutique winery: only choice wines will be produced in the future, bearing names such as "Don David" or "Altimus". This exclusivity is the hallmark of the country hotel as well. Offering the authentic experience of the vintner's way of life on a private farmhouse, without losing out on any of the comforts and amenities of a modern hotel. The plan even envisages Argentina's first wine spa, where the active ingredients of grapes are harnessed to a wellness regime. The leisure programme includes vineyard tours, photo expeditions, riding, trekking, and fishing trips. Regardless of which programme you opt for, the finest hours may well be those that begin at sunset, when real country cooking is served in the inviting dining rooms – with the estate's own fine wines.

Book to pack: "Imagining Argentina" by Lawrence Thornton

Bodega El Esteco de Cafayate	
Ruta 40 s/n	
4427 Cafayate	
Salta	
Argentina	
Tel. (54) 1147168000 and 80088 84667	
E-mail: fperkins@micheltorino.com.ar	
Website: www.micheltorino.com.ar	
Booking: www.great-escapes-hotels.com	

DIRECTIONS	Situated 120 km/75 miles (two and a half hours by road) south of Salta.
RATES	Double rooms US$ 135 for 2 persons.
ROOMS	25 double rooms.
FOOD	Argentine country food, with first-class wines.
HISTORY	A 19th-century winery with guest house accommodation added five years ago.
X-FACTOR	In vino veritas.

Dem Wein gewidmet

Man könnte meinen, in einer spanischen Altstadt zu sein:
Hinter mächtigen Torbögen liegen weiß getünchte Gebäude
mit Rundbögen, Glockentürmen und Patios, in denen Gera-
nien oder Rosen für süßen Duft und Farbe sorgen. Und
wirklich ist die kolonial angehauchte Architektur der Bodega
El Esteco de Cafayate dem Barrio de la Santa Cruz, dem historischen Zentrum Sevillas, nachempfunden – doch das
Umland holt einen schnell nach Südamerika zurück. Rings
um das Anwesen dehnt sich ein Weinanbaugebiet aus, das
bis zum Horizont oder zumindest bis zur Andenkordillere
im Hintergrund zu reichen scheint. Mehr als 340 Sonnentage, kühle Nächte und eine ideale Höhenlage von 1.700
Metern lassen in den Valles Calchaquíes erstklassige Trauben reifen – hier ansässige Winzer exportieren ihre Tropfen
in alle Welt. Die Bodega El Esteco de Cafayate (Insidern war
sie bislang auch als Bodega La Rosa bekannt) wurde 1892
von den ursprünglich katalanischen Brüdern David und Salvador Michel gegründet und wird derzeit zu einer Art »Bou-
tique-Winery« umstrukturiert: Nur noch Spitzenweine mit
klingenden Namen wie »Don David« oder »Altimus« sollen
künftig produziert werden. Ebenso exklusiv geht es auch im
angeschlossenen Landhotel zu. Hier soll man das Winzerle-
ben wie in einem privaten Farmhaus erleben, ohne auf die
Annehmlichkeiten eines modernen Hotels verzichten zu
müssen. Geplant ist sogar das erste Wein-Spa Argentiniens,
in dem die Wirkstoffe der Trauben für Wellness und Wohl-
befinden genutzt werden. Auf dem Entspannungsprogramm
stehen zudem Touren durch die Wineyards, Fotosafaris, Ausritte, Trekkings und Angelausflüge. Doch ganz egal, für welches Programm man sich entscheidet: Die vielleicht schönsten Stunden beginnen bei Sonnenuntergang, wenn in den
gemütlichen Gutsräumen echte Landhausküche serviert
wird – und dazu feine Weine aus eigenem Anbau im Glas
glänzen.

Buchtipp: »Wiedersehen in Argentinien« von Hubert Landes

Le goût du vin

On se croirait dans une vieille cité espagnole : derrière de
vastes portails s'élèvent des bâtiments blancs dotés d'arches
en plein cintre, de clochers et de patios dans lesquels des
géraniums ou des roses apportent des accents de couleur et
des odeurs suaves. L'architecture aux accents coloniaux de la
Bodega El Esteco de Cafayate est réellement inspirée de celle
du Barrio de la Santa Cruz, le cœur historique de Séville.
Mais l'illusion se dissipe rapidement car, autour de la propriété, les vignobles semblent se déployer jusqu'à la cordillère des Andes. Avec plus de 340 journées d'ensoleillement,
des nuits fraîches et une altitude de près de 1700 mètres au-
dessus du niveau de la mer, les Valles Calchaquies voient
mûrir des raisins de premier choix – les viticulteurs de la
région exportent leurs crus dans le monde entier.
La Bodega El Esteco de Cafayate (jusqu'ici Bodega La Rosa
pour les initiés), fondée en 1892 par les frères d'origine cata-
lane David et Salvador Michel, est en cours de restructura-
tion et ne produira bientôt plus que des vins exceptionnels
au doux nom de « Don David » ou « Altimus ». L'hôtel
annexe subit la même métamorphose luxueuse. Les hôtes
doivent vivre ici comme à la ferme sans renoncer aux com-
modités d'un hôtel moderne. On envisage même la création
du premier spa d'Argentine dans lequel les substances
actives du raisin seront utilisées pour la remise en forme
et le bien-être.
Le programme-détente prévoit aussi des randonnées à travers la région viticole, des safaris photo, du trekking et des
excursions de pêche. Mais les heures les plus douces seront
sans doute celles que l'on passe après le coucher du soleil
quand la bonne cuisine rustique est servie dans les salles
accueillantes – sans oublier les vins délectables produits
sur le terroir.

Livre à emporter : « La trame céleste » de Adolfo Bioy Casares

ANREISE	120 Kilometer (zweieinhalb Fahrtstunden) südlich von Salta gelegen.	ACCÈS	Situé à 20 kilomètres (deux heures et demie de voiture) au sud de Salta.
PREISE	Doppelzimmer US$ 135 für 2 Personen.	PRIX	Chambre double US$ 135 pour 2 personnes.
ZIMMER	25 Doppelzimmer.	CHAMBRES	25 chambres doubles.
KÜCHE	Argentinische Landhausküche, erstklassige Weine.	RESTAURATION	Cuisine de pays, vins de premier choix.
GESCHICHTE	Ein Weingut aus dem 19. Jahrhundert, seit fünf Jahren mit Gästehaus.	HISTOIRE	Un vignoble du 19e siècle, transformé en hôtel il y a cinq ans.
X-FAKTOR	In vino veritas.	LE « PETIT PLUS »	In vino veritas.

Roaming further afield...
Dos Lunas, Province Córdoba

Dos Lunas, Province Córdoba

Roaming further afield

It was at Mount Colchequin that the indigenous Comechin-gones suffered their worst moment. Faced on this rocky terrain with defeat at the hands of the Spanish, they leapt from the peak to their deaths, preferring to die with pride rather than on Spanish pikes. Happily, this onetime battleground is now a peaceful place. To gaze across the green and gently undulating country of Ongamira, where weather-rounded rocks repose like slumbering creatures of fantasy with russet-brown backs, is to behold a soft and tranquil landscape. And it is here that we find the Dos Lunas country hotel, in the heart of 3,000 hectares of what seems utterly unspoilt nature. For new arrivals, the best way to acclimatise to the vast and peaceful spaces of Córdoba province is to relax by the pool in the garden; but no later than day two you should be out and about, exploring the region. Take a long walk through the forests and hills, for instance, forever moving on from one breathtaking lookout point to the next. Or if you want to roam further afield, Dos Lunas offers horse riding – from short canters, to excursions into the mountains, to trekking expeditions lasting days. If you opt for the long version, you'll spend your nights camping in the open, listening to the guides' tales and guitar playing by the campfire. If you're a little weary on your return, and your muscles are aching, Dos Lunas has all the creature comfort you need, and hot baths to relax in. The establishment is also celebrated for its country cooking – from breakfast with home-baked break and honey from the region to barbecues by the pool, this is the taste of Argentina!

Book to pack: "Don Segundo Sombra" by Ricardo Güiraldes

Dos Lunas	
Alto Ongamira	
Province Córdoba	
Argentina	
Tel. and fax (54) 800 333 2666	
E-mail: doslunas@doslunas.com.ar	
Website: www.doslunas.com.ar	
Booking: www.great-escapes-hotels.com	

DIRECTIONS	Situated 120 km/75 miles north of Córdoba (domestic flights from Buenos Aires), 90 minutes by road. The transfer costs US$ 90.
RATES	Double room US$ 135 per person. Includes full board and all activities.
ROOMS	8 double rooms.
FOOD	Good, substantial fare, using regional produce.
HISTORY	A modern country hotel on historic ground.
X-FACTOR	Nature pure and simple – as far as the eye can see.

Ein weites Feld

Am Berg Colchequin musste der Stamm der Comechingones einst seine größte Niederlage hinnehmen: Die Indianer drohten auf dem felsigen Gelände den Kampf gegen die Spanier zu verlieren und stürzten sich vom Gipfel in den Tod, um zumindest mit Stolz zu sterben und nicht durch spanische Speere. Der einstige Kampfplatz präsentiert sich heute zum Glück friedvoll: Wer über das leicht gewellte und grüne Land von Ongamira blickt, in dem rund geschliffene Felsen wie schlafende Fantasiewesen mit rotbraunen Rücken liegen, sieht eine sanfte und stille Landschaft. Hier steht auch das Landhotel Dos Lunas – inmitten von 3.000 Hektar wie unberührt wirkender Natur. Neuankömmlinge gewöhnen sich am besten am runden Pool im Garten an die Ruhe und Weitläufigkeit der Provinz Córdoba; doch spätestens am zweiten Tag sollte man die Region aktiv erkunden. Zum Beispiel bei einem langen Spaziergang durch die Wälder und Hügel und immer auf der Suche nach einem Aussichtspunkt, der noch schöner als der vorhergehende ist. Wen es noch weiter hinaus zieht, für den bietet Dos Lunas Touren hoch zu Ross an – von kurzen Ausritten über Ausflüge in die Berge bis hin zu tagelangen Trekkings ist alles möglich. Wer sich für die Maxiversion entscheidet, campiert nachts im Freien, lauscht den Legenden der Guides und ihrem Gitarrenspiel am Lagerfeuer. Vielleicht schmerzen die Muskeln anschließend ein wenig und vielleicht kommt man ein bisschen müde zurück; doch Dos Lunas sorgt mit gemütlichem Komfort und heißen Bädern für Entspannung. Berühmt ist das Haus auch für seine Landhausküche – vom Frühstück mit selbst gebackenem Brot und regionalem Honig bis hin zum Barbecue am Pool: So schmeckt Argentinien!

Buchtipp: »Das Buch vom Gaucho Sombra« von Ricardo Güiraldes

Les grands espaces

C'est sur la montagne de Colchequin que la tribu des Comechingones a subi l'une de ses plus terribles défaites. Alors qu'ils étaient sur le point d'être vaincus par les Espagnols, les Indiens préférèrent se jeter dans le vide plutôt que de se rendre. Ils voulaient mourir dans la dignité et non pas par les lances de leurs ennemis. L'ancien champ de bataille a retrouvé aujourd'hui un aspect serein. Légèrement vallonné, le territoire d'Ongamira se distingue par sa douceur et sa tranquillité, les rochers aux formes arrondies ressemblent à des êtres fabuleux assoupis dont on ne verrait que le dos rougeâtre. C'est ici qu'est situé également l'hôtel de campagne Dos Lunas – au milieu d'une nature de 3000 hectares qui semble être restée intacte. Les nouveaux venus s'acclimateront au calme et à l'immensité de la province de Córdoba en se prélassant près de la piscine ronde dans le jardin. Mais après une journée de repos, nous leur recommandons de partir à la découverte de la région en faisant, par exemple, une longue promenade à travers les forêts et les collines, à la recherche des points de vue, tous plus beaux les uns que les autres. Pour celui qui désire s'aventurer plus loin, Dos Lunas propose des randonnées à cheval : petites virées dans les montagnes ou excursions de plusieurs jours, tout est possible. Si vous vous décidez pour la dernière solution, vous dormirez à la belle étoile, vous écouterez, allongé près du feu de camp, vos guides jouer de la guitare et vous conter les légendes du pays. Peut-être reviendrez-vous un peu fatigué et courbatu à Dos Lunas, mais avec son confort et ses bains chauds, l'hôtel vous invitera à la détente. Sa célèbre cuisine campagnarde vous redonnera aussi le punch nécessaire : petit déjeuner avec pain cuit maison et miel de la région, barbecue au bord de la piscine, c'est tout le goût de l'Argentine !

Livre à emporter : « Don Segundo Sombra » de Ricardo Güiraldes

ANREISE	120 Kilometer nördlich von Córdoba gelegen (dorthin Inlandsflüge ab Buenos Aires), Fahrtzeit 90 Minuten. Der Transfer kostet US$ 90.
PREISE	Doppelzimmer US$ 135 pro Person. Mit Vollpension und allen Aktivitäten.
ZIMMER	8 Doppelzimmer.
KÜCHE	Gut, kräftig und mit regionalen Produkten.
GESCHICHTE	Modernes Landhotel auf geschichtsträchtigem Boden.
X-FAKTOR	Natur pur – bis zum Horizont.

ACCÈS	Situé à 120 kilomètres au nord de Córdoba (vols intérieurs depuis Buenos Aires), trajet 90 minutes. Le transfert coûte US$ 90.
PRIX	Chambre double US$ 135 par personne, y compris pension complète et toutes les activités.
CHAMBRES	8 chambres doubles.
RESTAURATION	Bonne cuisine rustique avec des produits régionaux.
HISTOIRE	Hôtel de campagne sur un territoire chargé d'histoire.
LE « PETIT PLUS »	De la nature à perte de vue.

A good vintage...
Estancia Ancón, Mendoza

Estancia Ancón, Mendoza

A good vintage

Mendoza is in the Cuyo region in western Argentina and lies at the foot of the Andean Cordilleras. In the language of the indigenous peoples, "Cuyo" means "sandy soil", but don't let that fool you: with more than 300 days of sunshine a year, and sophisticated irrigation systems, Cuyo is a green and blossoming wonderland renowned throughout the world for its exceptional wines. One of its finest producers is the Estancia Ancón. The ivy-clad château, with its crannied architecture, vaulted ceilings, and round tower, would look more in place among the vineyards of France, you'd think, than in the rolling empty spaces of Argentina. And you wouldn't be too wrong, since the owners originally haled from Limoges and came to Mendoza in 1760. The Bombal family still manage the estate to this day – Lucila Bombal and her children keep a watchful eye on the wine-making to ensure that, for all the modern methods of production, the old vintner traditions are upheld. Since 1999 the Bombals have been taking guests at the château too: every year, from mid October to early May, connoisseurs of wine and of natural beauty move in to the six hotel rooms, which have dark gleaming parquet floors, furniture with a touch of the aristocratic, and a sparing deployment of knick-knacks. Vineyard trips and tastings are on offer, alongside walks amid the walnut and cherry orchards of the estate, or horse riding with the snow-capped Andes to marvel at. In the evenings, good home cooking is served, using produce mainly from the estate and washed down, of course, with estate wines.

Book to pack: "The Winners" by Julio Cortázar

Estancia Ancón

San José, Tupungato

5500 Mendoza

Argentina

Tel. (54) 261 488245

Tel. for bookings (54) 261 4200037

E-mail: bombal@arnet.com.ar

Website: www.estanciancon.com

Booking: www.great-escapes-hotels.com

DIRECTIONS	Situated 80 minutes by road southwest of Mendoza international airport (domestic flights from Buenos Aires), at an altitude of 1,300 metres/approx. 4,000 feet.
RATES	Double rooms US$ 360, single room US$ 250. Full board included.
ROOMS	5 double rooms and 1 single room. Open from 15 October to 1 May.
FOOD	Regional specialities using estate produce and served with estate wines.
HISTORY	The summer residence of the Bombals, built in 1933, has been a small hotel since 1999.
X-FACTOR	French-cum-South American style, and first-class wines.

Ein guter Jahrgang

Mendoza gehört zur Region Cuyo – im Westen Argentiniens und am Fuß der Andenkordillere gelegen. In der Sprache der Ureinwohner bedeutet Cuyo so viel wie »sandige Erde«, doch davon sollte man sich nicht täuschen lassen: Mehr als 300 Sonnentage im Jahr und ausgefeilte Bewässerungssysteme verwandeln Cuyo in ein blühendes und grünes Wunderland, das in aller Welt für seine ausgezeichneten Weine berühmt ist. Zu den besten Produzenten gehört die Estancia Ancón – mit ihrem Château unter einer dichten Efeudecke, das man ob seiner verwinkelten Architektur, seiner Gewölbedecken und seines Rundturms eher in Frankreichs Rebbergen als in der Weite Argentiniens vermuten würde. Dieser Eindruck kommt nicht von ungefähr, denn die Besitzer stammen ursprünglich aus Limoges und kamen anno 1760 nach Mendoza. Die Familie Bombal managt das Gut noch heute – Lucila Bombal und ihre Kinder wachen strengstens darüber, dass trotz moderner Produktionstechniken die alten Winzertraditionen erhalten bleiben. Seit 1999 empfangen die Bombals im Schloss auch Gäste: Jedes Jahr zwischen Mitte Oktober und Anfang Mai ziehen Wein- und Naturliebhaber in die sechs Hotelzimmer, die mit dunkel glänzendem Parkett, aristokratisch angehauchten Möbeln und ohne viel Nippes ausgestattet sind. Neben Ausflügen in die Rebberge und Degustationen stehen Spaziergänge über das herrliche Gelände voller Walnuss- und Kirschbäume auf dem Programm sowie Ausritte vor der Kulisse der schneebedeckten Anden. Abends verwöhnt man die Besucher mit Hausmannskost, für die hauptsächlich Produkte aus eigenem Anbau verwendet und die natürlich von eigenen Weinen begleitet werden.

Buchtipp: »Die Gewinner« von Julio Cortázar

Un bon cru

Située dans l'Ouest de l'Argentine au pied de la cordillère des Andes, Mendoza se trouve dans la région de Cuyo. Dans le dialecte indigène Cuyo signifie « terre de sable », mais ne nous laissons pas abuser par ce terme. En effet, plus de 300 jours de soleil par an et un judicieux système d'irrigation ont métamorphosé Cuyo en une région verdoyante connue dans le monde entier pour la qualité de ses vins. Estancia Ancón compte parmi les meilleurs producteurs, et quand on regarde son château recouvert d'une épaisse couche de lierre, avec ses plafonds voûtés et son donjon, on l'imaginerait plus dans les vignobles de France que sur les vastes étendues de l'Argentine. Cette impression n'est pas complètement fausse car les premiers propriétaires, qui arrivèrent à Mendoza en 1760, étaient originaires de Limoges. La famille Bombal gère son exploitation aujourd'hui encore – Lucila Bombal et ses enfants veillent au respect des traditions tout en employant des techniques de production modernes. Depuis 1999, le château reçoit aussi des hôtes : tous les ans, entre la mi-octobre et début mai, les amateurs de vin et de nature peuvent résider dans l'une des six chambres décorées sobrement, avec parquet ciré et meubles aristocratiques. À côté des excursions dans les vignobles et des dégustations, le château propose des promenades dans la magnifique propriété, où poussent une multitude de noyers et de cerisiers, ainsi que des randonnées à cheval avec pour décor les sommets neigeux des Andes. Le soir on flatte les papilles des hôtes avec une cuisine rustique, préparée principalement avec des produits maisons et accompagnée bien sûr des vins des vignobles alentour.

Livre à emporter : « Les gagnants » de Julio Cortázar

ANREISE	80 Fahrtminuten südwestlich des Internationalen Flughafens Mendoza gelegen (dorthin Inlandsflüge ab Buenos Aires), auf 1.300 Metern Höhe.
PREISE	Doppelzimmer US$ 360, Einzelzimmer US$ 250. Mit Vollpension.
ZIMMER	5 Doppelzimmer und 1 Einzelzimmer. Für Gäste geöffnet vom 15. Oktober bis 1. Mai.
KÜCHE	Regionale Spezialitäten aus eigenem Anbau und Weine aus eigener Produktion.
GESCHICHTE	Der 1933 erbaute Sommersitz der Bombals ist seit 1999 ein kleines Hotel.
X-FAKTOR	Französisch-südamerikanisches Flair und 1A-Weine.

ACCÈS	Situé à 80 minutes en voiture au sud-ouest de l'aéroport international de Mendoza (vols intérieurs depuis Buenos Aires), à une altitude de 1.300 mètres.
PRIX	Chambre double US$ 360, chambre simple US$ 250. En pension complète.
CHAMBRES	5 chambres doubles et 1 chambre simple. Hôtellerie ouverte du 15 octobre au 1er mai.
RESTAURATION	Spécialités régionales maisons.
HISTOIRE	La résidence d'été des Bombal, construite en 1933, a été transformée en un petit hôtel en 1999.
LE « PETIT PLUS »	Ambiance franco-sud-américaine et vins de première classe.

A natural beauty...
La Pascuala Delta Lodge, Province Buenos Aires

La Pascuala Delta Lodge, Province Buenos Aires

A natural beauty

Amazing to think town and country can be so close and yet so far apart: just a few miles out of Buenos Aires you come to the Paraná delta, an enchanting landscape of small waterways and lush vegetation, where life seems to move in slow motion, as if bedded on velvet. It's the perfect place to while away the days paddling a kayak on the river, watching the birds and listening to their shrill, wondrous calls, or fishing from the riverbank in a mood so peaceful that bristling appointments diaries and ceaselessly jangling mobiles seem a world away. In the heart of this idyllic realm, La Pascuala Delta Lodge awaits its guests. It's situated on the bank of the Arroyo Las Cañas, with marshlands around it that have largely remained unspoilt. The few stray buildings supported on stilts seem almost to hover above the water, and are linked by wooden walkways or bridges. Every one of the 15 bungalow suites has all the charisma of a private residence – for a few happy days, you are the owner of a humble lodging of understated luxury, with a dream veranda and views of the greenery. If you don't only want to admire the water from a dry haven, why not take time out on the river in a boat, or indeed *in* it? The only imperative rule is always to swim against the current – otherwise you'll be borne away from paradise all too swiftly...

Book to pack: "Mascaro, the American Hunter"
by Haroldo Conti

La Pascuala Delta Lodge	
c/o Montevideo 1938 3° C	
C1021AAH, Buenos Aires	
Argentina	
Tel. (54) 11 4728-1253 and -1395	
Fax (54) 11 4728-2070	
E-mail: lapascuala@anylink.com.ar	
Website: www.lapascuala.com	
Booking: www.great-escapes-hotels.com	

DIRECTIONS	Situated some 60 km/38 miles north of Buenos Aires. One-hour boat transfer from San Fernando/Tigre US$ 30 per person.
RATES	Suite US$ 150 per person per day, single occupancy US$ 175. Includes full board and water sports such as paddle-boats, kayaks, and fishing, as well as trekking. No children under 16.
ROOMS	15 bungalow suites for 2 people.
FOOD	Argentine specialities and wines.
HISTORY	Opened 1st April 2001.
X-FACTOR	Everything is in flow – feel good by the water.

Natürlich schön

So nahe können Stadt und Land nebeneinander liegen und
so fern können sich beide Welten sein: Man muss nur ein
paar Kilometer aus Buenos Aires hinausfahren und schon
erreicht man das Paraná-Delta, eine Märchenlandschaft mit
kleinen Wasserwegen und üppiger Vegetation, in der das
Leben noch in Zeitlupe und wie unter Samt gelegen abläuft.
Hier kann man seine Tage damit verbringen, mit dem Kajak
auf den Fluss hinaus zu paddeln, den Vögeln hinterher zu
sehen und ihren schrill-schönen Rufen zu lauschen oder mit
so viel Seelenruhe am Ufer zu angeln, als hätte man niemals
Wochen voller berstender Terminkalender und im Sekun-
dentakt klingelnder Handys erlebt. Inmitten dieses Idylls
wartet die La Pascuala Delta Lodge auf Gäste – am Ufer des
Arroyo Las Cañas gelegen und um sich herum eine Sumpf-
landschaft, die ihren ursprünglichen Charakter noch weitgehend erhalten konnte. Die einzelnen Gebäude scheinen
auf ihren Stelzen über dem Wasser zu schweben und sind
über hölzerne Stege oder Brücken miteinander verbunden.
Jede der 15 Bungalow-Suiten besitzt das Flair einer Privat-
adresse – für ein paar glückliche Tage ist man Besitzer eines
Häuschens mit dezentem Luxus und einer traumhaften Veranda mit Blick ins Grüne. Wer das Wasser nicht nur vom
Trockenen aus bewundern will, kann an Bootsausflügen teil-
nehmen oder ganz einfach im Fluss untertauchen. Dabei
gilt nur eine einzige Regel: Immer gegen die Strömung
schwimmen – sonst wird man allzu schnell vom Paradies
weggetrieben.

Buchtipp: »Op Oloop« von Juan Filloy

Des vacances au naturel

Buenos Aires, la capitale trépidante, ne se trouve qu'à
quelques kilomètres, et pourtant elle semble très loin d'ici.
En fait nous sommes dans un autre monde, celui du delta
du Paraná, véritable paysage de contes de fées avec ses canaux et sa végétation luxuriante. Ici, la vie passe encore au
ralenti, comme si elle glissait sur du velours. On peut passer
ses journées en kayac sur le fleuve à regarder les oiseaux et
écouter leurs beaux cris perçants ou pêcher sur les rives en
toute sérénité. Envolés les agendas bourrés des semaines
durant de rendez-vous urgents, oubliée la sonnerie incessan-
te des portables.
Située sur la rive de l'Arroyo Las Cañas, entourée d'un paysage de marécages qui a su préserver son caractère original,
la Pascuala Delta Lodge attend ses hôtes pour partager avec
eux ce site idyllique. Les constructions sur pilotis, reliées
entre elles par des passerelles en bois et des pontons, semblent flotter au-dessus de l'eau. Chaque suite-bungalow a
son caractère particulier – pendant quelques jours, on sera
l'heureux propriétaire d'une maisonnette au luxe sobre dotée
d'une véranda de rêve s'ouvrant sur la verdure. Et ceux qui
ne veulent pas se contenter d'admirer l'eau de loin peuvent
participer à des sorties en bateau ou tout simplement se
baigner, en veillant cependant à nager contre le courant –
sinon ils seraient trop vite entraînés loin de ce paradis.

**Livre à emporter : « La ballade du peuplier carolin » de
Haroldo Conti**

ANREISE	Rund 60 Kilometer nördlich von Buenos Aires gelegen. Einstündiger Bootstransfer ab San Fernando/Tigre US$ 30 pro Person.
PREISE	Suite US$ 150 pro Person und Tag, bei Einzelnutzung US$ 175. Mit Vollpension und Wassersport wie Tretboot, Kajak, Angeln sowie Trekking. Keine Kinder unter 16 Jahren.
ZIMMER	15 Bungalow-Suiten für je 2 Personen.
KÜCHE	Argentinische Spezialitäten und Weine.
GESCHICHTE	Am 1. April 2001 eröffnet.
X-FAKTOR	Alles fließt – Wohlfühlen am Wasser.

ACCÈS	Situé à 60 kilomètres au nord de Buenos Aires. À une heure de bateau de San Fernando/Tigre, US$ 30 par personne.
PRIX	Suite US$ 150 par jour et par personne, pour une seule personne US$ 175 (pension complète et sports aquatiques – pédalo, kajak, pêche – ainsi que trekking inclus). Pas d'enfants de moins de 16 ans.
CHAMBRES	15 suites-bungalows pour 2 personnes.
RESTAURATION	Spécialités et vins argentins.
HISTOIRE	Ouvert le 1er avril 2001.
LE « PETIT PLUS »	Au fil de l'eau.

King for a day...
Estancia La Candelaria, Province Buenos Aires

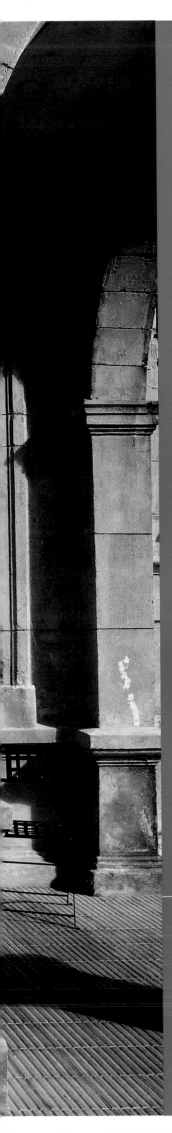

Estancia La Candelaria,
Province Buenos Aires

King for a day

At first glance you'd think this castle with its turrets, battlements, and high windows belonged in the Loire Valley, or maybe Eurodisney near Paris – if it weren't for the fact that it's in this breathtaking tropical garden. More than 240 different trees and plants grow here, such as palms, eucalyptus trees, or banana plants. A gleaming white bridge spans a modest watercourse, and the grass shines as if it had been sprayed with bright green paint. The park was created by the famous landscape architect Charles Thays, and the château fits into it perfectly. The residence was built in the mid-19th century by pharmacist and sheep breeder Don Orestes Piñeiro, who named it after his wife, Doña Candelaria Del Marmol. La Candelaria was the family's other world, their retreat in the solitude of the Argentine pampas, far from civilisation. And although the region is now perfectly accessible, and anything but backwoods, the château remains a quiet refuge to get away to. You reside in spacious rooms beneath coffered ceilings and crystal chandeliers. The floors are gleaming parquet or costly carpet, the armchairs are carved, and the beds have gilded bedsteads. La Candelaria is a return to a magnificent era long thought forgotten, and guests here can be king for a while. The pastimes all strike the right note of class, among them billiards, tennis, golf, and polo. The property still belongs to the same family, and while the owners may be deeply attached to the past, they also have a real sense of the present: all the sporting and leisure activities are included in the room price. This is Argentina all inclusive.

Book to pack: "Voices" by Antonio Porchia

Estancia La Candelaria	DIRECTIONS	Situated 115 km/75 miles northeast of Buenos Aires.
Ruta 205, km 114.5	RATES	From Double room in a bungalow US$ 220 up to a suite US$ 340. For 2 people. Includes full board and all activities.
Lobos, Buenos Aires		
Argentina	ROOMS	2 double rooms in bungalows, 1 double in the old mill, 2 double in the Casa del Sol, 8 double in colonial houses, 10 double and 2 suites in the château.
Tel. (54) 2227 424404		
Fax (54) 2227 494132		
E-mail: lacandelaria@isei.com.ar	FOOD	Refined Argentine and international cuisine.
Website: www.lacandelaria.com.ar	HISTORY	A picture-book retreat, family-owned since 1840.
Booking: www.great-escapes-hotels.com	X-FACTOR	My palace, my park, my polo pitch.

Heute ein König

Auf den ersten Blick würde man dieses Schloss mit seinen spitzen Türmen, Zinnen und hohen Fenstern eher im Tal der Loire oder im Disneyland bei Paris vermuten – stünde es nicht in diesem traumhaften tropischen Garten. Hier gedeihen mehr als 240 verschiedene Pflanzen wie Palmen, Eukalyptusbäume oder Bananenstauden, über einen kleinen Wasserlauf spannt sich eine strahlend weiße Brücke, und der Rasen leuchtet, als habe man ihn mit hellgrüner Farbe besprüht. Der Park trägt die Handschrift des berühmten Landschaftsarchitekten Charles Thays, und das Château passt dazu wie das Tüpfelchen auf dem i. Mitte des 19. Jahrhunderts ließ der Apotheker und Schafzüchter Don Orestes Piñeiro das Anwesen bauen und benannte es nach seiner Frau, Doña Candelaria Del Marmol. Mit La Candelaria schuf sich die Familie eine andere Welt – in der Einsamkeit der argentinischen Pampa und fern jeglicher Zivilisation gelegen. Und obwohl die Region inzwischen gut erschlossen und alles andere als hinterwäldlerisch ist, ist diese Adresse noch immer ein Fluchtpunkt und ein ruhiges Refugium. Hier residiert man in weiten Räumen unter Kassettendecken oder Kristalllüstern, schreitet über glänzendes Parkett oder wertvolle Teppiche, thront auf geschnitzten Lehnstühlen oder in goldumrahmten Betten. La Candelaria lässt eine prachtvolle und längst vergessen geglaubte Epoche wieder aufleben und verwandelt seine Gäste in Schlossherren auf Zeit. Zum standesgemäßen Vergnügen gehören auch Billard, Tennis, Golf und Polo – und dass die Besitzer (das Areal ist immer noch in Familienbesitz) trotz aller Liebe zur Vergangenheit längst in der Gegenwart angekommen sind, zeigt sich daran, dass alle Sport- und Freizeitaktivitäten im Zimmerpreis eingeschlossen sind: Das ist Argentinien *all inclusive*.

Buchtipp: »Verlassene Stimmen« von Antonio Porchia

Se sentir comme un roi

On pourrait croire au premier abord que ce château avec ses tours, ses créneaux et ses hautes fenêtres se trouve dans la Vallée de la Loire ou à Disneyland près de Paris, s'il n'était pas entouré de ces merveilleux jardins tropicaux, dans lesquels poussent plus de 240 espèces différentes de plantes, comme des palmiers, des eucalyptus et des bananiers. Un pont d'un blanc éclatant passe au-dessus d'un petit cours d'eau et la pelouse resplendit comme si on l'avait peinte de couleur verte. Le parc porte la signature du célèbre paysagiste Charles Thays et s'accorde parfaitement avec le château. C'est au milieu du 19ᵉ siècle que l'apothicaire et éleveur de moutons Don Orestes Piñeiro fit construire sa demeure et la baptisa d'après sa femme, Doña Candelaria Del Marmol. Avec La Candelaria la famille s'est créé un autre univers, dans la solitude de la pampa argentine et loin de toute civilisation. Et même si la région est maintenant bien développée et tout sauf sauvage, cette adresse demeure encore un refuge tranquille. Ici, on réside dans de larges pièces sous un plafond à cassettes et des lustres en cristal, on marche sur un parquet reluisant ou des tapis précieux, on trône sur des fauteuils en bois sculpté ou on se prélasse dans des lits dorés. La Candelaria fait revivre une époque somptueuse que l'on croyait depuis longtemps révolue et transforme pour un temps ses hôtes en châtelains. Pour se divertir dignement, on aura le choix entre le billard, le tennis, le golf et le polo. Malgré leur amour pour le passé, les propriétaires (la résidence est encore aux mains de la famille) ont les deux pieds dans le présent et cela se voit dans le fait que toutes les activités sportives ou non sont comprises dans le prix de la chambre : c'est l'Argentine *all inclusive*.

Livre à emporter : « Voix abandonnées » d'Antonio Porchia

ANREISE	115 Kilometer nordöstlich von Buenos Aires gelegen.
PREISE	Vom Doppelzimmer im Bungalow für US$ 220 bis zur Suite für US$ 340 für 2 Personen. Mit Vollpension und allen Aktivitäten.
ZIMMER	2 Doppelzimmer in Bungalows, 1 Doppelzimmer in der alten Mühle, 2 Doppelzimmer in der Casa del Sol, 8 Doppelzimmer in traditionellen Kolonialhäusern, 10 Doppelzimmer und 2 Suiten im Schloss.
KÜCHE	Verfeinerte argentinische und internationale Küche.
GESCHICHTE	Familienbesitz wie aus dem Bilderbuch – seit 1840.
X-FAKTOR	Mein Palast, mein Park, mein Polo-Feld.

ACCÈS	Situé à 115 kilomètres de Buenos Aires.
PRIX	A Partir de US$ 220 chambre double en bungalow, jusqu'à US$ 340 pour une suite. Pour 2 personnes, pension complète et toutes les activités comprises.
CHAMBRES	2 de chambres doubles en bungalow, 1 chambre double dans l'ancien moulin, 2 chambres doubles à la Casa del Sol, 8 chambres doubles dans les maisons coloniales traditionnelles, 10 chambres doubles et 2 suites au château.
RESTAURATION	Cuisine argentine et internationale de qualité.
HISTOIRE	Entre les mains de la famille depuis 1840.
LE « PETIT PLUS »	Mon palais, mon parc, mon terrain de polo.

Life in the sun...
Teh Rivers & Ten Lakes Lodge, Patagonia

Ten Rivers & Ten Lakes Lodge, Patagonia

Life in the sun

It was love at first sight. When young British actress Renée Dickinson went to Patagonia in the Thirties, she found her personal place to be. She had a lodge built of cypress wood in the densely forested hills of the Lanín National Park, with a view of Lago Lacar and the Andes that was lovelier by far than any theatre backdrop. She called the house "Arrayán", which means, in the language of the Mapuche, "The place where the rays of the setting sun fall". But Dickinson was to enjoy that sunlight for just four years. In 1943 she fell ill whilst travelling, and died in Buenos Aires, aged only 31. After her death, her brother Barney and his family took over the property and transformed it into one of the finest hotels in the country, the Ten Rivers & Ten Lakes Lodge. Celebrities and diplomats from all around the world have vacationed here and have enjoyed the fly-fishing – for the rivers and lakes of Patagonia are a true El Dorado of trout and salmon. If fishing isn't quite for you, the rugged and uncannily beautiful landscape is there to be discovered, on foot or on horseback, climbing or mountainbiking. Visit the mountain town of San Martín de los Andes, or go birdwatching. And whatever you choose to do with your day, in the evenings the Lodge coddles you with cosy luxury (cypress remains the dominant note) and culinary treats. The wine cellar can satisfy even the most demanding of sommeliers, and the cuisine wonderfully marries South American and Mediterranean fragrances and flavours – the lamb of Patagonia is legendary.

Book to pack: "Asleep in the sun" by Adolfo Bioy Casares

Ten Rivers & Ten Lakes Lodge	
Circuito Arrayán km 4	
Q8370DWT San Martín de los Andes	
Neuquén	
Argentina	
Tel. (54) 2972 425571 and 70	
E-mail: info@tenriverstenlakes.com	
Website: www.tenriverstenlakes.com	
Booking: www.great-escapes-hotels.com	

DIRECTIONS	Located near San Martín de los Andes, a 20-minute drive from Chapelco airport (domestic flights from Buenos Aires). Transfer is organised.
RATES	From US$ 450 per person per night. Full board and fly-fishing included (without fly-fishing: US$ 315).
ROOMS	3 double rooms, 1 apartment for 3 people (with living room and open fireplace).
FOOD	The restaurant serves South American and Mediterranean cuisine (with an emphasis on lamb and game).
HISTORY	An actress's dream house turned into a luxury lodge.
X-FACTOR	Active vacation and relaxation.

Sonnige Zeiten

Es war Liebe auf den ersten Blick. Als die junge britische Schauspielerin Renée Dickinson in den dreißiger Jahren nach Patagonien kam, fand sie ihren persönlichen *place to be*: In den dicht bewaldeten Hügeln des Lanín-Nationalparks ließ sie sich eine Lodge bauen; ganz aus Zypressenholz und mit einem Blick auf den Lago Lacar und die Anden, der schöner als jede Theaterkulisse war. Sie nannte das Haus »Arrayán«, was in der Sprache der Mapuche so viel bedeutet wie »Der Ort, auf den die Strahlen der untergehenden Sonne fallen« – doch sie durfte dieses Leuchten gerade einmal vier Jahre genießen. 1943 erkrankte sie während einer Reise und starb in Buenos Aires; nur 31 Jahre alt. Nach ihrem Tod übernahmen ihr Bruder Barney und seine Familie das Anwesen und verwandelten es in eine der schönsten Adressen des Landes, in die Ten Rivers & Ten Lakes Lodge. Berühmtheiten und Botschafter aus aller Welt verbrachten hier bereits ihren Urlaub und versuchten sich im Fliegenfischen – denn die Flüsse und Seen Patagoniens sind ein Eldorado für Forellen und Lachse. Wer sich mit dem nassen Element nicht anfreunden kann, entdeckt die raue und fast unwirklich schöne Landschaft beim Wandern und Reiten, Klettern und Mountainbiken, besichtigt das Gebirgsstädtchen San Martín de los Andes oder geht zum Birdwatching. Ganz egal, für welches Tagesprogramm man sich entscheidet: Abends verwöhnt die Lodge mit warmem Luxus (Zypressenholz ist noch immer das dominierende Element) und kulinarischen Festen: Der Weinkeller genügt selbst Ansprüchen großer Sommeliers, und die Küche verbindet südamerikanische und mediterrane Aromen – vor allem das patagonische Lamm ist legendär.

Buchtipp: »Schlaf in der Sonne« von Adolfo Bioy Casares

Les rayons du soleil couchant

Ce fut un vrai coup de foudre. Lorsque la jeune actrice britannique Renée Dickinson arriva en Patagonie dans les années 1930, elle sut tout de suite qu'elle allait y rester et se fit construire un lodge dans les collines boisées du parc national de Lanín. Sa maison en bois de cyprès offrait une vue incomparable sur le Lago Lacar et sur les Andes. La jeune femme la baptisa « Arrayán », ce qui signifie dans le dialecte des Mapuche « le lieu sur lequel tombent les rayons du soleil couchant ». Malheureusement, elle ne profita de cette lumière que quatre ans. Elle tomba malade lors d'un voyage en 1943 et mourut à Buenos Aires ; elle était âgée de 31 ans seulement. Après sa mort, son frère Barney et sa famille reprirent la maison et la transformèrent en l'une des plus belles adresses du pays, le Ten Rivers & Ten Lakes Lodge. Des personnalités et des ambassadeurs du monde entier y ont passé leurs vacances et se sont essayé à la pêche au lancer. Il faut dire aussi que les rivières et les lacs de Patagonie sont un El Dorado pour pêcheurs et regorgent de truites et de saumons. Si l'on n'aime pas trop se mouiller les pieds, on peut partir à la découverte de cette région rude et presque irréelle : à pied, à cheval, en faisant de l'escalade ou du V. T. T. On visitera aussi la petite ville montagneuse de San Martín de los Andes ou on partira observer les oiseaux. Quel que soit le programme de la journée, une chose est sûre : le soir, le lodge vous chouchoutera avec son luxe cosy (le bois de cyprès est encore l'élément dominant) et ses fêtes culinaires. La cave des vins satisfait les sommeliers les plus exigeants et la cuisine allie les arômes sud-américains et méditerranéens – en particulier l'agneau de Patagonie est légendaire.

Livre à emporter : « La trame céleste » de Adolfo Bioy Casares

ANREISE	Bei San Martín de los Andes gelegen, 20 Fahrtminuten vom Flughafen Chapelco entfernt (dorthin Inlandsflüge ab Buenos Aires). Transfer wird organisiert.	ACCÈS	Situé près de San Martín de los Andes, à 20 minutes en voiture de l'aéroport de Chapelco (vols intérieurs depuis Buenos Aires). Le transfert est organisé.
PREISE	Übernachtung ab US$ 450 pro Person. Mit Vollpension und Fliegenfischen (ohne Fliegenfischen: US$ 315).	PRIX	US$ 450 par personne. Pension complète et pêche au lancer comprises (sans pêche au lancer US$ 315).
ZIMMER	3 Doppelzimmer, 1 Apartment für 3 Personen (mit Wohnzimmer und offenem Kamin).	CHAMBRES	3 chambres doubles, 1 studio pour 3 personnes (avec salle de séjour et cheminée).
KÜCHE	Restaurant mit südamerikanischen und mediterranen Menüs (viel Lamm und Wild).	RESTAURATION	Restaurant proposant des menus sud-américains et méditerranéens (en particulier agneau et gibier).
GESCHICHTE	Das Traumhaus einer Schauspielerin wurde zur luxuriösen Lodge.	HISTOIRE	La maison de rêve d'une actrice a été transformée en lodge luxueux.
X-FAKTOR	Aktivurlaub und Ausspannen.	LE « PETIT PLUS »	Vacances actives et détente.

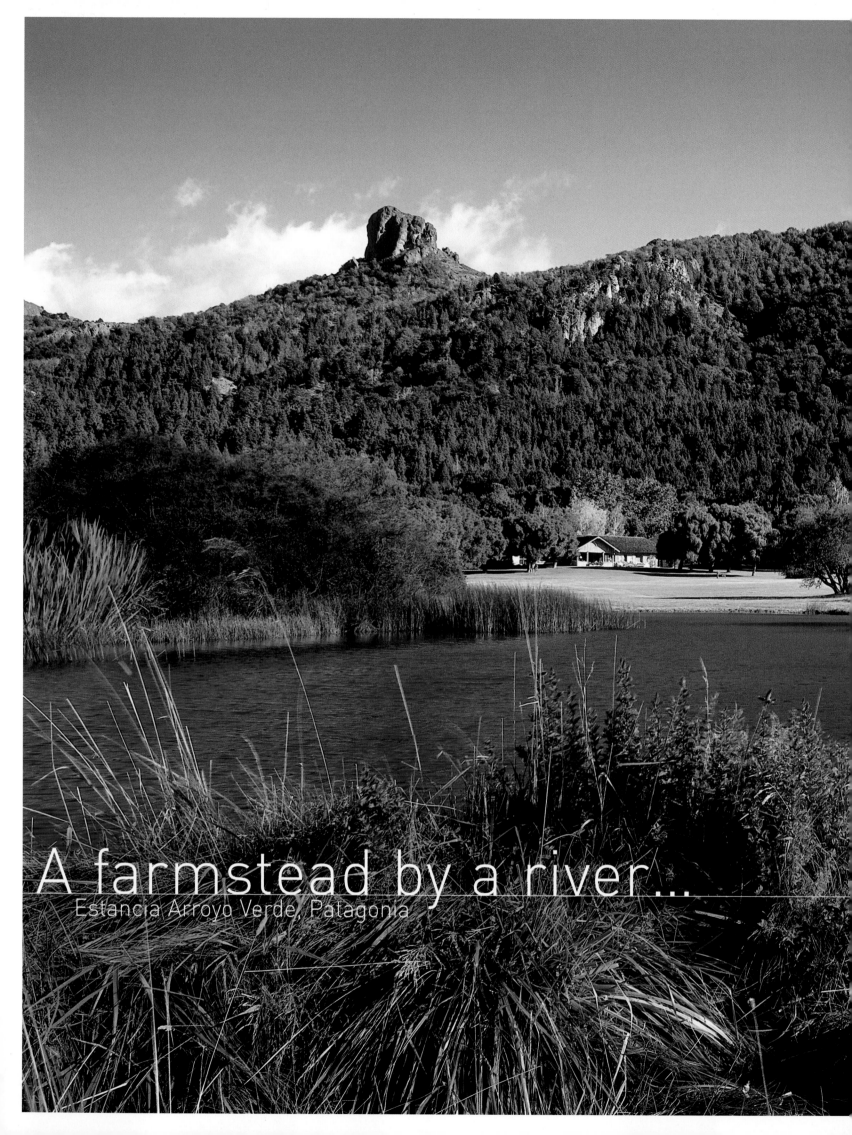

A farmstead by a river...
Estancia Arroyo Verde, Patagonia

Estancia Arroyo Verde, Patagonia

A farmstead by a river

The sparkling blue waters are crystal clear, and as it flows majestically through the valley it is brimful of salmon and trout – the Traful is every fly-fisher's dream. In the Nahuel Huapi National Park in northern Patagonia, where millions of years ago the earth was invisible beneath vast glaciers, the season opens on the second Saturday in November and runs till the third Sunday in April. Throughout those months the anglers are to be seen in their waders standing in the river, making their skilful (or in some cases not so skilful) casts and waiting patiently for the next bite. Most days the fish will weigh in at three to four pounds, and on a good day a ten-pounder will be reeled in from the Traful. If you like spending your time in the right kind of setting, among others who share your interests, book in to the Estancia Arroyo Verde and get a taste of Argentine country living at its best. Cattle and sheep graze the pastures at the foot of an impressive massif, and the stone and timber farmhouse itself is furnished in the South American country manner with deep armchairs, hunting trophies and knick-knacks. In the evenings, eat with silver cutlery off antique china, or barbecue down by the river if the weather's warm. For those who aren't here for the fishing alone, Arroyo Verde also offers riding and trekking in the Andes, or birdwatching in the land of the condor.

Book to pack: "Around the day in 80 worlds" by Julio Cortázar

Estancia Arroyo Verde	
c/o Meme Larivière	**DIRECTIONS** Situated 67 km/41 miles southeast of Bariloche airport.
Billinghurst 2586, 3° Piso	**RATES** Double rooms from US$ 490 to US$ 515 per person in the main building and chalet, respectively. Full board, airport transfer, and all activities included.
Buenos Aires	
Argentina	**ROOMS** 4 double rooms in the main building, 1 lakeside chalet for 2 to 4.
Tel. (54) 1148075535	
Fax (54) 1148017448	**FOOD** Home cooking; the picnics and barbecue evenings .
E-mail: info@estanciaarroyoverde.com.ar	**HISTORY** A ranch was transformed into an adventure playground for those seeking an active holiday.
Website: www.estanciaarroyoverde.com.ar	**X-FACTOR** One of South America's prime locations for fly-fishing.
Booking: www.great-escapes-hotels.com	

Die Farm am Fluss

Sein blau glitzerndes Wasser ist kristallklar, er fließt majestätisch durchs Tal und bringt ganze Schwärme von Lachsen
und Forellen mit sich – der Traful ist der Traum aller Flie-
genfischer. Im Norden Patagoniens, wo vor Millionen von
Jahren riesige Gletscher die Erde bedeckten und sich heute
der Nationalpark Nahuel Huapi ausdehnt, beginnt die Saison am zweiten Samstag im November und dauert bis zum
dritten Sonntag im April. Dann stehen die Angler in hohen
Gummistiefeln im Wasser, werfen mit (mehr oder weniger)
wohl geübten Bewegungen ihre langen Leinen aus und warten geduldig auf den nächsten Fang – drei bis vier Pfund
bringen die Fische an normalen Tagen auf die Waage, an
Glückstagen kann man aber durchaus auch einen satten
Zehnpfünder aus den Fluten ziehen. Wer standesgemäß und
unter Gleichgesinnten wohnen möchte, reserviert am besten
in der Estancia Arroyo Verde und erlebt dort das argentini-
sche Landleben *at its best*. Auf den Weiden am Fuß eines
beeindruckenden Felsmassivs werden Rinder und Schafe
gezüchtet, das Farmhaus aus Stein und Holz ist im südame-
rikanischen Countrystil mit viel Nippes, Jagdtrophäen sowie
tiefen Sesseln zum Versinken eingerichtet, und man isst
abends mit Silberbesteck von antikem Porzellan oder grillt
bei warmem Wetter am Flussufer. Für alle, die ihre Tage
nicht nur mit den Fischen verbringen wollen, bietet Arroyo
Verde auch Ausritte und Trekkingtouren in den Anden an
oder schickt sie zum Birdwatching auf den Spuren des
Condors.

Buchtipp: »Reise um den Tag in 80 Welten« von Julio Cortázar

Le ranch au bord du fleuve

Il coule majestueusement à travers la vallée, ses eaux sont
d'une pureté cristalline et elles regorgent de saumons et de
truites. Le Traful est bien le paradis des pêcheurs. Dans le
nord de la Patagonie, là où s'étendaient d'énormes glaciers
il y a plusieurs millions d'années et où se trouve aujourd'hui
le parc national de Nahuel Huapi, la saison de la pêche au
lancer commence le deuxième samedi du mois de novembre
pour se terminer le troisième dimanche du mois d'avril.
Pendant cette période, les pêcheurs qui ont enfilé leurs cuis-
sardes lancent leur ligne avec plus ou moins d'adresse et
attendent patiemment que le poisson morde. En général, les
poissons qu'ils attrapent pèsent entre trois et quatre livres,
ce qui n'est pas négligeable, mais les jours de chance ils
peuvent aussi avoir une belle prise qui pèsera ses dix livres
sur la balance. Celui qui désire résider dans un hôtel de qualité parmi des gens qui partagent ses goûts, sera bien avisé
de réserver une chambre à l'Estancia Arroyo Verde où il
pourra aussi découvrir la vie à la campagne sous son meilleur côté. Des élevages de bœufs et de moutons paissent
tranquillement dans les prairies au pied d'une formation
rocheuse impressionnante. Le ranch, construit en pierre et
en bois, présente un style campagnard sud-américain, avec
beaucoup de bibelots, de trophées de chasse et de fauteuils
dont la mollesse et la profondeur invitent au repos. Le soir,
on sort l'argenterie et la porcelaine ou, quand le temps s'y
prête, on organise un barbecue sur la rive du fleuve. Pour
ceux qui ne désirent pas s'adonner à la pêche toute la journée, Arroyo Verde propose aussi des randonnées à pied ou
à cheval dans les Andes ainsi que la possibilité de partir sur
les traces du condor.

**Livre à emporter : « Le tour du jour en 80 mondes »
de Julio Cortázar**

ANREISE	67 Kilometer südöstlich des Flughafens Bariloche.
PREISE	Doppelzimmer im Haupthaus US$ 490 pro Person, Doppelzimmer im Chalet US$ 515 pro Person. Mit Vollpension, Transfer ab/an Flughafen, allen Aktivitäten.
ZIMMER	4 Doppelzimmer im Haupthaus, 1 Chalet am See für 2 bis 4 Personen.
KÜCHE	Hausmannskost; Picknicks und Grillabende.
GESCHICHTE	Aus einer Ranch wurde ein Abenteuerspielplatz für Aktivurlauber.
X-FAKTOR	Einer der besten Plätze fürs Fliegenfischen in Südamerika.

ACCÈS	67 kilomètres au sud-est de l'aéroport de Bariloche.
PRIX	Chambre double dans le bâtiment principal US$ 490 par personne, chambre double dans le chalet US$ 515 par personne. Comprenant pension complète, trans-fert aéroport et toutes les activités.
CHAMBRES	4 chambres doubles dans le bâtiment principal, 1 cha-let au bord du lac pour 2 à 4 personnes.
RESTAURATION	Cuisine maison ; pique-niques et soirées barbecue.
HISTOIRE	Un ranch s'est transformé en terrain d'aventure pour touristes désirant des vacances actives.
LE « PETIT PLUS »	L'un des meilleurs endroits pour la pêche au lancer dans toute l'Amérique du Sud.

Close to the Ice Age...
Los Notros, Patagonia

Los Notros, Patagonia

Close to the Ice Age

The masses of ice glint a whitish-blue by day, and at evening glow orange. As if in slow motion they grind their way through the mountains, and tumble with a mighty roar into the waters of the Canal de los Témpanos. To stand before the Perito Moreno is to feel transported to some unreal science fiction scenario – and to experience one of the most arresting natural spectacles on earth. The Perito Moreno is the most famous of the 47 glaciers in Argentina's Los Glaciares National Park. It is a giant, soaring up to 60 metres (197 feet) out of the water, the surface as soft as frozen meringue and as pointed as billions of icy needles. If you prefer not to venture right up close, either by ship or on a trekking expedition, you can admire the glacier from a distance – for preference, from the terrace of the Los Notros Hotel. Viviana and Michel Biquard discovered the unique plot on the tip of the Magellan Peninsula in the late Eighties and built a house like a box in a theatre. Panoramic windows are the key feature even in the bathrooms. Not that that's the only way you're uniquely spoilt at Los Notros. Every one of the 32 rooms is differently furnished, with deep wing armchairs and iron bedsteads, hand-woven carpets and antique pictures. There is a cosy library where amateur students of glaciers will find all they wish to know about the Perito Moreno. There's a cigar lounge and a restaurant serving Argentine beef but also lamb, game, and fish. The herbs and spices are from the hotel's own garden, as are the desserts – the crème brûlée with a hint of lavender is surpassed only by the view of the glacier.

Book to pack: "The Old Patagonian" by Paul Theroux

Los Notros		
Bookings to: Arenales 1457, Piso 7°	DIRECTIONS	Situated 30 km/20 miles east of El Calafate airport. Transfer is organised.
C1061AAO	RATES	Cascade double room US$ 440 per person; Superior: US$ 520, Premium: US$ 590. Transfers, full board and National Park admission included.
Buenos Aires		
Argentina	ROOMS	12 Cascade double rooms, 8 Superior doubles, 12 Premium doubles.
Tel. (54) 1148143934		
Fax (54) 1148157645	FOOD	The regional specialities of Patagonia and Argentine wines.
E-mail: info@losnotros.com		
Website: www.losnotros.com	HISTORY	The only building on the tip of the Magellan Peninsula, built in the late 1980s.
Booking: www.great-escapes-hotels.com	X-FACTOR	The might of the glaciers on your doorstep.

Der Eiszeit so nah

Seine Eismassen glitzern tagsüber in Weiß-blau und glühen abends in Orange, sie schieben sich wie in Zeitlupe knirschend durch die Berge und stürzen von mächtigem Donner begleitet in die Fluten des Canal de los Témpanos – wer vor dem Perito Moreno steht, fühlt sich wie in einer irrealen Sciencefiction-Szene und erlebt doch eines der faszinierendsten Naturschauspiele der Erde. Der Perito Moreno ist der berühmteste von 47 Gletschern im argentinischen Nationalpark Los Glaciares; ein Gigant, dessen Oberfläche gleichzeitig so sanft wie gefrorenes Baiser und so spitz wie Milliarden eisiger Nadeln aussieht. Wer dem bis zu 60 Meter aus dem Wasser ragenden Gletscher nicht gleich per Schiff oder beim Trekking näher kommen möchte, kann ihn auch erst aus einiger Entfernung bewundern – am besten von der Terrasse des Hotels Los Notros aus. Viviana und Michel Biquard haben das einzigartige Grundstück an der Spitze der Magallanes-Halbinsel Ende der 80er Jahre entdeckt und hier ein Haus wie eine Theaterloge gebaut. Panoramafenster sind selbst in den Bädern das wichtigste Gestaltungselement, doch auch sonst verzichtet Los Notros nicht auf einmalige Erlebnisse. Jedes der 32 Zimmer ist unterschiedlich eingerichtet, mit tiefen Ohrensesseln und Eisenbetten, handgewebten Teppichen und antiken Bildern. Es gibt eine gemütliche Bibliothek, in der Hobby-Glaciologen alles über den Perito Moreno finden, eine Zigarrenlounge und ein Restaurant, in dem argentinisches Rindfleisch ebenso auf der Karte steht wie Lamm, Wild und Fisch. Verfeinert wird jedes Gericht mit Kräutern und Gewürzen aus dem eigenen Garten – das gilt sogar für die Nachspeisen: Die Crème brûlée mit einem Hauch Lavendel wird nur noch von der Aussicht auf den Gletscher übertroffen.

Buchtipp: »Im Feuerland« von Eduardo Belgrano Rawson

Se retrouver à l'ère glacière

Ses blocs de glace jettent dans la journée des lueurs bleutées et s'enflamment le soir dans des tons orangés, ils se poussent doucement les uns les autres en craquant, puis s'effondrent dans un effroyable bruit de tonnerre dans les eaux du Canal de los Témpanos – quand on se trouve devant le Perito Moreno, on a l'impression de voir une scène de science-fiction face au fascinant spectacle qu'il nous offre. Le Perito Moreno est le plus célèbre des 47 glaciers du parc national argentin de Los Glaciares. Il est un géant dont l'extérieur semble aussi moelleux qu'une meringue et aussi acéré que des milliards d'épines glacées. Celui qui ne désire pas se rapprocher en bateau ou en faisant du trekking de ce géant de 60 mètres, peut aussi le contempler de loin. Le mieux est encore de le faire de la terrasse de l'hôtel Los Notros. Après avoir découvert, dans les années 1980, ce terrain exceptionnel de la presqu'île de Magallanes, Viviana et Michel Biquard y ont construit une maison qui évoque une loge de théâtre. Même dans les salles de bains, les fenêtres panoramiques sont l'élément dominant bien que Los Nostros ne renonce pas à une décoration hors pair. Chacune des 32 chambres est aménagée de façon différente, avec de confortables bergères, des lits en fer, des tapis tissés à la main et des photos anciennes. Il y a une bibliothèque dans laquelle les amoureux des glaciers trouveront tous les renseignements sur le Perito Moreno, un fumoir et un restaurant qui propose au menu du bœuf argentin, de l'agneau, du gibier et du poisson. Chaque plat reçoit une saveur incomparable grâce aux fines herbes et aux épices du jardin et cela vaut aussi pour les desserts : la crème brûlée aromatisée à la lavande est un délice que seul la vue sur le glacier est capable de surpasser.

Livre à emporter : « Le naufragé des étoiles » de Eduardo Belgrano Rawson

ANREISE	30 Kilometer östlich des Flughafens El Calafate gelegen. Transfer wird organisiert.
PREISE	Doppelzimmer Cascade US$ 440 pro Person, Superior: US$ 520, Premium: US$ 590,00. Mit Transfers, Vollpension und Eintritt in den Nationalpark.
ZIMMER	12 Doppelzimmer Cascade, 8 Doppelzimmer Superior, 12 Doppelzimmer Premium.
KÜCHE	Regionale Spezialitäten aus Patagonien und argentinische Weine.
GESCHICHTE	Ende der 80er Jahre als einziges Gebäude an der Spitze der Magallanes-Halbinsel erbaut.
X-FAKTOR	Gletschergewalten direkt vor der Tür.

ACCÈS	Situé à 30 kilomètres à l'est de l'aéroport d'El Calafate. Le transfert est organisé.
PRIX	Chambre double Cascade US$ 440 par personne Superior : US$ 520, Premium : US$ 590. Transferts, pension complète et entrée dans le parc national compris.
CHAMBRES	12 chambres doubles Cascade, 8 chambres doubles Superior, 12 chambres doubles Premium.
RESTAURATION	Spécialités de Patagonie, bœuf et vins argentins.
HISTOIRE	Construit à la fin des années 1980. Seul bâtiment à la pointe de la presqu'île de Magallanes.
LE « PETIT PLUS »	Le spectacle grandiose du glacier devant la porte.

A summer residence in the so

Hotel Casa Real, Región Metropolitana

uth...

Hotel Casa Real,
Región Metropolitana

A summer residence in the south

When Domingo Fernández Concha established the Santa Rita winery in 1880, his aim for the future was not only to grow some of Chile's best wines – he also wanted to live in one of the nation's finest houses. So he had a luxury country residence built south of Santiago, in the Pompeian style, with majestic flights of steps, slender pillars, and high windows. He resided beneath richly ornamented wooden ceilings and crystal chandeliers, viewed his reflection in gilt-framed mirrors, and hung gleaming oil paintings on his walls. He even had a billiards table imported from Great Britain. And all of this grand style can be savoured to this day; for in 1996 the house became the Hotel Casa Real, offering guests a veritable journey into the past. Indeed, the grounds laid out in 1882 by French landscape architect Guillermo Renner may well be even finer than they originally were, having matured into an enchanting estate with century-old cedars, almond, olive, and lemon trees, and what may well be the largest bougainvillea on the entire continent. The hotel also has the Doña Paula Restaurant, named after the former owner, and an homage to Chile's independence hero Bernardo O'Higgins and his 120 soldiers, who sought refuge here after a fight with the Spanish. The finest products of the estate all carry "120" in their names, as in "120 Chardonnay" or "120 Sauvignon Blanc". Both are in fact among the best Chilean wines – just as Domingo Fernández Concha once hoped they would be.

Book to pack: "The House of the Spirits" by Isabel Allende

Hotel Casa Real	
Viña Santa Rita, Av. Padre Hurtado 0695	
Alto Jahuel/Buin	
Chile	
Tel. (56) 2 8219966	
Fax (56) 2 8219767	
E-mail: hotelcasareal@santarita.cl	
Website: www.santarita.com	
Booking: www.great-escapes-hotels.com	

DIRECTIONS	Situated 25 km/15 miles south of Santiago.
RATES	Double rooms from US$ 220 for 2 people, suites from US$ 250 for 2. Breakfast and winery tour included.
ROOMS	10 double rooms, 6 suites.
FOOD	The "Doña Paula" Restaurant serves very good regional and international cuisine. An excellent wine list, including the estate's own range of wines.
HISTORY	The property, dating from 1880, converted into a country hotel in 1996.
X-FACTOR	Lead the life of a wine-grower – on a choice estates.

Sommersitz im Süden

Als Domingo Fernández Concha 1880 das Weingut Santa Rita gründete, ging es ihm nicht nur darum, hier künftig einige der besten Weine Chiles anzubauen – er wollte auch in einem der schönsten Häuser der Nation wohnen. Südlich von Santiago ließ er ein Landhaus de luxe errichten; im pompeijanischen Stil, mit prachtvollen Freitreppen, schlanken Säulen und hohen Fenstern. Er residierte unter reich verzierten Holzdecken und Kristalllüstern, blickte in goldumrahmte Spiegel und auf glänzende Ölgemälde – und besaß sogar einen aus England importierten Billardtisch. All das hochherrschaftliche Flair kann man noch heute genießen, denn seit 1996 ist das Haus das Hotel Casa Real und lädt seine Gäste zu einer Reise in die Vergangenheit ein. Vielleicht noch schöner als anno dazumal ist der Park rund um das Anwesen, den der französische Landschaftsarchitekt Guillermo Renner 1882 anlegte – ein verwunschenes Fleckchen Erde mit jahrhundertealten Zedern, Mandel-, Oliven- und Zitronenbäumen sowie der wahrscheinlich größten Bougainvillea des Kontinents. Zum Hotel gehört außerdem das Doña Paula Restaurant, benannt nach seiner ehemaligen Eigentümerin und eine Hommage an Chiles Unabhängigkeitsheld Bernardo O'Higgins und seine 120 Soldaten, die hier nach einer Schlacht gegen die Spanier Unterschlupf suchten. Die besten Produkte des Hauses tragen alle ein »120« im Namen, zum Beispiel der »120 Chardonnay« oder der »120 Sauvignon Blanc«. Beide gehören übrigens zu den besten Weinen Chiles – ganz im Sinne von Domingo Fernández Concha.

Buchtipp: »Das Geisterhaus« von Isabel Allende

La magie du Sud

Lorsque Domingo Fernandez Concha a fondé le vignoble de Santa Rita en 1880, il ne voulait pas seulement produire ici quelques-uns des meilleurs vins du Chili. Il avait aussi l'intention d'habiter dans l'une des plus belles maisons du pays. Il fit édifier au sud de Santiagoune villa luxueuse de style pompéien, dotée de magnifiques perrons, de colonnes élancées et de hautes fenêtres. Les salons abritaient des plafonds lambrissés richement décorés et des lustres de cristal, des miroirs aux cadres dorés, des tableaux peints à l'huile – et même un billard importé d'Angleterre.

Cette ambiance aristocratique existe toujours. Devenue l'Hotel Casa Real en 1996, la maison invite ses hôtes à voyager dans le temps et à goûter les plaisirs d'une époque disparue. Le parc agencé en 1882 par le paysagiste français Guillermo Renner est peut-être encore plus beau qu'alors. C'est un endroit magique qui abrite des cèdres, des amandiers, des oliviers et des citronniers séculaires ainsi que probablement le plus grand bougainvillée du continent. Le Doña Paula Restaurant fait partie de l'hôtel. Il doit son nom à son ancienne propriétaire et rend hommage au héros de l'indépendance chilienne Bernardo O'Higgins et à ses 120 soldats qui vinrent se réfugier ici après une bataille contre les troupes espagnoles. Les meilleurs produits de la maison sont tous nommés « 120 » en l'honneur de ces patriotes, par exemple le « 120 Chardonnay » ou le « 120 Sauvignon Blanc ». Ces deux là font partie des meilleurs vins du Chili – Domingo Fernández Concha peut donc dormir tranquille.

Livre à emporter : « La maison aux esprits » d'Isabel Allende

ANREISE	25 Kilometer südlich von Santiago gelegen.
PREISE	Doppelzimmer ab US$ 220 für 2 Personen, Suite ab US$ 250 für 2 Personen. Mit Frühstück und Besichtigung des Weinguts.
ZIMMER	10 Doppelzimmer, 6 Suiten.
KÜCHE	»Doña Paula« Restaurant mit sehr guter regionaler und internationaler Küche. Ausgezeichnete Weinkarte, hauseigene Vinothek.
GESCHICHTE	Anwesen aus dem Jahr 1880, 1996 Umbau zum Landhotel.
X-FAKTOR	Wohnen wie ein Winzer – auf einem der besten Weingüter.

ACCÈS	Situé à 25 kilomètres au sud de Santiago.
PRIX	Chambre double à partir de US$ 220 pour deux personnes, suite à partir de US$ 250 pour deux personnes. Petit-déjeuner et visite du vignoble inclus.
CHAMBRES	10 chambres doubles, 6 suites.
RESTAURATION	Le « Doña Paula » Restaurant propose une savoureuse cuisine régionale et internationale. Remarquable carte des vins, la maison à sa propre cave.
HISTOIRE	Domaine datant de 1880, transformé en hôtel de campagne en 1996.
LE « PETIT PLUS »	Célébrer la « dive bouteille » dans l'un des meilleurs domaines viticoles.

Simply beautiful...
explora en Atacama, Atacama

explora en Atacama, Atacama

Simply beautiful

The country below this bleached-out sky is one of the barest and most arid on earth – and one of the most intriguing, too. One feature of the Atacama desert in northern Chile is the Salar de Atacama, a salt lake some 300 square kilometres (74,000 acres) in area, containing vast reserves of lithium and offering a home to rosy-coloured flamingos. There are also mysterious volcanoes affording a suitable challenge to the practised climber, and the Tatio geysers that send great jets of water aloft every morning. Not least among the attractions is the explora en Atacama hotel. Chilean architect Germán de Sol built it at an altitude of 2,400 metres (some 7,500 feet) hard by the oasis village of San Pedro de Atacama. With a main building and three courtyard groupings, it was conceived along the lines of a farmstead. Far from familiar civilisation, it affords every creature comfort, while at the same time reflecting the spartan simplicity of the landscape it is set in. The patios and buildings are linked by plain walkways and steps, large panoramic windows command views of the desert that can be enjoyed even from your bed, and the rooms have been done in regional materials such as black, natural stone. The mild temperatures are perfect for excursions or for the four long, simply-designed pools, massages in the "Casa del Agua" or the "Termas de Puritama", hot springs at an altitude of 3,100 metres (nearly ten thousand feet) some 30 kilometres or 20 miles away. Then at night the hotel has a special treat in store for its guests: on the new "Pueblo de Estrellas" observation platform there are three telescopes to scan the skies above the desert, a smooth expanse of blue-black velvet starred with glittering sequins.

Book to pack: "Clandestine in Chile: The Adventures of Miguel Littin" by Gabriel García Márquez

explora en Atacama	
Calle Domingo Atienza S/N,	
Ayllu de Larache	
Casilla 8	
San Pedro de Atacama, Chile	
Tel. (56) 55 851110	
Fax (56) 55 851115	
E-mail: reservexplora@explora.com	
Website: www.explora.com	
Booking: www.great-escapes-hotels.com	

DIRECTIONS	Situated 100 km/63 miles southeast of Calama (regular domestic flights from Santiago de Chile). The one-hour bus transfer is organised.
RATES	Three-night package US$ 1,300 per person in double rooms (7 nights US$ 2,440). Includes transfers, full board, and daily excursions.
ROOMS	50 double rooms.
FOOD	Healthy fare using produce chiefly from the region. At lunch and dinner there are two menus to choose from.
HISTORY	Opened 1st September 1998.
X-FACTOR	Unlock the secrets of the desert.

Schlicht schön

Die Landschaft unter dem weiß schraffierten Himmel ist eine der kargsten und trockensten der Erde – und dennoch eine der faszinierendsten. Die Atacamawüste im Norden Chiles besitzt den rund 300 Quadratkilometer bedeckenden Salzsee Salar de Atacama, der gewaltige Lithiumreserven birgt und Heimat der rosafarbenen Flamingos ist. Sie bietet geheimnisvolle Vulkane, die geübte Bergsteiger sogar bezwingen können, die Tatio-Geysire, die jeden Morgen Wasserfontänen in die Luft fauchen – und nicht zuletzt das Hotel explora en Atacama. Der chilenische Architekt Germán de Sol hat es auf 2.400 Metern Höhe am Rand des Oasendorfs San Pedro de Atacama gebaut und mit einem Haupthaus und drei Höfen wie eine Farm konzipiert. Fern aller gewohnten Zivilisation bietet es jeden Komfort, spiegelt aber zugleich Klarheit und Schlichtheit der umliegenden Landschaft wieder. Einfache Rampen und Treppen verbinden die Patios und die Gebäude, große Fensterfronten geben den Blick auf die Wüste frei (sogar vom Bett aus bietet sich ein zauberhaftes Panorama), und die Zimmer sind mit regionalen Materialien wie schwarzem Naturstein ausgestattet. Die milden Temperaturen genießt man bei Tagesausflügen, an den vier langgezogenen und schnörkellos designten Pools, bei Massagen in der »Casa del Agua« oder in den 30 Kilometer entfernten »Termas de Puritama«, den heißen Quellen auf 3.100 Metern Höhe. Nachts holt das Hotel seinen Gästen dann die Sterne vom Himmel: Von der neuen Plattform »Pueblo de Estrellas« aus kann man mit Hilfe dreier Teleskope einen Blick in den Himmel über der Wüste werfen, der wie schwarzblauer Samt voller glitzernder Pailletten wirkt.

Buchtipp: »Das Abenteuer des Miguel Littín« von Gabriel García Márquez

Beau tout simplement

Le paysage qui s'étend sous le ciel strié de blanc est l'un des plus pauvres et des plus arides de la Terre, et pourtant il est aussi l'un des plus fascinants. C'est sur ce désert d'Atacama, dans le nord du Chili, que se trouve le lac salé, Salar de Atacama, d'une surface de 300 kilomètres carrés, qui est à la fois une énorme réserve de lithium et un refuge pour les flamands roses. Le désert offre aussi ses volcans mystérieux que peuvent escalader des alpinistes expérimentés, ses geysers Tatio qui crachent tous les matins des fontaines d'eau dans les airs – et, last but not least, l'hôtel explora en Atacama. L'architecte chilien Germán de Sol l'a construit à 2.400 mètres d'altitude près du village de San Pedro de Atacama et l'a conçu comme un ranch avec un bâtiment principal et trois annexes. Loin de toute civilisation, il offre beaucoup de confort tout en reflétant la clarté et la sobriété du paysage environnant. Des rampes et des escaliers tout simples relient les patios et les bâtiments, des fenêtres panoramiques donnent sur le désert (on a même une vue splendide de son lit) et les chambres sont décorées avec des matériaux de la région, comme la pierre noire. On profitera des températures agréables pour faire des excursions d'une journée, pour se baigner dans l'un des quatre longs bassins, pour se faire masser dans la « Casa del Agua » ou encore pour se rendre aux « Termas de Puritama », des sources chaudes situées à trente kilomètres de l'hôtel, à 3100 mètres d'altitude. La nuit, l'hôtel fait descendre les étoiles du ciel tout spécialement pour ses clients : sur la nouvelle plate-forme « Pueblo de Estrellas », on peut ainsi à l'aide de trois télescopes regarder le ciel au-dessus du désert qui ressemble alors à du satin bleu foncé parsemé de paillettes étincelantes.

Livre à emporter : « L'aventure de Miguel Littín, clandestin au Chili » de Gabriel García Márquez

ANREISE	100 Kilometer südöstlich von Calama gelegen (dorthin regelmäßige Flugverbindungen ab Santiago de Chile). Einstündiger Bustransfer wird organisiert.
PREISE	Package mit 3 Nächten US$ 1.300 pro Person im Doppelzimmer (7 Nächte US$ 2.440). Mit Transfers, Vollpension und täglichen Exkursionen.
ZIMMER	50 Doppelzimmer.
KÜCHE	Gesunde Küche mit vorwiegend regionalen Produkten. Mittags und abends stehen jeweils zwei Menüs zur Auswahl.
GESCHICHTE	Am 1. September 1998 eröffnet.
X-FAKTOR	Den Geheimnissen der Wüste auf der Spur.

ACCÈS	Situé à 100 kilomètres au sud-est de Calama (vols réguliers depuis Santiago de Chile). Le transfert d'une heure en car est organisé.
PRIX	Forfait pour 3 nuits US$ 1.300 par personne en chambre double (7 nuits US$ 2.440). Transferts, pension complète et excursions quotidiennes comprises.
CHAMBRES	50 chambres doubles.
RESTAURATION	Cuisine saine préparée surtout avec des produits de la région. Deux menus au choix le midi et le soir.
HISTOIRE	Ouvert depuis le 1er septembre 1998.
LE « PETIT PLUS »	Sur les traces des mystères du désert.

North America

Canada • New York • Massachusetts
Florida • Hawaii • Texas
New Mexico • Arizona • California

Photos by Don Freeman   *Text by* Daisann McLane   *Edited by* Angelika Taschen

The Point **554** ●

Wheatleigh **560** ●

Langdon Hall **548** ●

● **568** The Wauwinet

"The world is a book and those
who do not travel read only one page."
St. Augustine

Little Palm Island Resort & Spa **576** ●

Timeless Country Life...
Langdon Hall, Cambridge, Ontario

Langdon Hall, Cambridge, Ontario

Timeless Country Life

The English country life used to be the exclusive province of the old moneyed and titled classes, but nowadays it seems like every other rock star and newly-minted dot-com zillionaire owns a grand estate with stables, gardens, and valets, the better to play lord or lady of the manor. The good news is that not all the gorgeous English country houses belong to Elton John and Madonna. About an hour's drive outside of Toronto is a 200 acre estate that's a near-perfect replica of an English country manse. Langdon Hall is an elegant, columned Federal revival mansion that was built in the 19th century as a summer home for the granddaughter of New York mogul John Jacob Astor. Like many such houses, it was so huge that when the great fortunes dissipated, the property became too expensive to maintain privately. Eventually Langdon Hall was converted to a hotel, and today it is a place where one can enjoy the British country life for a few days. The highlight of this Relais & Châteaux inn is its magnificent English garden, with four trails for strolling through flower beds or woods, and a lawn for playing, yes, croquet. Some contemporary touches, like a heated swimming pool, and a full-service spa, are balanced by some very old-school ones, like a traditional afternoon tea served in the conservatory. The rooms, with big beds, overstuffed chairs, and de luxe European-style bathrooms, have natural gas radiant heating under the hardwood floors, a touch of creature comfort as understated and luxurious as everything else in this picture perfect manor.

Book to Pack: "Pride and Prejudice" by Jane Austen.
Lives and loves of the landed gentry in the beginning of the 19th century - very often filmed.

Langdon Hall	
1 Langdon Drive	
Cambridge, Ontario N3H 4R8	
Canada	
Tel. +1 519 740 2100	
Fax +1 519 740 8161	
Email : info@langdonhall.ca	
Website: www.langdonhall.ca	
Booking: www.great-escapes-hotels.com	

DIRECTIONS	45 miles (70 km) west of Toronto Airport.
RATES	Rooms from US$259 to US$629.
ROOMS	53 guest rooms and suites.
FOOD	Dining room on premises; fine cuisine and regional dishes, indoor and outdoor dining. Continental breakfast.
HISTORY	Originally built in 1898 as a summer home for the granddaughter of U.S. millionare John Jacob Astor; renovated in 1987 as an inn.
X-FACTOR	A timelessly grand country estate, complete with croquet lawn.

Leben wie der Landadel

Das englische Landleben war lange ein Privileg des Geld- und sonstigen Adels. Heutzutage spielen nun aber auch gewöhnliche Rockstars und Dot-Com-Multimillionäre Lord oder Lady auf Landgütern mit Pferdeställen, Gartenanlagen und Dienern. Doch zum Glück gehören nicht alle dieser prächtigen Herrenhäuser einer Madonna oder einem Elton John. Ungefähr eine Autostunde außerhalb von Toronto in Kanada befindet sich auf einem 80 Hektar großen Grundstück eine originalgetreue Replika eines englischen Landgutes. Das mit Säulen verzierte elegante Herrenhaus »Langdon Hall« wurde im 19. Jahrhundert für die Enkelin des New Yorker Tycoons John Jacob Astor gebaut. Es ist wie die meisten solcher Gutsbesitze riesig, und als mit der Zeit das Familienvermögen zerrann, wurde der Unterhalt für die Familie zu kostspielig. Schließlich wurde »Langdon Hall« zu einem Hotel umfunktioniert, und die Gäste können hier für ein paar Tage den Lifestyle des britischen Landadels genießen. Das Schönste an diesem »Relais-&-Châteaux«-Hotel ist die englische Gartenanlage mit vier Pfaden, die durch Blumenbeete und Wälder führen. Dazu gehört ein Rasen, auf dem Krocket gespielt wird. Mit dem Umbau wurden ein paar Konzessionen an heutige Zeiten gemacht: Ein geheizter Swimming-Pool und ein Full-Service-Spa gehören dazu. Das Haus hält allerdings an seinen Traditionen fest. So wird ein Afternoon-Tea im Konservatorium serviert. Die Zimmer sind mit großen Betten, gepolsterten Stühlen und luxuriösen Badezimmern mit Bodenheizung ausgestattet. »Langdon Hall« ist ein schönes Beispiel für die Eleganz britischen Understatements.

Buchtipp: »Stolz und Vorurteil« von Jane Austen.
Leben und Lieben des englischen Landadels zu Beginn des 19. Jahrhunderts – mehrfach verfilmt.

La grande vie à la campagne

La campagne anglaise était autrefois l'apanage des vieilles familles fortunées et de l'aristocratie mais, de nos jours, il semblerait que toute rock star et nouveau super riche point-com se doivent de posséder son grand domaine avec écuries, parc et valets afin de mieux jouer au châtelain et à la châtelaine. Bonne nouvelle : toutes les sompteuses gentilhommières n'appartiennent pas à Elton John ou à Madonna. À une heure de route de Toronto, sur une propriété de 80 hectares, l'élégant « Langdon Hall », réplique d'un presbytère anglais revu et corrigé dans le style nordiste du 18e siècle, vous accueille sous son porche à colonnade. Le magnat new-yorkais John Jacob Astor le fit construire au 19e siècle comme résidence d'été pour sa petite-fille. Comme beaucoup de ces demeures immenses, une fois la fortune dilapidée, elle devint trop lourde à entretenir. Convertie en hôtel, on peut aujourd'hui y goûter aux joies distinguées de la campagne l'espace de quelques jours. Le joyau de ce bastion des « Relais & Châteaux » est le parc, avec son magnifique jardin à l'anglaise, son bois et sa pelouse où l'on joue, of course, au croquet. Les touches contemporaines telles que la piscine chauffée en plein air et le spa sophistiqué sont contrebalancées par les rituels traditionnels tel le thé de cinq heures servi dans le jardin d'hiver. Les chambres, équipées de grands lits, de profonds fauteuils et de belles salles de bain à l'européenne, sont chauffées au gaz naturel par le plancher, un détail aussi discret et luxueux que tout le reste dans ce manoir de carte postale.

Livre à emporter : « Orgueil et préjugés » de Jane Austen.
La vie et les amours de l'aristocratie anglaise au début du 19e siècle – plusieurs fois adapté au cinéma.

ANREISE	70 km westlich vom Flughafen Toronto.
PREISE	Zimmer zwischen 210 € und 510 €.
ZIMMER	53 Gästezimmer und Suiten.
KÜCHE	Speisesaal mit Terrasse; elegante Küche, regionale Gerichte. Kontinentales Frühstück.
GESCHICHTE	1898 als Sommerresidenz für die Enkelin von US-Millionär John Jacob Astor erbaut; 1987 renoviert und als Hotel eröffnet.
X-FAKTOR	Prächtiges klassisches Landgut mit einer Krocket-Rasenanlage.

ACCÈS	À 70 km à l'ouest de l'aéroport de Toronto.
PRIX	Chambres entre 210 € et 510 €.
CHAMBRES	53 chambres et suites.
RESTAURATION	Cuisine gastronomique et plats régionaux, servis dans la salle à manger ou en terrasse. Petit-déjeuner continental.
HISTOIRE	Construit en 1898 comme résidence d'été pour la petite-fille du millionnaire américain John Jacob Astor ; rénové en 1987 et converti en hôtel.
LE « PETIT PLUS »	L'atmosphère atemporelle d'une grande demeure de campagne, parfaite jusque dans sa pelouse de croquet.

Five Star Wilderness...
The Point, Saranac Lake

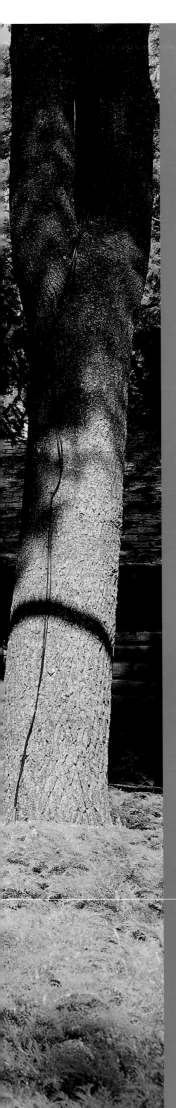

The Point, Saranac Lake

Five Star Wilderness

During the Gilded Age in the late 19th century, America became an industrial powerhouse. The economy was open and unregulated, and the rich were richer, relative to the rest of America's population, than they have ever been before or since. The names of the period's wealthiest and most prominent tycoons still resonate in U.S. history: Rockefeller, Morgan, Roosevelt. They built fabulous mansions in New York City, but preferred to spend weekend and summer vacations, in this era before air travel, in the remote Adirondack mountains of New York State.

The Point, located in the middle of the Adirondacks on the serene Saranac Lake, is one of the original "Great Camps" built by the industrial magnates of the era. The "camps" were an architectural fantasy of rustic living – the exteriors were roughhewn log facades, but inside, the appointments were as lush and expansive as a palace. The Point, originally built by William Avery Rockefeller, is a complex of cabin lodges fit for a king. Here, on 75 acres of pristine woodlands, giant stone fireplaces blaze in huge central halls with beamed ceilings. Fox, moose and deer heads line the walls. The rooms – here they're called "quarters"– are small private apartments, replete with fireplaces, Oriental rugs, marbled bathrooms with soaking tubs, and beds made from trunk posts that seem to be growing out of the room. A Relais & Châteaux resort, The Point is renowned for its impeccable high-level service to its guests – everything from breakfast in bed to a champagne lake cruise on a classic 33 foot mahogany launch. Here in the beautiful Adirondack woods, the whisper of pines mingles with the whisper of old money.

Book to pack: "The Rise of Theodore Roosevelt" by Edmund Morris.
The definitive, Pulitzer Prize winning biography of the U.S. president who was the Adirondack's most famous vacationer.

The Point P.O. Box 1327 Saranac Lake, NY 12983 USA Tel. +1 800 255 3530 and +1 518 891 5674 Fax +1 518 891 1152 Email: point@relaischateaux.com Website: www.thepointresort.com Booking: www.great-escapes-hotels.com	**DIRECTIONS** Located in the Adirondack Mountains about 310 miles (500 km) north of New York City. **RATES** Guestrooms starting at US$1250 per night, incl. full board. **ROOMS** 10 rooms and one suite. **FOOD** Sumptuous breakfasts, served in your private quarters, or in the resort's Great Hall. Five star lunches and dinners, served in the guests-only restaurant. Wines from the private cellar. **HISTORY** Originally "Camp Wonundra", a lavish "great camp" built by wealthy U.S. industrialist William Avery Rockefeller in the late 1800s. **X-FACTOR** Experience wilderness wrapped in luxury, just like a Gilded-Age New York millionaire.

Luxus in der Wildnis

Im späten 19. Jahrhundert brach in Amerika das Goldene Zeitalter an. Das Land entwickelte sich zu einer Industriemacht, die Möglichkeiten für Unternehmer schienen grenzenlos. Tycoons wie Rockefeller, Morgan und Roosevelt begründeten ihre Dynastien, schrieben amerikanische Geschichte und ließen sich in New York City sagenhafte Herrenhäuser bauen. An den Wochenenden und im Sommer zog es sie jedoch in die Abgeschiedenheit der Adirondack Mountains in New York State – damals auch ohne Flugverkehr schnell zu erreichen.

»The Point« am friedlichen Saranac Lake mitten in den Adirondacks, ist eines der »Great Camps«, wie sie damals von den Großindustriellen nach ihren Vorstellungen vom Landleben gebaut wurden. Von außen einfache Blockhütten, sind sie innen so protzig eingerichtet wie in einem Palast. »The Point«, einst der Landsitz von William Avery Rockefeller, besteht aus einer Ansammlung luxuriöser Holzhütten mitten in 30 Hektar unberührten Waldes. In jeder Unterkunft lodert in einem Steinkamin ein Feuer, rustikale Holzbalken stützen die Decken, und an den Wänden hängen ausgestopfte Fuchs-, Elch- und Hirschköpfe. Die Zimmer mit Kaminen, Orientteppichen, Marmorbadezimmern und Bettpfosten aus riesigen Baumstämmen, sind so groß wie Privat-Apartments. »The Point« gehört zur »Relais-&-Châteaux«-Gruppe und bietet entsprechend perfekten Service. Ob Frühstück im Bett oder Champagner-Fahrt auf dem See in einem der 33 Mahagoni-Boote – in den zauberhaften Wäldern von Adirondack lässt es sich so gut leben wie ein Rockefeller.

Buchtipp: »John D. Rockefeller, die Karriere des Wirtschafts-Titanen« von Ron Chernow.
Biografie über den ersten Milliardär der Geschichte.

Un palais en pleine forêt

À la fin du 19e siècle, l'Amérique connut un âge d'or économique qui fit d'elle une puissance industrielle. Jamais les riches n'avaient été aussi riches. Les plus grandes fortunes de l'époque sont entrées dans l'histoire : Rockefeller, Morgan, Roosevelt. Ces magnats bâtirent de fabuleux hôtels particuliers à Manhattan mais, en ces temps d'avant l'aviation, ils préféraient passer leurs week-ends et leurs étés dans les hauteurs isolées des Adirondacks.

Construit par William Avery Rockefeller sur les rives sereines du lac Saranac, « The Point » est l'un de ces « grands campements » des barons de l'industrie. Sorte de fantasme architectural de la vie rustique, leurs façades en rondins de bois brut cachaient des intérieurs aussi spacieux et pavillons dignes d'un roi. Éparpillés sur une trentaine d'hectares en pleine forêt, tous sont construits autour d'une immense salle centrale avec poutres apparentes et cheminées géantes en pierre. Des têtes de renards, d'élans et de cerfs ornent les murs. Les chambres (on les appelle des « quartiers ») sont de petits appartements privés avec cheminées, tapis persans, salles de bain en marbre, lits taillés dans des troncs qui semblent jaillir des murs. Membre des « Relais & Châteaux », « The Point » est renommé pour la qualité de son service impeccable, depuis ses petits déjeuners à ses croisières sur le lac arrosées au champagne dans une vedette en acajou de dix mètres de long. Ici, dans la splendeur de la forêt des Adirondacks, le murmure des pins se mêle à celui des vieilles fortunes.

Livre à emporter : « John D. Rockefeller » de Ron Chernow.
La biografie du premier milliadaire dans l'histoire.

ANREISE	Liegt in den Adirondack Mountains, zirka 500 km nördlich von New York City.
PREISE	Gästezimmer ab 1000 € pro Nacht, inkl. Vollpension.
ZIMMER	10 Zimmer und eine Suite.
KÜCHE	Reichhaltiges Frühstück in Privatgemächern oder der großen Halle. 5-Sterne-Restaurant für Mittag- und Abendessen, nur für Gäste. Weine aus dem Privatkeller.
GESCHICHTE	Das »Camp Wonundra« wurde im späten 19. Jahrhundert vom amerikanischen Industriellen William Avery Rockefeller gebaut.
X-FAKTOR	Wildnis und Luxus – Leben wie die amerikanischen Tycoons des Goldenen Zeitalters.

ACCÈS	Situé dans les montagnes Adirondacks, à environ 500 km au nord de New York.
PRIX	Chambres à partir de 1000 € la nuit, en pension complète.
CHAMBRES	10 chambres et une suite.
RESTAURATION	Somptueux petits-déjeuners, servis dans vos quartiers privés ou dans le grand hall du complexe. Déjeuners et dîners cinq étoiles, servis dans le restaurant réservé aux clients de l'hôtel.
HISTOIRE	S'appelait à l'origine « Camp Wonundra » et fut construit par William Avery Rockefeller à la fin du 19e siècle.
LE « PETIT PLUS »	Goûtez à la nature en vous drapant dans le luxe.

The Age of Innocence...
Wheatleigh, Lenox

Wheatleigh, Lenox

The Age of Innocence

In America the 1890s were a time when a small group of wealthy moguls controlled an enormous amount of money, money they spent, as nouveau riche do, unabashedly and ostentatiously. Historians refer to this time as the "Gilded Age," and the pre-eminent social chronicler of the period was the famed American novelist from Lenox, Massachusetts and New York City, Edith Wharton. Not far from Wharton's old home in Lenox is Wheatleigh, one of the grand, over-the-top country residences that defined the Gilded Age. It is a sprawling copy of a 16th century Florentine palazzo, built as a "summer cottage" by the son of a railroad mogul as a gift to his daughter, who had made a smart marriage to a Spanish Count. One hundred fifty artisans arrived from Italy to do the carvings and plaster work; the famed American landscape architect Frederick Law Olmstead designed the estate grounds. A multimillion dollar renovation in 2000 transformed Wheatleigh into a private resort, closer in design and feel to the tastes of our contemporary Gilded Age. The faux Italian touches are gone, muted soft colors and Asian fabrics are in, and the restaurant is regionally famous, with an award-winning wine list. Wheatleigh seems tailor-made for lovers and honeymooners, and not surprisingly, it is the setting for many wedding parties. We may not live in the Age of Innocence anymore, but at Wheatleigh we can go there for the weekend.

Book to Pack: "The Age of Innocence" by Edith Wharton.
The definitive chronicle of life among the wealthy during the Gilded Age.

Wheatleigh		
Hawthorne Road	DIRECTIONS	130 miles (210 km) west of Boston Logan International Airport.
Lenox, MA 01240		
USA	RATES	Rooms from US$485; suites from US$985.
	ROOMS	19 suites and guestrooms.
Tel. +1 413 637 0610	FOOD	Contemporary interpretations of classic French cuisine, served in the elegant main dining room.
Fax +1 413 637 4507		
Email: info@wheatleigh.com	HISTORY	Replica 16th century Florentine palazzo built in 1893.
Website: www.wheatleigh.com	X-FACTOR	Tastefully updated Gilded Age grandeur.
Booking: www.great-escapes-hotels.com		

Zeit der Unschuld

Die ersten Superreichen tauchten in Amerika gegen Ende des 19. Jahrhunderts auf. Sie kontrollierten riesige Summen und warfen das Geld mit großen Gesten zum Fenster hinaus – so wie es eben Neureiche tun. In den Geschichtsbüchern wird diese Zeit als das Goldene Zeitalter bezeichnet. Eine scharfe Beobachterin ihrer Zeit war die Romanautorin Edith Wharton aus Lenox, Massachusetts. Nicht weit entfernt von Whartons ehemaligem Zuhause in Lenox liegt »Wheatleigh«, ein großartiger Landsitz. Es wurde vom Erben eines Eisenbahn-Tycoons als Kopie eines florentinischen Palazzos aus dem 16. Jahrhundert als Hochzeitsgeschenk für seine Tochter erbaut. Die junge Dame hatte das Geschick, einen echten Grafen aus Spanien zu ehelichen. Für die Holzschnitzereien und Gipserarbeiten wurden hundertundfünfzig Handwerker aus Italien geholt, und der renommierte Landschaftsarchitekt Frederick Law Olmstead erhielt den Auftrag für das Design der Gartenanlagen. Heute ist »Wheatleigh« ein Privat-Resort, das 2000 aufwändig für mehrere Millionen restauriert und dem heutigen Geschmack angepasst wurde. Die allzu kitschigen Imitationen italienischer Dekors wurden entfernt und durch zurückhaltende Eleganz in sanften Tönen ersetzt. Das Hotel-Restaurant mit ausgezeichneter Weinliste gehört zu den besten der Region und hat sich landesweit einen Namen gemacht. Verliebte Paare und Frischverheiratete finden in »Wheatleigh« ein perfektes Liebesnest – kein Wunder: Hier finden immer wieder Hochzeitsfeiern statt.

Buchtipp: »Zeit der Unschuld« von Edith Wharton.
Die Chronik über das Leben der Wohlhabenden in Amerika im Goldenen Zeitalter.

L'âge de l'innocence

À la fin du 19e siècle, un petit groupe de grands capitalistes dépensaient sans compter et avec ostentation, à l'instar de tous les nouveaux riches. Les historiens parlent « d'âge d'or » de l'Amérique, dont la grande chroniqueuse mondaine fut la célèbre romancière Edith Wharton, qui partageait son temps entre New York et Lennox, dans le Massachusetts. « Weatleigh » se trouve non loin de son ancienne demeure. Cette gigantesque copie d'un palais florentin du 16e siècle, une de ces grandioses résidences d'été délirantes emblématiques de l'époque, fut offerte en cadeau de noces par un magnat du chemin de fer à sa fille, bien mariée à un comte espagnol. Cent cinquante artisans arrivèrent d'Italie pour réaliser les stucs et les sculptures ; le célèbre paysagiste américain Frederick Law Olmstead dessina le parc. En 2000, une coûteuse rénovation la transforma en hôtel de luxe, dans un style et une atmosphère plus proches de notre propre conception de l'âge d'or. Les touches italianisantes ont disparu, remplacées par des tons plus doux et des étoffes d'Orient. Son restaurant et sa cave primée sont connus dans la région. L'endroit semble avoir été conçu sur-mesure pour les amoureux et les lunes de miel. De fait, il accueille de nombreux banquets de mariage. On ne vit peut-être plus à l'âge de l'innocence, mais on peut la retrouver le temps d'un week-end à « Weatleigh ».

Livre à emporter : « L'Âge de l'innocence » d'Edith Wharton.
La chronique de la vie parmi les riches pendant l'âge d'or de l'Amérique.

ANREISE	210 km westlich vom internationalen Flughafen Boston Logan.
PREISE	Zimmer ab 390 €; Suiten ab 790 €.
ZIMMER	19 Suiten und Gästezimmer.
KÜCHE	Klassisch französische Küche, neu interpretiert, im eleganten Speisesaal serviert.
GESCHICHTE	Replika eines florentinischen Palazzos von 1893 aus dem 16. Jahrhundert.
X-FAKTOR	Geschmackvolle Grandezza auf die heutige Zeit getrimmt.

ACCÈS	À 210 km à l'ouest de l'aéroport international Boston Logan.
PRIX	Chambres à partir de 390 € ; suites à partir de 790 €.
CHAMBRES	19 suites et chambres.
RESTAURATION	Interprétation contemporaine de classiques de la gastronomie française, servie dans l'élégante salle à manger principale.
HISTOIRE	Réplique d'un palais florentin du 16e siècle construit en 1893.
LE « PETIT PLUS »	La grandeur de l'âge d'or élégamment remise au goût du jour.

A Rose is a Rose...
The Wauwinet, Nantucket

The Wauwinet, Nantucket

A Rose is a Rose

Siasconset – pronounced "Skon-set" by the locals – is at the far end of Nantucket Island from the town, and from the ferry pier. Quiet and low, the fishing village faces eastwards, towards the endless sea and Europe beyond. Nantucket is known for its grey-shingled cottages, covered with vines of pink roses, which were originally built by the sea captains and sailors who moved here during the 1800s, when whale oil was a prized commodity. Whaling ships sailed out into the cold Atlantic Ocean, sometimes for months. Back then, Nantucket was a wealthy place, but life was not always rose-covered: many of the cottages had a tiny cupola on the roof, ringed by a railing, so that nervous sea captain's wives could look out to sea and try to spot approaching ships – and ship-wrecks (the cupolas were called "widow's walks"). After the invention of electric lighting, Nantucket's commercial life faded and was replaced by tourism; it was, famously, a sum-mer retreat for America's "old money" families. There were few hotels or inns in the main village, and in Siasconset only one, the Wauwinet. Remodelled and reopened as an exclu-sive inn in 1988, the Wauwinet has preserved the charm of a way of life that is disappearing, as Nantucket's real estate development runs rampant. Peaceful, its garden bursting with flowers, it commands amazing views from its location between two private beaches, one on the Atlantic and one on Nantucket Bay. A wildlife preserve is right next door, so the birdwatching from the white wicker chairs on the front lawn is excellent. Inside the rooms are pretty and filled with sun-light and good books; the restaurant downstairs, Topper's, is among the best on the island. Whether you arrange a sail, a picnic, or a boat trip into town, worldly cares will fade into the distance. From the Wauwinet, life seems covered in roses.

Book to Pack: "Moby Dick" by Herman Melville.
The fabled quest for the great white whale captures the atmosphere of Nantucket in its heyday.

The Wauwinet	
120 Wauwinet Road	
Nantucket, MA 02584	
USA	
Tel. +1 508 228 0145	
Fax +1 508 325 0657	
Email: email@wauwinet.com	
Website: www.wauwinet.com	
Booking: www.great-escapes-hotels.com	

DIRECTIONS	On Nantucket Island, 9 miles (15 km) from Nantucket Town.
RATES	From US$260 per night.
ROOMS	35 rooms and cottages.
FOOD	Fine dining, emphasis on local seafood at Topper's restaurant, open for breakfast, lunch and dinner.
HISTORY	Originally the Wauwinet House, an inn opened in the mid-1900s. Property remodelled in 1988.
X-FACTOR	Charm, squared: the quintessential rose-covered Nantucket cottage.

Eine Rose ist eine Rose

Siasconset (»Skon-set« ausgesprochen) am östlichen Ende von Nantucket Island, Massachusetts, liegt abgelegen. Vom stillen Fischerdorf mit den typischen rosenüberwachsenen, grauen Schindel-Cottages kann man den Blick übers weite Meer schweifen lassen. Die Cottages wurden im 19. Jahrhundert von Seeleuten gebaut, die nach Nantucket zogen, um ihr Glück zu suchen. Damals blühte der Handel mit Walfischöl, und mit ihren Schiffen segelten sie zum Walfang hinaus in den kalten Atlantik. Manchmal blieben sie monatelang auf hoher See. Die Ehefrauen der Seeleute bangten um das Leben ihrer Männer und guckten bange durch die kleinen Kuppeln auf den Dächern der Cottages, um die ankommenden Schiffe zu erspähen. Statt stolzer Schiffe sahen sie manchmal auch Wracks ankommen. Deshalb werden die Kuppeln auch »Witwengänge« genannt. Mit dem Aufkommen der Elektrizität veränderte sich Nantucket. Aus der Fischerinsel wurde ein Touristenort. Vor allem wohlhabende Familien reisten zur Sommerfrische nach Nantucket. Erste Hotels wurden gebaut wie das »Wauwinet« in Siasconset. 1988 wurde es umgebaut und als exklusives Gasthaus wiedereröffnet. Der Immobilienboom der letzten Jahrzehnte hat das Gesicht der Insel verändert, doch das »Wauwinet« hat noch immer den Charme von früher. Es liegt zwischen zwei Privatstränden, neben einem Naturschutzgebiet inmitten eines blühenden Garten, und der Blick auf die Nantucket Bay ist so zauberhaft wie die lichtdurchfluteten Zimmer. Der schönste Zeitvertrieb in Nantucket: Segeln oder Picknicks. Was man auch unternimmt, der Alltag erscheint wunderbar weit weg.

Buchtipp: »Moby Dick« von Herman Melville.
Die Fabel über die Suche nach dem großen weißen Walfisch beschreibt die Atmosphäre des alten Nantucket.

Une rose est une rose

Siasconet (prononcez « Skon-set ») se trouve à l'autre bout de la ville et du débarcadère de Nantucket. Ce paisible village de pêcheurs fait face à l'océan et à l'Europe. L'île est connue pour ses cottages aux bardeaux gris couverts de rosiers grimpants construits par des marins au début du 19e siècle quand l'huile de baleine était une denrée précieuse. Les baleiniers s'aventuraient dans l'Atlantique glacé pendant des mois. Nantucket était alors prospère mais la vie n'y était pas toujours rose. Bon nombre de cottages sont surmontés d'une coupole ceinte d'une rambarde (une « promenade de veuve ») d'où les femmes de capitaines scrutaient l'horizon pour repérer les navires rentrant... ou les naufrages. Avec l'avènement de l'électricité, le commerce a cédé le pas au tourisme. Les vieilles fortunes d'Amérique établirent ici leurs résidences d'été. L'île ne compte qu'une poignée d'hôtels et Siasconet un seul, le « Wauwinet ». Rénové en 1988, tranquille et entouré d'un jardin fleuri, il conserve le charme d'un mode de vie en voie d'extinction tandis que sévit le développement immobilier. Situé entre deux plages, l'une sur l'Atlantique, l'autre sur la baie de Nantucket, il jouit de vues spectaculaires. Depuis les fauteuils en osier blanc sur la pelouse, on peut observer les oiseaux de la réserve naturelle tout à côté. Ses jolies chambres claires sont remplies de bons livres. Son restaurant, « Topper's », est un des meilleurs de l'île. Que vous envisagiez une promenade en mer, un pique-nique ou une virée en ville, vos soucis s'envoleront car, au « Wauwinet ». la vie semble un tapis de roses.

Livre à emporter : « Moby Dick » d'Herman Melville.
La quête fabuleuse de la grande baleine blanche restitue fort bien l'atmosphère de la grande époque de Nantucket.

ANREISE	15 km vom Hauptort Nantucket.
PREISE	Ab 210 € pro Nacht.
ZIMMER	35 Zimmer und Cottages.
KÜCHE	Das Gourmetrestaurant »Topper's« mit lokalen Fischspezialitäten gehört zu den besten der Insel. Morgens, mittags und abends geöffnet.
GESCHICHTE	Mitte des 20. Jahrhunderts als Gasthaus »Wauwinet House« gebaut. 1988 renoviert.
X-FAKTOR	Nantucket-Charme mit typischen rosenbedeckten Schindel-Cottages.

ACCÈS	Sur l'île de Nantucket, à 15 km de la ville de Nantucket.
PRIX	À partir de 210 € la nuit.
CHAMBRES	35 chambres et cottages.
RESTAURATION	Le restaurant « Topper's », ouvert pour le déjeuner et le dîner, propose une bonne cuisine avec des spécialités à base des produits de la mer locaux.
HISTOIRE	Initialement connue comme la « Wauwinet House », une auberge ouverte vers le milieu du 20e siècle, rénovée en 1988.
LE « PETIT PLUS »	Le charme bien ordonné, la quintessence du cottage fleuri de Nantucket.

Your Own Key...
Little Palm Island, Little Torch Key

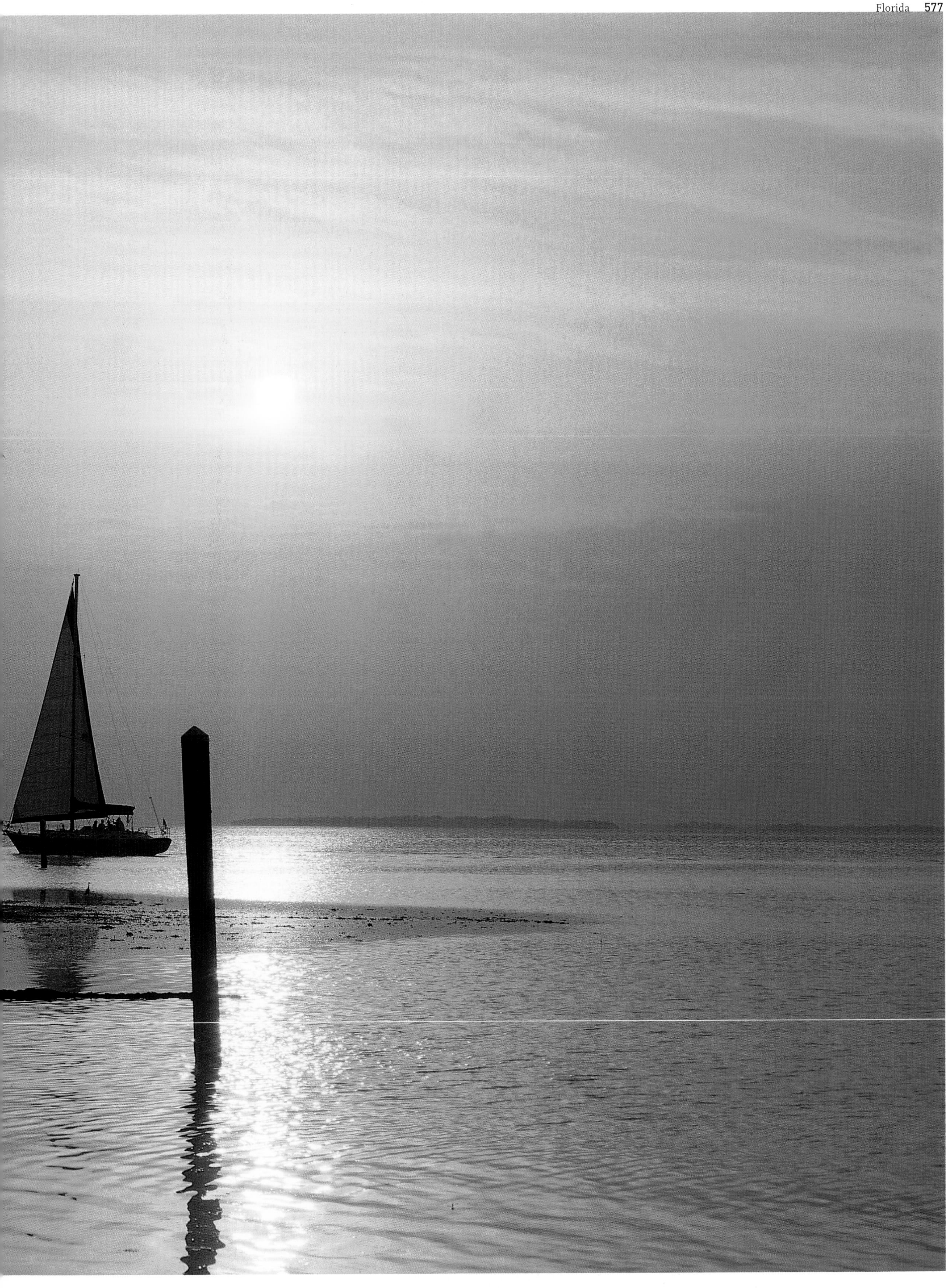

Little Palm Island, Little Torch Key

Your Own Key

As you drive south from Miami on US 1, the road narrows to a two lane highway, one of the most dramatic stretches of road in the country. The highway is actually a long causeway that seems to leapfrog over open ocean, as it passes through one small sandy island after another. This chain of little islands, the Florida Keys, is the southernmost point in the United States, and as you continue southward, it often feels as if you are going to drive right off the edge of the continent. The air is thick and humid, the landscape wild. Birds and waterfowl swoop overhead – the Everglades National Park is close by – and, occasionally in the early mornings, shy little deer the size of dogs (Key Deer, an endangered species) feed by the roadside.

Little Palm Island resort is located on Little Torch Key a private island accessible only by the launch that carries guests over to the resort from the mainland. It is just three miles offshore, but it feels a million miles away. The resort boasts twenty eight varieties of lush palm trees, white sand beaches, aquamarine ocean – and no cellphones, televisions or clocks to spoil the illusion that you have washed up in Tonga, or Fiji. There are twenty eight large seaside cottages, decorated in one of three tropical themes: Indonesian, Polynesian, British Colonial. Whichever you choose, you can be sure it will have a king bed draped in billowy mosquito netting, the fragrance of jasmine, the sound of birds, and solitude.

Book to pack: "The Empty Copper Sea" by John D. MacDonald. A murder potboiler set in the Keys by Florida's most renowned noir thriller writer.

Little Palm Island Resort & Spa	
28500 Overseas Highway	
Little Torch Key, FL 33042	
USA	
Tel. +1 305 872 2524	
Email: contactus@littlepalmisland.com	
Website: www.littlepalmisland.com	
Booking: www.great-escapes-hotels.com	

DIRECTIONS	Located on Little Torch Key, an island about 125 miles (200 km) south of Miami International Airport. Access to the island is by private plane or boat only.
RATES	From US$945 a night for a cottage.
ROOMS	28 thatched-roof oceanfront bungalows and two grand suites.
FOOD	The Dining Room restaurant serves "Floribbean" cuisine – elegantly presented local seafood specialties.
HISTORY	A private island that used to belong to a Florida politician. Converted in 1988 to a private resort.
X-FACTOR	Lush Caribbean-like tropical solitude, without leaving the continental USA.

Reif für die Insel

Die US 1 mündet südlich von Miami in eine schmale, zwei-spurige Überlandstraße und gehört zu den zauberhaftesten Straßenstrecken des Landes. Eigentlich ein langer Damm, reiht sie über den offenen Ozean hinweg kleine, sandige Inseln zu einer Kette auf. Die Florida Keys bilden den süd-lichsten Punkt der Vereinigten Staaten, und wer auf dem Damm weiter in diese Richtung fährt, glaubt gleich über den Horizont zu kippen. Die Luft ist schwer und feucht, die Landschaft wild. Im Sturzflug rasen einem Vögel über den Kopf – der »Everglades National Park« ist in der Nähe –, und manchmal kann man am frühen Morgen fressendes »Key Deer« am Straßenrand beobachten, ein vor dem Aussterben bedrohtes Kleinwild, das nicht größer ist als ein Hund.

Das Resort »Little Palm Island« auf der Privatinsel »Little Torch Key« ist nur per Schiff zu erreichen. Die Strecke ist zwar nur knapp fünf Kilometer lang, doch man hat das Gefühl, tausende von Kilometern weit weg zu sein. Im Resort zeigen dann 28 verschiedene üppige Palmenarten, weiße Sandstrände und der aquamarine Ozean ihre ganze Pracht, sodass man sich auf Tonga oder Fidschi glaubt. Weder Handys, Fernseher noch Uhren stören diese Illusion. Entsprechend sind auch die 28 großzügigen Strand-Cottages eingerichtet: im indonesischen, polynesischen oder briti-schen Kolonialstil. In den Cottages stehen große Kingsize-Doppelbetten, die in Moskitonetze eingehüllt sind. Überall schwebt der Duft von Jasminblüten, und einzig der Gesang der Vögel durchbricht die Ruhe.

Buchtipp: »Der dunkelschwarze Betrug« von John D. MacDonald. Kriminalroman aus der Feder des bekanntesten Thriller-Autors Floridas.

Une île rien que pour vous

Quand vous descendez l'US1 vers le sud à partir de Miami, la chaussée rétrécit pour former la route à deux voies la plus spectaculaire du pays. Elle devient en fait une longue passe-relle qui semble jouer à saute-mouton sur l'océan ouvert, rebondissant d'une île sablonneuse à l'autre. Cette chaîne d'îlots, les « Keys » de Floride, constitue le point le plus méridional des États-Unis. À mesure que l'on avance, on a l'impression qu'on va tomber du bout du continent. L'air est lourd et humide, les paysages sont luxuriants. Le « parc national des Everglades » est tout près : les oiseaux abondent et parfois, le matin, on voit de petits cervidés de la taille d'un chien (les cerfs des Keys, une espèce en voie de disparition) brouter sur le bord de la route.

« Little Palm Island » est située sur « Little Torch Key », une île privée accessible uniquement par la vedette de l'hôtel qui fait la navette avec la terre ferme. Elle ne se trouve qu'à cinq kilomètres environ de la côte mais semble perdue au milieu de nulle part. L'établissement est fier de ses vingt-huit espè-ces de palmiers, de ses plages de sable blanc, de son eau tur-quoise et aucun téléphone portable, poste de télévision ni pendule ne viennent gâcher l'illusion d'avoir échoué sur les rivages de Tonga ou de Fiji. Les vingt-huit grands bungalows qui donnent sur la mer sont décorés dans un thème tropical : indonésien, polynésien ou colonial britannique. Quel que soit votre choix, vous pouvez compter sur un grand lit drapé d'une ample moustiquaire, le parfum du jasmin, le chant des oiseaux et la solitude.

Livre à emporter : « Le combat pour l'île » de John D. MacDonald. Une histoire de meurtre située dans les Keys, par le plus célèbre des auteurs de polars de Floride.

ANREISE	Etwa 200 km südlich vom internationalen Flughafen Miami. Nur mit einem Privatflugzeug oder per Schiff zu erreichen.
PREISE	Ein Cottage kostet ab 765 € pro Nacht.
ZIMMER	28 Strand-Bungalows mit Strohdächern, zwei große Suiten.
KÜCHE	Restaurant mit »Floribbean« Küche – elegant präsentier-te Seafood-Spezialitäten.
GESCHICHTE	Die Privatinsel gehörte einem lokalen Politiker. 1988 wurde daraus ein Resort.
X-FAKTOR	Abgeschiedenheit in üppiger, tropischer Karibik-Landschaft.

ACCÈS	L'île de « Little Torch Key », se trouve à environ 200 km au sud de l'aéroport international de Miami. On accè-de uniquement par avion ou bateau privé.
PRIX	À partir de 765 € la nuit pour un bungalow.
CHAMBRES	28 bungalows avec un toit en chaume donnant sur l'o-céan et deux grandes suites.
RESTAURATION	Le restaurant propose une cuisine « floribéenne »: des spécialités de poissons et fruits de mer élégamment présentées.
HISTOIRE	Une île privée qui appartenait autrefois à un politicien de Floride. Convertie en hôtel en 1988.
LE « PETIT PLUS »	Une tranquillité tropicale absolue.

Home of the Hula...

Molokai Ranch, Maunaloa, Molokai

Molokai Ranch, Maunaloa, Molokai

Home of the Hula

The native Hawaiians on the tiny island of Molokai claim to have invented the signature, hip-swaying dance of the islands, the hula. And so, every year, they hold an island-wide festival celebrating this dance that is one of Hawaii's greatest cultural treasures. In the hula, the movements of the arms and hands tell a story; the hulas of Molokai tell a very happy story, one of a Hawaiian island rich in culture, few in tourists, where the islands of today remain the islands of yesterday's dreams. Molokai island is so remote that for years it was mainly known to Hawaiians as the site of an old leper colony (it is still possible to visit the isolated settlement, which now is home to fewer than 100 people). The Molokai Ranch and Lodge is the only major resort on the island, and occupies its most stunning white sand beach, where you can kayak in the warm, gentle waters and – if you are lucky – meet some green sea turtles along the way. The resort combines two styles of accommodation. The main lodge has spacious, air conditioned rooms. But it is at the Beach Village where you can best experience the old-fashioned, pre-tourism Hawaii, sleeping in a tent on a wooden platform. Here, your bed can catch the ocean breezes, and your shower has a little portal open to the sky. If, under the moonlight you feel moved to do your own Hawaiian hula, only the stars will know.

Book to pack: "Hawaii" by James A. Michener.
The classic, grand epic about Hawaiian history and life.

Molokai Lodge and Beach Village	DIRECTIONS	10 miles (16 km) west of Molokai's Hoolehua Airport.
100 Maunaloa Highway	RATES	Air conditioned guest rooms from US$398; from US$268 for a bungalow-like tent on a wooden platform in the Beach Village.
Maunaloa, HI 96770		
USA		
Tel. +1 808 660 2824	ROOMS	22 guest rooms in the Lodge, 40 "tentalows" in the Beach Village.
Fax +1 808 552 2773	FOOD	A la carte dinners in the lodge's Maunaloa Room and Paniolo Lounge, buffet-style open-air dining at the Ranch's Kaupoa Dining Pavilion.
Email: info@molokairanch.com		
Website: www.molokairanch.com	HISTORY	A 65,000 acre ranch, founded more than 100 years ago.
Booking: www.great-escapes-hotels.com	X-FACTOR	Savor what is perhaps the last unspoiled, un-touristy Hawaiian island.

Heimat des Hula-Tanzes

Der Hula-Tanz stammt aus der kleinen Hawaii-Insel Molokai. Darauf sind die Inselbewohner so stolz, dass sie jedes Jahr zu Ehren des hüfteschwingenden Tanzes ein Festival organisieren. Der Hula gehört zu den großen kulturellen Schätzen Hawaiis, durch Bewegungen mit Armen und Händen werden Geschichten aus dem Inselreich erzählt. Molokai gibt dafür besonders schönen Stoff her. Die Insel hat ein reiches kulturelle Erbe, und nur wenige Touristen verirren sich dorthin. Molokai ist so paradiesisch geblieben, wie man sich Hawaii in seinen Träumen vorstellt. Sogar die Einheimischen kennen die abgelegene Insel nur als ehemalige Leprakolonie. Die fast verlassene Siedlung mit weniger als hundert Bewohnern kann man übrigens besichtigen. Die »Molokai Ranch and Lodge« ist das einzige Resort auf der ganzen Insel. Den größten Teil des wunderschönen weißen Sandstrandes nimmt die Anlage für sich ein. Das Meer hier ist ruhig, fast friedlich, und die Wassertemperaturen sind angenehm warm. Ein schöner Ort, um Kajakfahrten zu unternehmen. Mit etwas Glück entdeckt man dabei sogar eine der grünen Meeresschildkröten. Das Resort besteht aus zwei Teilen. Die Hauptlodge mit großzügigen Zimmern und Air-Conditioning und das »Beach Village« im Stil des ursprünglichen Hawaii. Hier stehen auf Holzplattformen bungalowartige Zelte, durch die sanfte Ozeanbrisen wehen. Und in der Dusche gibt es eine kleine Luke, die den Blick auf den Himmel freigibt. Der perfekte Ort, um unter freiem Sternenhimmel etwas Hula zu tanzen.

Buchtipp: »Hawaii« von James A. Michener.
Klassiker und großartiges Epos über Hawaii.

Le berceau du hula

Les natifs de la minuscule Molokai affirment avoir inventé le hula, la fameuse danse des îles Hawaï caractérisée par une ondulation frénétique des hanches. C'est pourquoi, chaque année, toute l'île organise un festival qui célèbre ce monument de la culture hawaïenne. Dans le hula, les mouvements des bras et des mains racontent une histoire. Celle de Molokai est très heureuse : une riche culture, peu de touristes, une atmosphère d'île de rêve comme on n'en fait plus. Molokai est si éloignée que, pendant des années, la plupart des Hawaïens ne la connaissaient que comme le site d'une vieille léproserie (on peut encore visiter la colonie qui compte désormais moins d'une centaine d'occupants). Le « Molokai Ranch and Lodge » est le seul grand hôtel de l'île et monopolise ses plus belles plages au sable d'un blanc aveuglant. On peut se promener en kayak dans ses eaux chaudes et calmes et, avec un peu de chance, apercevoir la carapace verte de tortues marines. L'hôtel offre deux types d'hébergement. Le bâtiment principal propose des chambres spacieuses avec air conditionné, mais c'est dans le village sur la plage que vous pourrez goûtez au mieux le Hawaï d'avant l'ère du tourisme, en dormant sous une tente perchée sur une plate-forme en bois. Ici, votre lit est caressé par la brise marine et vous prenez votre douche en regardant le ciel. Et si, sous le clair de lune, il vous vient l'envie d'expérimenter votre propre version du hula, vous n'aurez que les étoiles pour témoins.

Livre à emporter : « Hawaï » de James A. Michener.
Un classique, la grande histoire héroïque d'Hawaï.

ANREISE	16 km westlich vom Flughafen Hoolehua auf Molokai.
PREISE	Gästezimmer mit Air-Conditioning in der Hauptlodge ab 320 €; bungalowähnliche Zelte auf Holzplattform im »Beach Village« ab 215 €.
ZIMMER	22 Gästezimmer in der Lodge, 40 »Tentalows« im »Beach Village«.
KÜCHE	Büffet und à-la-Carte-Gerichte im »Maunaloa Room« und in der »Paniolo Lounge« der Lodge. Freiluftbüffet im »Kaupoa Dining Pavillon«.
GESCHICHTE	Die Ranch auf 26 000 Hektar ist über 100 Jahre alt.
X-FAKTOR	Ursprüngliche Hawaii-Insel ohne Touristenmassen.

ACCÈS	À 16 km à l'ouest de l'aéroport Hoolehua, sur Molokai.
PRIX	Chambres avec air conditionné à partir de 320 € ; un bungalow / tente sur une plate-forme en bois dans le « Beach Village » à partir de 215 €.
CHAMBRES	22 chambres dans la Lodge, 40 « tentalows » dans le « Beach Village ».
RESTAURATION	Menu à la carte dans la «salle Maunaloa» et la « Paniolo Lounge » de la Lodge ; buffet en plein air dans le «Kaupoa Dining Pavillon » du ranch.
HISTOIRE	Un ranch de près de 26 000 hectares fondé il y a plus d'un siècle.
LE « PETIT PLUS »	La dernière île hawaïenne préservée du tourisme.

Big Bend...
Cibolo Creek Ranch, Marfa

Cibolo Creek Ranch, Marfa

Big Bend

The legend is that the Cibolo Creek Ranch got its start as a getaway hideout. In the American West of the mid-1800s, gunfight duels were still more popular, and cheaper, than courts and lawyers for resolving disputes. But the duel winners usually had to run from justice, so after Milton Faver shot his rival, he quickly fled to the most remote and isolated place he could find, in order to start a new life. Today, Faver's old ranch – 32,000 acres straddling the Rio Grande river where it makes its "big bend" at the Texas-Mexico border – provides a different kind of refuge, an escape to the lost romance of the American West. It remains as remote as it was in the old wild West days (arrival here involves a three and a half hour drive or a private plane), but the working cattle ranch has been painstakingly restored as a luxury retreat. There are beautiful details here: Mexican carnival masks adorn the walls, original broad wooden beams secure the ceilings. Late at night, huddled under a colourful Southwestern blanket in your room in one of three historic adobe forts, you may hear wild boars rooting around in the sagebrush. Daylight activities at the ranch range from the old-fashioned to the modern. There are horses or 4-wheel drive vehicles to ride across the high mesas, a heated swimming pool and Jacuzzi to relax in. Or you can fast-forward to the ultra-contemporary, and drive a half hour north to visit Donald Judd's cool aluminium sculpture installations at the Chinati Foundation in Marfa. Being a fugitive from justice probably never was this much fun.

Book to pack: "Riders of the Purple Sage" by Zane Grey.
The early 20th century classic by the famous Western genre novelist.

Cibolo Creek Ranch	
HCR 67, PO Box 44	
Marfa, TX 79843	
USA	
Tel. +1 432 229 3737	
Fax +1 432 229 3653	
Email: reservations@cibolocreekranch.com	
Website: www.cibolocreekranch.com	
Booking: www.great-escapes-hotels.com	

DIRECTIONS	The ranch is located a 225 miles (360 km) southwest of Midland (Texas) Airport, and 214 miles (340 km) southeast of El Paso (Texas) airport.
RATES	Rooms from US$450 a night, incl. three meals daily.
ROOMS	34 guest rooms in the fort buildings and guest house.
FOOD	Eclectic cuisine, using local ingredients like antelope and quail, and Mexican-Texas inspired dishes.
HISTORY	Cibolo's three historic frontier forts date back to the mid 19th Century. The property was restored and opened as a guest resort in 1994.
X-FACTOR	Luxurious and authentic immersion in the solitude and wilderness of the old Texas frontier.

Leben wie ein Cowboy

Im 18. Jahrhundert pflegte man im Westen Amerikas Streitereien nicht am Gericht zu regeln, sondern ganz unkompliziert mit einem Pistolen-Duell. Eine damals beliebte Methode und dazu noch kostengünstig. Wer aus einem solchen Duell als Sieger hervorkam, musste sich meist vor dem Gesetz verstecken. So etwa Milton Faver. Er streckte seinen Rivalen nieder und floh an den abgelegensten Ort, den er finden konnte, um dort ein neues Leben zu beginnen. Heute ist Favers 13 000 Hektar große »Cibolo Creek Ranch« entlang des Rio Grande an der texanisch-mexikanischen Grenze eine romantische Erinnerung an den Wilden Westen. Die Ranch liegt genauso abgeschieden wie damals und ist mit dem Auto von Midland oder El Paso in dreieinhalb Stunden zu erreichen, sonst nur mit einem Privatflugzeug. Auf der »Cibolo Creek Ranch« wird immer noch Viehzucht betrieben, auch wenn heute daraus ein sorgfältig umgebautes Luxus-Resort geworden ist. Ganz im traditionellen Ranch-Stil zieren Karnevalsmasken aus Mexiko die Wände und rustikale, breite Holzbalken stützen die Decken. Spät nachts kann man sogar draußen in der Wüste Wildschweine hören, während man in einem Zimmer der historischen Adobe-Forts unter einer Folklore-Bettdecke kuschelt. Bei Tage vertreibt man sich die Zeit mit einer Fahrt im traditionellen Vierspänner hoch auf den Tafelbergen. Oder man entspannt im geheizten Pool oder Jacuzzi. Ein Leckerbissen für Kulturfans liegt eine halbe Stunde weiter nördlich: Die Chinati Foundation in Marfa mit den spektakulären Aluminium-Skulpturen des Künstlers Donald Judd.

Buchtipp: »Desperados« von Zane Grey.
Klassischer Western-Roman aus dem frühen 20. Jahrhundert.

Le grand coude

La légende veut que le « Cibolo Creek Ranch » ait été la planque d'un hors-la-loi en cavale. Dans le Far West du milieu du 19e siècle, il était plus simple – et meilleur marché – de régler ses litiges par un duel au revolver qu'en recourant aux tribunaux. Le hic, c'était que le vainqueur avait ensuite la justice aux trousses. C'est ainsi qu'après avoir abattu son rival, Milton Faver se réfugia dans le lieu le plus perdu qu'il trouva afin d'y refaire sa vie. Aujourd'hui, son ranch – 13 000 hectares à cheval sur le Rio Grande là où il décrit un « grand coude » : à la frontière entre le Mexique et le Texas, offre un autre type d'évasion : une plongée dans l'atmosphère romantique de la conquête de l'Ouest. Le lieu est toujours aussi isolé (on y accède après trois heures et demie de route ou en avion privé), mais la ferme et ses enclos à bestiaux ont été restaurés et convertis en luxueux complexe hôtelier. Les détails ont été soignés : masques de carnaval mexicains aux murs, plafonds en poutres apparentes. Tard dans la nuit, blotti sous une couverture indienne dans votre chambre située dans une des trois bâtisses fortifiées en adobe, vous entendrez peut-être les cochons sauvages fouiller la terre sous les armoises. Le jour, les activités vont du traditionnel à l'avant-garde. On peut explorer les hautes mesas à cheval ou en quatre-quatre, se détendre dans la piscine chauffée et le jacuzzi ; ou encore se projeter en avant dans l'ultramoderne en allant voir les sculptures en aluminium de Donald Judd à la « Chinati Foundation » de Marfa. Jamais être en cavale n'aura été aussi plaisant.

Livre à emporter : « La Cabane perdue » de Louis L'Amour.
Un classique par un des plus grands auteurs de westerns adventures.

ANFAHRT	Die Ranch liegt 360 km südwestlich vom Flughafen in Midland, Texas, und 340 km südöstlich vom Flughafen in El Paso, Texas.
PREISE	Zimmer ab 360 € pro Nacht, inkl. drei Mahlzeiten.
ZIMMER	34 Gästezimmer verteilt auf drei Forts und ein Cottage.
KÜCHE	Vielseitige Küche mit lokalen Zutaten wie Antilope oder Wachtel; Tex-Mex-Gerichte.
GESCHICHTE	Drei historische Grenz-Forts aus der Mitte des 19. Jahrhunderts. 1994 Umbau und Eröffnung als Luxus-Resort.
X-FAKTOR	Eine geschichtsträchtige und luxuriöse Welt mitten in der wilden Einsamkeit des Grenzgebietes zu Mexiko.

ACCÈS	Le ranch est situé à 360 km au sud-ouest de l'aéroport de Midland (Texas), et à 340 km au sud-est de celui d'El Paso (Texas).
PRIX	Chambres à partir de 360 € la nuit, en pension complète.
CHAMBRES	34 chambres dans trois bâtiments fortifiés et un chalet.
RESTAURATION	Cuisine éclectique à base de produits locaux comme l'antilope et la caille, plus des plats tex-mex.
HISTOIRE	Les trois forts de « Cibolo Creek Ranch » gardaient la frontière au milieu du 19e siècle. La propriété a été restaurée et convertie en complexe hôtelier en 1994.
LE « PETIT PLUS »	Une immersion luxueuse et authentique dans la solitude et la nature sauvage du Texas.

Five Star Dharma...
El Monte Sagrado, Taos

El Monte Sagrado, Taos

Five Star Dharma

The 1960s are long gone, but its visionaries and healers and hippies can still be found living – indeed, thriving – in American outposts like Taos, New Mexico. Taos is mystic central, and mysticism, it seems, attracts prosperity. Taos today is one of the richest towns in the Southwest. It boasts of having more massage therapists per capita than any other place in the U.S. It's no surprise that Taos is also home to the only luxury resort spa constructed around a Navajo (Native American) Sacred Circle. El Monte Sagrado is the brainchild of Tom Worrell, a philanthropist cum environmentalist, whose dream was to construct an ecologically sound luxury retreat in the desert at the foot of the Sangre de Cristo mountains. There is no doubt that he has created a unique oasis; El Monte is a marvellous fantasy enclave of adobe buildings, pools and fountains that burble gently and constantly. But, fear not – everything at El Monte is designed to be 100% eco-sensitive: the water is constantly recycled by something called a "Living Machine", and it is purified with a non-chlorine substance. There is a Native American sweat lodge in the resort's spa, which aims to, according to Worrell, "help people identify their own self." The treatments include a "life reading" massage and an "Egyptian Anointing" which involves chakras and gemstones and hot oils. There's also an animal therapy session for those interested in learning to talk to their pets. "If something works," asks Worrell, "Why ask why?"

Book to Pack: "The Teachings of Don Juan" by Carlos Castaneda.
Words of wisdom from a Native American shaman. This book is the bible of the New Age movement.

El Monte Sagrado	
317 Kit Carson Road	
Taos, NM 87571	
USA	
Tel. +1 505 758 3502	
Fax +1 505 737 2985	
Email: info@elmontesagrado.com	
Website: www.elmontesagrado.com	
Booking: www.great-escapes-hotels.com	

DIRECTIONS	9 miles (15 KM) northwest of Taos Municipal Airport.
RATES	From US$325 per night.
ROOMS	36 suites and casitas (little houses).
FOOD	De La Tierra restaurant, serving organic gourmet dishes like "Yak Chili".
HISTORY	The resort was opened in 2003 by Tom Worrell, a maverick philanthropist and environmentalist.
X-FACTOR	Recharge your mystical and spiritual batteries in the southwest's most luxurious eco-resort.

Fünf-Sterne-Dharma

Die Sechziger sind längst vorbei, doch noch immer gibt es Visionäre, Heiler und Hippies aus der Zeit. Eine Hochburg dieser Zunft ist Taos in New Mexico. Taos ist ein Zentrum für Esoterik und hat damit seinen Wohlstand begründet. Die Stadt gehört zu den wohlhabendsten im Südwesten der Vereinigten Staaten und brüstet sich gerne damit, die höchste Dichte an Masseuren im ganzen Land zu haben. Taos kann auch mit dem einzigen Luxus-Spa aufwarten, das rund um eine heilige Stätte der Navajo-Indianer gebaut wurde. Der Gründer von »El Monte Sagrado«, der Philanthrop und Umweltschützer Tom Worrell, hat hier seinen Traum von einem ökologisch verträglichen Luxus-Retreat verwirklicht. Mitten in der Wüste, am Fuße der »Sangre de Cristo Mountains«, schuf er eine einzigartige Oase. »El Monte« ist eine zauberhafte Traumwelt aus Lehmziegel-Häusern, Pools und Brunnen, aus denen sanft das Wasser plätschert. Trotz der Annehmlichkeiten ist hier alles hundertprozentig umweltverträglich: So wird das Wasser dauernd wiederaufbereitet und mit einer chlorfreien Substanz gereinigt. Im Spa gibt es eine rituelle Indianer-Sauna, eine »Sweat Lodge« die, gemäß Worrell, »helfen soll, sein Innerstes zu erkennen«. Unter den Behandlungen findet man auch »Life-Reading«-Massagen und »Egyptian Anointing«, eine ägyptische Chakra-Ölung mit Edelsteinen und heißen Ölen. Auch Haustierhalter kommen zum Zug: In einer speziellen Therapiestunde lernt man, mit Tieren zu kommunzieren. »Es funktioniert«, versichert Worrell.

Buchtipp: »Die Lehren des Don Juan« von Carlos Castaneda. Weisheiten eines Indianer-Schamanen. Das Buch ist die Bibel der New-Age-Bewegung.

Le dharma cinq étoiles

Les années soixante sont loin mais les visionnaires, guérisseurs et hippys continuent de s'épanouir dans des avant-postes tels que Taos, au Nouveau-Mexique. Cette Mecque du mysticisme doit attirer la prospérité car elle est aujourd'hui l'une des agglomérations les plus riches du Sud-Ouest américain. Elle se targue de compter plus de massothérapeutes par habitant que n'importe quelle autre ville des États-Unis. Il n'y a donc rien d'étonnant à ce qu'elle abrite le seul spa de grand standing construit autour d'un « cercle sacré » navajo. « El Monte Sagrado » est l'œuvre de Tom Worrell, philanthrope et écologiste qui rêvait de bâtir une retraite de luxe respectueuse de l'environnement dans le désert au pied du massif de « Sangre de Cristo ». Il a su créer un lieu de rêve : une merveilleuse oasis de bâtiments en adobe, de bassins et de fontaines qui gargouillent doucement. Mais n'ayez crainte, tout à « El Monte » a été conçu dans le plus grand respect de la nature : l'eau est recyclée en permanence par une « machine vivante » et purifiée par une substance sans chlore. Il y a une « hutte de sudation rituelle » qui, selon Worrell, « aide chacun à identifier son moi ». Les traitements incluent un « massage de lecture de vie » et des « onctions égyptiennes » qui font intervenir les chakras, des gemmes et des huiles chaudes. Il existe même des séances de thérapie animale pour ceux qui souhaitent apprendre à communiquer avec leurs matous et toutous chéris. « Si ça marche, il ne faut pas chercher à savoir pourquoi », déclare Worrell.

Livre à emporter : « Le Voyage à Ixtlan : les leçons de Don Juan » de Carlos Castaneda. Des perles de sagesse offertes par un shaman amérindien. Bible du mouvement New Age.

ANREISE	15 km nordwestlich vom Flughafen Taos.
PREISE	Ab 260 € pro Nacht.
ZIMMER	36 Suiten und Casitas (kleine Häuser).
KÜCHE	Im Restaurant »De La Tierra« gibt's Bio-Gourmetgerichte wie »Yak Chili«.
GESCHICHTE	Das Resort wurde 2003 vom Philanthropen und Umweltschützer Tom Worrell gegründet.
X-FAKTOR	Auftanken in einem der luxuriösesten Öko-Resorts Amerikas.

ACCÈS	À 15 km au nord-ouest de l'aéroport municipal de Taos.
PRIX	À partir de 260 € la nuit.
CHAMBRES	36 suites et « casitas » (petites maisons).
RESTAURATION	Le restaurant « De La Tierra » sert des plats gastronomiques bios tels que le « Chili au yack ».
HISTOIRE	L'hôtel a été ouvert en 2003 par Tom Worrell, un philanthrope et écologiste anticonformiste.
LE « PETIT PLUS »	Rechargez vos batteries mystiques et spirituelles dans l'hôtel écologique le plus luxueux du Sud-Ouest.

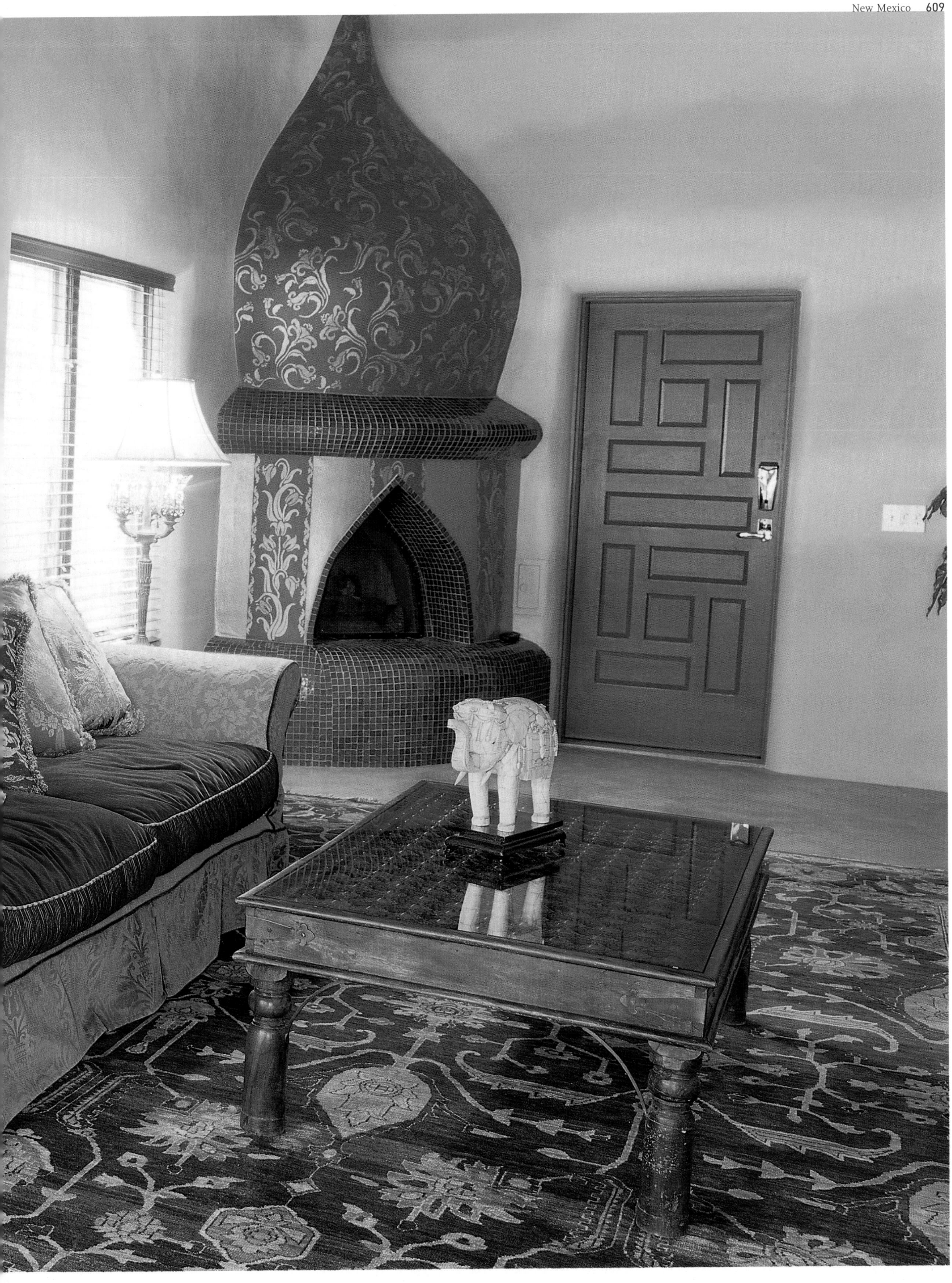

Great Spirits...
The Mabel Dodge Luhan House, Taos

The Mabel Dodge Luhan House, Taos

Great Spirits

The guest list of the Mabel Dodge Luhan house reads like an intellectual, cultural and artistic history of the twentieth century: Carl Jung, Willa Cather, Georgia O'Keeffe, Ansel Adams, Edmund Wilson, Aldous Huxley, Martha Graham. It was D.H. Lawrence who painted the vibrant red, yellow and blue stained glass windows that surround the bed in the main bedroom; Willa Cather, the well-known American novelist, came to Mabel Dodge Luhan's house to write. There are few places in America where a guest can sleep surrounded by so many great bohemian spirits of the past. Mabel Dodge Luhan, a socialite and patron of the arts from New York City's Greenwich Village, came to Taos in 1918, and soon afterwards married her fourth husband, Tony Luhan, a Pueblo Indian. Together they built this quirky adobe house full of windows to let in the brilliant blue light of the Taos, New Mexico sun. Their friends came, and stayed, and wrote, painted, and talked. That time has long passed, but something of that bright bohemian spirit remains in the sunsplashed spaces of this house, which is now open to guests as a bed and breakfast. Sit in a quiet corner by the window, and see if you can hear the whispers of dazzling conversations past.

Book to Pack: "The Rainbow" by D.H. Lawrence.
Novel by one of the Mabel Dodge Luhan house's most famous guests.

The Mabel Dodge Luhan House	
240 Morada Lane, PO Box 558	
Taos, NM 87571	
USA	
Tel. +1 505 751 9686	
Fax +1 505 737 0365	
Email: mabel@mabeldodgeluhan.com	
Website: www.mabeldodgeluhan.com	
Booking: www.great-escapes-hotels.com	

DIRECTIONS	9 miles (15 km) northwest of Taos Municipal Airport.
RATES	From US$95 a night.
ROOMS	11 rooms.
FOOD	Breakfasts only, served in the original dining room.
HISTORY	Built by the bohemian "new woman" Mabel Dodge Luhan and her husband Tony in the 1920s, the house became a magnet for the great intellectuals and writers of the period.
X-FACTOR	Sleep in an architectural treasure of a house, filled with the spirits of extraordinary intellectuals and artists.

Berühmte Gäste

Die Gästeliste des » Mabel-Dodge-Luhan«-Hauses liest sich wie das »Who is Who« der Intelligenzija und Künstlerszene des zwanzigsten Jahrhunderts. Carl Jung war hier, Willa Cather, Georgia O'Keeffe, Ansel Adams, Edmund Wilson, Aldous Huxley und Martha Graham. D.H. Lawrence griff hier sogar zum Pinsel und malte die Fensterscheiben im großen Schlafzimmer knallrot, gelb und blau. Willa Cather, eine amerikanische Romanautorin, reiste ins Haus von Mabel Dodge Luhan, um zu schreiben. Es gibt nur wenige Orte in Amerika, die von so viel Künstlergeist beseelt sind. Mabel Dodge Luhan, Dame der Gesellschaft und Kunstmäzenin aus Greenwich Village in New York, kam 1918 nach Taos, New Mexico, und heiratete kurz nach ihrer Ankunft Ehemann Nummer Vier, Tony Luhan, einen Pueblo-Indianer. Zusammen bauten sie ein eigenwilliges Lehmziegel-Haus mit vielen Fenstern, durch die das strahlend blaue Licht von Taos hineinströmt. Oft kamen Freunde des Paares zu Besuch, schrieben, malten und diskutierten. Das ist zwar längst Vergangenheit, doch noch immer schwebt etwas von diesem Künstlergeist durch die sonnendurchfluteten Räume des heutigen »Bed and Breakfast«. Und schaut man zum Fenster hinaus, kann man wunderbar von vergangenen Zeiten träumen.

Buchtipp: »Der Regenbogen« von D.H. Lawrence.
Novelle von einem der berühmtesten Gästen vom »Mabel-Dodge-Luhan«-Haus

Les grands esprits

La liste des hôtes de la « Mabel Dodge Luhan House » ressemble à une histoire intellectuelle, culturelle et artistique du 20e siècle : Carl Jung, Willa Cather, Georgia O'Keeffe, Ansel Adams, Edmund Wilson, Aldous Huxley, Martha Graham. Les vitraux rouges, jaunes et bleus qui entourent le lit dans la chambre principale furent réalisés par D. H. Lawrence. La célèbre romancière américaine Willa Cather vint s'y installer pour écrire. Il existe peu d'endroits aux États-Unis où l'on peut s'endormir bercé par les fantômes de tant de grands esprits bohèmes du passé. La New-Yorkaise Mabel Dodge, grande mondaine et mécène, quitta le Greenwich Village pour s'installer à Taos en 1918 où elle rencontra peu après son quatrième mari, Tony Luhan, un Indien Pueblo. Ensemble, ils construisirent cette demeure excentrique en adobe pleine de fenêtres pour laisser entrer le soleil du Nouveau-Mexique. Leurs amis vinrent et restèrent, écrivant, peignant, discutant. Cette époque est loin maintenant mais il subsiste quelque chose de cette ambiance inspirée et bohème dans ces espaces inondés d'une belle lumière bleutée. La maison est désormais convertie en maison d'hôtes. Asseyez-vous dans un petit coin tranquille près d'une fenêtre et essayez d'entendre le murmure des conversations brillantes du passé.

Livre à emporter : « L'Arc-en-ciel » de D.H. Lawrence.
Roman de l'un des invités les plus célèbres de « Mabel Dodge Luhan House ».

ANREISE	15 km nordwestlich vom Flughafen Taos.
PREISE	Ab 75 € pro Nacht.
ZIMMER	11 Zimmer.
KÜCHE	Nur Frühstück im Speisezimmer.
GESCHICHTE	Das Haus der unkonventionellen Mabel Dodge Luhan und ihrem Mann Tony aus den 1920er Jahren war Anziehungspunkt für die großen Intellektuellen und Schriftsteller der Zeit.
X-FAKTOR	Außergewöhnliche Architektur erfüllt von dem Geist und Animus Intellektueller und Künstler.

ACCÈS	15 km au nord-ouest de l'aéroport municipal de Taos.
PRIX	À partir de 75 € la nuit.
CHAMBRES	11 chambres.
RESTAURATION	Petits-déjeuners uniquement, servis dans la salle à manger qui a conservé son décor original.
HISTOIRE	Construite par la « nouvelle femme » bohème Mabel Dodge Luhan et son mari Tony dans les années vingt, la maison devint un lieu de rencontre des grands intellectuels et écrivains de l'époque.
LE « PETIT PLUS »	Dormez dans un trésor architectural, une demeure peuplée par les fantômes d'intellectuels et d'artistes extraordinaires.

Wild West Rocks...
Hotel Congress, Tucson

The Hotel Congress, Tucson

Wild West Rocks

"Everybody, eventually, ends up at the Hotel Congress," proclaims a Tucson lifestyle magazine. "Everybody", in this case, is the crème de la crème of this desert city's bohemian scene, from college students, to poets, to musicians. In the lower part of the hotel, there's a well-known rock and roll venue, Club Congress. The hotel's 40 rooms – iron bedsteads, ceiling fans – are conveniently located upstairs, above the hotel bars and the club, so you don't have to worry about how you're getting home from the party. Though it has a young, hipster feel, the Hotel Congress is rich in history, atmosphere, and ghosts. It was built in 1919, to cater to the railroad and cattle ranchers who made this southern Arizona town near the Mexican border boom at the turn of the 19th century. The lobby, with velvet curtains, leather chairs, and glass-windowed doors, looks straight out of a Wild West movie, or a Bob Dylan ballad. When the famous bank robber John Dillinger was running away from the police in 1934, he picked the Hotel Congress to hide out in. He stayed for a couple of weeks, then he got caught. But you don't have to be.

Book to pack: "The Dillinger Days" by John Toland.
Another American criminal case turned into a happy legend. History told like a story.

Hotel Congress
311 East Congress Street
Tucson, AZ 85701
USA
Tel. +1 520 622 8848
Fax: +1 520 792 6366
Email: reservations@hotelcongress.com
Website: www.hotelcongress.com
Booking: www.great-escapes-hotels.com

DIRECTIONS	Located in downtown Tucson, Arizona about 7.5 miles (12 km) north of Tucson International Airport.
RATES	Prices range from US$25 (for a bed in the youth hostel rooms) to US$99 a night.
ROOMS	40 rooms, with double or twin beds. A few of the rooms have bunk beds and are shared, youth hostel style.
FOOD	The Cup Café serves breakfast, lunch and dinner – dishes from Indian to French. The Tap Room is the original hotel bar.
HISTORY	Built in 1919 when Tucson was still a small railroad and cattle town at the edge of America's wild West. The hotel was gangster John Dillinger's hideout in 1934.
X-FACTOR	Rock and roll hipsters meet outlaw chic.

Rock'n'Roll im Wilden Westen

In Tucson, Arizona, kommt kein Hippie um das »Hotel Congress« herum. Hier verkehren College-Studenten, Poeten und Musiker. Kurz, die ganze junge Szene der Wüstenstadt. Anziehungspunkt ist der »Club Congress« im Erdgeschoss des Hotels, der sich als der Ort für Rock'n'Roll weitum einen Namen gemacht hat. Für Hotelgäste ist dieser Umstand sehr praktisch: Nach der Party müssen sie nur schnell die Treppe hochklettern – und schon sind sie in ihren Betten. Ihnen stehen im ersten Stockwerk, direkt über dem Club und der Bar, 40 Zimmer mit altmodischen Eisenbetten und Deckenventilatoren zur Verfügung. Das »Hotel Congress« ist seit 1919 Teil der Stadtgeschichte. An der Wende vom 19. zum 20. Jahrhundert herrschte in Tucson Aufbruchstimmung: Eisenbahnbau und Viehzucht verhalfen der Stadt im Süden Arizonas zu ihrer Blüte. Der Geist längst vergangener Zeiten ist im »Congress« überall zu spüren. Samtvorhänge, verglaste Türen und Ledersessel in der Lobby erinnern an alte Western-Filme. Auch Bob Dylan würde ganz gut hierher passen. Und selbstverständlich kann das Hotel, wie es sich für den Wilden Westen gehört, mit einer ordentlichen Räubergeschichte aufwarten. 1934 versteckte sich hier der berüchtigte Bankräuber John Dillinger mit seiner Gang wochenlang vor der Polizei und wurde dann erwischt.

Buchtipp: »The Dillinger Days« von John Toland.
Und wieder ein amerikanischer Krimineller, der zur Legende geworden ist. Geschichte im Krimi-Format.

Les rockeurs de l'Ouest

« Tout le monde, un jour ou l'autre, atterrit à l'hôtel Congress », proclame un magazine de Tucson. « Tout le monde », en l'occurrence, c'est la crème des cercles bohèmes de cette ville du désert : étudiants, poètes ou musiciens. Le rez-de-chaussée abrite un club célèbre, le « Club Congress », on l'on écoute du rock. Les 40 chambres (lits en fer forgé, ventilateurs de plafond) se trouvent à l'étage, au-dessus des bars et du club de l'hôtel, si bien que « boire ou conduire » n'est plus un choix cornélien. En dépit de son ambiance jeune et branchée, l'« Hotel Congress » a une histoire riche chargée de fantômes. Il a été construit en 1919 pour accueillir les voyageurs du nouveau chemin de fer et les éleveurs de bétail à l'époque où cette ville du sud de l'Arizona proche de la frontière mexicaine était en plein essor. Le hall, avec ses rideaux en velours, ses fauteuils en cuir et ses portes vitrées, semble tout droit sorti d'un western ou d'une ballade de Bob Dylan. En 1934, John Dillinger, le célèbre braqueur de banques, vint s'y planquer. Il y séjourna plusieurs semaines avant de se laisser piéger. Mais vous n'êtes pas obligé d'en faire autant.

Livre à emporter : « Dillinger » de John Toland.
Encore une affaire criminelle américaine transformée en légende positive. Se lit comme un roman.

ANREISE	Im Zentrum der Stadt, etwa 12 km nördlich vom internationalen Flughafen Tucson, Arizona.	
PREISE	Zwischen 20 € (Bett im Schlafsaal) und 80 € pro Nacht.	
ZIMMER	40 Zimmer, meist mit Einzel- oder Doppelbetten. Ein paar Zimmer haben Etagenbetten.	
KÜCHE	Frühstück, Mittag- und Abendessen im »Cup Café«. Verschiedene Gerichte aus Indien, Amerika und Frankreich. Nicht verpassen: Ein Drink im »Tap Room«.	
GESCHICHTE	Erbaut 1919, als Tucson noch eine kleine Eisenbahn-Stadt mitten im Wildem Westen war. 1934 diente dem landesweit bekannten Gangster John Dillinger als Versteck.	
X-FAKTOR	Unkonventioneller Rock'n'Roll-Schick.	

ACCÈS	Situé au centre de Tucson, dans l'Arizona, à environ 12 km au nord de l'aéroport international de Tucson.	
PRIX	À partir de 20 € jusqu'à 80 € la nuit.	
CHAMBRES	40 chambres, certaines avec un grand lit, d'autres des lits jumeaux. Plusieurs chambres ont des lits superposés.	
RESTAURATION	Le « Cup Café » sert le petit-déjeuner, le déjeuner et le dîner. Jouez des coudes jusqu'au comptoir de la « Tap Room », le vieux bar de l'hôtel.	
HISTOIRE	Construit en 1919. Le fameux bandit John Dillinger s'y réfugia avec son gang en 1934.	
LE « PETIT PLUS »	La « rock'n'roll » attitude rencontre le chic canaille.	

Melting into Morocco...

Korakia Pensione, Palm Springs

Korakia Pensione, Palm Springs

Melting into Morocco

Romantic escape is something that many luxury lodgings promise, but few hotels in the world deliver it as effortlessly, and with such perfect detail, as Palm Springs's Korakia Pensione. Here, you pull off the California Interstate highway, pass through the whitewashed gates, and suddenly you are thousands of miles away in Tangiers. Maybe it's because the dry heat and endless sunshine of the Palm Springs desert so closely resemble the white-hot Moroccan sky of Paul Bowles. Or perhaps it is simply because the two original 1924 villas that now form the Pensione were built as marvellous dreams themselves, the fantasies of a Scottish painter named Gordon Coutts. He longed to live in Tangier, but his American wife didn't want to leave the U.S., so he constructed a Tangier of his fantasies in Palm Springs, and baptized it "Dar Marroc". Coutts's artist's retreat attracted a mixed crowd of 1920s bohemians and the hoi palloi – including, it is said, Winston Churchill, who painted in the villa's studio. After Coutts's death the villa languished until it was resurrected by another romantic, owner Douglas Smith, who restored the dilapidated property to its original lush North African/Mediterranean ambience.

The rooms are furnished with pieces collected by the owner from Afghanistan and Thailand. Every one is airy, bright, and whitewashed, and many open to cool, tiled patios. Step through arched portals into courtyards where tiled fountains gently burble, and purple and pink bougainvilla droops overhead: at the Korakia, you may be sleeping in California, but you are dreaming in Morocco.

Book to pack: "The Sheltering Sky" by Paul Bowles.
A journey to the heart of Morocco.

Korakia Pensione
257 S. Patencio Road
Palm Springs, CA 92262
USA
Tel. +1 760 864 6411
Fax +1 760 864 4147
Website: www.korakia.com
Booking: www.great-escapes-hotels.com

DIRECTIONS	Located in downtown Palm Springs, about 110 miles (180 km) drive east of Los Angeles Airport and 2.7 miles (4.3 km) west of Palm Springs Airport.
RATES	Rooms starting at US$139 per night. The Orchard House rents for US$599.
ROOMS	27 rooms and the Orchard House, a one-bedroom house.
FOOD	No dining room; some rooms with kitchens. Breakfast is included and served in the rooms, poolside or in the garden. Moroccan mint tea is served evenings.
HISTORY	1924 Moroccan-style artist's villa restored to its original splendour and opened as a hotel in 1992.
X-FACTOR	Lose yourself in Tangiers without leaving California.

Abstecher nach Marokko

Was viele Luxus-Herbergen versprechen, haben nur ganz
wenige: Charme. Eine der schönen Ausnahmen ist die
»Korakia Pensione« in Palm Springs. Hier wurde mit wun-
derbarer Leichtigkeit und Liebe zum Detail eine zauberhafte
Welt erschaffen. Bereits die Ankunft ist reizvoll: Man fährt
noch ganz normal auf der Haupstraße, durch einen großen,
kalkweißen Torbogen, und plötzlich scheint man im marok-
kanischen Tanger statt in Kalifornien zu sein. Die trockene
Hitze und endlos scheinende Sonne über der Wüste von
Palm Springs erinnern an die Beschreibung des gleißend
weißen Himmels Marokko. Paul Bowles marokkanische
Sehnsüchte weckt auch der Geist des schottischen Malers
Gordon Coutts, der durch die »Korakia Pensione« weht.
Coutts sehnte sich nach Tanger, doch seine amerikanische
Gattin wollte unter nicht aus den USA wegziehen. Ein
Dilemma, das Coutts 1924 pragmatisch mit dem Bau zweier
Villen im marokkanischen Stil löste. Diese Fantasiewelt mit-
ten in der Wüste Südkaliforniens taufte er »Dar Marroc«. Zu
seinen Lebzeiten wurde seine Fantasiewelt von den unter-
schiedlichsten Gästen besucht – Bohemiens, ganz normale
Leute, aber auch Persönlichkeiten wie Winston Churchill,
der sich im Studio der größeren Villa der Malerei gewidmet
haben soll. Nach Coutts' Ableben kümmerte sich lange Zeit
niemand mehr um »Dar Marroc«. Der heutige Besitzer
Douglas Smith nahm sich dann des verfallenen Anwesens
an und verwandelte es zurück in den marokkanischen
Traum von damals. Die Zimmer hat er mit Möbeln und
Objekten aus Afghanistan und Thailand eingerichtet. Die
Wände sind kalkweiß gestrichen, die Räume luftig und hell.
Aus einem gekachelten Brunnen, der mit violetten und
roten Bougainvillea überwuchert ist, plätschert sanft das
Wasser. Willkommen in Marokko!

Buchtipp: »Himmel über der Wüste« von Paul Bowles.
Eine Reise in das Innere Marokkos.

Un rêve marocain

De nombreux hôtels de luxe dans le monde vous promettent
un dépaysement romantique mais peu tiennent parole aussi
bien que la « Korakia Pensione » à Palm Springs. En sortant
de la route principale, on franchit un portail blanchi à la
chaux et, soudain, on se retrouve à des milliers de kilomètres de là, à Tanger. C'est peut-être parce que la chaleur
sèche et le soleil impitoyable du désert rappellent le ciel
chauffé à blanc du Maroc de Paul Bowles. À moins que ce
ne soit simplement parce que les deux villas qui forment la
« Korakia Pensione » furent construites en 1924 comme
deux merveilleux mirages, fantasmes du peintre écossais
Gordon Coutts. Il rêvait de vivre à Tanger mais son épouse
américaine refusait de quitter les États-Unis. Il s'est donc
construit un Tanger issu tout droit de son imagination à
Palm Springs et l'a baptisé « Dar Marroc ». Dans les années
vingt, ce refuge d'artistes attira une clique bohème et certaines sommités dont, paraît-il, Winston Churchill qui aurait
peint dans l'atelier. Après la mort de Coutts, les lieux tombè-
rent à l'abandon jusqu'à ce qu'un autre romantique, Douglas
Smith, ne les ressuscite et ne leur rende leur voluptueuse
atmosphère nord-africaine/méditerranéenne.
Dans les chambres, toutes spacieuses, claires et blanches,
les meubles ont été rapportés d'Afghanistan et de Thaïlande
par les propriétaires. Beaucoup donnent sur de frais patios
carrelés. Des arches s'ouvrent sur des cours où glougloutent
des fontaines en céramique sous des masses de bougainvil-
lées roses et violettes : à « Korakia », on s'endort en
Californie mais on rêve au Maroc.

Livre à emporter : «Un thé au Sahara» de Paul Bowles.
Un voyage au cœur du Maroc.

ANREISE	4,3 km westlich vom Flughafen Palm Springs.
PREISE	Zimmer mit Küche ab 110 € pro Nacht, das »Orchard House« kostet 485 € pro Nacht.
ZIMMER	27 Zimmer; das »Orchard House« mit Schlafzimmer.
KÜCHE	Eigenes Restaurant. In den Zimmern kann man kleine Mahlzeiten zubereiten. Frühstück wird in den Zimmern, am Pool oder im Garten unter Zitronenbäumen gereicht. Abends wird marokkanischer Pfefferminz-Tee serviert.
GESCHICHTE	Marokkanische Villa, Baujahr 1924. 1992 stilgerecht renoviert und als Hotel eröffnet.
X-FAKTOR	Eine kalifornische Reise nach Tanger.

ACCÈS	4,3 km à l'ouest du aéroport celui de Palm Springs.
PRIX	Le prix des chambres commence à partir de 110 € la nuit. La Orchard House se loue 485 €.
CHAMBRES	27 chambres, plus l'Orchard House, une maison indivi- duelle avec une chambre à coucher.
RESTAURATION	Pas de salle à manger; dans les chambres équipées de cuisine on peut préparer des repas simples. Le petit- déjeuner est compris. Du thé à la menthe est servi le soir.
HISTOIRE	Une villa d'artiste de style marocain datant de 1924, restaurée et convertie en hôtel en 1992.
LE « PETIT PLUS »	Perdez-vous dans Tanger sans quitter la Californie.

Cabin Fever...
Deetjen's Big Sur Inn, Big Sur

Deetjen's Big Sur Inn, Big Sur

Cabin Fever

The first thing you notice, walking up to the main cabin at Deetjen's Big Sur Inn, is the stillness. Tall redwood trees rustle in the breeze, the Pacific Ocean crashes mightily on the rocky cliffs far below. As you check into your room, a Deetjen's clerk hands you an information sheet that advises "Be Considerate. Our walls are paper thin and your neighbor can almost hear you breathe." But the warning seems needless, for here in the middle of redwoods, sea, rocks and spirit, the very atmosphere seems to encourage guests to lower their voices, to listen to one of America's most celebrated natural landscapes. When the two-lane highway was first built along this part of the California coast, on cliffs and bluffs above the ocean, a Norwegian immigrant named Helmuth Deetjen opened a few hand built wooden cabins to shelter travellers making the fabled drive between Los Angeles and San Francisco. As time passed, he built more cabins in his rustic old-world style (the balustrades are hand-carved), and his retreat attracted not only passing sightseers, but the bohemians of San Francisco, the writers and artists and free spirits of the Beat Generation and beyond. Henry Miller hung out here (his old house, now a library, is a few miles up the road), When Deetjen died, his heirs turned the inn into a non-profit organization, in order to keep prices low and preserve the low-key, authentic character of the place. There are no tvs, phones or broadband Internet connections in a Deetjen's cabin room, but there might be a Buddha, and there certainly will be a little diary, where guests can write notes to each other across the decades, like this one: "I never thought I'd sleep in a bed where so many neurotics and bad poets slept before me...otherwise it is very peaceful here. Goodnight"

Book to Pack: "Big Sur and the Oranges of Hieronymous Bosch" by Henry Miller.
The great American novelist's meditation on his life in Big Sur.

Deetjen's Big Sur Inn	
48865 Highway 1	
Big Sur, CA 93920	
USA	
Tel. +1 831 667 2377	
Fax +1 831 667 0466	
Website: www.deetjens.com	
Booking: www.great-escapes-hotels.com	

DIRECTIONS	30 miles (50 km) south of Carmel, California on U.S. Highway 1.
RATES	Rooms from US$75 .
ROOMS	18 rooms, one small house.
FOOD	Breakfasts and continental-style dinners served in the inn's rustic dining room with fireplace.
HISTORY	Built by Norwegian immigrant Helmuth Deetjen on his land in the 1930s.
X-FACTOR	An oasis of stillness and simplicity in one of America's most famous landscapes.

Rustikaler Hüttenzauber

Die Ruhe im »Deetjen's Big Sur Inn« wird einzig vom Rascheln der Bäume und den Wellen, die an die felsigen Klippen des Pazifiks peitschen, gestört. An der Rezeption bekommt der Gast gleich ein Blatt in die Hand gedrückt: »Bitte nehmen Sie Rücksicht auf die anderen Gäste. Unsere Wände sind so dünn wie Papier, ihr Zimmernachbar kann Sie atmen hören.« Der Hinweis entpuppt sich schnell als hinfällig. Die friedliche Atmosphäre lässt automatisch die Stimme senken, und man lauscht andächtig auf die Natur. Als die Straße entlang der Steilküste zwischen Los Angeles und San Francisco gebaut wurde, entwickelte der Norweger Helmuth Deetjen hoch über dem Ozean ein paar rustikale Holzhütten für die Reisenden. Der Ort lockte nicht nur Ausflügler, sondern auch die Künstlerszene der Beat Generation an. Henry Miller pflegte sich hier aufzuhalten (sein ehemaliges Haus, heute eine Bibliothek, steht wenige Kilometer weiter oben). Deetjens Erben gründeten nach seinem Tod eine gemeinnützige Stiftung, um die Zimmerpreise tief zu halten und den authentischen Charakter des Ortes zu bewahren. Fernseher, Telefone oder Internet-Anschlüsse sucht man hier vergebens. Dafür findet man Buddha-Statuen und ein Tagebuch, mit dem die Gäste über die Jahrzehnte hinweg untereinander kommunizieren: »Nicht im Traum hätte ich daran gedacht, einmal eine Nacht in einem Bett zu verbringen, in dem so viele Neurotiker und schlechte Dichter geschlafen haben«, schrieb ein Gast. »Dennoch ist es hier sehr friedlich.«

Buchtipp: »Big Sur und die Orangen des Hieronymus Bosch« von Henry Miller.
Reflektionen Millers über seine Zeit in Big Sur.

L'appel de la nature

Ce qui frappe d'abord, c'est le calme. Le frémissement des hauts séquoias, les puissantes vagues du Pacifique qui s'écrasent au pied des falaises. Avec votre clef, le réceptionniste vous remet une note : « Soyez prévenants. Nos cloisons sont si fines que votre voisin peut presque vous entendre respirer ». C'est inutile car tout ici incite spontanément à baisser la voix et à tendre l'oreille pour écouter l'un des paysages naturels les plus célèbres d'Amérique. Quand la première route a été tracée le long de cette partie de la côte, un Norvégien, Helmut Deetjen, a construit quelques cabanes en bois pour les voyageurs qui effectuaient ce trajet mythique entre Los Angeles et San Francisco. Au fil du temps, il s'est agrandi tout en conservant son style rustique à l'ancienne (avec des balustrades sculptées) et sa retraite a attiré, outre les touristes, la bohème de San Francisco : écrivains, artistes et autres libres penseurs de la génération beat et des suivantes. Henry Miller était un voisin (sa maison, devenue bibliothèque, est à deux pas). À la mort de Deetjen, ses héritiers ont transformé l'hôtel en organisation à but non lucratif afin de conserver des tarifs bas et préserver l'authenticité des lieux. On ne trouve ni télé, ni téléphone ni Internet à haut débit dans les chambres mais, éventuellement, un bouddha et, à coup sûr, un journal où les hôtes peuvent se laisser des messages d'une décennie à l'autre, tel que celui-ci : « Je n'aurais jamais cru dormir un jour dans un lit qui a vu passer tant de névrosés et de mauvais poètes. À part ça… c'est très paisible ici. Bonne nuit. »

Livre à emporter : « Big Sur, sur les Oranges de Jérôme Bosch » d'Henry Miller.
Une méditation du grand romancier américain sur sa vie à Big Sur.

ANREISE	50 km südlich von Carmel, Kalifornien, am US Highway 1.
PREISE	Zimmer ab 60 €.
ZIMMER	18 Zimmer, ein kleines Haus.
KÜCHE	Frühstück und kontinentales Abendessen im rustikalen Speisesaal mit Kamin.
GESCHICHTE	In den dreißiger Jahren vom norwegischen Einwanderer Helmuth Deetjen erbaut.
X-FAKTOR	Eine Oase der Ruhe und Einfachheit in einer der berühmtesten Landschaften Amerikas.

ACCÈS	À 50 km au sud de Carmel, en Californie, sur l'U.S. Highway 1.
PRIX	Chambres à partir de 60 €.
CHAMBRES	18 chambres, une petite maison.
RESTAURATION	Cuisine continentale ; les petits-déjeuners et dîners sont servis dans la salle à manger rustique de l'auberge, devant la cheminée.
HISTOIRE	Construit par un immigré norvégien, Helmuth Deetjen, sur ses terres dans les années 1930.
LE « PETIT PLUS »	Un havre de calme et de simplicité dans l'un des plus célèbres paysages des États-Unis.

American Pie...
Madonna Inn, San Luis Obispo

Madonna Inn, San Luis Obispo

American Pie

To be honest, the Madonna Inn is not everybody's cup of tea. Some travellers, pulling their car off the Interstate highway into the Madonna Inn parking lot, take one look at the giddy building, with its rollicking spiral staircases, multiple balconies, pink, faux-Tudor towers with cupolas and turn the car around and continue driving towards San Francisco. For other travellers, a quick lunch in the Inn's Copper Café, a surreal explosion of bright stained glass, imitation roses, and dozens of Christmas trees that blink and sparkle 365 days of the year, is enough exposure to the Madonna's singular aesthetic. How much kitsch is too much? Fans of the Madonna Inn would say you can never have enough – they relish their nights in one of the Inn's 109 rooms, no two alike. They dream of emerald green carpets, or zebra patterned bedspreads, and read by the light of smiling gold cherub chandeliers. Alex and Phyllis Madonna, the owners, opened their roadside inn on Christmas eve in 1958, and have been decorating and redecorating the place according to their own peculiar vision and taste ever since. The Madonna Inn's location – it is on the highway near San Luis Obispo, exactly halfway between San Francisco and Los Angeles, means that the next customer is always just an exit ramp away. Come to Madonna Inn for the homemade apple pie, or the Danish pastry, baked on the premises; then stay for the cheese.

Book to Pack: "Against Interpretation" by Susan Sontag. Contains "Notes On Camp", Sontag's seminal essay about kitsch.

Madonna Inn

100 Madonna Road

San Luis Obispo, CA 93405

USA

Tel. +1 800 543-9666 or 805 543-3000

Fax +1 805 543-1800

Email: info@madonnainn.com

Website: www.madonnainn.com

Booking: www.great-escapes-hotels.com

DIRECTIONS	Located just off U.S. Highway 101, about 2 miles (3 km) south of the U.S. 1 junction, midway between San Francisco and Los Angeles.
RATES	From US$137 for a single room.
ROOMS	109 rooms, each decorated differently.
FOOD	Classic American steaks and salads at Gold Rush Steak House; American coffeeshop-style dining (breakfast, lunch, dinner, fresh pastries) at the Copper Café.
HISTORY	Family run roadside inn, opened 1958.
X-FACTOR	Kitsch so thick you can almost eat it with a spoon.

Zuckersüßer Kitsch

Das »Madonna Inn« ist nicht jedermanns Sache. Manche fahren vom Interstate 101 kurz auf den Parkplatz des »Madonna Inn«, werfen einen Blick auf das schwindelerregende Gebäude mit spiralförmigen Treppen, unzähligen Balkonen, rosa Disneyland-Türmen und fahren dann schnurstracks weiter Richtung San Francisco. Andere bestaunen bei einem kurzen Mittagessen das exzentrische Dekor des »Copper Café« mit seinen knallbunten Fenstergläsern, künstlichen Rosen und einem Dutzend Weihnachtsbäumen, die das ganze Jahr über blinken und funkeln. Einzig eingefleischte Fans kriegen nie genug vom zuckersüßen Kitsch und genießen die Nächte in einem der 109 völlig unterschiedlich eingerichteten Zimmer in vollen Zügen. Dabei träumen sie von smaragdgrünen Teppichen, Bettdecken mit Zebramuster und lesen ein Buch unter dem Licht goldener Lüster, von denen Cherubine herunterlächeln. Alex und Phyllis Madonna eröffneten ihr Gasthaus an Heiligabend 1958 und richteten es im Laufe der Zeit immer wieder anders, aber immer nach ihrem eigenwilligen Geschmack, ein. Das »Madonna Inn« liegt direkt am Highway 101 in der Nähe von San Luis Obispo, ziemlich genau in der Mitte zwischen San Franciso und Los Angeles. Und wer befürchtet, hier an Reizüberflutung zu leiden, sollte statt einer Übernachtung wenigstens Apfelkuchen oder Dänisch Plunder aus der hauseigenen Bäckerei ausprobieren.

Buchtipp: »Kunst und Antikunst« von Susan Sontag. Ein wegweisendes Essay über Kitsch.

Chantilly à l'américaine.

Pour être sincère, le « Madonna Inn » n'est pas pour tous les goûts. Certains voyageurs s'arrêtent sur le parking de l'hôtel, jettent un regard sur le bâtiment vertigineux avec ses délirants escaliers en colimaçon, ses nombreux balcons, ses tourelles roses en faux Tudor surmontées de coupoles, et font aussitôt marche arrière pour reprendre la route vers San Francisco. D'autres limiteront leur immersion dans l'esthétique singulière du « Madonna Inn » à un bref déjeuner dans son « Copper Café », une explosion surréaliste de vitraux vivement colorés, de roses artificielles et de dizaines de sapins de Noël qui scintillent et clignotent 365 jours par an. Jusqu'où peut-on aller dans le kitsch ? Les fans du « Madonna Inn » vous répondront qu'on ne l'est jamais assez. Ils savourent leurs nuits dans l'une des 109 chambres, toutes différentes. Ils rêvent de moquette vert émeraude, de dessus-de-lit en zèbre et bouquinent à la lumière de lustres dorés ornés de chérubins à l'air ravi. Alex et Phyllis Madonna, les propriétaires, ont ouvert cet hôtel en bordure de route la nuit de Noël 1958 et n'ont cessé depuis de le décorer et de le re-décorer selon leur vision et leurs goûts particuliers. Son emplacement, près de San Luis Obispo, exactement à mi-chemin entre San Francisco et Los Angeles, en fait une halte de choix pour ceux qui prennent la route. Venez à « Madonna Inn » pour goûter sa tarte aux pommes faite maison ou ses pâtisseries viennoises, restez pour le fromage.

Livre à emporter : « Le Kitsch : un catalogue raisonné du mauvais goût » de Gillo Dorflès.
Une compilation d'études sur le kitsch sous toutes ses formes, dont une signée du célèbre essayiste autrichien Hermann Broch.

ANREISE	Rund 3 km südlich der Kreuzung US-Highway 101 und US 1 zwischen San Francisco und Los Angeles.
PREISE	Ab 110 € für ein Einzelzimmer.
ZIMMER	109 Zimmer, jedes verschieden eingerichtet.
KÜCHE	Steaks mit Salat im »Gold Rush Steak House«; amerikanisches Coffeeshop-Menü (Frühstück, Mittag- und Abendessen, hausgemachtes Gebäck) im »Copper Café«.
GESCHICHTE	Seit 1958 Hotel im Familienbesitz.
X-FAKTOR	Kitsch – so klebrig wie Sirup.

ACCÈS	Situé en bordure du Highway 101, à environ 3 km au sud de l'U.S. 1 junction, à mi-chemin entre San Francisco et Los Angeles.
PRIX	À partir de 110 € pour une chambre simple.
CHAMBRES	109 chambres, chacune décorée différemment.
RESTAURATION	Cuisine classique américaine : steaks et salades dans le « Gold Rush Steak » House ; cuisine typique de cafeteria américaine (petit-déjeuner, déjeuner, dîner, pâtisseries faites maison) au « Copper Café ».
HISTOIRE	Hôtel familial en bordure de la route, ouvert en 1958.
LE « PETIT PLUS »	Un kitsch si dense qu'on pourrait presque le manger à la petite cuillère.

Grapes of Style...
The Carneros Inn, Napa

The Carneros Inn, Napa

Grapes of Style

Napa Valley has always been a wine-growing center, but lately it has turned into something else: the U.S. capital of the Good Life. Only in the last ten or fifteen years has American culture embraced, wholeheartedly, things epicurean. But thanks to visionary chefs like California's Alice Waters, we are now a nation that knows about soft cheeses, field greens, and the culinary advantages of allowing four-legged creatures to range freely. Napa is the epicentre of the U.S. epicurean revolution, and it is often called the American Tuscany, or Loire Valley, because it is home to the largest concentration of American wineries. Food has followed the wine to Napa, and nowadays the area is renowned as much for its superb restaurants as for its vino. Travelers come here to indulge, to eat, drink and enjoy the fruits of the abundant Napa soil. The Carneros Inn, the newest resort in the area, is something of an anomaly for Napa. While many of the local wineries and lodgings take their stylistic and thematic cues from older European models, this inn, viewed from a distance, looks like a dust-beaten collection of American farmworker's shanties, the sort of place the migrant field hands of John Steinbeck's Grapes of Wrath might have stayed in. But the "agri-chic" aesthetic of this resort development is deceptive; inside the plain, rustic farm cottages with their tin mailboxes and stovepipe chimneys, the Good Life awaits. Open the doors, and the shanty becomes a breezy palace of hardwood floors, vaulted ceilings, wood-burning fireplaces, and showers that open to the stars. From the French windows in your bedroom, the rows of vineyards seem to stretch on forever (which they do: most of Napa's most famous wineries are a stone's throw away from the rocking chair on your front porch.)

Book to Pack: "The Grapes of Wrath" by John Steinbeck. An American classic from one of the literary giants of Northern California.

The Carneros Inn
4048 Sonoma Highway
Napa, CA 94559
USA
Tel. +1 707 299 4900
Fax +1 707 299 4950
Email: info@thecarnerosinn.com
Website: www.thecarnerosinn.com
Booking: www.great-escapes-hotels.com

DIRECTIONS	Located about 50 miles (80 km) north of San Francisco on Highway 12-121.
RATES	US$325 to US$1,200.
ROOMS	86 guest cottages, each with private patio and garden.
FOOD	The Hilltop Dining Room serves haute California cuisine; the Boon Fly Café serves a more informal breakfast and lunch.
HISTORY	A new resort, opened in 2003: modular tin-roofed guest cottages, built on the site of a former trailer park.
X-FACTOR	Enjoy the "agri-chic" rustic-modernism of Napa valley's newest resort.

Früchte des Genusses

Im Napa Valley wurde, lange bevor es internationale Aner-
kennung fand, Wein angebaut. Doch erst die Entwicklung
zu einer Top-Weinregion machte aus Napa Amerikas wichtigste Lifestyle-Destination. Bis vor zehn, fünfzehn Jahren
waren in den Vereinigten Staaten kulinarische Genüsse wie
Weichkäse, Bio-Gemüse und Fleisch aus Freiland-Tierhal-
tung nahezu unbekannt. Erst weitsichtige Meisterköche wie
Alice Waters vom legendären Restaurant »Chez Panisse« in
Berkeley bei San Francisco weckten die Begeisterung der
Amerikaner für diese Tafelfreuden. Napa ist das Zentrum
der Genussrevolution und wird gerne mit der Toskana oder
dem Loire-Tal verglichen. Nicht zuletzt weil hier landesweit
die höchste Dichte an Weingütern zu finden ist. Sicher aber
auch, weil Napa heute neben Spitzenweinen auch eine aus-
gezeichnete Küche bietet. Viele der Weingüter und Gast-
häuser orientieren sich an europäischen Stilvorbildern.
Ungewöhnlich ist von daher das »Carneros Inn«, das neuste
Resort in Napa. Die Ansammlung traditioneller amerikanischer Landwirtschafts-Baracken erinnert an das Leben der
Landarbeiter, das John Steinbeck in seinem Werk »Früchte
des Zorns« beschreibt. Doch der »Agro-Schick« des Resorts
täuscht. Die einfachen, rustikalen Cottages mit den typisch
amerikanischen Briefkästen aus halbrundem Blech und altmodischen Ofenrohren sind innen luxuriös mit Parkett,
gewölbten Decken, Kaminen und Duschen mit Dachluken
ausgestattet. Und durch die Sprossenfenster kann man den
Blick über die endlosen Weinreben schweifen lassen.

Buchtipp: »Früchte des Zorns« von John Steinbeck

Klassiker der modernen US-amerikanischen Literatur, 1940
mit dem Pulitzer-Preis ausgezeichnet.

Les raisins du bien-être

La vallée de Napa a toujours été une région viticole mais,
récemment, elle est devenue la capitale U. S. de l'art de
vivre. Depuis une dizaine d'années, les Américains s'aban-
donnent sans réserve aux plaisirs épicuriens. Grâce à des
chefs visionnaires tels qu'Alice Waters, ils se sont familiari-
sés avec les fromages à pâte molle, les légumes verts et les
avantages culinaires du bétail élevé en liberté. Épicentre de
cette révolution, Napa est surnommée la Toscane ou la vallée
de la Loire américaine en raison de ses nombreux vignobles.
La gastronomie a suivi et, aujourd'hui, elle est également
renommée pour ses grands restaurants. Les voyageurs viennent ici pour la bonne chère et jouir des fruits de son sol
généreux.
Le « Carneros Inn », récemment inauguré, se distingue des
autres établissements vinicoles et hôtels de la région qui
s'inspirent de modèles européens plus anciens. De loin, il
ressemble à un ensemble de baraques agricoles balayées par
la poussière, du genre qui abritaient les journaliers des
« Raisins de la colère ». Mais son esthétique « agro-chic » est
trompeuse : à l'intérieur des bungalows rustiques, avec leur
boîtes aux lettres en fer blanc et leurs cheminées en tuyau
de poêle, la belle vie vous attend. En ouvrant la porte, vous
découvrez un luxe joyeux, des planchers lustrés, des plafonds voûtés, de grandes cheminées et des douches ouvertes
sur les étoiles. Depuis la baie vitrée de votre chambre, les
vignes s'étendent à perte de vue (la plupart des plus célèbres
vignobles de Napa se trouvent à un jet de pierre du rocking-
chair sur votre véranda).

Livre à emporter : « Les raisins de la colère » de John Steinbeck.

Un classique de la littérature américaine par l'un de ses plus
dignes représentants.

ANREISE	Ungefähr 80 km nördlich von San Francisco auf dem Highway 12-121.	ACCÈS	Situé à environ 80 km au nord de San Francisco sur le Highway 12-121.
PREISE	Zwischen 260 € und 960 €.	PRIX	Entre 260 € et 960 €.
ZIMMER	86 Gästecottages, jedes mit Privatterrasse und Garten.	CHAMBRES	86 bungalows, chacun avec un patio et un jardin privés.
KÜCHE	Der »Hilltop Dining Room« serviert erstklassige kalifornische Küche; im »Boon Fly Café« gibt's Frühstück und Mittagessen in zwangloser Umgebung.	RESTAURATION	Le « Hilltop Dining Room » sert de la haute cuisine californienne ; le « Boon Fly Café » propose des petits-déjeuners et déjeuners plus simples.
GESCHICHTE	Ein neues Resort, 2003 eröffnet, modulare Cottages mit Blechdächern auf einem ehemaligen Campingplatz.	HISTOIRE	Nouvel établissement ouvert en 2003 : bungalows modulaires avec toit en fer, construit sur le site d'un ancien village de mobiles homes.
X-FAKTOR	Rustikal-moderner »Landwirtschafts-Schick«.	LE « PETIT PLUS »	Goûtez au modernisme rustique « agro-chic » du dernier-né des établissements de la vallée de Napa.

Haute Springs...
Calistoga Ranch, Calistoga

Calistoga Ranch, Calistoga

Haute Springs

Napa Valley is best known, of course, for wine, but the name Calistoga is famous on the West Coast because it is a popular brand of mineral water – it is the Vichy, the Perrier of California. In the town of Calistoga, which is located in the northern end of Napa, modest wooden houses and early 20th century public buildings line a main street that appears like something out of an old sepia-toned California postcard. Until recently, Calistoga's main draw was the little inexpensive motels where weekend visitors could take the curative spring waters, and immerse themselves up to the neck in Calistoga's famous, spongy, warm mud baths. But when the Calistoga Ranch, a sister property of nearby Auberge du Soleil, opened in 2004, funky Calistoga became a haute spring. The Ranch, an exclusive retreat of 46 individual lodges located on 157 acres in a valley canyon, has mineral water baths, a spa, and a private-label vineyard. The lodges on the property are spread out, for solitude, and they are large and airy, with floor to ceiling windows that provide endless views of surrounding vineyards, and blur the boundaries between in- and outdoors. So in-tune are the lodges to the natural setting, that many were constructed around the twisted, ancient oak trees that dot the property. Sit back in your lodge, admire the ancient oak that emerges from beneath your deck, and enjoy a glass of your favorite Calistoga beverage: wine, or water.

Book to Pack: "The Accidental Connoisseur: An Irreverent Journey Through the Wine World" by Lawrence Osborne. 2004 American bestseller that chronicles the author's journey through wineries in France, Italy and California.

Calistoga Ranch
580 Lommel Road
Calistoga, CA 94515
USA
Tel. +1 707-254-2800
Fax +1 707-254-2888
Email : info@calistogaranch.com
Website: www.calistogaranch.com
Booking: www.great-escapes-hotels.com

DIRECTIONS	70 miles (115 km) north of San Francisco International Airport.
RATES	From US$450 to US$1025.
ROOMS	46 guest lodges.
FOOD	Dining in the Lakehouse, featuring fine California cuisine and private-label wines, or privately in one's own lodge.
HISTORY	Newly built, opened in 2004.
X-FACTOR	Maximum opulence in California wine country.

Premium-Quelle

Das Napa Valley kennt man vor allem wegen seiner Weine. Doch es gibt dort auch andere Schätze. Zum Beispiel Mineralwasser aus den Quellen von Calistoga am nördlichen Ende des Napa Valley. An der US-Westküste ist es so bekannt wie Perrier oder Vichy in Frankreich. Bescheidene Holzhäuser und Gebäude aus dem frühen 20. Jahrhundert säumen die Hauptstraße des Ortes – eine Szenerie wie auf einer alten, vergilbten Postkarte. Noch bis vor kurzem waren in Calistoga preisgünstige Motels und Wochenendgäste, die Heilwasser tranken und ihre Körper in warme Schlammbäder steckten, die einzige Attraktion. Mit der Eröffnung der »Calistoga Ranch« 2004, die zum nahegelegenen Luxusresort »Auberge du Soleil« gehört, ist das bis dahin unglamouröse Calistoga zur Erstklasse-Destination geworden. Die Ranch, ein exklusives Retreat in einer Schlucht auf 63 Hektar, besteht aus 46 individuellen Lodges, Mineralwasserbädern, einem Spa und einem privaten Weinberg. Die Lodges sind über das ganze Grundstück verteilt, sodass man ungestört bleibt. Sie sind alle groß, luftig mit raumhohen Fenstern, durch die man freie Sicht auf die Rebberge genießt. Manche sind sogar um knorrige, alte Eichen herum gebaut. Hier verwischt Innen- und Außenraum zu einem harmonischen Ganzen.

Buchtipp: »Die Architektur des Weines. Baukunst und Weinbau im Bordeaux und im Napa-Valley« von Dirk Meyhöfer. Illustrierte Geschichte über amerikanische Weinbauern wie Robert Mondavi und ihre Zusammenarbeit mit Winzern aus dem Bordeaux.

Baigner dans le luxe

La vallée de Napa est surtout renommée pour ses vins mais Calistoga est connue sur toute la côte Ouest comme une eau minérale, équivalent californien de la Vichy ou du Perrier. Dans la ville du même nom, tout au nord de la vallée, de modestes maisons en bois et des bâtiments publics du début du 20e siècle bordent une rue principale qui semble sortie d'une vieille carte postale sépia. Jusqu'à récemment, son attrait principal était ses hôtels bon marché accueillant les visiteurs venus prendre les eaux le temps d'un week-end et barboter dans ses célèbres bains de boue chauds. Mais depuis que le «Caligosta Ranch», pendant de «l'Auberge du Soleil» voisine, a ouvert ses portes en 2004, Caligosta la malodorante a découvert le grand luxe. Cette élégante retraite de 46 bungalows individuels éparpillés sur 63 hectares au creux d'un canyon possède des thermes minérales, un centre de beauté et son propre vignoble. Spacieux, les bungalows sont éloignés les uns des autres pour préserver l'intimité, avec des baies vitrées qui offrent des vues à l'infini sur les vignes, brouillant les limites entre l'intérieur et l'extérieur. Ils sont tellement en harmonie avec leur environnement que certains sont construits autour des vieux chênes qui parsèment le domaine. Asseyez-vous confortablement, contemplez les troncs anciens qui émergent sous votre terrasse et savourez votre boisson de Calistoga préférée, vin ou eau.

Livre à emporter : «Guide Paumard des grands vins du Monde 2005-2006» de Bruno Paumard. Guide pratique et sans complaisance signé d'un expert œnologue.

ANREISE	115 km nördlich vom internationalen Flughafen San Francisco.
PREISE	Zwischen 360 € und 820 €.
ZIMMER	46 Gästelodges.
KÜCHE	Erstklassige kalifornische Küche und Weine vom hauseigenen Weinberg im »Lakehouse«. Mahlzeiten werden auf Wunsch auch in den Gästelodges serviert.
GESCHICHTE	Neues Resort, 2004 eröffnet.
X-FAKTOR	Üppiges Leben im kalifornischen Weingebiet.

ACCÈS	À 115 km au nord de l'aéroport international de San Francisco.
PRIX	Entre 360 € et 820 €.
CHAMBRES	46 bungalows individuels.
RESTAURATION	On peut dîner dans le «Lakehouse», qui propose un menu gastronomique californien arrosé de crus locaux, ou se faire servir dans ses appartements.
HISTOIRE	Récemment construit, inauguré en 2004.
LE «PETIT PLUS»	L'opulence maximum dans le pays des vins californiens.

Europe

Africa

Asia

Photo Credits | Fotonachweis
Crédits photographiques

South America

416–543

All 15 hotels are exclusively photographed by the photographer Tuca Reinés, São Paulo, www.tucareines.com.br for the book published by TASCHEN.

North America

544–669

All 15 hotels are exclusively photographed by the photographer Don Freeman, New York, www.donfreemanphoto.com for the book published by TASCHEN.

Photo Credits | Fotonachweis
Crédits photographiques

© 2009 TASCHEN GmbH
Hohenzollernring 53, D-50672 Köln
www.taschen.com

To stay informed about upcoming TASCHEN titles, please request our magazine at www.taschen.com/magazine or write to TASCHEN, Hohenzollernring 53, D-50672 Cologne, Germany; contact@taschen.com; Fax: +49-221-254919. We will be happy to send you a free copy of our magazine, which is filled with information about all of our books.

EDITOR AND LAYOUT: Angelika Taschen, Berlin
PROJECT MANAGER: Stephanie Bischoff, Cologne
LITHOGRAPH MANAGER: Thomas Grell, Cologne
TEXT: Shelley-Maree Cassidy, New Zealand (Europe and Africa); Christiane Reiter, Hamburg (Asia and South America); Daisann McLane, New York (North America)
FRENCH TRANSLATION: Delphine Nègre-Bouvet, Paris (Europe); Philippe Safavi, Paris (North America); Michèle Schreyer, Cologne (Asia and South America); Thérèse Chatelain–Südkamp, Cologne (Asia and South America); Stéphanie Tabone for LocTeam, S.L., Barcelona (Africa)
GERMAN TRANSLATION: Claudia Egdorf, Düsseldorf (Europe); Gabriele-Sabine Gugetzer, Hamburg (Europe); Simone Ott Caduff, California (North America); Sylvia Still for LocTeam, S. L., Barcelona (Africa)
ENGLISH TRANSLATION: Cathy Lara, Berlin (Asia); Sophie Lovell, Berlin (Asia); Michael Hulse, Warwick (South America)
DESIGN: Lambert und Lambert, Düsseldorf
PRINTED IN China
ISBN 978-3-8365-0999-2